Trading the Fruits of the Land

African Studies Centre
Research Series
11/1997

Trading the Fruits of the Land

Horticultural Marketing Channels in Kenya

Tjalling Dijkstra

Routledge
Taylor & Francis Group

LONDON AND NEW YORK

First published 1997 by Ashgate Publishing

Reissued 2018 by Routledge
2 Park Square, Milton Park, Abingdon, Oxon OX14 4RN
52 Vanderbilt Avenue, New York, NY 10017

Routledge is an imprint of the Taylor & Francis Group, an informa business

Publisher's Note
The publisher has gone to great lengths to ensure the quality of this reprint but points out that some imperfections in the original copies may be apparent.

Disclaimer
The publisher has made every effort to trace copyright holders and welcomes correspondence from those they have been unable to contact.

A Library of Congress record exists under LC control number: 98141816

Cover photograph:: A Kenyan horticultural trader (photo: Fred Hoogervorst/HH)

ISBN 13: 978-1-138-36443-1 (hbk)
ISBN 13: 978-0-429-43134-0 (ebk)

To the people of Kenya
and
to José,
with love

Contents

List of maps

List of figures

List of boxes

List of tables

List of Appendices

Currency rates

1990: KSh 1 = $ 0.04; KSh 1 = Fl 0.08
1991: KSh 1 = $ 0.04; KSh 1 = Fl 0.07
1992: KSh 1 = $ 0.03; KSh 1 = Fl 0.06
1993: KSh 1 = $ 0.02; KSh 1 = Fl 0.04

Acknowledgements

The fieldwork for the present study was carried out as part of a research project on horticultural production and marketing in Kenya. The project was set up under the auspices of the Food and Nutrition Studies Programme (FNSP), a joint effort of the Ministry of Planning and National Development in Nairobi and the African Studies Centre in Leiden, and was financed by the Netherlands Ministry of Foreign Affairs. After the completion of the project, the African Studies Centre gave me the opportunity to reanalyse the gathered data and write a book on the topic. The Department of Marketing and Marketing Research at Wageningen Agricultural University agreed to supervise the process in collaboration with the African Studies Centre.

Both the FNSP phase and the book phase have been successfully brought to a close thanks to the cooperation, dedication and enthusiasm of many people. I would like to express my sincere gratitude to all of them. I will mention a number of them in particular.

A first word of thanks goes to Prof. Dr. Ir. M. T. G. Meulenberg and Dr. A. van Tilburg of Wageningen Agricultural University and to Prof. Dr. J. C. Hoorweg of the African Studies Centre. When I visited Prof. Meulenberg and Dr. Aad van Tilburg for the first time, I had only vague ideas about the book. Many visits followed in which we chose relevant theories and analytic frameworks, and eventually a model was born (the latter to my own surprise). Anytime I wanted to show new findings or discuss the next step in my battle with the data I was welcome. Prof. Meulenberg and Aad, I am extremely grateful for the confidence you showed in me and for your dedication throughout the process.

The support of Prof. Jan Hoorweg dates from long before it had even come into my mind to write this book. As the godfather of the FNSP programme, he supervised my first steps in Kenya and encouraged me in developing the project on horticultural production and marketing. His enthusiasm and love for Kenya were not lost on me, and always made me eager to go back. Later, in Leiden, he helped me think about what direction the book would take, and he read my numerous drafts. Jan, many thanks for your immense support all these years.

Many people in Kenya were involved in the FNSP project. The first I would like to mention is Mr. Tom Magori, my Kenyan counterpart from Egerton University. We were a good team, coping with impassable roads, lost enumerators, broken-down computers, car accidents, half-answered questionnaires and expenses without receipts. Thanks for the fruitful cooperation.

During the fieldwork we received extensive support from the staff of the FNSP office. I would especially like to thank Mr. Jan Capon, Mr. Rebson Dzala and Mr. Joseph Abich.

The real hardships were borne by the CBS enumerators who interviewed the farmers, and by the research assistants from Egerton University who worked with the xiv

traders. The CBS people included Mr. G. Gichuhi, Mr. J. Muturi, Mr. F. Kimani, Mr. D. Mwangi, Mr. D. M. Bosire, Mr. R. O. Mbeche, Mr. E. N. Kinyanjui, Mr. J. O. Masea, Mr. P.O. Nyamongo, Mr. D. M. Mwashighadi, Mr. H. Mwabili, Mr. S. W. Ndolo, Mr. S. Mwachugu, and Mr. J. Ngolo. The research assistants from Egerton University were Mr. J. Lagat, Mr. J. Ouma, Mr. F. R. Ndago, Mr. G. O. G. Nyambane, Ms. J. K. Mogire, Mr. J. J. Osoro, Mr. B. M. Omayio, Ms. Z. Challa, Mr. S. Mazera and Mr. M. M. Masai. All were dedicated to their tasks, for which I am still grateful.

In Leiden at the African Studies Centre I was privileged to work in a stimulating atmosphere amongst fine colleagues. I would like to thank a few of them by name. Willem Veerman was always willing to solve my real and imaginary hardware and software problems. Nina Tellegen and Annette van Andel were my comrades in arms when it came to methodological questions and statistics. Laurens van der Laan was my local consultant on agricultural marketing theory, and a valued source of knowledge on the economic history of Africa. Dick Foeken and Marcel Rutten have been companionable and supportive office mates. The staff of the library and of secretariat rendered assistance whenever necessary. Nel van Betlehem made the maps and Michael Dallas edited the text.

On the home front, my partner in life José Bouwens shared all my ups and downs, setbacks and victories, for which I love her. This book is dedicated to her and to the people of Kenya.

Introduction

1

1.1. Exploration of the problem

At the World Food Summit of November 1996, which was organized by the Food and Agriculture Organization of the United Nations, food marketing in developing countries was one of the central themes. In a document prepared for the summit, the reason for this focus was made clear: the road to food security is impeded by malfunctioning marketing systems (FAO, 1995). This is certainly true for Africa. The demand for food is rising because an increasing number of people are unable to produce their own food. Population growth, rural-urban migration, land pressure and land degradation are among the factors behind this process. While the demand for food is rising, the supply is hampered by inefficiencies in production, collection, processing and distribution. Scarcity of inputs, poor infrastructure, lack of financial intermediaries and unstable political environments are some of the explanatory factors.

African governments in the 1960s and 1970s tried to solve food marketing inefficiencies, particularly for storables such as grains. They replaced private-sector collection and distribution systems by state-controlled ones. In so doing they threw away the good with the bad. The cure also proved worse than the disease. In the 1980s, governments began putting their faith again in the hands of the free market, the same free market that had all along been shaping private trade systems for perishables such as vegetables, fruits and tubers.

Present African governments are trying to keep pace with new developments in private food trade. They generally believe that state interventions should be avoided. At the same time, they understand that allowing resources to be allocated by the market may not always yield the desired results. Government regulations may be necessary, but will only be effective when based on a profound knowledge of the structure of private trade systems and of the factors that determine their long-term development. The present book contributes to this knowledge for the trade of vegetables, fruits and tubers (so-called horticultural commodities).

1

Kenya as a case study

Kenya is taken here as a case study. Horticultural commodities are produced by millions of Kenyan smallholders and are consumed by large sections of the rural and urban population. Marketing structures have developed without any significant government involvement, and within a relatively stable political environment. Marketing channels are comprised of a wide variety of intermediaries. Small petty traders carry vegetables, fruits and tubers on their heads to the nearest market, while large wholesalers hire transporters to carry horticultural commodities by truck from one side of the country to the other. Export traders charter whole cargo planes to fly produce to other parts of the world.

Knowledge about the Kenyan horticultural sector is limited. Government studies of food marketing have dealt largely with grains. There are two reasons for this. First, grain is a strategic commodity in the struggle for national food self-sufficiency. Second, the marketing system for grains, which until recently was monopolized by a marketing board, has been exhibiting politically unacceptable inefficiencies. Both these factors justify the attention paid to grains, but they do not warrant the knowledge gap that exists when it comes to vegetables, fruits and tubers.[1] Besides being sources of indispensable nutrients, these commodities bring income, employment and foreign exchange to the Kenyan population.

The horticultural marketing system in Kenya is more highly developed than those in many other African countries, and the present situation may give an indication of future developments in these countries. At the same time the Kenyan system is far from perfect. Various constraints reduce its efficiency and effectiveness. Most of them are typical for many other African countries as well as Kenya. Analysing them could therefore contribute to a better understanding of horticultural marketing constraints in various parts of Africa, and eventually to better performance in horticultural marketing systems.

The marketing channel approach

Horticultural marketing in Kenya will be studied here by means of a marketing channel approach, meaning that all successive actors and institutions involved in getting produce from the farms to the consumers will be taken into account. The analysis examines not only transactions in market places, but also those elsewhere, such as at the farm gate. That creates a clearer picture of the entire channel. Constraints on the exchange process at each marketing level can be investigated. The findings can be of use in improving the efficiency and effectiveness of the channels.

Many commodities change hands in more than one market place before reaching the consumer. The marketing channel concept enables us to clarify the function of each market place, and to explain under which circumstances a market place will develop which kind of functions. This knowledge can be useful in planning new market places or upgrading existing ones.

For a particular commodity, different types of marketing channels can exist. Together these channels form a marketing structure. Some channels in the structure can be

---

[1] Not only policy studies by the government but also scholarly studies by local universities have rarely dealt with the marketing of horticultural commodities during the past few decades. This contrasts with the late 1960s and 1970s, when researchers at the University of Nairobi carried out a number of studies on the subject (Wilson, 1969, 1973; Maritim, 1976; Mbogho, 1977; Ngeno, 1978; Durr & Lorenzl, 1980).

vertically differentiated to a greater extent than others. The degree of differentiation in marketing channels is influenced by specific factors in the marketing environment. The challenge in the present study is to relate the degree of vertical differentiation to these explanatory factors. The findings can lead to a better understanding of the current marketing structures in developing countries, and can help to predict structural changes ensuing from expected changes in the marketing environment.

1.2. Research objective and questions

The horticultural sector is of major importance to Kenya, and improved knowledge of the marketing system can help enhance the performance of the sector. The present study seeks to expand this knowledge. The objective is to analyse the structure and development of horticultural marketing channels in Kenya.

Kenyan farmers that produce horticultural commodities for the market will be described first. They are the raison d'être of the marketing channels. Knowing them will increase understanding of the marketing system.

The subsequent focus will be on the marketing channels themselves. The first research question is: What actors and institutions operate in the channels and what are their characteristics? Traders, agents and facilitating intermediaries will be examined. Specific focus is on collecting wholesalers. In Kenya, as in many other developing countries, they operate in the most problematic and least understood part of the channel. Special attention will be devoted to their efficiency. The development of rural assembly markets, in which collecting wholesalers operate, will also be investigated. Special reference is made to transport and information costs.

What factors determine the degree of vertical differentiation in Kenyan horticultural marketing channels? This is the second and central research question. The most important factors to be investigated are the size of the consumer population and transport times from farms to consumer centres. A historical analysis of food trade in Sub-Saharan Africa helps to identify them.

1.3. Research methodology

The analyses in the present study are based primarily on primary data. Surveys were carried out as part of a research project on horticultural production and marketing in Kenya. This project was part of the Food and Nutrition Studies Programme (FNSP), a joint effort of the Ministry of Planning and National Development in Nairobi, and the African Studies Centre in Leiden.[2]

The surveys were carried out by enumerators of the Central Bureau of Statistics and students from Egerton University, under supervision of one researcher from Egerton

---

[2] For a review of research results and published reports during the 1985-1992 period, see Hoorweg (1993).

4

Map 1. Surveyed districts

provincial boundary
district boundary

University and one from the African Studies Centre. The project results were published as FNSP reports (Dijkstra & Magori, 1991, 1992a, 1992b, 1994a, 1994b, 1995b).

The farm survey

A farm survey was carried out in Nyandarua, Taita Taveta and Kisii Districts. These were selected because they were known for their horticultural output, and because their location would provide information on different parts of Kenya. Nyandarua is located in the central highlands, Kisii in western Kenya, and Taita Taveta halfway between the central highlands and the coast. Map 1 shows their location. The map depicts the situation at the time of the survey. Kisii District is smaller today than shown on the map due to a redrawing of district boundaries.

In each of the three selected districts, the rural areas suitable for horticulture were identified. In Taita Taveta two areas with greatly divergent agro-ecological conditions were encountered, each with its own kind of horticulture (rainfed or irrigated). Taita Taveta was therefore divided into two separate research areas, the Taita Hills and Taveta Division. Four research areas were thus distinguished: Nyandarua, Kisii, Taita and Taveta.

In each research area, horticultural farmers were sampled in a multi-stage sampling procedure. First, clusters were sampled randomly in the areas suitable for horticulture, using a list of existing CBS clusters. Maps 2 to 4 show the locations of the clusters within each district. The next step differed from one district to another. In Nyandarua a relatively recent listing existed of all households located in the clusters. The large majority of the households were presumed to sell horticultural commodities. A systematic sample of 240 households was taken from the list and all of them were interviewed. The six households that turned out not to sell horticultural commodities were removed from the sample when the characteristics of commercial horticultural farmers were analysed.

In Kisii, Taita and Taveta, existing listings were relatively old and the involvement of households in commercial horticulture was expected to be lower than in Nyandarua. Therefore, new household listings were compiled in the sampled clusters. During the listing, households were asked whether they had sold horticultural commodities in the year under consideration. After the listing was finalized, a systematic sample was drawn from the listed households which had been found to be involved in commercial horticulture.[3] Table 1.1 shows the number of listed, households, and listed and sampled households with horticultural sales.

For the purpose of the survey, households were defined in accordance with the definition of the Kenyan CBS: a household is a group of people who live together in the same dwelling unit or homestead, and eat together (share the same cooking pot) (CBS, 1994b). Normally these people are related by blood or marriage, but this is not necessarily the case. All members are answerable to the same head. Horticultural commodities were defined as all vegetables, fruits and tubers which were traded fresh (and were therefore perishable). Beans were not regarded as horticulture, with the exception of those eaten fresh

---

[3]   In all four research areas substitution was applied. In the event of nonexistent households or repeated no response, these households were replaced by other ones. Less than 5 per cent of the sampled households had to be substituted.

Map 2. Nyandarua District and part of Nakuru District

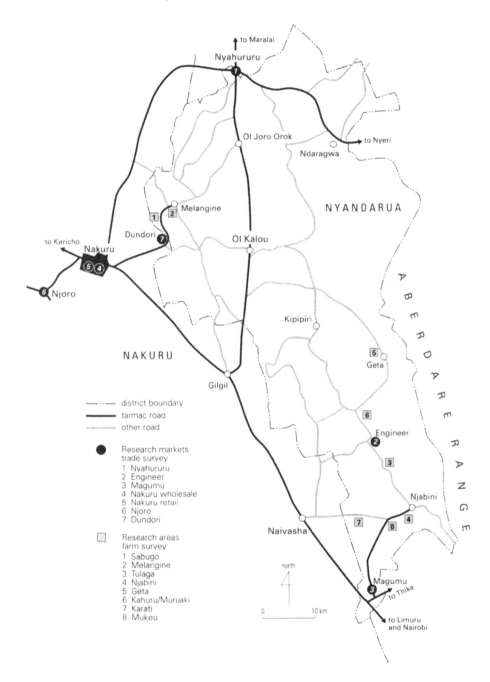

Table 1.1. Listed and sampled households in the farm survey per district

District (Province)	all listed households	listed hh's with horticultural sales	sampled hh's with horticultural sales
Nyandarua (Central)	[240]	[234]	234
Kisii (Nyanza)	1,289	1,016	144
Taita Taveta (Coast)			
- Taita Hills	563	351	87
- Taveta Division	544	182	38

(e.g. French beans). Cut flowers are also part of horticulture, but none of the farmers in the survey areas cultivated them.

The farm survey was carried out between August 1990 and March 1992. Farmers were visited once, and asked about farm and off-farm activities in the current or previous year. The enumerators used standardized questionnaires.

The trade survey

Parallel to the farm survey, a trade survey was carried out in 18 market places, located in 15 population centres in five Kenyan districts. Some of the centres were located in the horticultural production areas of the same districts examined in the farm survey. Others were located outside such production areas in the same or other districts. The market places and their locations are listed in Table 1.2, and shown in Maps 2 to 4.

The survey was carried out during harvesting periods, when the bulk of the horticultural commodities entered the market. Market places in large urban centres were operational six days a week, while the others had two official market days a week. Outside these two days trade was limited. Each market place was surveyed once, on an official market day.

In each market place, horticultural traders were selected by systematic sampling, and were interviewed by means of a standardized questionnaire.[4] It is important to note that the trade area of the market place was usually bigger than the demarcated selling area. The fenced area was often too small, or there was no fence at all, and selling in front of the market was not uncommon. Market masters adapted to this situation and also collected market fees from traders who displayed their commodities on the ground outside the official selling area. In our survey, everyone who had paid market fees was considered to be part of the market place.

---

4   Each enumerator began in a different part of the market and interviewed, for example, every fifth trader (depending on the total number of traders selling in the market place and the targeted number of interviews). If a trader refused to cooperate or was busy dealing with a customer, the next trader was approached. In small markets, the aim was to interview at least 20 traders. In the Kongowea wholesale market in Mombasa, only horticultural traders who sold commodities from Taita Taveta were included in the sampling (such in accordance with the aims of the FNSP project at the time). In the other markets all horticultural traders selling produce were included.

Map 3. Kisii District

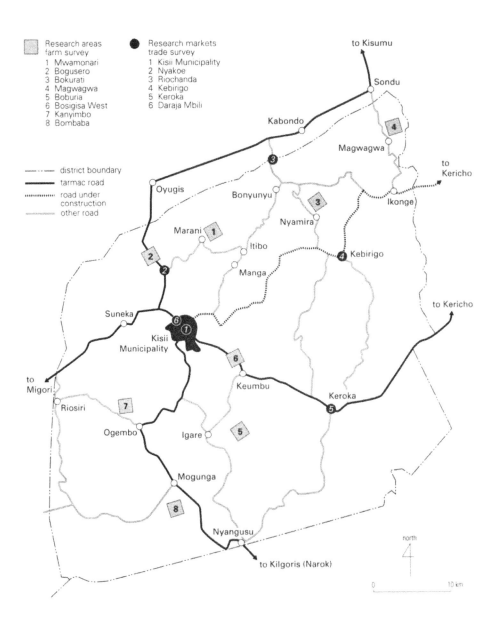

Table 1.2. Location, total trader population and sample size of surveyed market places

District (Province)	market centre	market place	trader population*	sample size
Nyandarua (Central)	Nyahururu	Nyahururu	50	21
	Engineer	Engineer	25	21
	Magumu	Magumu	75	30
Nakuru (Rift Valley)	Nakuru	wholesale market	803	96
		retail market	90	24
	Njoro	Njoro	160	31
	Dundori	Dundori	45	19
Taita Taveta (Coast)	Voi	Voi	184	57
	Taveta	Taveta	452	95
	Wundanyi	Wundanyi	199	56
Kisii (Nyanza)	Kisii	Municipal market	137	39
		Daraja Mbili	286	41
	Nyakoe	Nyakoe	225	27
	Riochanda	Riochanda	307	37
	Kebirigo	Kebirigo	74	38
	Keroka	Keroka	127	35
Mombasa (Coast)	Mombasa	Kongowea wholesale market	343	40
		Majengo retail market	106	59

* The size of the trader population is the number of farmer-traders and professional traders selling produce in the market place on the day of the survey.

Table 1.2 shows the number of traders questioned per market place and the total horticultural trader population in the market on the day of the survey. The figures refer to traders who offered produce for sale. Traders who came from elsewhere to buy commodities were neither counted nor sampled.

In addition to the general trade survey, some smaller surveys were carried out. One of them focused on collecting wholesalers operating in Nyandarua District. Another was carried out by an MA student from Wageningen Agricultural University, who gathered detailed information in the Nakuru and Njoro markets (Van den Berg, 1994). A third survey collected background information on traders in three market places in Taita Taveta District (Voi, Wundanyi and Mgambonyi).

1.4. Scope of the study

The present study examines horticultural farmers and horticultural marketing intermediaries. Their behaviour is analysed from an economic point of view. It is realized, however, that social, psychological, political and religious motives may play a role, too. Consumers are regarded as willing buyers of produce, because we are dealing with a sellers market. Horticultural commodities normally sell as long as they reach a retail outlet. Marketing constraints are found mainly in earlier parts of the channel.

Map 4. Taita Taveta District

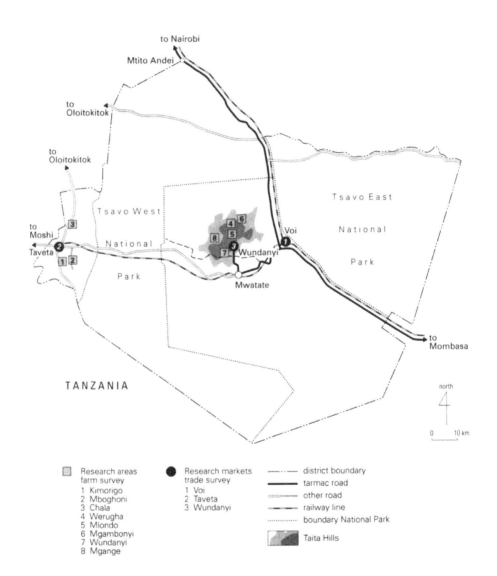

to Nairobi

Mtito Andei

to
Oloitokitok

to
Oloitokitok

Tsavo East

Tsavo West

National

to
Moshi

National

Taveta

Voi

Park

Wundanyi

Park

Mwatate

to
Mombasa

TANZANIA

north

0   10 km

▨ Research areas farm survey	● Research markets trade survey	—·—·— district boundary
1 Kimorigo	1 Voi	━━━ tarmac road
2 Mboghoni	2 Taveta	═══ other road
3 Chala	3 Wundanyi	━┃━┃━ railway line
4 Werugha		·········· boundary National Park
5 Miondo		
6 Mgambonyi		▨ Taita Hills
7 Wundanyi		
8 Mgange		

The analyses focus on marketing channels for fresh produce. By far the largest part of the Kenyan horticultural commodities are marketed fresh, and only relatively small quantities are processed. Horticultural processors will be examined in brief.

When we deal with horticultural farmers, our unit of analysis is the household. Households decide to sell part of their horticultural produce in some certain way. It is realized that the decision processes are subject to certain intra-household mechanisms. When we deal with horticultural marketing intermediaries, the unit of analysis is the actor or the institution.

The farm and trade surveys were cross-sectional. Most of the questions dealt with the situation on the day of the interview. Some questions related to the past (with a maximum recall period of one year). Market places were surveyed during the main harvesting period in that region. As a consequence, markets in different regions were surveyed in different parts of the year, or in successive years (August 1990 - March 1992). The years under consideration experienced normal horticultural harvests. The value of the Kenyan shilling declined during the research period, but it was generally observed that this did not affect prices for horticultural commodities.

Farmers and traders were willing to cooperate, and did not find it a problem to discuss their businesses. This was, at least in part, thanks to the enumerators. Local CBS personnel carried out the farm survey. They knew the farmers and spoke the local language. Farmers knew from experience that their answers would not be used for tax purposes. Egerton students carried out the trade survey. In most cases they came from the survey area and spoke the local language. The fact that they were 'just' students reassured the traders.

1.5. Outline of the book

Figure 1.1 visualizes the structure of the book. Chapters 2 and 3 are introductory chapters, and provide information needed for the analyses later on. Chapter 4 discusses relevant aspects of marketing channel theory, and Chapters 5 to 8 contain the actual analysis of the structure and development of horticultural marketing channels in Kenya. Here follows a summary of contents of each chapter in brief.

Chapter 2 gives a short history of food trade in Sub-Saharan Africa, covering the pre-colonial, colonial and post-independence period. This furnishes a historical framework for the analysis of horticultural marketing that follows. It shows that urbanization, transport developments and government policies have to be taken into account when explaining the development of food marketing channels in Africa.

Chapter 3 provides an introduction to the horticultural sector in Kenya in general and in the research areas in particular. After a brief explanation of the national situation, the focus is on Nyandarua, Kisii, Taita and Taveta. The history of commercial horticulture in the research areas is discussed, and its present importance in terms of income is shown. The sustainability of the horticultural enterprise is shown to be threatened by production problems.

Chapter 4 looks at aspects of marketing channel analysis relevant to the present study. In the first part, definitions are given of a marketing channel, channel structure and

12

Figure 1.1. Structure of the book

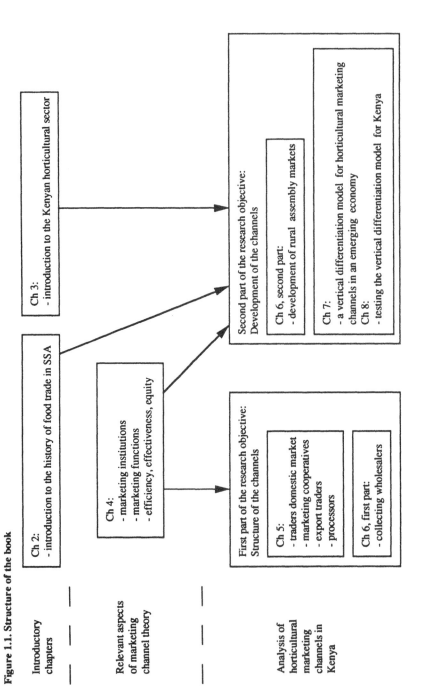

Note: Arrows indicate that aspects of one chapter are used as input to another chapter.

channel environment. It is explained how a marketing channel can be described. Reference is made to horticultural marketing channels in Sub-Saharan Africa. In the second part of the chapter, efficiency, effectiveness and equity are introduced as concepts for understanding vertical differentiation and integration processes in marketing channels. Relevant concepts such as functional spin-off, entry barriers, place, time and form convenience, and power are explained. Again, reference is made to horticultural marketing on the African continent.

Chapter 5 is the first of four chapters to analyse horticultural marketing channels in Kenya. The various actors and institutions are introduced here. The chapter begins with traders, agents and facilitating intermediaries. Then horticultural marketing cooperatives are examined, analysing the difference between success and failure. Horticultural export traders are observed and their business strategies are explained. Horticultural processors are briefly looked at, with a focus on their problems in producing for the world market. The chapter ends with some comments on the structure, conduct and performance of the horticultural marketing system.

Chapter 6 focuses on one specific stage of the marketing channels, the collection of produce in the production areas and transport to wholesale markets in urban centres. The first part of the chapter shows the importance of collecting wholesalers, and the efficiency of their mediation, which benefits both distributing wholesalers and farmers. The second part of the chapter analyses the development of rural assembly markets, showing how they reduce transport and information costs at the collection stage.

Chapter 7 is the first of two chapters that deal with vertical differentiation in Kenyan horticultural marketing channels. A model is developed with five explanatory factors: number of inhabitants of the market centre served by the channel, population density of the rural hinterland of this centre, transport time of the commodity, keeping qualities of the commodity, and turnover of the trader involved. Hypotheses about the impact of each factor are proposed. The unit of analysis, sample size and composition are discussed, and variables are specified.

In Chapter 8 the vertical differentiation model proposed in Chapter 7 is tested. First, a brief introduction is given to the types of analyses used (binomial and multinomial logistic regression), and the analytic procedure is explained. The model is tested twice: once analysing trade flows with known terminal markets, and once analysing all trade flows but excluding rural assembly markets. Conclusions are drawn at the end of the chapter. The final chapter provides a summary and general conclusions.

2

Food Trade in Sub-Saharan Africa: from the Pre-Colonial Past to the Structural Adjustment Era[1]

This chapter deals with food trade in pre-colonial, colonial and post-independence Sub-Saharan Africa. It provides a broad historical framework for the present study. As will be shown, the development of food trade is closely related to urbanization and urban growth. Other factors are also at work, however. They will be identified, to be examined later when the development of horticultural marketing channels is traced.

2.1. The pre-colonial period

In the beginning
The first forms of exchange between African communities probably go back as far as the Early Stone Age. Food items were already part of the deal: 'The exchange of bright or useful stones and honey for meat, and occasionally even womenfolk, probably marked the gatherings of foraging peoples' (Mokhtar, 1990, 386). With the beginning of agriculture at the start of the Neolithic era (the New Stone Age), such exchanges became more regular. Although much of the trade was probably still on a relatively restricted scale and local in scope, it included a wide range of commodities including 'salt, certain types of stone and later iron tools, beads, shells, possibly plants for medicinal or ritual use, meat for arable communities, and grains and root crops for pastoral groups, specialized utensils or substances like poisons for fishing or hunting, dried fish and all sorts of objects with a scarcity value such as strange seeds, animal claws, teeth, curious stones, bones, etc. which might have a magical significance' (Mokhtar, 1990, 387).

---

[1] An earlier version of this chapter was published by the author as an ASC Working Paper (vol. 22/ 1995) entitled 'Food Trade and Urbanization in Sub-Saharan Africa. From the Early Stone Age to the Structural Adjustment Era'.

As Hopkins (1973) explains for West Africa, and Gray & Birmingham (1970) for the eastern and central part of the continent, exchange took place even while production was primarily intended for subsistence. It resulted from households' production strategies, and from variations in the natural and human micro-environment:

> The basic aim of most households was to secure the products needed to maintain their customary standards of living. In order to reach this target each household tried to plant the amount of crops needed for survival in what, from experience, was known to be a poor year. In planning for disaster, there would be more crops available in an average year than the household could consume. Sometimes these crops were stored for future use, but this was not always possible with perishable varieties. Sometimes they were consumed in harvest 'festivals', but there were limitations to the amount of food which one community could eat in a short period of time. Sometimes, if neighbouring villages lacked foodstuffs, local produce was traded (Hopkins, 1973, 54).

In some cases, households planned their production of foodstuffs and crafts with a certain amount of exchange in mind. Trade of this kind was made possible by the presence of complementary needs within regions: 'Variations in natural resources did not have to be profound for local trade to develop, though marketing activity was especially intense on the borders of ecological zones' (Hopkins, 1973, 54). Those borders existed at the edges of savannah and forest, but also along the banks of major rivers. In the central Zaire basin, for instance, a brisk trade in river fish for inland agricultural products existed.[2]

Agriculture led to the rise of urban settlements. The oldest ruin in western Africa (Dar Tichitt) is thought to be 'a stalled early form of proto-urban settlement occurring at the time of the Neolithic Revolution on the southern Sahara border' (Coquery-Vidrovitch, 1991, 22). It dates back from 3800 to 2300 years.

The presence of urban settlements led to the rise of a class of merchants who organized the supply of food. However, some of the townspeople had residential bases in the countryside, and lived only intermittently in the urban centres, thus reducing the urban demand for agricultural commodities. Moreover, elites (and armies, for that matter) relied at least partly on non-market provision of food. They were supported in kind by slave cultivators, clients and requisitions from the subordinate population (Guyer, 1987).[3]

Long-distance trade
Not all food came from within the direct sphere of influence of the elites. Long-distance trade developed all over Africa. In **West Africa**, the Saharan salt mines and Sahelian commercial towns, which existed already before the Christian era, were almost entirely dependent on savannah agriculture (Tarver & Miller, 1993; Meillassoux, 1971).[4]

---

2   'Although inland people fished in small streams, their catches did not satisfy their needs. Conversely, the fishing societies of the central Zaire basin grew crops, but the conflicting demands of fishing and farming prevented them from growing adequate supplies' (Harms, 1981, 20).

3   Non-market provision was not only common among urban elites, as in parts of West Africa, but also among rural elites, such as the royalty who lived in mobile villages in some of the central parts of the African continent (Guyer, 1987).

4   Meillassoux gives an example of this dependency that dates back to the 14th century (the Teghaza salt mines receiving dates from Morocco and millet from Sudan). Hopkins (1973) gives an example dating from the 12th century (Timbuktu 'imported' grain, vegetables and livestock) and one from the 15th

Commodities passed through the hands of several merchants before arriving at their destination. This was related to the limited capacity of carriers to travel across different ecological zones: camels were used in the Sahara but stopped at the Niger, donkeys moved from the Sahel to the edges of the forest, and men were mainly used south of the savannah. The merchants tended to sell their goods at the relay points.[5] Livestock, dairy produce and salt were traded at the Sahara-savannah border in exchange for millet and cloth. In return, livestock, salt, dried fish, potash and cloth were traded at the savannah-forest border in exchange for slaves, ivory, ironware, cloth and kola nuts.[6] Finally, various foodstuffs and manufactures were traded in for fish and sea salt at the coastal settlements (Hopkins, 1973).

A relay point could form the beginning of urbanization (Meillassoux, 1971). Even if it became a prime trading city, however, it remained only a small-sized settlement where the major part of the population went on cultivating (Coquery-Vidrovitch, 1991).

In addition to relay points, rest places developed along caravan routes. They were mainly centres of trade for sellers of cooked food. Rest places could evolve into major market centres if they were on an important route. On the other hand, they could become inconsequential because of diversion of trade routes or destruction by war (Falola, 1991). Everywhere in West Africa, long-distance trade suffered considerably from civil, intertribal and interstate warfare on caravan routes (McGowan, 1990).

Markets and urban centres were not common in **East Africa**, except among the coastal Swahili settlements. But this does not mean that long-distance trade was absent. Trade was not conducted through regular markets, 'but in ad hoc gatherings at a caravan halt, or by visiting a particular place of commercial interest, such as a centre of salt or iron production' (Roberts, 1970, 64).[7] As articles of intertribal trade, salt and iron were especially important in the Northern interlacustrine region (now Uganda), along with bark-cloth and wild coffee beans (Tosh, 1970). In western Tanzania, salt and iron were traded along with pottery, dried fish, forest products and cattle.[8] According to Roberts (1970, 47) the trade may well have involved exchanges over 'considerable distances'. According to Wagner (1993, 159) trade linkages were prominently based on 'economic and utilitarian goals'.

An important exception to the basically marketless interior of East Africa were periodic markets at interethnic boundaries. Transactions could be safely carried out at these markets, even during tribal warfare. In western Kenya, for instance, 'a truce would be organized to enable the women folk to go to the market, the opposing warriors remaining at a distance at either side of the market. There would be mainly a bartering of foodstuffs and also there would be exchange of cattle in the payment of bride price. The elders controlled

---

century (long distance trade in millet, rice and livestock within the empire of Mali). Evidence from earlier periods does not seem to be available.

5   Relays did not only mark ecological boundaries but could also mark ethnic boundaries, as in the particular case of southern Ivory Coast (Meillassoux, 1971).

6   Kola nuts are important commodities in West Africa. Their bitter-sweet liquid acts as a stimulant and an antidote against thirst. They are also used for social functions as well as rituals (Adebayo, 1991). The kola trade already existed well before the 16th century (Lovejoy, 1980).

7   Not only the present hinterlands of Kenya and Tanzania lacked well-established markets, but also Uganda (Middleton, 1962).

8   Nearer to the Tanzanian coast tobacco was probably the most widely traded agricultural product (Iliffe, 1979).

the market and extracted dues' (Fearn, 1955, 29, as quoted by Obudho & Waller, 1976, 10).[9] Exchanges often had a regional and interzonal character, as cattle from the lowlands was exchanged for grain and root crops grown upland (Cohen, 1983). The periodic markets remained weakly organized compared to the caravan towns that would arise later on (Obudho & Waller, 1976).

Well-established markets did exist in the coastal Swahili settlements of East Africa. They were supplied with inland products by specific groups such as the 'Nyika'.[10] The latter sent their caravans from the coastal area to the north and northwest to trade with the Kamba, bringing back a variety of items including ivory, gum copal, honey, beeswax, grain, food stuffs, timber for building dhows, a special kind of beer, game meat, saliferous sand, tobacco and bark bags. In exchange they obtained salt, beads, cloth, iron hoes, and other coastal goods (Lamphear, 1970).

Long-distance trade not only developed in West and East Africa but also in **central Africa**, for instance in the Zaire basin. 'The Bobangi, in particular, mounted long distance expeditions by canoe. During those ventures they came into contact with other river peoples and acted as long distance commercial carriers' (Birmingham, 1981, 141). As in West Africa, commodities passed through the hands of several merchants before arriving at their destination. The Tonga in southern Central Africa (now Zambia), for instance, had valuable supplies of salt with which they could purchase goods of external origin. Items like shells, beads, and cloth came 'from farther afield and reached the Tonga after multiple exchanges had taken place among neighbours who were trading in fish, grain, game, ochre, building materials and specialized food items' (Birmingham, 1981, 127). Both in Zambia and Malawi, salt, iron, and copper were part of 'complex inter-regional bartering networks, which were based on a comparatively steady, but informally structured demand for raw materials' (Fagan, 1970, 25).[11] Permanent markets and urban centres, however, were not characteristic for the region before the arrival of the Europeans (Rotweg, 1962; Birmingham, 1981).

Although local trade in Sub-Saharan Africa had its own rationale, it was connected to long-distance trading through the sale of supplies to passing caravans and, to a lesser extent, through the distribution of goods that caravans delivered. People along the caravan routes found it profitable to produce crops for sale, and when commercial contacts increased it became easier to make up for local deficiencies through trade (Gray & Birmingham, 1970; Hopkins, 1973).

---

[9] Both in East Africa and elsewhere, local traders were predominantly women because of their immunity during wars. In Yorubaland (Nigeria), 'even during the earliest tribal wars, the mutual need to hold markets seems normally to have been recognised sufficiently to allow transactions to be safely carried out on neutral territory: the women would go to the market, the opposing warriors remaining at a distance on either side' (Hodder, 1969, 24). Women were also immune among the Lugbara of Uganda, trading commodities like fish with other ethnic groups. The women 'were able to travel freely, even moving between groups which were fighting one another.' Men were also involved in trade, especially of iron and poisons. They moved, however, 'along lines of kinship from one tribe to another' (Middleton, 1962, 563).

[10] The semi-arid wasteland which runs just inland parallel to much of the Kenyan Coast was called the 'nyika'. Arab and Swahili residents from the coastal towns referred to Giriyama and other ethnic groups who lived in this area and traded with them as the Nyika (Lamphear, 1970).

[11] Long-distance trade of iron and salt was absent in the central Zaire basin, because the resources were distributed rather evenly throughout the region (Harms, 1981).

In addition to local trade, two other types of trade were connected to the regionally determined long-distance trade networks. The first was specific for West Africa and concerned trans-Saharan trade. The internal system of long-distance trade in West Africa made the development of trans-Saharan trade possible (Mokhtar, 1990). Dating back as far as 1000 BC, it included a large range of items, but few of them were food. Gold, slaves, expensive cloth, pepper, ivory, kola nuts, leather goods, and in the 19th century ostrich feathers, were carried to the north, while textiles, copper, preserved foodstuffs, glassware, beads and miscellaneous 'fancy goods' went south (Hopkins, 1973).

The second type of trade that made use of existing regional networks was the overseas trade. Both the trade with the Arab Mediterranean world and the Atlantic trade inserted themselves into existing regional and even local networks (Coquery-Vidrovitch, 1991).

Overseas trade

The Portuguese were the first to open up trans-Atlantic trade routes from **West Africa** in the late 15th century, followed by the French, Danish, Dutch and British in the 17th century (Gugler & Flanagan, 1978).[12] Until the 19th century the main exports from West Africa were slaves, gold, ivory, timber, dyewoods, beeswax, gum, leather, indigo and pepper (Meillassoux, 1971; Northrup, 1978, Hopkins, 1973). Slave trade became the prime focus in the 18th century, causing local warfare, disorder and even the rise of an entirely new state on the Slave Coast (Dahomey).[13] According to Hopkins (1973), however, the trade of commodities such as gold, camwood, beeswax and gum continued, not only to supplement the trade of slaves but also as viable exports in their own right.

Overseas and local trade were interrelated. Searing (1993) studied the 18th century slave trade concluding that the demand for food by the slave caravans not only stimulated local grain trade, but that grain supplies even determined the geographical origins of slaves sold to Atlantic merchants. When a region experienced a grain shortage due to a famine or high regional demand, the area exported fewer slaves.[14]

The overseas slave trade was abolished in the course of the 19th century.[15] In consequence, the West African product mix shifted to palm oil, rubber, groundnuts, wood, hides and rice (Meillassoux, 1971; Mark, 1986).

The overseas trade stimulated urban growth. Multicentred urban networks came up or expanded in Yorubaland, Hausaland, Ashanti, Dahomey, in the Volta and Niger hinterland and in the Wolof kingdoms (Coquery-Vidrovitch, 1991). Food trade flourished in

---

[12] The early trade of the Portuguese consisted of two kinds of activities. They carried bulk goods from one part of the coast to the other, converting their profits into gold, ivory, and pepper for remittance to Lisbon. In addition, they carried Mediterranean manufactures, especially North African textiles, to Africa. In West Africa this cut into existing markets accustomed to trans-Saharan trade (Birmingham, 1981).

[13] Law (1991) has shown that the rise of Dahomey in the 17th century was linked to the growth of the European slave trade, and that Dahoman military organization was clearly geared to gathering slaves.

[14] Slaves were used for gum extraction in the desert region. They had to be fed with savannah grain. An increase in gum production reduced the grain available for slave caravans that travelled through the savannah area. Grain was cultivated not only by peasants but also by slave labour on large-scale farms. Hence, grain production and gum extraction cut into the available supply of slaves for export (Searing, 1993; Roberts, 1980).

[15] In 1807, the British were the first to make slave trade illegal. It took until the end of the 1860s before the Atlantic slave trade was entirely suppressed (Hopkins, 1973).

these networks. According to Guyer (1987), however, not the urban dwellers but the caravans participating in the export trade were the prime initiators of the rise in food demand. The porters that carried crops to the coast for export were the most rapidly expanding consumer group. There were enormous numbers of them, and 'unlike the retainers and clients of earlier periods, porterage crews had no authority behind them to ensure free support from village populations. They had to be fed along the line of march, through some kind of commercial transaction' (Guyer, 1987, 27).[16]

As well as urban residents and porters, the crews of docking ships and the slaves that were put to work on local plantations had to be fed by bought food. The latter were a significant group. Plantation production was pushed by an increasing demand for export commodities. In Senegambia, groundnuts were cultivated on a large scale in the Atlantic coastal region and the Senegal River Valley (Searing, 1993). Elsewhere in West Africa, large-scale production of palm oil emerged alongside peasant production of the commodity.[17] The slaves that could no longer be sold to the Europeans because of the abolition of the slave trade were put to work on oil palm plantations, producing and transporting the oil (Meillassoux, 1971). The rise in palm oil production led to shortages of food in the oil palm belt, which in turn stimulated regional food trade in yams, cattle, fruit and grain (Northrup, 1978).

Market places were the centre of most food transactions. They exhibited a high level of competition, and operated within efficient distribution systems (Hopkins, 1973). Gold dust, cowries, strips of cloth, and copper and iron rods functioned as general-purpose currencies (Arhin, 1990; Hopkins, 1973). Prices were subject to short-term fluctuations reflecting the balance of supply and demand, but overall they tended to rise.[18] In the large towns, continuous markets were found, while elsewhere markets were usually held at intervals of between two and eight days (Hopkins, 1973). Some African states played an active role in market development. In Asante on the Gold Coast, for instance, an elaborate system of border markets, customs duties, state-sponsored traders, and state loans for trading existed (Wilks, 1975).[19]

Overseas trade in **East Africa** dates back as far as the first millennium BC, when colonies of Greeks, Egyptians, Arabs, and possibly Indians existed on the Ethiopian coast (Abir, 1970). Aksum, the oldest still-existing city of Sub-Saharan Africa, was a major

---

[16] Guyer (1987) observes that wage levels and food prices were already in place by the time colonial governments became major employers of porters in the late 19th century. She quotes Daaku (1971), who recorded wage payment and food purchase in cowries in Ashanti (West Africa) in the 17th century, and Iliffe (1979) who describes 19th-century trading caravans in East Africa as internally differentiated organizations with guards, personal servants, cooks, guides, porters, and slaves, each with their own mode of remuneration.

[17] Large- and small-scale entrepreneurs were involved in the production and trading of palm oil in Dahomey, Yorubaland, Lagos and Igboland, among other places (Law, 1995).

[18] The expansion of European trade between the mid-17th and mid-18th centuries had led to an uncontrolled importation of cowry shells that caused inflation of prices both in European trade and in the domestic markets. In the second half of the 19th century the situation repeated itself, leading to the so-called Great Inflation (Law, 1992).

[19] The king of Asante was also a large slave trader. According to Spaulding and Kapteijns (1987, 5), he practised 'a royally administered export commerce in slaves'. The same was true for the kings of Dahomey, Kazembe and late Keira Dar Fur.

trading town in Eritrea at that time (Hance, 1970).[20] From the end of the first millennium AD, Muslim trading towns began to develop on the western coast of the Red Sea, in the Gulf of Aden, and further down the East African coast (Abir, 1970; Hrbek, 1992).[21] Arab and Persian settlers became involved in exporting slaves and ivory from the hinterland, and locally produced skins, hides, precious gums, ghee and ostrich feathers (Lewis, 1962). Indian merchants were the principle suppliers of cotton, cloth, beads and sundry manufactured articles, and buyers of ivory, gold, iron, gum copal, ambergris, incense, and, later on, slaves (Mangat, 1969).[22]

In the late 16th century, Portugal conquered various independent Swahili states on the East African coast. The Portuguese, however, were not so much interested in inland trade as in a secure port of call for vessels sailing between Goa and East Africa (Berg, 1968). Towards the end of the 17th century they were expelled from East Africa by the Sultan of Oman, who ruled the coast until the arrival of the British.[23]

Meanwhile, the Arabian, Persian and Indian traders continued their business. Initially, local groups like the 'Nyika' and Kamba in Kenya and the Nyamwezi in Tanzania supplied them with export commodities and food.[24] Much of the long-distance trade was cut off in the latter half of the 19th century due to raiding by tribes such as the Maasai, Shambala and Galla. As far as the coastal cities were concerned, it was at this time that direct Arab trading caravans became necessary to obtain the trade goods formerly supplied by local ethnic groups, and permanent caravan towns arose where caravan traders could procure fresh supplies of water and food and take a rest (Obudho, 1983; Obudho & Waller, 1976).[25] The caravans did not end at the shores of Lake Tanganyika, but penetrated further into the central part of the continent.

Apart from ports and caravan towns, 19th-century urbanization was not as common in East Africa as in West Africa. Some ethnic groups had capital cities (e.g. the Lunda and the Kuba), others had military camps, but according to Coquery-Vidrovitch (1991, 31), the rest of the people 'probably scattered in the bush in precarious settlements as to escape slave raiders and pillage or were decimated by the spread of rising epidemic diseases (such as sleeping sickness) all along the Rift encouraged by the progress of penetration.'

---

[20] Blocks of salt and coined money were already used as currencies. 'The use of salt as currency was a common phenomenon in Africa and can be explained by a general scarcity of salt .... The coastal salt plains of northern Ethiopia were therefore probably an important asset to the people of Axum and helped to foster their commercial activity and sponsor caravan trade' (Abir, 1970, 119).

[21] Around 1500 AD, coastal Muslim settlements in East Africa were Mogadishu, Marka and Brava (in the present Somalia), Lamu, Malindi and Mombasa (in the present Kenya), Zanzibar, Kilwa (in the present Tanzania), and Sofala (in the present Mozambique) (Hrbek, 1992).

[22] 'By the tenth century India and China were the most important markets for East African ivory' (Mokhtar, 1990, 312). The trading of slaves by the Indians possibly followed the expansion of Islam into the Indian subcontinent after the 14th century (Mangat, 1969).

[23] In 1832, Zanzibar town became the capital of the Omani empire instead of Mombasa (Berg, 1968).

[24] The Nyamwezi, who had accumulated their capital in the internal trade of western Tanzania, were important long-distance traders of iron, salt, hoes, cloth, food, and other local staples (Birmingham, 1981). Their caravans travelled all the way from eastern Zaire to the coast from the early 19th century onwards (Berg, 1968).

[25] In West Kenya these towns appeared in the second half of the 18th century. Mumias was the most important one, being one of the five major interior caravan towns that still exist in today's Kenya. The other four were Taveta, Dagoretti, Machakos and Tsavo (Obudho & Waller, 1976).

Similarly to 19th-century West Africa, export crop plantations developed in East Africa. They were, however, not situated on the mainland but on islands in the Indian Ocean. Arab settlers in Zanzibar and Pemba went into plantation-wise production of cloves. Earlier on, in the second half of the 18th century, sugar plantations had been established on the islands of Mauritius and Réunion.[26] All these plantations made use of slaves brought in from the East and Southeast African mainland (Alpers, 1968).[27] The demand for slaves became one of the main reasons for the growing importance of caravan trade, boosting the development of caravan towns along the routes as places for resting and procuring fresh food supplies (Obudho, 1983). Thus, plantation production did not stimulate food trade on the mainland because slaves had to be fed while working, as was the case in West Africa, but because they had to be fed on their way to the plantations on the islands.

The Portuguese were the first Europeans to arrive in **central Africa**. They landed on the coast of Angola towards the end of the 15th century, and started to export slaves and ivory from the central Zaire basin in the second half of the 16th century (Birmingham, 1970; Harms, 1981). Their arrival in central Zaire changed political entities such as the large Kongo kingdom, which until that time did not have an established market network. After a century of overseas contact, 'a relatively high level of craft specialisation had developed among potters, weavers, salt-makers, fishermen, blacksmiths and coppersmiths, all of whom traded part of their output, either by the traditional flow of goods through the tribute network, or by the increasing use of regular marketplaces' (Birmingham, 1981, 29). Tragically, these changes were bound to the increasing wealth of the ruling elite and the trading class involved in the slave trade.

The Portuguese were also the first Europeans to land on the shores of Mozambique in the early years of the 16th century, subsequently penetrating the hinterland by river.[28] They continued as far as Zumbo along the Zambezi, at the border with the present Zambia, where they started to trade with African ethnic groups like the Yao and the Bisa (John, 1970).[29] Later, in the second half of the 18th century, Scottish, Dutch and Indian traders travelled up the Zambezi in the direction of Lake Malawi, both to look for ivory and to purchase commodities such as sesame seeds in exchange for cloth, hoes, and other foreign goods (Mandala, 1990).[30]

In the 19th century, commerce and Christianity travelled hand in hand. Missionaries in areas such as southern Malawi and Namibia encouraged the local people to grow tobacco, thus boosting market development. Mission stations developed into market centres with schools, hospitals and trading companies. Examples are Windhoek in Namibia, which was

---

[26] The Dutch introduced sugar cane to Mauritius in the 17th century. The French created the first sugar factory and sugar estate on the island in 1740. The sugar production was limited: 3,000 tonnes in 1803. After the British took over in 1810, production rapidly increased to 34,000 tonnes in 1830 (North-Coombes, 1993).

[27] In addition to the mainland, Madagascar supplied slaves, together with rice and cattle that was needed to feed the slaves on the plantations of the other islands (Campbell, 1993).

[28] Vasco da Gama anchored off Kilwa in 1498, making it one of Portugal's strongholds until Malindi and Mombasa became more important (Berg, 1968).

[29] At the limit of the foreigners' trading frontier, 'the vital trading initiative seems to have come from the Africans', just as in the case of the Kamba and Nyamwezi East Africa (Sutherland-Harris, 1970, 231).

[30] Indians acted as itinerant traders, as well purchasing foodstuffs for their own consumption and for resale on the lower Zambezi and the coast (Mandala, 1990).

established by missionaries as early as the 1850s, and Blantyre in Malawi, established in the 1870s (Gibson, 1962; Van Dijk, 1992).

While overseas trade was generally connected to regional trade, such was not the case at the Cape of South Africa. Here, Dutch settlers arrived as early as the 1650s with the initial aim of growing wheat for the ships of the Dutch East India Company (Omer-Cooper, 1978). Later on, in the 18th century, they began exporting surplus wool and wine to Europe (Ross, 1986). The commodities were produced on the settlers' farms with the help of slave labour instead of being purchased from local ethnic groups.[31]

2.2. The colonial period

The European conquest of Africa took place largely between 1874 and 1905. 'Frontiers of trade and belief, of white settlement, and the linked scourges of famine and epidemic disease' moved on in the process of 'the scramble for Africa' (Lonsdale, 1985, 682). 'In 1879 more than 90 per cent of the continent was ruled by Africans. By 1900 all but a tiny fraction of it was being governed by European powers' (Oliver & Atmore, 1967, 103).

Under colonial rule the process of urbanization and market development continued. According to Coquery-Vidrovitch (1991, 35-36) 'colonisers tried to use and adapt previous settlements, towns, villages, or clusters of villages (such as Swahili harbours, Yoruba towns, or marketplaces and villages close to the river, for instance Kinshasa and Brazzaville) just because their needs were more or less the same as before.' When existing facilities were found unsuitable, new colonial towns might be established to serve as administrative or commercial centres.

Settler farmers and mining economies
Colonial rule meant a pronounced difference in the case of settler farmers and mining economies. Non-African farmers settled in South Africa, Southern Rhodesia (now Zimbabwe) and Kenya. In the central highland regions of Kenya, urbanization and market development can be directly attributed to the settlers. The newly established urban centres were regarded as bases for administrative and commercial activities rather than as centres for permanent African settlement. They were, however, encircled by settlements of African migrants (Obudho, 1983).[32] The centres had marketing functions with regard to the collection of local produce for export, the distribution of imported goods and the trade of local food. African and non-African traders were officially segregated. Non-African food and non-food traders were allowed to establish themselves only in the urban areas, townships and trading centres, while African traders could establish themselves 'anywhere in the bush' (Rimmer, 1983, quoting a report of the East African Royal Commission).

The British colonial administration in Nairobi imposed a hut tax and later a poll tax to get local Africans to work on settler farms as wage labourers (Low, 1965; Wrigley,

---

[31] One commodity that was initially purchased from local Africans, especially the Khoi, was meat. It was not exported, however (Omer-Cooper, 1978).

[32] In contrast, 'Africans in the indigenous West African cities during the colonial period purchased urban property, erected city dwellings, and moved freely between rural and urban areas' (Chandler & Tarver, 1993, 253).

1965).[33] In fertile regions away from the settler areas, it thought to generate taxes and bring economic development by promoting cash crops among Africans.[34] Coffee and cotton appeared suitable for peasant production and were successfully pushed.[35] The peasant crop was carried by rail to Mombasa together with the settler output. Only the collection stage called for additional efforts. The challenge was taken up by Indians and Arabs, who collected the cash crops at periodic markets in the production areas (Obudho & Waller, 1976). According to Ehrlich (1965), who studied Uganda, the Indians played a crucial role because they were both willing purchasers of export products and sellers of trade goods, thus creating new incentives for further production.[36] However, the administration also played its part. It encouraged the establishment of additional periodic markets and trading centres by improving roads (Obudho & Waller, 1976). The new markets and centres streamlined export trade, stimulated sales of import goods and facilitated local trade in food.

Trading centres emerge not only as a result of improved roads but also of new laws. In 1936, the colonial authorities in Nairobi declared that from then on 'all townships belonged to the central government, the trading centres belonged to the local government, and the periodic markets were left to the Locational Authority' (Obudho & Waller, 1967, 44). In the years that followed, many local governments established new trading centres. At the same time, new periodic markets sprang up around newly introduced mills for grinding maize.

Mining had at least as much impact on African urbanization and food trade as the arrival of non-African settlers. The biggest mining industries developed in South Africa, Rhodesia, Angola and Belgian Congo.[37] In South Africa the discovery of diamonds and gold in the 1860s and 1870s changed an economy that was basically agricultural and pastoral in nature into one based on mining and industry (Omer-Cooper, 1987). The greatly increased demand for African labour could not be met from within the areas of white

---

[33] The poll tax was introduced to catch the youths who did not qualify as householders (Wrigley, 1965). A similar tax was introduced by the British-administered territories in Southern Africa (Wild, 1992).

[34] According to Rimmer (1983, 146) the colonial administrators went for taxes to 'discharge their responsibilities without dependence on grudgingly given metropolitan subventions'.

[35] Coffee production was promoted among African smallholders on the western shores of Lake Victoria, but discouraged in the central highlands of Kenya and around Mount Kilimanjaro to protect the white settlers (Wrigley, 1965; Brett, 1973). Although technically speaking there were no legislative sanctions against African coffee cultivation in the settler areas, custom and bureaucratic obstruction excluded it (Talbott, 1990).

[36] In the Uganda protectorate cotton became the most important smallholder cash crop (Ehrlich, 1965).

[37] Gold, diamonds, coal and iron ore were mined in South Africa, copper, zinc, and lead in Northern Rhodesia (presently Zambia), and iron ore, gold, asbestos and chrome in Southern Rhodesia (presently Zimbabwe). In the Belgian Congo, copper, cobalt, and zinc were mined, together with gold and diamonds, which were also found in Angola (Katzenellenbogen, 1975; Pedler, 1975). Mining activities also took place in West Africa. Tin and coal were found in Nigeria, diamonds and iron in Sierra Leone, diamonds and bauxite in Ghana, and bauxite in various parts of French West Africa. According to Katzenellenbogen (1975), however, mining never had as much impact on the West African economies during the colonial period as it did in the Southern African economies. In addition to Southern and West Africa, some relatively small gold mining activities were developed in East Africa, especially in the Lake Victoria regions of Kenya, Uganda and Tanganyika (Iliffe, 1979; Pedler, 1975). In all parts of Africa colonial governments relied on private enterprise for the development of the mineral resources. The only major exception was the coal mine that was an enterprise of the Nigerian railway (Pedler, 1975).

occupation and control alone.[38] Migrant labourers settled in camps near the mines, that rapidly developed into towns and eventually cities (Chandler & Tarver, 1993). The expanding consumer populations created new markets for food, providing new opportunities not only for white commercial farmers but also for African peasants, who greatly expanded their commercial production (Omer-Cooper, 1987). Wild (1992), who discusses Southern Rhodesia (colonial Zimbabwe), explains that market gardening was quite common among African farmers living near urban settlements. The market gardeners hawked their pumpkins, grains, fowls, eggs and so forth in the European residential and business areas.

Food-supply policies of the colonial administrations
British colonial administrations became directly involved in the marketing of food when they allowed African farmers to pay their taxes in rice, beans and maize as an alternative to cash. In addition, the administrations bought surpluses for distribution to prisons, marine, army and police, and for sale to civil servants in urban centres (Kalinga, 1990).[39]

Both public institutions and private employers provided their workers with food. The bulk purchases by public and private employers stimulated large-scale production and wholesale trade. In Kenya, for instance, where a large African labour force worked on European coffee plantations, some settlers concentrated on maize production. Although some maize was exported, most was directed to plantation and other labourers in the domestic market (Wrigley, 1965).

Taxation in kind was applied not only by the authorities in the British administered territories but also in parts of the French, Belgian and Portuguese empires, particularly in the low-density areas of central Africa. A 'requisition regime', with local chiefs as intermediaries, was introduced because of the lack of an indigenous market system that could be expanded, the limited means of transport, and the non-existence of commercial farmers. The chiefs were ordered to regularly supply specified kinds and quantities of food to cities, worksites, porterage crews and administrative headquarters (Guyer, 1987, 32).

In West Africa, the supply of food to wage labourers was left to the existing indigenous marketing systems. As a consequence, the process of institutional market development gained further momentum in this region. Colonialism tended to favour the growth of daily food markets and their transformation into permanent retail trading places. At the same time, buying points for the collection of cash crops multiplied (Meillassoux, 1971).[40] The spacing of markets became more uniform, whereby, according to Hogendorn (1975), the location and periodicity of a market was related to the density of the population, allowing for anomalies due to the absence of exchanges, the interference of past economic phenomena, or social and political factors.

---

[38] The labourers had to be drawn to a large extent from African-occupied areas and still independent African states within South Africa, Mozambique and Southern Rhodesia (Omer-Cooper, 1987).

[39] Both the food buying and the payment of workers in food were part of a policy to control newly introduced European currencies (which were in denominations too large for everyday food purchases), and simultaneously to maintain low food prices. Low food prices were especially important when consumer populations were big, as in the mining and settler economies (Guyer, 1987).

[40] The most important African-produced export crops during this period were palm oil (in various countries bordering on the Atlantic Ocean), groundnuts (Senegal and the Gambia), cocoa (the Gold Coast and western Nigeria) and cotton (northern Nigeria) (Hogendorn, 1975).

Hogendorn does not mention the purchasing power of a population. In colonial Gambia, however, purchasing power was at least as important as population density (Barrett, 1988). Purchasing power was associated with groundnut cultivation. The commercial production of groundnuts led to a lack of food self-sufficiency among the farm households involved, and consequently food had to be purchased in market places. In areas with high groundnut production, market places flourished, whereas they were absent in areas without commercial groundnut production.

In addition to supplies from the African continent, some of the colonial territories depended on food imports, such as rice from the Orient (Kalinga, 1989). Imported food fed a large proportion of the mining workers during the mineral boom in Southern Africa. In Senegal and the Gambia, rice imports from Indochina were needed to feed the urban population because farmers had specialized in peanut production (Guyer, 1987). Rice was imported in smaller quantities in a self-sufficient country such as Malawi, where Europeans and Indians preferred Burmese and Thai rice to the locally produced variety (Kalinga, 1990).

New boundaries and transport networks
The introduction of new, artificial boundaries between colonial territories affected the development of market centres and trade networks. While freighting became easier, faster and relatively cheaper within territories, trade across international boundaries became more difficult in some cases.

Within colonies, internal security allowed traders to go further away from home. Among the notable large-scale movements in West Africa were those of Ibo traders who travelled from their homelands east of the Niger to the north of Nigeria, and Hausa butchers from the north who went to markets throughout the south. Many traders from Lagos had stalls in the markets of Ashanti, and the Kwahus from the highlands near Nkawkaw were well represented in the Accra markets. There were fewer of these kinds of movements in East Africa, but there were some. Luos from western Kenya, for instance, were a major trading group in Mombasa, and Somali traders from Somalia and northeastern Kenya travelled about the countryside far from their homes (Pedler, 1975).

Trade across colonial borders could become more difficult. In West Africa, the long-distance trade of salt and kola nuts that cut across French to British territories declined (Adebayo, 1991). A combination of new borders and the increasing importance of overseas export trade caused the decline of many of the old towns in the Saharan region. A famous town like Timbuktu in today's landlocked Mali 'succumbed entirely to a second economic desiccation' (Gugler & Flanagan, 1978, 27).

The development of coastal market centres was determined by their accessibility from the sea and by the productivity of their hinterlands (Gugler & Flanagan, 1978). The fate of market centres between the coast and the production areas was in the hands of the colonial authorities, which had to decide on the improvement of local transportation networks. The trajectory of a new railway line or the improvement of a road governed the rise of certain centres and the decline of others.[41] River ports and smaller seaports were usually among the

---

[41] Newly built railways in colonial Africa had three purposes: (i) to connect an administrative centre on the seacoast with an interior area for political and military control; (ii) to reach areas of mineral exploitation; and (iii) to reach areas of potential agricultural production (Salau, 1979). The British built railways in

losers. They were robbed of their hinterlands 'as spreading networks of railroads and roadways swept up and funnelled export commodities to those few larger coastal ports destined to become the focal points of national economies' (Gugler & Flanagan, 1978, 28).[42]

From depression to growth

In the 1930s the world economy was struck by a depression that affected African economies through the falling prices of their export commodities. In West Africa, some of the peasant farmers reacted by retreating into subsistence, e.g. growing millet instead of groundnuts. Farmers with tree crops such as cocoa and coffee planted fewer new trees, and at particularly critical times they withheld supplies in the hope of forcing buyers to offer higher prices (Hopkins, 1973). The lower purchasing power of the rural population and retreat into subsistence production reduced food trade in the periodic markets.

In the settler communities, white farmers were at least partly sheltered from falling commodity prices by increased market regulation, including preferential access to markets, credit, and government services (Adedeji, 1984). The prices of export commodities of local African farmers (sesame, beans, hides, skins and ghee) fell more drastically than those of European cash crops. In addition, tens of thousands of Africans lost their jobs on settler farms. Despite the ensuing reduction in household incomes, the colonial administration did not adjust the tax obligations of the Africans (Kanogo, 1989). As in West Africa, domestic food trade followed the depression in export trade.

Food market controls cumulated in the settler economies during the Second World War. New committees and so-called commodity control boards were formed in the first two years of the war, controlling the whole economy including the production and marketing of maize. The authorities introduced a guaranteed price for settler-produced maize, bought the commodity in bulk, and introduced compulsory African labour to guarantee production on the settler farms (Bennett, 1965; Zeleza, 1989).[43]

After the war and the recovery in the international economy, the world demand for African commodities and minerals rose rapidly (Adedeji, 1984). At the same time, colonial administrations began to explore indirect interventions rather than direct controls. In French Africa, any hitherto existing direct controls on population movements were abolished

---

South Africa, Bechuanaland (Botswana), Rhodesia (Zimbabwe, Zambia), Nyasaland (Malawi), Kenya and Uganda, Sudan, Sierra Leone, Nigeria, and the Gold Coast (Ghana). The French built them in French Sudan (Senegal, Mali), French Guinea, Dahomey (Benin), Ivory Coast and Upper Volta (Burkina Faso), French Equatorial Africa (Congo, Central African Republic), and on three Islands in the Indian Ocean (Madagascar, Réunion, Mauritius). The Italians built railways in Ethiopia, Eritrea and to a lesser extent Somaliland; the Germans in Southwest Africa (Namibia), Tanganyika, Kamerun (Cameroon) and Togoland; the Belgians in the Belgian Congo; the Portuguese in Angola and Mozambique (Durrant et al., 1981; Wiener, 1931). The railways were usually built by the state, but sometimes a private company took the initiative. An example of a private initiative was the railway line that was built by a German company in Kamerun (now Anglophone Cameroon), going inland from the port of Bonaberi to a distance of about 160 km. It provided the company with transport through the difficult forest zone to the savannah belt (Gann, 1975).

[42] River ports played a major role during the early days of transoceanic trade (Noah, 1989).

[43] Maize produced by African peasants was also bought at a guaranteed price, but it was approximately half the price settlers received (Zeleza, 1989).

(Guyer, 1987). This stimulated urban growth.[44] Farmers increased their production of food commodities to meet the growing needs of the urban population. Rural periodic markets functioned as collection points for food commodities destined for urban daily markets. In addition they served a rural population that was experiencing increasing purchasing power due to the rising prices for export crops such as groundnuts, coffee and cotton.[45]

In East Africa, British colonial administrations continued to use their powers to control population movements and determine the establishment and location of markets. They concentrated on the development of periodic markets 'since it was discovered that they would help more in the economic development of the district than would gazetted towns' (Obudho & Waller, 1976, 55).[46] In the export trade, Marketing Boards took over the role of the commodity control boards (Bennett, 1965).

In the East and Southern African settler economies, the activities of African traders remained largely restricted to the 'reserves'. Wild (1992) showed for Zimbabwe that African traders did very well in these rural areas. Towards the end of the 1950s they had firmly established their hold on rural trading at the expense of European businessmen. In the urban areas, segregation politics hampered the development of African enterprises. However, here the Asians eroded European control on domestic trade, taking over most of the general stores in the traditional European enclaves (Jones-Dube, 1991).[47]

2.3. The post-independence period

In 1960, 16 African states became independent, followed by many others in quick succession during the following years.[48] The new independent nations were confronted with

---

44 The rate of urbanization had remained modest in Sub-Saharan Africa prior to World War II. In 1920, only two to three per cent of the African population lived in towns, and forty per cent of these were Nigerians who had lived in towns for more than a hundred years (Vennetier, 1972). After World War II the rate of urbanization accelerated, reaching its peak during the post-independence period (Elkan & Van Zwanenberg, 1975).

45 Prices in the rural market places were not always lower than in the urban market places. Collecting traders came to periodic markets from distant places to buy large quantities of one product but did not generally bring produce from other areas. The latter produce was brought to the market by a few local traders. As a consequence, periodic markets had a limited range of foodstuffs from other parts of the country for sale at high prices, in contrast with daily markets in urban centres that offered a wider range at more competitive prices (Lawson, 1971). Market places were not always the linchpin of the food trade. So-called landlord systems also existed, whereby buyers and sellers of commodities like kola, fish, cattle, sheep and goats, onions and natron were received in the houses of powerful landlords (Hill, 1971; Hodder, 1971).

46 The most active markets were also made auction centres where cattle could be exchanged in addition to produce. In some parts of western Kenya, new periodic markets were established as part of a plan to redistribute the population (Obudho & Waller, 1976).

47 Indian and European 'general trading stores', which could be wholesale- or retail-oriented, had already been in competition since the pre-war period, not only in settler economies but also in other British colonies such as Malawi (Power, 1993). The British had brought the Indians to East Africa to work on the railways at the end of the 18th century.

48 In 1960 Cameroon, the Central African Republic, Chad, Congo-Brazzaville, Congo-Leopoldville (now Congo), Dahomey (now Benin), Gabon, the Ivory Coast, Mali, Mauritania, Nigeria, Senegal, Somalia, Togo and Upper Volta (now Burkina Faso). In 1961 Sierra Leone and Tanganyika (now Tanzania). In 1962 Burundi, Rwanda and Uganda. In 1963 Kenya. In 1964 Nyasaland (now Malawi), and Northern Rhodesia (now Zambia). In 1965 the Gambia. In 1966 Bechuanaland (now Botswana) and Basutoland

a steady population growth and increasing urbanization. The region was not highly urbanized by global standards, but the urbanization process gathered momentum very rapidly.[49] Six major factors have influenced the urbanization process in post-independence Africa. The first two are endogenous — population growth and rural exodus (Appendix 2.1 summarizes the causes of the rural exodus).[50] The other four are exogenous (White, 1989). One of them is drought, as in 1983/84. The others are related to the global economy. There were price increases of petrol in the 1970s, which were followed in the first half of the 1980s by an appreciation of the US dollar in which oil is priced. There was also the slowdown of the global economy, and the adverse trend in the terms of trade for exporters of primary goods. These international factors led to a concentration of industries and a decline in per capita agricultural production, aggravated by the urban bias in governments' policies.[51]

Government interventions in food production and marketing
The growth of urban centres and the relatively high purchasing power of the urban population boosted the flow of food from the countryside to the cities.[52] Many African governments believed that these flows should be regulated by the state in order to control inflation and replace traditional and private-sector distribution systems that were thought to be inefficient (Manu, 1992). Marketing boards were established in Anglophone Africa, Offices de Commercialisation and Caisses de Stabilisation in Francophone Africa, and Empresas de Comercalização Agrícola in Portuguese-speaking countries, to deal with the collection, storage and distribution of selected food commodities. Most organizations focused on durable crops such as millet, sorghum, rice, and maize, leaving aside perishable crops.[53] In the first half of the 1980s, as many as 29 African countries south of the Sahara

---

(now Lesotho) (Dudley, 1984). Prior to 1960, Ghana was the first and only colony in Sub-Saharan Africa to become independent, in 1957 (Due, 1971).

[49] Today the rate of growth of the urban population in Africa is the highest in the world (UN, 1989). Interregional differences are considerable, however, with higher levels of urban population prevailing in Southern Africa (Kosinski & Clarke, 1982). In 1989, South Africa had the highest urban population as a percentage of the total population (59%), followed by Zambia, the Central African Republic, Liberia, and Mauritania (45% to 50%) (World Bank, 1991). Burundi and Rwanda were the least urbanized (5% to 10%). Cross-country comparisons should, however, be made with caution, because the figures are based on divergent national definitions of what is urban. Between 1980 and 1989, the average annual growth rates of the urban population were the highest in Mozambique, Tanzania and Botswana (10% to 11%) and the lowest in Mali and Sudan (3% to 4%) (World Bank, 1991).

[50] A third endogenous factor involves changing classifications of urban areas, but the contribution of this factor is minimal (UN, 1989).

[51] The international factors also caused increasing national debts, negative balances of payment, and the reliance of many African countries on food aid and concessionary capital (White, 1989). The human crush that resulted from the rural-urban migration 'often added to the frantic political scene in which one-party states were emerging, and where politicians who had lost out in the zero-sum game of African politics, plotted how to compromise with the ruling cliques or overthrow them' (Skinner, 1986, 194).

[52] Purchasing power is most important in the cases of meat, vegetables and fruits, as the general urban trend towards a higher consumption of these commodities is basically conditioned by a rising level of income. This does not mean that urban dwellers are always better off. Nutritional deprivation among the urban poor can be greater than in rural areas due to the closer link between food consumption and purchasing power (Delisle, 1991).

[53] The grain marketing boards succeeded the raw material marketing boards that had already been established under colonial rule in the 1940s and 1950s to deal with commodities like cocoa, coffee, cotton, and oil seeds for export (Dijkstra & Van der Laan, 1990) (see also Section 2.2).

(60%) had one or more marketing boards that were actively involved in the cereal trade (FAO, 1985). In six cases, grain marketing boards had an official monopoly in the domestic market.[54]

Many African countries tried to tackle the increasing need for food not only through market intervention, but also by intervening at the production stage. In the former settler areas of Kenya, many of the large-scale farms were subdivided to parcel out land to small-scale producers.[55] The number of large-scale farms dropped from 4000 in 1960 to less than 400 in 1982 (Odingo, 1971; CBS, 1984).[56]

Africans not only settled on former European farms but also in areas that had hitherto sporadically been used for agriculture. These settlement schemes, which became quite common all over Sub-Saharan Africa, were not merely aimed at increasing commercial food production and the food self-sufficiency of rural households, but also at tackling the problems of (1) displaced persons, landless families and squatters in the rural areas, and (2) unemployment and the rise of a lumpenproletariat in the urban centres (Hill, 1977; Hoorweg et al., 1991). The farmers in the schemes were subject to scheduled production and mandatory marketing arrangements, or were treated like any other small-scale producer.[57]

In some countries, government interventions at the production stage were more drastic. In Tanzania, a forced villagization programme was carried out to increase both yields and the total marketed output (Bryceson, 1993). Between 1973 and 1977, approximately 60 per cent of the rural population was moved into villages. On the marketing side, all cereal trade was monopolized by the National Milling Cooperation, but later cooperative unions were reinstated in an attempt to remedy rising urban food shortages caused by marketing inefficiencies.[58]

Villagization and cooperative production were also forced upon peasant farmers in Mozambique and Ethiopia. In 1976, the FRELIMO government nationalized all land, and in the subsequent five years it relocated one million Mozambicans to communal villages (Davison, 1986). The Marxist government in Ethiopia instituted sweeping land reforms in 1975 which dissolved all existing tenancy and abolished private ownership (Krishnan,

---

[54] Congo-Brazzaville, Gambia, Guinea, Kenya, Mozambique and Zambia (FAO, 1985). Some of these countries had socialist regimes, others had not. The monopoly of the board usually referred to interdistrict and interregional trade, excluding local retail trade, which remained the domain of private traders. The boards were not only responsible for trade, but also for the maintenance of strategic reserves, and in some cases for the actual running of market places. The ADMARC in Malawi, for instance, had an extensive countrywide network of some 1,139 markets (Kaluwa & Chilowa, 1991).

[55] The first settlement schemes were already initiated two years prior to independence 'to facilitate an orderly transfer of land from European to African ownership with little or no drop in productivity' (Odingo, 1971, 188).

[56] The remaining large-scale farms included individually owned farms (many of them absently owned), group-owned farms (including partnership, company and cooperative farms), and farms of the Agricultural Development Corporation (a Kenyan parastatal responsible for the purchase of farms from Europeans and reselling to Africans) (Foeken & Verstrate, 1992; Foeken & Tellegen, 1994).

[57] Four basic types of settlement schemes can be distinguished: schemes with individual holdings, compulsory marketing schemes, schemes with scheduled production, and schemes in which production is collectively organized (Chambers, 1969). In Kenya, the first two are most common (Hoorweg et al., 1991).

[58] The National Milling Cooperation was accorded a monopoly in 1975, after which existing cooperatives were abolished in 1976. In 1983 urban food shortages became so acute that the government had to introduce a party-supervised rationing system in Dar es Salaam. In 1984, cooperative unions were re-established (Bryceson, 1993).

1994). Peasant Associations, Service Cooperatives and Producer Cooperatives were established, and villagization, resettlement, and forced quota deliveries of cereals to the Agricultural Marketing Cooperation were introduced (Habtu, 1994).[59]

Communist and socialist regimes were also in favour of large-scale production on state farms. Nkrumah, the first president of Ghana, sought to make the country a showpiece of African development through mechanized agriculture (Due, 1971). Over 200 state farms were established, which focused on export crops like cacao and food crops like rice. In Benin, the Marxist regime established state farms in the 1970s that produced export crops like French beans and groundnuts, and food crops like maize and rice (Godin, 1986). Large farms were also run by the state in Ethiopia, Mozambique and Angola (Krishnan, 1994; Davison, 1986; Azam et al., 1994). The governments in the latter two countries nationalized plantations that were neglected or abandoned by the Portuguese to form state plantations.[60]

Negative intervention results

The results of government interventions in food production and trade were negative in most cases. In Tanzania, the reinstated cooperatives did nothing to improve the finances or operations of the country's grain marketing. Marketing inefficiency caused huge financial losses among the cooperative unions, which the state eventually paid for through explicit subsidies or enormous bank overdrafts with inflationary consequences (Bryceson, 1993). The main effect was a massive transfer of resources away from peasant farmers (Ellis, 1983, as quoted by Fleming & Antony, 1991).

In Ethiopia, explicit and implicit taxes discouraged farm production (Krishnan, 1994). The system of compulsory deliveries of grains induced farm households to switch towards production of goods that were not covered by the quota system (Aredo, 1994).[61] The inability of the Agricultural Marketing Corporation to carry out the necessary interregional stock movements disadvantaged both consumers in the deficit areas and producers in the surplus areas.[62] Moreover, the subsequent disinvestment in land had disastrous environmental effects (Habtu, 1994). Small-scale production was also hampered by the government's favouritism to state farms. While these farms covered only 4 per cent of the arable land, they received 75 per cent of the available fertilizer and 88 per cent of the improved seeds (Krishnan, 1994). Despite their relatively high input levels, they used the land less efficiently than small-scale producers (Statistisches Bundesamt, 1990).

State farms were also a manifest failure in Ghana, Angola, Benin, and Mozambique. The contribution of Ghanaian state farms to the food supplies of the local peasants was

---

[59] Private ownership of land was also abolished in Angola in 1975. In contrast with Ethiopia and Mozambique, the Angolan government did not relocate peasant farmers or force them into cooperatives. Smallholders could rent land from the state for 90 years (Azam et al., 1994).

[60] Under capitalist regimes private plantations were more common. Like most of the state farms, they focused either on traditional export crops like rubber (e.g. Firestone in Liberia), tea and coffee (e.g. Brooke Bond in Kenya), or on food crops for export like palm oil (e.g. Unilever in Cameroon and Zaire), pineapples (e.g. Del Monte in Kenya), and bananas (e.g. United Brands in Ivory Coast and Cameroon) (Dinham & Hines, 1983).

[61] The farmers also dumped inferior-quality produce onto the Agricultural Marketing Corporation, which was responsible for the compulsory purchases of farm products (Fleming & Antony, 1991).

[62] The consumers had to pay more while the producers received less (Fleming & Antony, 1991).

negligible (Konings, 1986). Most of the farms were phased out by as early as 1970.[63] In Angola, much of the land of the state farms had been appropriated for individual household farming by the early 1980s, and almost all cattle had been absorbed into smallholder herds. The remaining state farms were dependent on state subsidies to cover sizeable deficits, and basically supplied the military forces (Azam et al., 1994). In Benin, the production of the state farms was reduced to practically zero at the beginning of the 1980s, because of mismanagement and lack of spare parts and capital (Godin, 1986). In Mozambique, the bulk of the total agricultural output still came from peasant production, although the FRELIMO government placed priority on state-farm production to the neglect of peasants.[64] Peasant collectivization was not an overwhelming success under the Marxist regime either. Although one million Mozambicans had been relocated to communal villages by 1981, only 70,000 were involved in agricultural cooperatives (Davison, 1986).

Not only state farms and cooperatives failed to achieve their objectives in Sub-Saharan Africa, the same was true of grain marketing boards. In the 1970s it became increasingly clear that statutory food marketing authorities (including the grain marketing boards) were acting according to a hidden agenda that aimed to keep prices low in order to pacify urban populations (Hesp & Van der Laan, 1985, Fleming & Antony, 1991). They were rather effective at transferring producers' surpluses both to the state and the urban consumers.[65] The outcome was, however, achieved at a tremendous cost, notably a reduction in the rate of agricultural and rural development (Fleming & Antony, 1991).[66] In Ghana the results were widespread shortages of food, smuggling, hoarding and corruption. Interventions created a class of newly rich people who had preferential access to government officials (Manu, 1992). In Zimbabwe, incomes among poor rural consumers were effectively reduced by as much as 30 per cent because 100,000 tonnes of expensive commercial maize meal were brought into rural areas annually, at the same time that local grain was being carried out through the state marketing channel (Jayne & Chisvo, 1991).[67] The same circuitous movement of grain was common, for instance, in Malawi, where grain was moved by ADMARC from regions in the north to the strategic grain silos in Lilongwe to be stored, and then moved back in the hungry season for distribution. The operation caused large financial deficits to the parastatal (Kaluwa & Chilowa, 1991).

---

[63] In the aftermath of the first Ghanaian coup, many of Nkrumah's programmes were dismantled as quickly as possible. The state farms were no exception. By June 1968 the number of state farms had been halved and the labour force had been reduced by three quarters (Hill, 1977). By mid-1970 only 38 farms had survived, including three rice farms (Due, 1971).

[64] In 1985, state farms were responsible for 28% of the total agricultural output (largely cash crops for export) in the central region of Mozambique, while 12% came from cooperatives and 60% from peasants (Davison, 1986).

[65] Schiff & Valdés (1992), who studied Ivory Coast, Ghana and Zambia, calculated that as a result of the combined effect of direct and indirect price interventions, there was a huge transfer of income from agriculture towards the government and the rest of the non-agricultural economy in these countries, representing a staggering 96% of their agricultural GDP between 1960 and 1984.

[66] Schiff & Valdés (1992) associated high taxation of agriculture through direct and indirect price interventions statistically with lower agricultural and overall growth rates.

[67] The system was very costly in terms of transport and storage, especially because the price system failed to synchronize supply and demand for grains. Unit handling costs increased because of a vast depot network that was dictated mainly by social and political considerations. Weak accountability processes and the bureaucratic nature of the marketing board further contributed to the high marketing margins (Jiriyengwa, 1993; Takavaraha, 1993).

Many grain marketing boards had to face a financial crisis sooner or later. The NCPB of Kenya had billions of shillings of outstanding debts in 1987. Farmers were complaining about excessive payment delays, while commercial banks were unwilling to extend any further credit to the board. The financial problems resulted not only from allocative and operational inefficiencies, but also from the Treasury's reluctance to finance the exceptional losses made by the board in carrying out its price stabilization and food security objectives (Smith, 1992).[68] The wide trade margin which the board had to set to accommodate its high costs further encouraged informal sector markets and private sector trading, reducing the board's ability to achieve its food security objectives (Smith, 1992).[69]

In Mali the monopoly of the grain marketing board was likewise more fictional than real. The OPAM handled only 20 to 40 per cent of the total grain market in the country (Staatz et al., 1989). Meanwhile, the repression of private trade, while not sufficient to eliminate it, did increase transaction costs. OPAM's official monopoly and its system of official prices also acted as major disincentives to domestic grain production.[70]

Structural adjustment

All in all, the involvement of the state in primary agricultural marketing placed an enormous burden on the African economies.[71] This did not remain unnoticed, all the more because it appeared to be part of a general problem of inefficiency and ineffectiveness of public sector activities. The situation was seriously questioned for the first time in the mid-1970s, when agricultural stagnation, a hostile external economic environment, and an internal debt crisis was impairing the macroeconomic performance of most African countries. The fact that many such countries were unable to recover from the 1974 oil crisis was blamed at least partly on their large public sectors, which, it was argued, robbed these economies of the flexibility they needed to achieve the necessary adjustments (Najib & Nindi, 1988).

Although changes were generally thought necessary, they took off very slowly in the following years.[72] They gained momentum, however, after the second oil crisis in 1979. Governments had to look desperately for foreign financiers, who set their conditions (Najib

---

[68] The allocative inefficiencies stemmed from the various types of administrative controls in operation, while the operational inefficiencies stemmed predominantly from the board's monopoly position, which encouraged managerial slackness and rent-seeking activities. The board's costs were also inflated by the expansion of the depot and buying centre network, a threefold increase in the number of employees between 1980 and 1987, and the need to finance the strategic reserve of maize (Bates, 1989; Smith, 1992).

[69] The policy of stringent movement regulations aggravated an already substantial regional and seasonal food price variation in rural Kenya, simultaneously raising the profitability of private trade and placing restrictions on it (Meilink, 1987).

[70] Other similarities with boards in other countries were mismanagement and accumulating deficits (Staatz et al., 1989).

[71] African farmers, for instance, received a significantly smaller part of the final consumer price than Asian farmers, even taking into account the higher transport and related marketing costs on the African continent (Ahmed, 1988).

[72] The slow implementation of reforms was related to a number of widely observed factors: vested interests and political factors, an unwillingness to give up direct patronage benefits; the beliefs prevalent in many countries that markets would not work, that peasants would be exploited, etc.; the fact that short-term gains might be small; that some ethnic groups or foreigners would be the prime beneficiaries; that piecemeal reform was difficult since complex systems were often at stake; that reformers often did a poor job; and that donor assistance could sometimes allow governments to avoid hard choices (Berg, 1985).

& Nindi, 1988). Structural adjustment was recommended, grain marketing liberalization being one of the central components (Shepherd, 1989).

Senegal's parastatal for cereals (ONCAD) was liquidated as early as 1980,[73] while grain marketing in Mali was gradually deregulated from 1981 onwards.[74] Many countries followed in subsequent years. Deregulation took place in Burkina Faso, Kenya, Tanzania, Madagascar, Malawi, Zimbabwe, Somalia, and Ethiopia, while grain marketing boards were phased out in Nigeria, Zambia, Zaire, Ivory Coast and Sierra Leone (Antony & Fleming, 1991; Reusse, 1987).[75] In some countries the process went very gradually, as in Tanzania, where grain trade deregulation started in 1984, only to be completed in 1990. The buying monopoly of the Tanzanian cooperative unions was phased out by gradually allowing private traders to handle larger quantities of grain, and eventually permitting them to purchase directly from the farmers instead of dealing with farmers' societies (Coulter & Golob, 1992). In other countries the road of adjustment was more circuitous. The Zambian government dissolved the poorly performing NAMBOARD in 1989, transferring its marketing functions to cooperative unions (as in Tanzania five years earlier). The unions, however, were unable to operate efficiently under a pricing structure based on huge subsidies to maize meal consumers. Eventually, all consumer subsidies were abolished in 1991, and the remaining restrictions on maize marketing were removed (Jones & Beynon, 1992).

The first results of the deregulation of the African grain trade have been encouraging. To mention but a few, in Tanzania liberalization improved the efficiency of resource allocation, stimulated private enterprise and contributed towards production surpluses (Coulter & Golob, 1992); in Mali, liberalization stimulated entry into grain marketing, led to an increase in specialization and scale of operations, and reduced premiums demanded by merchants (Staatz et al., 1989); in Madagascar, liberalization led to growing competitiveness and effectiveness, which significantly diminished rice price differences between surplus and deficit areas (Berg, 1989).

Nevertheless, the deregulation process has also exposed the weaknesses of African economies. Due to the long period of suppression in Tanzania, the system which has emerged from liberalization exhibits many inefficiencies:

> Wholesale traders characteristically have little capital, handle small volumes (not more than a truckload at a time), and do not invest in vehicles or interseasonal storage of grains. Their operation is hampered by the poor state of the roads, a shortage of vehicles, a lack of market infrastructure, and above all the absence of any source of formal credit for private trading operations. There is limited integration of the country's different markets, with restricted spatial flows reflected

---

73 The core activity of the Senegalese ONCAD was groundnut marketing, while millet marketing and supplying inputs were additional activities. ONCAD's dissolution brought greater participation by private enterprise in the millet market, but not in the groundnut market, where cooperatives and other parastatals filled the gap (Hoogervorst et al., 1988; Van der Laan & Van Haaren, 1990).

74 In exchange for the Malian government's agreement to abolish the state's legal monopoly on grain trade and to encourage private sector marketing, international agencies and donors pledged long-term shipments of food aid to supply the urban areas with grain during the transition period (Staatz et al., 1989).

75 In Madagascar the deregulated commodity was rice, and in Zimbabwe it was wheat. In other countries more than one type of grain was involved. The phased-out marketing boards in Ivory Coast and Sierra Leone dealt with rice, and in Zaire with maize. The others dealt with more than one type of grain.

by high regional price fluctuations. Lack of market information and systems of communication between markets have increased the risk of trading (Coulter & Golob, 1992, 421).

In Mali, similar and other constraints hamper most wholesalers in responding fully to the opportunities created by the grain trade liberalization; notably these are a shortage of working capital, lack of political connections, and the riskiness of the trade.[76] The latter derives from demand and supply instability, regulatory uncertainty, and the unenforceable nature of contracts.[77] In Madagascar, deregulation of the rice market has been impeded by ambiguous regulations, continuing limits on free entry, attempts at cartelization, and tenacious resistance of existing stakeholders and institutions. Additional structural constraints are poor roads, weak extension services, and inadequate credit systems and input supply arrangements (Berg, 1989). In Malawi the liberalization of food trade has affected food supplies to households in remote areas. These areas have experienced the closure of uneconomic ADMARC buying-and-selling points, while private traders have been reluctant to penetrate them.[78] Even where such traders do operate, they typically purchase for sale in other areas, leaving food-deficit households with access to fewer alternative sources of food (Kaluwa & Chilowa, 1991; Kandoole, 1991).[79]

On the basis of these and other experiences, it is now generally agreed that simply eliminating government controls and allowing resources to be allocated by the market may not yield the desired results. African governments have to play a role in creating the institutional framework within which efficient and effective grain markets can emerge. Primary factors in accelerating the development of private trading are (1) the development of market places, storage structures and rural financial markets, (2) long-term infrastructural policies to reduce transport costs, and (3) investment in market support systems, marketing research, and quality grades and standards.[80]

Other food commodities
Prior to structural adjustment, marketing boards dealt with grain trade in over half of the African countries south of the Sahara. At the same time, other, less strategic food commodities were hardly handled by parastatals. A few exceptions did exist.

---

[76] Political connections were important in the beginning because sales contracts with the OPAM were initially awarded not by an open bidding process but through personal contacts. Obtaining a contract to supply OPAM was very lucrative, because OPAM was buying grain at an official producer price that was considerably higher than the open market price (Staatz et al., 1989).

[77] Regulatory uncertainty exists when officials do not apply formal regulations, e.g. negotiating tax payments for the benefit of official and trader, or harassing traders that respect all regulations.

[78] Traders have not replaced ADMARC in areas that were abandoned as a result of the rationalization of economic activities. Both ADMARC and private traders are competing in accessible areas. This has had adverse effects in most remote areas in terms of access to inputs and markets (Mtawali, 1993).

[79] Apart from alternative food crops, these households presently have to rely on other farmers who are able to buy or grow and store excess maize. These surplus farmers realize high margins by trading maize for labour when the labour supply is high (the hungry season) and maize is short in supply. 'By neglecting their own farms, short-term food deficit farmers can find themselves in chronic deficit situations' (Kaluwa & Chilowa, 1991, 116).

[80] For a discussion on these factors see Santorum & Tibaijika (1992), Dias et al. (1991), Kaluwa & Chilowa (1991), Takavarasha (1993), Shawa (1993), Von Braun & Paulino (1990), Coulter & Golob (1992), Beynon et al. (1992).

Trade in sugar was monopolized by the state in Burkina Faso, Ivory Coast, Mali, Kenya, Tanzania and Zambia (FAO, 1985). Importation of foreign sugar was usually more important than the collection of local production. Domestic production was insufficient either because of unfavourable agro-ecological conditions, or, as in the case of Tanzania and Kenya, because of poor performance of the government-controlled sugar industry.[81] The sugar sectors have been reformed or are being reformed now.[82]

Trade of processed fluid milk was monopolized in Kenya by a national cooperative and in Zambia and Swaziland by a dairy board (FAO, 1985). The Kenya Cooperative Creamery (KCC) had a monopoly on milk sales in urban centres by virtue of a law that forbade trade of raw milk in cities. The milk market was liberalized in 1992 after the milk collection and marketing system of the KCC had broken down (Jaffee, 1995).[83] Private traders responded to the new situation by capturing a major share of the urban market.[84]

Kenyan and Zambian parastatals at one time monopolized commercial slaughtering of beef cattle (FAO, 1985). The Kenya Meat Commission (KMC) had a legal monopoly over commercial slaughter in the 1960s, but lost it in the 1970s. From then on, the KMC was supposed to concentrate on slaughter for export and export trade, while private firms took care of the domestic market. It did not become a very successful exporter, however (Evangelou, 1984; Rutten, 1992).[85]

Trade in vegetables, fruits and tubers was not monopolized in any African country during the post-independence period. The commodities were left to the free market. As a consequence, demographic, physical, and sociocultural circumstances determined the trade process, rather than political or legal ones. We will look into these circumstances (marketing channel environments) in various chapters of the present work. A few short remarks will do here. The sociocultural environment affects producers' sales decisions, traders' trading practices, and consumers' eating habits (see Section 4.1). As for the demographic environment, most transactions are concentrated in market places. The spatial organization of

---

81 The main causes of the disappointing performance of the Tanzanian sugar industry were (1) a shortage of foreign exchange (in combination with a high foreign exchange component in both operating and replacement costs), (2) an unfavourable pricing policy, and (3) deficiencies in management (NDC, 1992). In Kenya the reasons were more or less similar: (1) rising input costs, (2) a poor policy environment that provided disincentives to farmers, and (3) inefficient state-run sugar factories (Chalon, 1994). The processing capacity of Kenya's sugar factories potentially could meet domestic demand (PAM, 1995).

82 The Tanzanian reforms, which took off in 1986, included liberalization of prices, foreign exchange measures, and institutional reforms (NDC, 1992). The Kenyan reforms were announced in 1992. All sugar factories were listed for privatization (Chalon, 1994). Prices were decontrolled in 1993.

83 In early 1992 the Kenya Cooperative Creamery (KCC) was no longer able to meet urban demand because of a drought in the production areas, a liquidity crisis which led to payment delays of 3 to 4 months, and the inability to reconstitute large quantities of imported powered milk due to a lack of butter oil. As a consequence, the government was forced to relax controls on private milk distribution, including those on raw milk sales in cities (Jaffee, 1995).

84 In Nairobi the KCC's sales of fluid milk (pasteurized and sterilized [UHT]) fell from 400,000 litres/day in early 1982 to 230,000 litres/day in early 1993 (Jaffee, 1995).

85 The KMC had to receive its supplies from the Livestock Marketing Division (LMD), another parastatal responsible for the purchase of stock in pastoralist areas. However, the LMD was unable to compete with private traders who offered higher prices and direct payment (Evangelou, 1984; Rutten, 1992). The KMC has failed where the Botswana Meat Commission (BMC), which has a monopoly on beef exports from Botswana, has succeeded. According to Abbott (1987), the success of the BMC has been in its relationship with the Botswana government: it has received strong backing, without being pressured to take decisions that are politically desirable but economically costly.

these market places tends to follow population distributions (Section 4.5). Population distributions change with urbanization. In West Africa, urbanization and urban growth have moulded the trade of food (including horticultural commodities), as well as the location of market places, since pre-colonial days (Section 2.1). In most other parts of Sub-Saharan Africa, the urbanization process started during the colonial period, as did its effect on indigenous food systems. The settler economies were the only exception: urbanization and urban growth did occur, but segregation policies of colonial governments curtailed the possibilities of indigenous food traders to respond to increasing urban demands (Section 2.2). Here, a direct relation between urbanization and the trade in food (including horticultural commodities) could only develop after independence.

In addition to the demographic environment, the physical environment has played a major role in the development of post-independence horticultural trade (Section 5.6 and Chapter 6). That relation dates back to the pre-colonial period, when the structure of long-distance food trade was determined by transport conditions in various agro-ecological zones, and by the presence of things like navigable rivers (Section 2.1). In the colonial period the building of railways and the improvement of roads determined the emergence of new trade routes and market places for both export crops and food crops (Section 2.2).

Up to the 1970s, the purchasing power of consumers also played an important role in the development of food trade. This factor dates back to the long-distance caravans that traversed pre-colonial Africa. The traders were in need of large amounts of food and had considerable purchasing power, thus generating local food trade (Section 2.1). During the colonial period the introduction of cash crops increased the purchasing power of African farmers, further stimulating local trade in food (Section 2.2). Purchasing power lost importance as stimulating factor after the first oil crisis in 1974. The reason is that, on the whole, the purchasing power of the African population has not improved since that time. Between 1975 and 1993, per capita private consumption in Sub-Saharan Africa decreased on average 0.8 per cent per year (at current prices) (World Bank, 1995). Differences between countries do exist, but most had to cope with a decline, and none showed the kind of growth figures that were common for developing countries in East Asia (in Section 7.1 we will look in more detail at purchasing-power indicators for Kenya).[86]

2.4. Concluding remarks on food trade in Sub-Saharan Africa

The previous sections have traced the development of food trade in Sub-Saharan Africa. Various factors have influenced this development. The first is urbanization. From the very beginning of agriculture in the New Stone Age, a relationship has existed between urbanization and market development. Agriculture made urban settlements possible, which in turn led to the rise of a class of merchants who began trading food with the townspeople. Thus, urbanization gave rise to marketing channels. However, initially the non-market

---

[86] During the same period the average annual growth in per capita private consumption for East Asia and the Pacific was 5.3 per cent (World Bank, 1995). According to the World Bank, the highest average annual growth rate in the East was found in China: 6.6 per cent. The top of the class of Sub-Saharan Africa was Chad: 1.9 per cent.

provision of food remained common. Moreover, food trade also developed in regions of Africa without urban centres. Factors of importance in those areas were agro-ecological differences, interethnic boundaries, and a demand for specific raw materials like salt and iron ore which were traded in exchange for food and other commodities.

Once established, the development of local and regional food marketing networks was stimulated by the growth of trans-Saharan trade with the Mediterranean countries and of overseas trade with the Middle and Far East. Later still, Europe and the Americas came to be the most important export destinations and European traders the leading intermediaries. The trans-Atlantic trade led to a rapid growth of urban centres and a further intensification of regional and local food trade.

During the colonial period, the same process of export-led town and market development continued, with two exceptions. In the settler economies, new centres of food trade arose due to segregation policies. In the mining economies, urban centres inhabited by a new class of consumers sprang up around the mines. Elsewhere, food production and trade were stimulated by taxation in kind and by the rising purchasing power of farmers involved in cash crop production. Trade flows and the locations of market centres were affected by the improvement of local transportation networks.

After independence, urbanization and urban growth resumed their role as a catalyst of market development, as prior to the rise of the trans-Atlantic trade. However, the actual structure of food production and marketing systems was often governed by government policies. In many countries, cooperatives, state farms and marketing boards were used to stimulate, regulate or monopolize production and trade, especially of grains. Perishables were thought less strategic, and the trade in these commodities was seen as too risky for successful government intervention. Grain trade was again deregulated in most countries in the 1980s and 1990s, after two decades of disastrous experiments. Policymakers started to put their faith in the free market, reinventing the importance of private trade.

All in all, the development of food trade in Sub-Saharan Africa has varied in relation to population distributions (urbanization and urban growth), transport, purchasing power and government policies. Purchasing power was important in the late pre-colonial period and the colonial period, but has declined in significance during the post-independence period (especially in the 1970s and 1980s) due to stagnating per capita incomes. Government policies have affected grains in particular, while being of lesser consequence for vegetables, fruits, tubers and other perishables.

3

Horticulture in Kenya, with Special Reference to the Research Areas[1]

The present chapter will discuss the production of horticultural commodities in Kenya. In the first two sections Kenya will be introduced, and the national horticultural picture will be drawn. In subsequent sections the research areas will be presented, and some aspects of the horticultural enterprise in these areas will be analysed.

3.1. Kenya

Kenya belongs to the middle-income countries of Sub-Saharan Africa. In 1992, it had a per capita GNP of $310. Mozambique had the lowest per capita GNP of Sub-Saharan Africa ($ 60) and Botswana the highest ($ 2,790) (World Bank, 1994). Kenya has one of the fastest growing populations of the continent, having witnessed a 40 per cent population increase in ten years' time. The annual growth rate was 3.4 per cent between 1979 and 1989 (CBS, 1981, 1994b).[2] Only Ivory Coast had a higher population growth rate during that period (3.8 per cent) (World Bank, 1994). Overall, Kenya's average population density is not particularly high compared to other African countries. In 1989, the average population density for the whole country was 36 persons per square kilometre (CBS, 1994b). Countries such as Nigeria, Burundi, Uganda and Gambia had densities over twice as high (UN, 1993). However, by far the largest part of Kenya consists of sparsely populated dry lowlands, and 18 per cent of the land accommodates 80 per cent of the population: in 1989, 17.1 million people lived on 103,150 sq km of land, while the remaining 4.3 million lived on 478,630 sq km (CBS, 1994b). Population concentrations can be found in the highland areas of central and western Kenya and along the shores of Lake Victoria and the Indian Ocean.

---

1   An earlier version of this chapter has been published by the author in the *Scandinavian Journal of Development Alternatives and Area Studies*, Vol. 16. no. 1, 1997, pp. 49-74: 'Commercial Horticulture by African Smallholders: A Success Story from the Highlands of Kenya.'
2   The two most recent population censuses were carried out in 1979 and 1989.

Over 80 per cent of the people live in rural areas (CBS, 1994c). Agriculture is their main activity and source of cash income. Traditional export crops for smallholder production are coffee, tea, pyrethrum and cotton. Many farmers have turned away from those crops, though, because of low producer prices and excessive delays in payment by the marketing boards that monopolize the trade.[3] Horticulture has become a popular alternative because it brings fair prices and immediate returns. The market prospects for vegetables, fruits and tubers are favourable as a result of ongoing urban growth. The share of the Kenyan population classified as urban increased from 15 per cent in 1979 to 18 per cent ten years later. In 1989, 3.9 million people lived in urban centres in Kenya, compared to 2.3 million in 1979 (CBS, 1994c).

3.2. Horticulture: the national picture

The Kenyan climates and soils are suitable for growing a large variety of vegetables, fruits and flowers (Table 3.1). The commodities are used as staple food (potatoes, bananas), are served as a supplement with *ugali* (tomatoes, onions, kale), or are grown for export

Table 3.1. Major horticultural commodities in Kenya

Vegetables and tubers	Artichokes	Cauliflower	Lettuce
	Asparagus	Celery	Okra
	Baby marrows	Chillies	Onions
	Beetroot	Cucumbers	Potatoes
	Brinjals	Dudi	Radishes
	Brussels sprouts	Galka	Snake gourds
	Cabbages	Karela	Spinach
	Capsicums	Kohlrabi	Turia
	Carrots	Kale	Turnips
Fruits	Avocados	Limes	Plums
	Apples	Mangoes	Pomelos
	Bananas	Mulberries	Strawberries
	Cape Gooseberries	Oranges	Sweet melons
	Figs	Papayas	Tangerines
	Grapes	Passion fruit	Tomatoes
	Guavas	Pears	Tree tomatoes
	Lemons	Pineapples	Watermelons
Cut-flowers	Alstroemerias	Lilies	Solidasters
	Ammi majus	Moluccella	Spray carnations
	Arabicum	Orchids	Standard carnations
	Chrysanthemums	Ornithogalums	Statice
	Delphiniums	Roses	Tuberoses

Note: Appendix 3.1 provides an extended list of vegetables and fruits, including their common and botanical names.

---

3   In the second half of the 1980s and first half of the 1990s, payment delays for coffee and cotton became extreme. Payments to coffee farmers (by the Coffee Board of Kenya through the Kenya Planters' Co-operative Union) and to cotton farmers (by the Cotton Lint and Seed Marketing Board) would often take more than a year (Weekly Review, 1990; Dijkstra, 1990).

purposes (French beans, avocados, cut flowers). Many of them were known in Kenya before the colonial period, but others were introduced by European settlers (potatoes, cabbages) or more recently by Kenyan research institutes (apples, strawberries).

Horticulture occupies eleven per cent of the total arable land, ranking third after maize cultivation,[4] and dairy farming. By comparison, coffee and tea account for only three per cent and two per cent respectively of arable land (Nyamiaka, 1995). According to Nyamiaka (1995), approximately 210,000 hectares of land were under production for fruits, vegetables and cut flowers in 1991 (Table 3.2).[5] He does not mention the land under production of tubers.

Almost all horticulture in Kenya is rain-fed and concentrated in the highland areas. The only exceptions are the small-scale production of citrus fruits and mangoes in the coastal

Table 3.2. Production of vegetables, fruits and cut flowers in Kenya, 1991

Crops	Hectares	Production in Tonnes
Fruits:		
Bananas	75,714	1,026,276
Citrus	19,287	190,875
Mangoes	10,173	93,994
Pineapples	8,322	378,705
Avocados	1,562	18,710
Passion fruit	1,463	16,256
Papayas	4,400	44,593
Apples	388	3,727
Pears	521	8,059
Plums	808	5,550
Others	1,910	12,885
Total	124,548	1,799,630
Vegetables:		
Cabbages	23,049	363,861
Tomatoes	9,292	118,414
Kale	18,178	220,532
Onions	7,086	73,140
Carrots	5,255	63,030
Brinjals	1,343	13,985
French beans	5,939	28,645
Chillies	1,432	9,443
Garden peas	6,752	31,643
Asian vegetables	2,299	37,187
Traditional vegetables	3,949	13,342
Others	1,961	19,492
Total	86,535	992,714
Cut flowers:		
Total	638	16,405

Source: Nyamiaka, 1995.

---

4   Part of the maize is intercropped with beans. The beans are normally intended for drying. They are not included in the area under horticulture.
5   Appendix 3.2 specifies the hectarage under cut flowers (including cut foliage).

region, and some large-scale farms and settlement schemes with irrigated production near rivers and lakes in the dry lowlands.[6] Table 3.3 lists all horticultural production areas and Map 5 shows the districts involved.[7]

Most small-scale horticultural farmers focus on production for family consumption and for the domestic market. The limited number of large-scale farms in the country concentrate mainly on production for export. Sometimes small-scale out-growers are contracted, for instance for French beans and so-called Asian vegetables (chilli peppers, okra, eggplants etc.), but they are relatively few in number. Horticultural exports make up approximately five per cent of the total volume of horticultural commodities marketed in the country (HCDA, 1990).[8] It can be concluded that commercial horticulture in Kenya is first and foremost rain-fed production for the domestic market by smallholders in the highland regions.

3.3. Smallholder horticulture in Nyandarua, Kisii and Taita Taveta

Three Districts were selected to study commercial horticulture among smallholders in more detail: Nyandarua, Kisii and Taita Taveta (see Section 1.3).[9] Nyandarua was occupied by pastoralists (Masai) during pre-colonial days (Rutten, 1992).[10] Later it was brought under cultivation by non-African settlers and became part of the White Highlands. The settler farms were located on the Kinangop plateau, which covers the lower parts of the present Nyandarua District; they measured 400 to 800 hectares each. The farmers cultivated cereals and pyrethrum and kept dairy cattle and sheep (Odingo, 1971).[11]

After independence (in 1963) most settlers were bought out, and most farms were subdivided by the government to be allocated to small-scale producers, mainly of Kikuyu ethnic origin. Later, additional settlement schemes were established in the forest reserves higher up the slopes of the Aberdare Range that borders the district to the east. The population density in the district remained relatively low compared to other parts of the Kenyan highlands.

Horticulture has been of major importance to small-scale producers from the moment they settled in the district. Coffee and tea cannot be cultivated at this high altitude (over 2400 metres). By 1970 about half the total area under cultivation in the settlement schemes was being used to grow Irish potatoes, cabbages, green peas and other horticultural commodities. In the next two decades the relative importance of horticulture remained roughly the same,

---

6   See Foeken et al. (1989), Hoorweg et al. (1991) and Hoorweg et al. (1995) on the coastal region, and Ruigu (1988) on large-scale irrigation schemes.

7   The map shows district boundaries as they existed in 1990.

8   The estimate dates back to 1990. More recent figures are not available, but the export percentage has increased one or two per cent at best since then. Large differences exist from one commodity to another: by far the bulk of the marketed French beans and cut flowers are exported, while many other commodities are not exported at all (see Section 5.4 on horticultural exports).

9   Appendix 3.3 provides some information on the altitude, rainfall, soil and population density in the research areas.

10   Some parts of Nyandarua still bear Masai names (Ol Kalou, Ol Joro Orok).

11   Pyrethrum is a naturally occurring insecticide. Traditionally it was used widely in domestic, institutional and commercial applications. Nowadays its uses are more restricted as a consequence of historical supply problems and the availability of cheap synthetic alternatives (Robbins, 1984).

Table 3.3. Horticultural production areas in Kenya

Production area	Altitude	Type of production (rainfall p.a.)	Major vegetables domestic market	Major vegetables export market	Minor vegetables	Fruits
A) Kiambu, Machakos, Nairobi	800-2400 metres	rain-fed (1500-2000 mm) Machakos: irrigated (1) (600-1000 mm)	cabbage, carrot, Irish potato, kale, (spring) onion, tomato	brinjal, capsicum, chilli, okra, French bean, karela	broccoli, pea, Brussels sprout, cauliflower, courgette, lettuce, spinach, cucumber	mango, citrus, papaya, banana, pineapple, passion fruit, avocado
B) Baringo, Nyandarua, Nakuru	2100-2800 metres Lake Naivasha: 1900 metres Lake Baringo: 1000 metres	Molo, Nyandarua: rain-fed (1200-1800 mm) Lake Naivasha, Lake Baringo: irrigated (400-600 mm)	cabbage, carrot, Irish potato, kale, (spring) onion, garden pea	capsicum, chilli, courgette, French bean, cut flowers (2)	broccoli, spinach, Brussels sprout, cauliflower, courgette, lettuce, cucumber (2)	plum, apple, pear
C) Embu, Meru Nyeri, Muranga, Kirinyaga	800-2500 metres	1200-2500 m: rain-fed (1000-2000 mm) 800-1200 m: irrigated (3) (400-800 mm)	cabbage, carrot, Irish potato, kale, onion, tomato (4)	brinjal, capsicum, French bean (5)		banana, orange, papaya, pineapple
D) Kisii, South Nyanza	1100-2200 metres	rain-fed (Kisii: 1200-2100 mm; S. Nyanza: 700-1800 mm)	cabbage, kale, onion, tomato			banana, pineapple, passion fruit
E) Busia, Siaya, Kakamega, Bungoma, Kisumu	Busia, Kisumu, Siaya: 1100-1500 metres Bungoma, Kakamega: 1200-2000 metres	rain-fed (Bungoma, Busia, Kakamega: 1100-2000 mm; Kisumu, Siaya: 700-1800 mm) Lake Victoria: irrigated	cabbage, kale, (spring) onion, tomato	French bean (tinned)		mango, banana, passion fruit, orange

Table 3.3, continued

F) Trans Nzoia	1600-2200 metres	rain-fed and irrigated (6) (900-1400 mm)		citrus, apple, avocado
G) Kilifi, Kwale	0-500 metres	rain-fed and irrigated (7) (400-1400 mm) (8)	brinjal, capsicum, onion, tomato	mango, citrus, cashew nut
H) Taita-Taveta	600-1000 metres Taita Hills: 1200-1700 metres	Taita Hills: rain-fed (800-1500 mm) Taveta, Voi: irrigated (400-600 mm)	cabbage, carrot, kale, onion, tomato	banana, mango, passion fruit
I) Oloitokitok	1800-2000 metres	irrigated (600-800 mm)	onion, tomato	
J) Garissa	200-300 metres	irrigated (250-500 mm)		banana, citrus, melon

Source: MOA, 1989.

Notes:

(1) mainly along Athi-River/Yatta Furrow
(2) export and minor vegetables especially under irrigation at Lake Naivasha
(3) including Kibirigwi irrigation scheme
(4) English potatoes especially in Meru
(5) export produce especially in Muranga
(6) usually large-scale farming
(7) irrigated horticulture particularly in case of vegetables
(8) high rainfall usually restricted to a narrow strip along the coast

44

Map 5. Horticultural production areas in Kenya

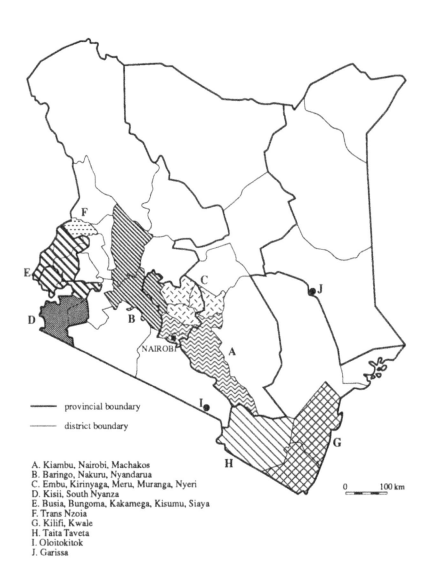

——— provincial boundary

——— district boundary

A. Kiambu, Nairobi, Machakos
B. Baringo, Nakuru, Nyandarua
C. Embu, Kirinyaga, Meru, Muranga, Nyeri
D. Kisii, South Nyanza
E. Busia, Bungoma, Kakamega, Kisumu, Siaya
F. Trans Nzoia
G. Kilifi, Kwale
H. Taita Taveta
I. Oloitokitok
J. Garissa

0   100 km

while the total area under cultivation increased by about one third.[12] The district had developed into one of the chief suppliers of potatoes and cabbages to the Nairobi market, a 100 km to 140 km journey from the production area.

Seventy per cent of the total area of Nyandarua District is suitable for horticulture. The remaining parts have to cope with frequent night frosts, unreliable rain and waterlogging (Jaetzold and Schmidt, 1983). The district's climate favours cultivation of temperate vegetables and fruits. The end of the long rains and the start of the short rains usually overlap, allowing two successful vegetable crops a year, and three with some luck. Maize is hardly grown in the areas suitable for horticulture because of its very long growth season of up to a year and its susceptibility to frost damage. Potatoes are the main staple food. In addition to horticulture, pyrethrum is grown as a cash crop, and graded cows (Frisian Holsteins) are kept to sell milk.

Kisii District is inhabited by the Gusii, who were traditionally mixed agriculturists-pastoralists.[13] They settled in the area in the 19th century, after being pushed out of the Kano plains and away from the shores of Lake Victoria, where they had arrived in the 16th century. During the colonial period, the area was part of the 'reserves'. The British administrators introduced coffee for smallholder production on an experimental basis in the 1930s, and tea and pyrethrum in the 1950s (Carlsen, 1980). In the course of time, farm sizes shrank substantially due to population growth and the subdivision of holdings as part of the inheritance system. At present, Kisii is among the most densely populated rural areas of Kenya (average density 554 persons per sq km).

Eighty per cent of the district is suitable for horticulture, with the remaining part lacking appropriate soils (Jaetzold and Schmidt, 1983). Although Kisii receives rain almost throughout the year (allowing three successive crops), two vegetable crop cycles per annum are most common. By far the most important horticultural commodity in the area are bananas, which are harvested more or less continuously. They are usually cultivated in monocultures, enriching the scenery with banana forests.[14]

The area under bananas more than quadrupled between 1970 and 1991, while the area under tea increased more gradually and the areas under coffee and pyrethrum declined during the same two decades.[15] Increasing scarcity of land and selling prices that were thought to be fair stimulated the cash crop production of bananas.[16] The bunches find their way to urban centres in western Kenya, the Rift Valley and the central highlands close to 370

---

[12] In 1970, 21,500 ha out of 40,300 ha was being used for horticulture (MFP, 1971). In 1991, the total area under cultivation had increased to 55,800 ha, of which 23,600 ha was used for horticulture (OVPMPND, 1994c).

[13] Kisii District in today's Kenya is smaller than the area discussed in this book because of a redrawing of district boundaries.

[14] Two types of bananas are grown: cooking bananas (Musa paradisiana), which are cooked and mashed before being eaten, and sweet bananas (Musa sapientum), usually consumed fresh. The cooking type is more common in Kisii.

[15] The area under bananas increased from 5,400 ha in 1970 to 20,000 in 1985 and approx. 24,000 in 1991. The area under tea rose from 6,200 ha in 1970 to approx. 15,000 ha in 1991, while the area under coffee declined from 11,100 ha to less than 7,000 ha, and the area under pyrethrum from 5,300 ha to approx. 4,000 ha (MFP, 1971; MPND, 1989; OVPMPND, 1994a; OVPMPND, 1994b).

[16] In contrast with bananas, tea and coffee cannot be intercropped with food crops without drastically reducing their yields.

km down the road. Some even reach Mombasa after an 850 km journey. Notwithstanding the importance of bananas, maize is the Gusii's staple food.

Taita Taveta is a district with two centres of agricultural production: the wet, foggy Taita Hills and the farmland around the Taveta springs in the otherwise dry lowlands. The Taita, who now occupy the Taita Hills, settled in the area in the 16th century after migrating southwards from Somalia together with other Bantu-speaking groups. They were agriculturists who in the 19th century started to sell surplus produce such as sugar cane, beans, dried cassava, sweet potatoes and gourds to passing caravans in exchange for cloth, metal objects and other items (Hollis, 1975). In the 1890s the missionaries introduced coffee (Nazzaro, 1974).

The Taita became further drawn into the cash economy by working for colonial officers who had established an administrative centre in the hills at Wundanyi, and for private companies that had received large concessions at the foot of the hills, which they turned into sisal plantations.[17] After independence, wage labour remained an important source of income to households in the region. The tourist industry along the coast and in the game parks that surround the Taita Hills developed into a new major employer.[18]

In the early 1940s the Taita were already growing vegetables for the Mombasa market, 170 km away. Cabbage was the most important crop. In 1941, colonial officers established a cooperative which collected the produce to be transported by truck to Voi, where it was loaded onto trains to Mombasa (African World, 1954).[19] In 1965 the newly independent government finished bituminizing the Voi-Mombasa road, which made possible direct transport to the coast by road (GOK, 1964, 1966). Since then, the hills have developed into one of the chief suppliers of the Mombasa market, not only for cabbages but also for highly perishable commodities such as tomatoes and capsicums. Most farmers produce two horticultural crops a year, though the area under production is smaller during the short rains because maize has priority at that time.[20] Some irrigated production takes place outside the rainy seasons with water diverted from small streams that run down the hills. As in Kisii, holdings have become quite small due to population pressure and because many slopes are too rocky and steep to cultivate.

In Taveta, the initial community was formed by refugees and immigrants from a number of population groups in the Kilimanjaro area who entered the Taveta forest seeking security and economic subsistence in the 17th century.[21] They practised subsistence agriculture, growing bananas and yams under irrigation by means of water from a local river and springs. With the arrival of caravans in the early 19th century, the Taveta started to obtain cloth, beads, weapons and ammunition from traders in exchange for bananas, honey, yams, tomatoes, sugar cane, tobacco, legumes, mangoes, maize, sweet corn, millet,

---

[17] Concessions were in high demand because of the Mombasa-Nairobi railway line that passed through the area and had a station at Voi (Nazzaro, 1974).

[18] Since 1987 tourism generates more foreign exchange per year than traditional export crops such as coffee and tea (CBS 1988, 1994a).

[19] African farmers who participated in the cooperative (the Taita Vegetable Growers' Cooperative Society) were exempted from military service (Wolf, 1985). The society was liquidated in 1959 (see Appendix 5.4, case 3).

[20] Horticulture has priority during the long rains. Few farmers plant maize then because they believe it does not do well in that season.

[21] The pre-colonial and colonial history of Taveta is based on Frontera (1978).

pumpkins, and a number of edible vines. The cultivation of the last six items was introduced to the area by the traders.

During the colonial period the Taveta area lost much of its importance as a centre of trade and agriculture. The Taveta started to grow cotton, introduced by the colonial authorities, but initially only enough to pay their taxes and make a few purchases of cloth and agricultural implements. The railroad line to Taveta, built before the First World War, prompted a substantial demand for hardwood, threatening the future of the forest. The focus of European settlers in the Taveta area on sisal production in the 1930s led to alienation of the greater part of the land of the Taveta, especially the grazing grounds outside the forest, and to importation of large numbers of non-indigenous peoples to work on the plantations.

After independence, Taveta remained a relatively isolated spot on the border with Tanzania, the nearest tarmac road ending 80 kilometres away at the foot of the Taita Hills. Nevertheless, the area developed into the chief supplier of bananas to the Mombasa market. The fruits are cultivated in monocultures on large irrigated plots, to be harvested throughout the year and carried to the coast by means of heavy trucks. Tomatoes and onions are also grown under irrigation, while mango, lemon and orange trees grow on the higher parts. Some bananas and onions find their way to Nairobi by rail.

The history of the three research areas shows that commercial horticulture did not develop overnight but evolved gradually over the past decades. Favourable agro-ecological circumstances and increasing land shortage in the production areas, in combination with growing urban demand and improvement of interregional road networks, have fostered the development process. The substantial purchasing power of consumer groups in large urban centres such as Nairobi and Mombasa allowed for long supply lines with transport distances of up to 850 km. In Nyandarua, commercial horticulture developed without much competition from other income-generating activities. In Kisii coffee and tea, and in Taveta cotton, competed for the same land, and in Taita employment opportunities competed for the same labour. Nevertheless, horticulture has developed into a major source of income to rural households in all four regions.

3.4. Some aspects of horticultural farming in the research areas

A core activity in terms of income
Farm surveys were carried out in the areas suitable for horticulture in Nyandarua, Kisii, Taita and Taveta. In Nyandarua, over 95 per cent of the households interviewed were found to sell horticultural commodities, in Kisii 79 per cent, and in Taita 63 per cent (see Section 1.3).[22] In Taveta 74 per cent of the households with access to irrigation water sold horticultural commodities.[23]

In all four research areas, high participation in commercial horticulture was revealed not only in clusters near all-weather roads but also in those which were regularly cut off from the world by heavy showers. Impassable roads were a recurrent problem in such

---

[22] Almost all rural households in the research areas owned at least some land to farm on. Landless households were scarcely found.
[23] Horticultural production without irrigation was not possible in the area. Forty-five per cent of the listed households had access to irrigation water.

clusters, but this kept few rural households from embarking on the enterprise. Commercial horticulture was not just something for the rural elite on prime locations, but an income-generating activity for the majority of the rural population in the surveyed areas.

In each of the four regions, commercial horticulture was on average the most important source of farm cash revenues for the households involved (Appendix 3.4). A traditional cash crop like coffee, which was grown in Kisii and Taita, hardly generated income, due to low prices on the international market which caused farmers to neglect their coffee trees.[24] Cotton, which was traditionally grown in Taveta, did not generate much income either, partly because of low world market prices and partly because of mismanagement by the cotton marketing board (see Section 3.1). Most farmers no longer took the trouble to grow the crop. The only export crop of any income significance at the time of the survey was tea, which was grown in Kisii.[25]

As a percentage of total household cash income, commercial horticulture was of roughly the same importance for low-income, middle-income and high-income households in Nyandarua, while being of distinctly greater significance for low-income households with horticultural sales in Kisii, Taita and Taveta (Appendix 3.6). This confirms that the horticultural enterprise was a core activity for broad segments of the rural population, including poorer households.

In the Nyandarua research area, commercial horticulture was even a source of income to the very poor. This was not the case in Kisii, Taita and Taveta. The poorest three to five per cent of the households in the latter regions did not sell horticultural commodities, nor were they involved in any other cash-generating activity. They used their land to grow crops for private consumption and did not have off-farm employment. They were thus highly vulnerable, living in a cash economy without earning money.[26]

Specialization

Although commercial horticulture was a successful income-generating activity in the research areas, it also faced serious problems. One severe problem at the production stage involved produce losses from pests and diseases. The latter spread because of specialization and lack

---

24   It was forbidden by law at that time to uproot coffee trees. Farmers therefore neglected them, interplanting them with food crops like maize and bananas, or sometimes killing them with salt.

25   Besides horticultural commodities, livestock contributed substantially to the farm revenues, especially in Nyandarua, where graded cows were found in most compounds and the selling of milk to the national dairy cooperative (Kenya Cooperative Creameries) was common. Off-farm employment was a major contributor to household cash income in all four regions, but only in Taita did it exceed the importance of horticulture (Appendix 3.4). In absolute terms, Nyandarua farmers earned at least as much money through horticultural sales as horticultural farmers in Kisii, Taita and Taveta earned with all their activities put together. This is to a large extent due to the possibility of growing three vegetable crops a year, as well as the larger size of the Nyandarua holdings (11.0 acres compared to 2.9 acres in Kisii, 3.4 acres in Taita and 2.9 acres in Taveta).

26   The percentages are based on the household listings and additional surveys in Kisii, Taita and Taveta among households without horticultural sales. The latter were sampled from the household listings. Owing to external circumstances, the sample sizes were relatively small (25 in Kisii, 22 in Taita and 16 in Taveta). In Kisii 16%, in Taita 14% and in Taveta 6% of the households without horticultural sales did not have any cash income in 1991. They represented 3% (Kisii), 5% (Taita) and 3% (Taveta) of all listed households in the regions. All households without cash income owned at least some land, which means that landless poor were not yet a problem in the research areas. The limited number of households without land in the research areas usually came from elsewhere and had moved to the region because the household head was stationed there as a teacher, extension worker etc.

of crop rotation. The relative importance of crops in terms of value and acreage was not always the same, but the composition of the average horticultural cash income gives an indication of farmers' specialization (lack of diversification). At the time of the survey, about 85 per cent of the average horticultural cash income in Nyandarua and Kisii came from two crops, namely potatoes and cabbages (Nyandarua), and bananas and kale (Kisii) (Table 3.4).[27] In Taveta the situation was not much different, with three crops providing about 80 per cent of the horticultural revenues.[28] Taita was the only area with a somewhat more diversified assortment: the two most important crops, tomatoes and cabbage, supplied less than 50 per cent of the average horticultural cash income, while 85 per cent of the revenues came from a total of nine different crops. The assortment of the Taita farmers even included fairly unknown vegetables such as baby marrow, cauliflower and lettuce, which were in demand from tourist hotels along the Kenyan coast (Table 3.4).

Input problems
Disease and pest problems were exacerbated by failing crop protection. Either farmers lacked knowledge, using the wrong chemicals or spraying too late, or they had the knowledge but not the money to buy the proper pesticides and fungicides. Credit to buy horticultural inputs was generally hard to obtain. Neither commercial banks, the Kenya Cooperative Bank nor the Agricultural Finance Corporation (a parastatal) were willing to issue loans to small-scale horticultural farmers, even when the latter possessed a title deed that could serve as security.

While chemical and fertilizer use were already low in the 1980s, the situation worsened in the early 1990s. Input costs rose sharply at that time due to the depreciation of the Kenya shilling and decreasing subsidies on farm inputs as part of Structural Adjustment. Pesticides, fungicides and fertilizers more or less doubled in price within two years' time. Farmers responded by cutting back on their use, leading to a further increase in pests and diseases.

Many horticultural farmers shied away from buying certified seeds in the early 1990s because of recurrent quality problems. The germination rate of seeds produced by the Kenya Seed Company, which still possessed a monopoly at that time, had deteriorated. Farmers and retailers blamed the seed company for supplying poor quality, while the seed company blamed the retailers for improper storage and the farmers for 'burying the seeds', that is, sowing them too deep.

Quality problems also occurred in the case of chemicals. Farmers were offered fake pesticides and fungicides in some rural markets, causing them to lose faith in such inputs. Well known is the story about Royco soup which was once sold as a pesticide in one of the local market places of Kisii. The dried soup was sold in the chemical's original packaging material. Once sprayed with this solution, the crop smelled nice while the pests flourished away.

---

[27] Farmers had been cultivating these commodities on the same plots for years, and bacterial wilt, late blight and eelworms (in the case of potatoes) and banana weevil, nematodes and Panama disease (in the case of bananas) were a constant and ever-increasing threat.

[28] Bananas had been cultivated under irrigation on the same plots for decades, and pests and diseases threatened to wipe out the entire crop.

Table 3.4. Composition of the average horticultural cash income of households selling horticultural commodities, by survey area, 1991

Nyandarua (n=229)		Kisii (n=144)		Taita (n=87)		Taveta (n=38)	
crop	%	crop	%	crop	%	crop	%
Irish potatoes	73	bananas	75	tomatoes	29	bananas	48
cabbages	14	kale	10	cabbage	20	tomatoes	19
spring onions	8	local leafy vegetables*	5	kale	12	onions	12
green peas	2	tomatoes	4	Irish potatoes	9	mangoes	5
plums	1	pineapples	1	spinach	3	lemons	4
pears	1	cabbage	1	avocados	3	oranges	3
other	1	other	1	passion fruit	3	Asian vegetables**	3
				lettuce	3	kale	3
				carrots	3	papaya	2
				French beans	2	avocado	2
				sweet pepper	2	other	1
				baby marrow	2		
				bananas	2		
				cucumber	1		
				cauliflower	1		
				other	5		

* The most important local leafy vegetables in Kisii were black nightshade, Amaranthus, spider flower, pumpkin leaves and cowpea leaves.
** Asian vegetables grown in Taveta at the time of the survey were chillies, brinjals and okra.

Future perspectives

Horticulture has brought rising incomes to broad sections of the rural population as well as diversification within the agricultural sector — two key aspects of rural development.[29] Continued growth in Kenya's urban population will lead to a further rise in the demand for horticultural commodities (see Section 3.1). Therefore market prospects are good, and commercial horticulture is expected to be a key source of income for the surveyed households in the years to come.

In Nyandarua there is no real alternative, because agro-ecological conditions do not permit cultivation of other cash crops, except pyrethrum. The demand for pyrethrum on the world market is declining in the wake of cheap synthetic alternatives.

Horticulture offers a more reliable source of income than coffee in Kisii or cotton in Taveta. Both crops are plagued by fluctuating world market prices and red tape at the collection stage of the marketing system. In Kisii, pressures on land make coffee and tea less attractive to smallholders. The crops are perennial, and intercropping with food crops such as maize and bananas reduces their yields drastically. In contrast, most horticultural crops can be grown in sequence with maize, and some even together with maize, without reducing yields.

In Taita, the coastal tourist industry formerly offered an attractive alternative to farm work. Since the first half of the 1990s, however, the industry's image has been tarnished by ethnic clashes and insecurity in the country, and it is no longer the source of jobs it used to be. No one can predict how long Kenya will remain a fashionable tourist destination.[30] The Kenyan government was formerly another major source of off-farm jobs, but in the 1990s it has been cutting expenditures as part of structural adjustment policies. Nowadays many college graduates wind up working on farms rather than sitting in government offices.[31]

The foregoing arguments demonstrate why commercial horticulture is expected to offer a more sustainable source of income in the research areas than export crops or (formal) off-farm employment. However, the sustainability of the horticultural enterprise can be threatened from within. The rise of commercial horticulture initially led to diversification in the agricultural sector. When it proved profitable, farmers started to forget other agricultural crops. This is not necessarily a problem, since horticultural crops are extremely varied in

---

[29] According to Sterkenburg (1987), rural development comprises growth of production and productivity, and diversification within the agricultural sector; expansion of rural industries; improvement of employment; increase in income for broad segments of the rural population; expansion and amelioration of agricultural and community services; and improvement of environmental conservation. Other authors have added more abstract notions like the improvement of health, human welfare, justice and equality, and the strengthening of local initiatives (Carr-Hill, 1990; Chole, 1991; Yimam, 1990). In the case of horticulture, in our study this labour-intensive enterprise had created not only income opportunities for farmers, but also new employment opportunities for local casual labourers at both the production stage (planting, weeding, harvesting) and the marketing stage (carrying produce to the road, loading trucks). Whether it had also improved health and human welfare cannot be judged with certainty, but the horticultural revenues the households earned had at least better prepared them for the potential misfortunes of human life.

[30] Countries such as South Africa and Gambia are becoming major competitors in the tourist market.

[31] Other people try to make a living through employment or self-employment in small-scale enterprises in the informal sector. Small-scale enterprise employment in Kenya is, however, heavily concentrated in urban areas (Livingstone, 1991). It is less common among rural households, including those in the Taita Hills. For a discussion on rural employment in Sub-Saharan Africa see Bryceson & Van der Laan (1994) and Bryceson (1996). For a bibliography on the subject see Tellegen (1993).

nature. Nonetheless the research found that farmers tend to confine themselves to a few horticultural commodities (e.g. potatoes in Nyandarua and bananas in Kisii and Taveta), making their farming as poorly diversified and as vulnerable as before.

4

Marketing Channel Analysis: Relevant Aspects for Horticultural Trade in Sub-Saharan Africa

The present chapter provides a theoretical framework for the analyses of horticultural marketing channels in the following chapters. In the first two sections, various concepts related to marketing channel analysis are introduced, and their relevance with regard to horticultural trade in Sub-Saharan Africa is analysed. In the subsequent four sections, relevant theories on the development of marketing channels are discussed. The theories use efficiency, effectiveness or equity as criteria.

4.1. Defining marketing channel, structure and environment

Stern et al. (1996, 1) view marketing channels (or channels of distribution) as 'sets of interdependent organizations involved in the process of making a product or service available for use or consumption.' Kohls & Uhl (1990, 529) define them as 'alternative routes of product flows from producers to consumers.' Kohls & Uhl focus on the marketing of agricultural products, as is the case in the present book. Their marketing channel starts at the farmer's gate and ends at the consumer's front door. Some of the products are processed on their way to the end users, while other products reach them without undergoing any form changes. The latter is most commonly the case with horticultural commodities in Sub-Saharan Africa.

For a particular commodity, various marketing channels form a marketing structure. The marketing structure is embedded in a marketing environment which consists of a number of subsystems. One such subsystem is the political and legal environment. It encompasses not only government policies and national laws, but also regulatory agencies, consumer advocacy organizations and trade associations which operate in so-called parallel political networks and represent the interests of consumer-citizens and specific constituency organizations.[1] Other environmental subsystems are the demographic environment, the economic environment, the physical (or natural) environment, the technological environment, and the sociocultural environment (Kotler, 1988, 1997).

The political and legal environment in Sub-Saharan Africa

Some components of the marketing environment have a larger impact than others on the horticultural marketing channels in Sub-Saharan Africa. The political and legal forces are generally weak. According to Van Tilburg et al. (1989), who looked into vegetable marketing in various developing countries, interventions in the horticultural subsector are generally avoided by national governments because of the risky nature of the operations. The perishability of the commodities requires a degree of flexibility more suited to private entrepreneurs than to parastatals. In addition, Abbott & Creupelandt (1966) have pointed out that off-season storage requires cold storage and processing facilities. These have been scarce so far.

Intervention is also thought unnecessary because vegetables, fruits and tubers are not regarded as strategic commodities. In Kenya, for instance, both horticultural commodities and maize show large seasonal supply fluctuations. The national government, through one of its marketing boards, tries to equalize seasonal maize supplies in the country by maintaining a national reserve stock, while not considering such policies for potatoes, cabbages etc.[2]

If African governments refrain from intervention in horticultural trading, neither do they introduce incentives policies. Improvement of market places and access roads to production areas, for instance, have low priority. Programmes to support beginning horticultural entrepreneurs with credit or training are lacking. Research into subjects such as post-harvest handling and appropriate packaging materials is limited (see also Section 5.6).

National laws which might try to regulate food marketing in Sub-Saharan countries usually have a limited impact on horticultural trade, because most of the fruit and vegetable traders operate in the so-called informal sector without being registered as entrepreneurs. Even the strong-arm method of law enforcement at roadblocks and in market places usually fails, because of the susceptibility of policemen to bribes. For that matter, law enforcement has also been a problem in the case of controlled commodities such as cereals (see Section 2.3).

The parallel political framework is not yet well developed when it comes to horticultural trade in developing countries. Specialized regulatory bodies that might, for instance, adjudicate conflicts among channel members are absent. Consumer advocacy organizations are only found in a few African countries. Kenya has a consumers'

---

[1] Failure to achieve acceptable and favourable exchange arrangements with the actors in the parallel political networks can hamper channel members' ability to achieve their marketing objectives and reach their target segments of consumers (Hutt et al., 1986). See also Stern & Reve (1980), Achrol et al. (1983), Arndt (1983).

[2] For past policies of the Kenyan government on maize prices and stocks, see for example Hesselmark & Lorenzl (1976), Gsaenger & Schmidt (1977) and Meilink (1985, 1987). For the performance of cereal marketing boards in Africa, see Section 2.3.

association, but its bureau is staffed by a director and his secretary who, when focusing on food, deal with complaints of contaminated milk, unsound maize meal and other types of processed food that have gone bad. Fresh horticultural commodities are normally outside their scope of interest. Trade unions of food traders are rare in Sub-Saharan Africa, because they are prohibited in some countries, and because the majority of the food traders are rural-based and communication networks are underdeveloped.

Under certain circumstances, the political environment does have a heavy impact on horticultural marketing in African countries, notably in the event of political unrest leading to national or regional insecurity. To give an example: tribal clashes in Kenya in the first half of the 1990s, which were largely politically inspired, caused the government to seal off Molo, one of the major supply areas of potatoes in the country. Those farmers who had not abandoned their homes were unable to sell their crop because nobody was allowed to enter the region, including the traders who otherwise came to buy the potatoes to carry them to Nairobi and elsewhere.

The demographic and economic environments in Sub-Saharan Africa
Under normal circumstances, the demographic and economic environments have a much bigger impact on horticultural trade in Sub-Saharan Africa than the political and legal one. Population growth, changing population distributions, and the rising purchasing power of consumers have their effect. This has already been shown in Chapter 2, and will be analysed further in Chapters 7 and 8. It therefore does not need further attention here.

The physical and technological environments in Sub-Saharan Africa
The physical environment is also of major importance. In most African countries the state of the roads limits the distances perishables can be transported. Bumpy roads and muddy market places reduce quality, increase produce losses and raise transport costs, as will be discussed in more detail in Chapter 5.

The technological environment is less important because most of the horticultural commodities are eaten fresh without prior processing. Fresh commodities are seldom cooled. The absence of cooling facilities is not only related to the technological environment but also to the economic one. Cooling would make horticultural commodities too expensive for large parts of the African population.

In the case of horticultural commodities such as tomatoes and leafy vegetables, absence of cooling leads to large seasonal supply fluctuations, which in turn have their bearing on the marketing channels. In the case of tubers such as potatoes such fluctuations may be less extreme because of the possibility of storage in pits.

The sociocultural environment in Sub-Saharan Africa
The sociocultural environment is of major importance in Sub-Saharan Africa. Social and cultural values determine people's relations to others, to institutions, and to society. One may add ethnic values as a third component, because ethnic thinking influences people's everyday behaviour in Africa.

The majority of the horticultural producers are peasant households that function both as a family and an enterprise, as a consumption and a production unit. Sales decisions may be based on risk aversion, profit maximization or other considerations. The peasants may operate within so-called interlocked markets, which means that the terms of exchange in one market (e.g. selling of output) are contractually tied to those in other markets (e.g. supply of inputs and credit) (Ellis, 1993).

In addition to most rural African households, some urban households produce their own food (practising so-called urban agriculture).[3] Others have access to land in their native rural areas, although rural relatives usually farm it (Andrae, 1992).[4] When food prices increase and access to food is reduced, poor urban households in particular tend to fall back on their rural connections.[5] In general, urban households try to stick to their traditional diet, which means that trade flows often follow migration patterns.

Social and cultural values are important to horticultural traders as well as to food traders in general. In rural areas, retailing is a women's affair and food trading is a part-time activity. Studies in such places as Bungoma (Kenya) and Borno (Nigeria) have shown that full-time professional food traders are scarce (Lado, 1991; Porter, 1984; Porter 1986). Farming is the most common other income-generating activity of the traders.

The reason why rural food retailers are females is determined by history and culture, as has been explained in Chapter 2 and will be discussed again in Chapter 5. The women tend to be involved part-time because of both farming activities and domestic obligations. Turrittin (1988) has shown that male traders in rural Mali have more time to go to the market than female ones, even when the women are beyond child-bearing age and have daughters-in-law to assist them in household matters.

The impact of the social environment on food trade in rural areas becomes clear once more when we look at rural market places. Larson (1991) describes rural periodic markets in northern Togo where young men flirt with young women who may one day be their wives, where people come from far and wide to meet old friends and relatives, where chiefs make their appearance to mingle with their people and frequently make important announcements, where minor court cases are tried by the chief and his council, and where government officials broadcast propaganda and information or sell tickets in the state lottery. The sphere that characterizes these market places determines the way buyers and sellers deal with each other. According to Seierup (1994), who looked at horticultural traders and small-scale entrepreneurs in Kenya in general, a fairly large number of the steady customers of these entrepreneurs are related to them through mutual or overlapping ties in the rural community.

In urban African markets, full-time professional food traders are more common than in rural areas. This does not, however, make the social environment less important. Van Donge (1992), who studied Waluguru traders in Dar es Salaam, Tanzania, found that marrying someone from another trading family was used to extend the economic network.

---

3   Urban agriculture has been found to be of importance in Nairobi, for instance (Freeman, 1988), Kampala (Maxwell & Zziwa, 1992) and Lomé (Schilter, 1991).

4   Things are changing, however. In African countries with a high level of commercialization of farmland, like Kenya, families are not always prepared to share their rural sources with those who have left for work in the cities (Kongstad & Mikkelsen, 1983, as quoted by Andrae, 1992). In addition to land, urban households may own livestock which is managed by their rural kinsmen. This is common in Somalia, for instance (Little, 1992).

5   'Exchanges often take place between urban and rural branches of extended families, with rural relatives bringing food for their urban kin in exchange for urban manufactured goods or services, such as a place to stay' (Von Braun et al., 1993, 13-14).

In contrast with rural areas, both women and men are involved in the urban food trade.[6] Various studies suggest that the female traders are of specific age groups or classes. Hansen (1989), for instance, showed that food-trading women in Lusaka, Zambia, tended to be either middle-aged married women who were beyond their childbearing age or single heads of households. Sandee & Weijland (1986) showed that horticultural trade in Swaziland was especially important among female-headed households.

Seierup (1994, 16) characterized female horticultural traders and, more generally, female 'open air' entrepreneurs in Kenya as 'a unified group in the sense that the majority of them use business surpluses for daily basic consumption needs. It is the widow who wants to feed her children, the disabled person who might be unable to marry and has to make a living on his/her own, and it is the wife in the poor urban-based family trying to earn a little extra for survival.'

4.2. Description of marketing channels

Authors like Revzan (1967), Bucklin (1970) and Mallen (1977) have combined elements of the institutional and functional approach to describe marketing channels and structures by means of marketing intermediaries, marketing functions and flows, and channel length, breadth and multiplicity.[7]

Marketing intermediaries
Four groups of marketing intermediaries can be distinguished: merchants, agents, brokers and facilitating intermediaries. The merchants take title to the merchandise, the brokers and agents restrict themselves to the negotiation of title, and the facilitating intermediaries assist the merchants in their marketing activities. Those dealing with horticultural trade in Africa usually refer to merchants as traders.

Each group of marketing intermediaries can be divided into smaller subgroups. The distinction between wholesale traders and retail traders is well known: wholesaling includes all activities involved in selling goods to those who buy for resale or for business use (Kotler, 1997). In the analysis of horticultural trade in developing countries, wholesale traders are usually subdivided into rural assembling traders, collecting wholesalers and distributing wholesalers.[8] Rural assembling traders accumulate produce in the production areas to sell to collecting wholesalers, who carry the commodities to large towns. On arrival,

---

6   The women are involved to a lesser extent in wholesaling, but they dominate retailing. In the urban food markets of Tanzania, for instance, 'women traders generally dealt in the grain commodities produced in their hinterland and traded smaller quantities than the men' (Bryceson, 1993, 120). In the peri-urban area of Maputo, Mozambique, over 95 per cent of the small-scale vegetable retailers are women (Little & De Coloane, 1992). In Kampala, Uganda, food-trading street hawkers are predominantly women, while male street hawkers focus on non-food items (Nyakaana, 1993).
7   For a review of the evolution of marketing channel theory, see Meulenberg (1989, 1997).
8   See for instance Shechambo (1993) on Tanzania, Moustier (1992) on Congo-Brazzaville, Central African Republic and Madagascar, Van Tilburg (1981) on Indonesia, Boekholt et al. (1983) on India, Torres & Lantican (1977) on the Philippines, and De Morrée (1985) on Colombia. In some of the studies, collecting wholesalers are called interregional traders. Region, however, is a rather ambiguous term.

they sell them to distributing wholesalers, who in turn sell to retailers.[9] The retailers may have a fixed base (either a stall, a shop or a place on the ground), or they may be hawkers carry their produce around (e.g. on a large platter on their head).

In addition to traders, agents also operate in the marketing channel. In the case of horticultural commodities in Sub-Saharan Africa, purchasing agents are most common. They generally have a long-standing relationship with buyers and make purchases for them (Kotler, 1997). They operate in the horticultural production areas, where most of them buy on behalf of collecting wholesalers and some on behalf of processing industries. In addition to purchasing agents, commission agents may sometimes be found. Commission agents take physical possession of products and negotiate sales in a central market place on behalf of a producer (Kotler, 1997). The majority of the horticultural producers, however, are peasant farmers whose output is too low to attract this type of agents.

Some brokers may be also found in large urban markets. In contrast with agents, who represent buyers or sellers on a rather permanent basis, brokers bring buyers and sellers together and assist in negotiations on a more ad hoc basis. They may, for instance, negotiate sales in a horticultural wholesale market on behalf of large distributing wholesalers. Some brokers may operate as auctioneers, auctioning produce on behalf of collecting wholesalers.

Traders not only use agents but also facilitating intermediaries. Kotler (1988, 1997) refers to three types of facilitators: first, physical distribution firms, including warehousing firms and transportation firms; second, marketing service companies, including marketing research firms, advertising agencies, media firms, and marketing consultancy firms; and third, financial intermediaries, including banks, credit companies, insurance companies, and other firms that help finance and/or insure risks associated with the buying and selling of goods.

In horticultural marketing in Sub-Saharan Africa, transportation firms are the most common intermediaries. Warehousing firms are scarcely found because of the perishability of the commodities and relatively high costs of cold storage. Marketing service companies such as advertising agencies are insignificant, except in the case of a few processed horticultural commodities (e.g. tomato ketchup).

Financial intermediaries such as commercial banks are present in Sub-Saharan Africa, but they are not very eager to finance the activities of individual horticultural traders. They find the risks too high and ask for collaterals that most of the traders lack. Consequently, horticultural traders have developed their own savings and credit associations (see Section 5.2). Business insurance is still far beyond the scope of horticultural traders and insurance companies in Africa. The insuring of trucks by transportation firms is the only exception.

---

[9] A wholesale institution that has been absent in African horticultural trade, while being a chief actor in many other food commodities, is the marketing board (see Sections 2.3 and 4.1).

Marketing functions and flows

Channel members carry out marketing functions, or, put differently, participate in marketing flows. Kotler (1997) delineates nine functions/flows:

1. Information	collection and dissemination of market information
2. Promotion	development and dissemination of persuasive communications about offers
3. Negotiation	attempts to reach final agreement on price and other items of the offer
4. Ordering	backward communication of intentions to buy
5. Financing	acquisition and allocation of funds required to finance the carrying of inventory
6. Risk taking	assumption of risks in connection with carrying out channel work
7. Physical possession	successive storage and movement of physical products (product flow)
8. Payment	payment of bills
9. Ownership	actual transfer of title[10]

When dealing with horticultural marketing channels in Sub-Saharan Africa, one can bring these nine functions back to six: information, negotiation/ordering, financing, risk taking, physical possession (transport and storage) and payment/ownership. Promotion is omitted because it is of minor importance (as explained earlier). Ordering is subordinate to negotiation. Both functions are performed by the same market intermediaries during the same meetings. Negotiation is the most important of the two because a successful negotiation process will almost inevitably lead to immediate placement of an order. Ownership is closely related to payment. Payments are carried out by traders without interference from banks. Titles change hands when payments are made, which means that the payment flow is the exact reverse of the title flow. In other words, in analysing the payment function we cover the ownership function, too.

The payment function arises because of the exchange of ownership rights. The same is true of the information and negotiation functions. The costs generated by these functions are so-called transaction costs.[11] Eggertsson (1990) distinguishes six activities that give rise to transaction costs: (1) information search, (2) negotiation, (3) the making of contracts, (4) the monitoring of contractual partners, (5) the enforcement of contracts, and (6) the protection of property rights against third party encroachment (e.g. protection against pirates in the case of illegal trade). The third to fifth activities, which are all related to contracts, are relatively unimportant in African horticultural trade, because most of the transactions take place in a spot market, and traders demand cash on delivery.[12] The sixth, protection of

---

[10] Other authors distinguish three categories of functions: exchange functions (buying and selling), physical supply functions (transportation, storage) and facilitating functions (financing, risk taking, marketing information, standardization and grading) (Meulenberg, 1989).

[11] According to Eggertsson's (1990) definition, transaction costs are costs that arise when individuals exchange ownership rights to economic assets and enforce their exclusive rights. See also Carlton & Perloff (1994) on transaction costs in general, and De Janvry & Sadoulet (1994), Ensminger (1992), Nabli & Nugent (1989) and Shechambo (1993) on transaction costs in developing countries.

[12] The only exception is the export trade (see Section 5.4).

property rights, is also unimportant because all people are allowed to trade horticultural commodities, and traders do not have their own brands.

Channel length, breadth and multiplicity
A marketing channel can be characterized by its length and breadth, and a marketing structure by its multiplicity. Channel length refers to the number of channel levels, and channel breadth to the number of institutions at a given level in a given geographical area. Multiplicity concerns the number of marketing channels in a marketing structure.

The length, breadth and multiplicity of horticultural marketing channels in Sub-Saharan Africa varies considerably. A channel may have only one intermediate level (rural retailers who buy their produce from farmers), or as many as four (rural assembling traders, collecting wholesalers, distributing wholesalers, urban retailers). The breadth may vary from a couple of collecting wholesalers in isolated production areas, to dozens of retailers in rural markets and hundreds of retailers in urban centres.

Multiplicity of channels is quite common. Farmers sell, for instance, to collecting wholesalers who then sell to distributing wholesalers. Within the same marketing structure, other farmers may bypass the collecting wholesalers to sell to distributing wholesalers, or directly to retailers. In the course of time, some channels disappear while others become more important.

4.3. Differentiation and re-integration of marketing channels

Marketing channels do not appear out of the blue but develop along certain lines. At the start only self-sufficient non-surplus producers are present, with no middlemen required. Marketing channels develop when a surplus in production occurs above a farmer's household requirements. Producers start to exchange commodities to other goods or money; a direct marketing channel is born. The exchange gets concentrated in central market places because of so-called place and time utility. By using a central market place each seller has to make fewer trips to meet all his customers (place utility), and buyers and sellers meet when commodities are ready for exchange (time utility) (Alderson, 1967).

At the next step, marketing intermediaries enter the chain and the direct marketing channels alter into indirect ones, causing vertical differentiation. Eventually, the vertical differentiation process comes to an end, and marketing channels start to re-integrate again. Vertical coordination occurs, including administered systems, based on informal collaboration on inclusive goals, or contractual systems, based on contractual agreements. In addition, channels may change into corporate systems, whereby members of different levels are owned and operated by one and the same organization.[13] Vertical coordination and integration lead to so-called Vertical Marketing Systems (VMSs), in which open-market activities are limited. This contrasts with Conventional Marketing Channels (CMCs), in which channel coordination is achieved primarily through bargaining and negotiation among actors.

---

[13] Stern et al. (1996) call corporate systems 'hard' vertical integration, and administered and contractual systems 'soft' vertical integration.

When looking at Sub-Saharan Africa, scores of small producers sell small quantities of horticultural commodities either directly to consumers or through professional traders. Marketing channels are still in a process of vertical differentiation; vertical re-integration is not yet a wide-spread phenomenon. According to Van Tilburg et al. (1989, 1), the channels can best be characterized as Conventional Marketing Channels: the actors in the chain are 'usually selling and buying together with many competitors, are separated by markets, and the allocation of resources is guided by "the invisible hand" of prices resulting from quantities supplied and demanded.' Elements of vertical coordination and integration may exist, however. Examples are contract farming (see Section 5.4), cooperative marketing by farmer groups (Section 5.3), and integrated production and wholesaling (Section 5.4).

As noted, the development of horticultural marketing channels in Sub-Saharan Africa is primarily a process of vertical differentiation. The following three sections of the present chapter will look into efficiency, effectiveness and equity theories that may explain this process.

4.4. Marketing channel development: efficiency

Vertical differentiation of conventional marketing channels can be explained in terms of efficiency, meaning that structural changes are the result of cost-minimization policies by channel members. Professional traders start to mediate between producer and consumer because they are able to improve the efficiency of the marketing process. In addition to time and place utility (see previous section), they create possession utility because transactions can be carried out at lower costs by them than through direct exchange (Alderson, 1967). Their mediation decreases the total number of transactions in the system (minimum transaction criterion), and allows economies of scale.[14]

When the number of professional traders in the system increases, the number of transactions can be reduced further by vertical differentiation into wholesale and retail trade. Wholesale trade may arise because of economies of scale in accumulation, but also because of what Alderson (1967) calls discrepancy of assortments. At the collecting wholesale level commodities may, for instance, be assorted in relation to physical handling characteristics during transport, while at the retail level they are assorted in relation to consumer preferences of the target group.

All in all, the role of wholesale traders is sorting out, accumulation, allocation and assorting, and that of retailers is allocation and assorting.[15] The relative importance of each function differs from one situation to another. In Kenyan horticultural trade, for instance, the sorting functions are relatively unimportant, as will be shown in Section 5.2.

---

[14] When producers deal directly with consumers, the number of bits in any flow is small. When traders enter the system they can aggregate bits from various producers, thus transporting produce in quantities sufficient to exploit economies of scale (Bucklin, 1972). They may also obtain economies of scale with regard to other marketing functions such as storage, information and negotiation.

[15] Sorting out involves breaking down a heterogeneous supply into separate stocks that are relatively homogeneous, notably through the grading of produce. Allocation refers to the breaking down of supplies into smaller lots. Assorting involves the building up of an assortment of associated products for sale (wholesalers building assortments of goods for retailers, and retailers building up assortments for consumers) (Stern et al., 1996).

The functional spin-off concept

Stigler (1951) and Mallen (1973, 1977) developed a theory that predicts the rise of new market intermediaries on the basis of cost developments in their marketing functions. The fundamental premise is that given a specific level of demand, traders will try to maximize profits by designing or selecting a channel that will generate *the lowest total average cost* for them.

The average costs of most marketing functions decrease with increasing volume, because of economies of scale. Decreasing average cost curves lead to a spinning off of functions by small entrepreneurs. The transport function is a good example. African horticultural producers are small-scale farmers (see Sections 3.3 and 3.4). If we assume that transporters face the same transport cost curve as these farmers, an individual farmer at his or her low volume will have higher average transport costs than a transporter who can combine the volumes of a number of producers and thus benefit from economies of scale. If the farmer in turn benefits from the lower average transport costs of the transporter, the farmer's total average cost will decline if the transport function is spun off.

A similar reasoning may also apply to other functions. It has to be noted, however, that the spinning off of certain functions may inevitably lead to the spinning off of other closely related ones. In Section 4.2 it was shown that in Sub-Saharan horticultural marketing the ordering and negotiation functions are interrelated, as are the payment and ownership functions. As a result six major marketing functions were distinguished: information, negotiation/ordering, financing, risk taking, physical possession (transport and storage) and payment/ownership. The last function is a crucial one to the extent that spinning off the payment/ownership function inevitably means spinning off all marketing functions. This happens, for instance, when a farmer does not take produce to the market but sells the commodities to a trader at the farm gate. The trader takes over all marketing functions from the farmer. The spinning off of all functions results in a more differentiated marketing channel. We will come back to this in Section 6.2 when we look at potato farmers in Nyandarua who sell their produce to collecting wholesalers instead of going to Nairobi themselves.

Barriers to entry

As said, the spin-off concept is based on the premise of cost minimization. Initially, it was believed that perfect competition was required to make market intermediaries minimize their costs (Bain, 1959). Later, Baumol et al. (1988) argued in their theory of contestable markets that imperfect competition was not a problem as long as entry and exit barriers were absent. Potential competitors could then enter the marketing channel as soon as 'monopoly profits' were observed, and existing competitors could leave the channel whenever profits came under pressure. The only possible barrier to entry would be so-called sunk costs: investments such as research and infrastructure that lose their value when they leave the market.

Among horticultural traders in Sub-Saharan Africa, sunk costs are usually low. Exit barriers are generally absent but entry barriers may exist. Porter (1980) distinguishes various sources of barriers to entry. Some are more relevant to us than others. Government policies, for instance, do not usually form entry barriers in horticultural trade (see Section 4.1, the political and legal environment). In contrast, economies of scale can be an entry barrier, especially in interregional trade when established wholesalers use large trucks. If a potential wholesaler wants to enter the chain he will have to start with the same scale of operations, because the use of a smaller vehicle will entail higher transport costs per selling unit. Lack of capital may also be an entry barrier in this respect, because hiring a truck and financing a truckload of produce require money. As pointed out earlier, commercial banks are not eager to issue loans to horticultural traders.

Product differentiation is not a real entry barrier to horticultural trade. Consumers may favour certain varieties, but all traders can include those varieties in their assortment if the want. In theory, traders can differentiate on the basis of services and quality. Services, however, are usually absent in horticultural trade. Most horticultural traders will not refund money when customers want to return bought produce, nor do they offer any kind of after-sales service, if such would even be possible. Quality is a matter of careful buying, since traders do not process bought commodities. Therefore, accumulated buying experience might serve as an entry barrier. Highly perishable commodities such as tomatoes and bananas may look fine to a layman and still turn black within a few days. Packaging experience is also needed, given the rough roads and the recurrent scarcity of packaging materials. Finally, negotiation experience is required to get a good price and avoid being cheated by other traders. After all, selling units are not standardized and prices are determined transaction by transaction.

Potential customers do not face major switching costs. Access to distribution channels may, however, be a problem, for instance because of existing customer relations between collecting wholesalers and distributing wholesalers or between farmers and collecting wholesalers. Many distributing wholesalers in urban centres attach importance to regular supplies, and may therefore cherish their existing suppliers who have shown to be reliable. Small-scale farmers are very suspicious when dealing with traders. They may not want to try their luck with a new unknown collecting wholesaler when customer relations with known wholesalers are satisfactory. Besides, the latter may be financing part of the farmers' crops, which ties the farmers' hands and makes switching to other traders difficult.[16]

A potential entrant's trepidation about the reactions of existing competitors may be an entry barrier, especially in urban wholesale markets where horticultural traders are often thought to be unscrupulous and hostile to new entrants. In the production areas, negative expectations by farmers about the reactions of collecting wholesalers may deter any decision to go into trade themselves. Farmers may believe that the collecting wholesalers they dealt with will persuade distributing wholesalers to boycott them, thus leaving them with unsaleable produce on arrival in the urban centre. They may also be afraid that if the experiment fails, collecting wholesalers will give them the cold shoulder and leave them with unsaleable produce on the farm.

In sum, entry barriers to horticultural trade in Sub-Saharan Africa may be related to economies of scale, capital requirements, cumulated experience, access to distribution channels and potential entrants' expectations. The chances of encountering entry barriers are especially real at the collecting wholesale level.

---

[16] See Section 4.1 on interlocked markets.

4.5. Marketing channel development: effectiveness

The development of marketing channels can also be assessed by analysing their effectiveness. The price of a commodity being equal, consumers prefer to deal with a marketing channel that provides a higher level of spatial, time and/or form convenience. Thus, a marketing channel may develop because consumers demand more convenience — in other words, a higher service output (Stern et al., 1996). In the long run, an effective channel will stimulate latent demand.

Spatial convenience: development of market places
The spatial convenience factor of the service output of a marketing channel refers to the development of market places. According to gravity models used in marketing research, the attractiveness of a city's shopping area to consumers from elsewhere is somehow related to the population size of the city and the distance to the city. One of the first models was developed by Reilly in the 1930s. His goal was to explain the relative attractiveness of two different cities' shopping areas for those consumers who lived in a town in between them. He proposed that the proportion of that trade that is attracted by city A relative to city B is equal to the population size of city A relative to city B, times the squared reciprocal of the distance from the intermediate town to city A relative to city B (Reilly, 1931, as quoted by Sheth et. al., 1988).

In the 1960s Huff (1964) developed a model predicting the probability of a consumer from a given point of origin travelling to a particular shopping centre. Size of the shopping centre (measured by the square foot of area devoted to the sale of a particular class of goods) and travel time were the two explanatory variables. Huff did not develop his model with an eye to Africa, but his use of travel time instead of distance is certainly appropriate when dealing with that continent. Two cities may be located at the same distance from an intermediate town, while due to divergent road conditions travelling to one of them takes twice as long as to the other.[17]

Population size and transport distance feature not only in gravity models used in marketing research but also in central place theory used in geographical research. The location of trading centres is said to be related to the minimum population required to bring about the offering of a certain good for sale, and the maximum distance over which people will travel to purchase a good offered at a central place.[18] Central place theory has been tested in Africa during the last few decades, and it was shown that we have to be careful in applying it. According to Obudho (1983) consumers are not supplied with goods and services from a central place, but central place functions are performed by mobile agents who move from place to place and thus give rise to periodic markets. Wambugu (1994) showed that, in Nyeri District (Kenya), the spatial organization of such periodic market places follows the distribution of the population. Lado (1991), however, came to a different conclusion for Bungoma District (Kenya). Some of the markets in that district developed into assembly points of local farm produce destined for large urban centres outside the area.

---

17   For a discussion of regional-spatial analysis in marketing, see also Revzan (1971), Grether (1983) and Timmermans (1993).
18   Pioneers of the central place theory were Berry & Garrison (1958).

The so-called rural assembly markets show a closer relationship with the distribution of agricultural production in the district than with the distribution of the population. Akasaka (1992) and Hollier (1980) showed for southwest Mali and west Cameroon respectively that the location of rural assembly markets in surplus areas was related to the demands of collecting wholesalers: markets that they could easily access by vehicle and where they could collect large quantities of a commodity at a time developed as collection points.[19] The development of rural assembly markets for horticultural commodities in Kenya will be discussed in Sections 6.3 to 6.7.

Time convenience: timing of market days
In the rural areas of Sub-Saharan Africa, the periodic nature of markets affects the time convenience of consumers. Timing of periodic markets is to some extent related to their place in a so-called market ring, composed of markets that operate on successive days. The itineraries of the traders that operate in the ring are thought to be determined by the aim that no hamlet or other settlement is far away from a market for any more than a few days.[20] Other factors are also at stake, however. In many regions one day is set aside for religious functions, but in some regions this day is generally chosen as market day because the market is located at the same site as the church or chapel (Lado, 1991). The assembly function of some rural markets also has its effects: their timing is at least partly related to the timing of market days in the urban centres served by these assembly markets. For instance, if Sunday is a day of rest in the urban centre, the assembly market will be more likely to operate on Friday than on Saturday. Generally, market places in cities operate six or seven days a week. The time convenience to the urban consumers is higher than to rural consumers: they can do their shopping almost whenever they want.

Form convenience: quality
In Sub-Saharan Africa where horticultural commodities are not usually processed, nor treated or pre-packed for retailing, form convenience refers largely to quality. In the USA and Europe, poor-quality vegetables, fruits and tubers hardly enter the marketing chain, but in developing countries this stage has not been reached yet, and trader policies to raise minimum quality standards are still subject to debate. We will look at problems of quality deterioration and produce losses in the course of horticultural marketing processes in Section 5.6.

---

[19] Near national boundaries, assembly markets develop in centres that are accessible by road or rail from both sides of the border. See Nkera & Schoepf (1991), Meagher (1990), and Fodouop (1988) for examples of cross-border trade of horticultural commodities and other foodstuffs.

[20] As a result, successive markets would not normally be adjacent ones. Early research on this matter was carried out by Hodder (1969) in Yorubaland (Nigeria), Ukwu (1969) in Iboland (Nigeria) and Skinner (1964) in China.

4.6. Marketing channel development: equity

As well as in terms of efficiency and effectiveness, the development of marketing channels can also be analysed by assessing equity. Equity refers to the division of power in the marketing channel and to the ways market segments are served.

Power in the marketing channel
In a marketing channel context, power typically is defined as a channel member's ability to influence the perceptions, behaviour and/or decision-making of another channel member (Anderson et. al., 1987). Changes in the division of power are related at least in part to members' perceptions about the present situation. French & Raven (1959) were the first to distinguish five types of perception-based power: reward power, coercive power, legitimate power and referent power. Each type may feature in horticultural marketing channels in Sub-Saharan Africa. Reward power and coercive power may play a role in isolated production areas where few traders operate. The farmers regard themselves as price takers and the traders they deal with as price setters. According to the farmers' perceptions, the traders have the power to offer a better price, for instance, if the farmers are loyal to them. Whether the traders are indeed price setters is less important than the perception of the farmers. Farmers may also believe that traders have the power to punish them if they try to bypass them and take the produce to an urban centre themselves. This belief slows down possible trends of forward integration.

Legitimate and reference power may play a role in horticultural trade as a consequence of social and ethnic constructs. Two examples: if a potential buyer lives in the same community as a seller, and the buyer has a higher social status than the seller (e.g. belongs to the family of the chief), this may give him legitimate power. Second, if a potential buyer belongs to the same ethnic group as a seller, while the majority of his competitors belong to another ethnic group, this may give him reference power.

Expert power may also play a role, as when farmers expect traders to have more up-to-date knowledge about demand and supply in the urban markets than they themselves have, or when traders assume that transporters have more knowledge about maintenance costs and related transport charges than they themselves.

Porter (1980) gives an extensive list of circumstances that determine the power of buyers and sellers who deal with each other in the marketing channel.[21] Some of the circumstances he mentions are characteristic for the collecting wholesale of horticultural commodities in most of Sub-Saharan Africa. Collecting wholesalers may be expected to be powerful when dealing with farmers because: they purchase large volumes relative to farmer

---

21 According to Porter (1980) a buyer is more powerful if (1) he purchases large volumes relative to sellers' sales; (2) the products he purchases from the sellers represent a significant fraction of his costs or purchases (making him more price-sensitive and purchase-selective); (3) the products he purchases from the sellers are standard or undifferentiated (which makes it easier to switch to other sellers); (4) he faces few switching costs (which would lock him to the seller); (5) he earns low profits (high profits would make him less price-sensitive and might give him a longer view towards preserving the health of his sellers); (6) he poses a credible threat to backward integration (is in a position to demand bargaining concessions); (7) the quality of the produce supplied by the sellers is unimportant for the quality of the buyer's products (making the buyer less price-sensitive); (8) the buyer has full information (about demand, actual market prices and even suppliers' costs).

sales; the commodities they purchase from the farmers represent a significant fraction of their cost; they buy undifferentiated commodities; they face few switching costs; and they have full market information.

Both French & Raven and Porter look at individual buyers and sellers. Actors who operate at the same level in the marketing chain may also cooperate to change the division of power in the channel. Farmers, for instance, could organize themselves into a horticultural marketing cooperative to increase sellers' sales relative to buyers' purchased quantities. Mutual cooperation increases their countervailing power.[22] Horticultural marketing cooperatives are, however, rare in Sub-Saharan Africa, as was explained in Section 2.3 and will be shown for Kenya in Section 5.3.

Not only farmers but also traders may cooperate to increase their power. They may, for instance, agree on maximum prices paid to suppliers and/or minimum prices demanded from buyers (thus forming price cartels). The chances to successfully hold prices below or above the competitive level are greater when there is a high degree of market concentration and products are homogeneous (Scherer & Ross, 1990). In Sub-Saharan horticultural trade, a high degree of market concentration may especially occur at the collection stage. The chances for collecting traders to come up with a successful price cartel are greater when most farmers in a given area specialize in a few horticultural commodities, making the supply relatively homogeneous. In the Kenyan research areas this was indeed the case, as shown in Section 3.3. Nevertheless, price cartels were not found, as will be explained in Section 5.6.

Equity in serving market segments
When a country develops, the equity in serving market segments may change for the better or the worse. The growth of urban centres and the rising purchasing power of urban citizens may, for instance, drain supplies from the countryside. As a consequence, prices in the rural areas rise, and households which hitherto have bought some of their requirements may no longer be able to do so.

The same may happen when developing countries start to export horticultural commodities. Fruits and vegetables previously destined for local consumption may rise in price when exportation becomes feasible. Whether such developments will indeed occur will be shown for Kenya in Section 5.4.

---

[22] Etgar (1976) defined the power of a channel member or of a group of members in a conventional marketing channel as a function of (1) his (their) power sources, (2) the degree of dependency of other channel members upon him (them), and (3) the countervailing power of those channel members whom he (they) wish(es) to influence. Heide & John (1988) defined dependency as the extent of the replaceability of the exchange partner.

Horticultural Marketing Channels in Kenya: Actors and Institutions

5.1. Introduction

In Chapter 4, the actors and institutions that operate in horticultural marketing channels in Sub-Saharan Africa were briefly introduced. In the present chapter the focus is on Kenyan channels. Actors and institutions will be looked at in some detail, with a focus on their characteristics and mode of operation. This will be preceded by a few examples of horticultural marketing channels which show the diversity in channels that exists. The examples are derived from the research areas.

The shortest marketing channel, found in all production areas, consists of a farmer-trader who goes to a small rural market on foot or by public minibus *(matatu)* to sell vegetables or fruits from her own farm to local consumers. The channel has a second level if the farmer does not sell her produce to consumers but to one or more retailers. She may do so in the market place itself or early in the morning at the gate of the market place. Instead of the farmer coming to the market gate, the retailer may also come to the farm gate. The retailer lives near the farmer, and before going to the market she passes by the farmer to purchase supplies. The retailer may carry additional supplies from her own farm.

When additional trade levels are present, the diversity in channels becomes greater and more region-specific. In Nyandarua, purchasing agents may deliver bags with cabbages to a collecting wholesaler, who fills his 7-tonne truck and takes the commodities to Wakulima wholesale market in Nairobi to sell to wholesalers and retailers. Another collecting wholesaler may buy directly from the farmers, and, on arrival at Wakulima, sell the entire load to a collecting wholesaler from the coast, who transfers the produce to another truck and takes it to the Kongowea wholesale market in Mombasa. Here the cabbages may be sold either to a distributing wholesaler or directly to retailers from Mombasa and nearby towns.

In Kisii, purchasing agents and small rural assembling traders without a store may bring banana bunches on foot to a bigger rural assembling trader with a store. The latter sells the bananas on to a collecting wholesaler from Nairobi, who transports them by hired 7-tonne truck to the capital. A colleague from the production area may employ agents herself and transport the produce straight from the farms to Nairobi, or even all the way to Mombasa.

In Taveta, rural assembling traders may bring tomatoes by pick-up trucks to Taveta market to sell to a collecting wholesaler from Mombasa. The latter hires space in a 7-tonne truck after sorting the tomatoes according to ripeness and repackaging them in large wooden boxes. The truck is shared with other collecting wholesalers, each trader paying in accordance with the number of units transported. On arrival in Kongowea wholesale market, Mombasa, the boxes are sold to distributing wholesalers and retailers from Mombasa or other coastal towns like Kilifi.

Another collecting wholesaler in Taveta may hire a pick-up truck to collect banana bunches near the farms, using purchasing agents to organize the harvesting and carry the produce to the collection point. He brings the bunches to the railway station in Taveta to be loaded into a goods wagon. Kenya Railways charges the wholesaler per bunch. Produce from several wholesalers is put into one wagon after the bunches are marked with a different sign for each trader. On arrival in Nairobi, the bananas are sold to distributing wholesalers and retailers at the railway station or from a store in town.

In another part of Taveta, there is an export trader who buys French beans from farmers three days a week at a specific collection point. The beans are graded and packed before going on transport to Nairobi by truck. In Nairobi the beans are stored in a cold store before being brought to the airport and flown to retailers in London.

In the Taita Hills, a local wholesaler may go to the farms to buy a large assortment of vegetables, including tomatoes, cabbages, baby marrows, sweet peppers, kale, leeks, carrots and Irish potatoes. She takes the produce in baskets to one of the main roads that traverse the hills and waits for a transporter, who comes by on certain days of the week. The transporter collects the produce of a large number of wholesalers, charging them an amount per kilogram after weighing the baskets with a scale. The wholesalers themselves travel to Mombasa by *matatu*. When the truck arrives in the Kongowea wholesale market at Mombasa, the baskets are weighed again to make sure no produce has disappeared on the way.

In the same hills, a truck owned by the local horticultural marketing cooperative assembles various kinds of vegetables from member-farmers at collection points. The produce is brought to the compound of the cooperative, where the commodities are sorted, graded and repacked. They are then carried to the Kongowea wholesale market, where the cooperative has a rented stall. Retailers, ship chandlers, hotels and other institutions come to buy the commodities.

5.2. Traders, agents and facilitating intermediaries in the domestic market

Traders and market places

Five types of horticultural market places can be distinguished in Kenya, each with its own mixture of trader types. The smallest horticultural markets are informal rural retail markets.[1] They are not registered and have no facilities at all. The market is periodic, with one or two market days a week. The number of traders is limited. Most are farmer-traders, selling produce cultivated on their own farms.

Next in hierarchy are the registered rural retail markets. They are also periodic, but in the bigger ones some trade may also take place outside official market days. Farmer-traders and professional retailers are the main sellers, and consumers the main buyers. Often very few facilities are available to the traders there, with permanent stalls, toilets and a proper drainage system being absent. The market fees collected by the County Council are rarely used to improve the market place. Some rural retail markets develop into rural assembly markets, where farmer-traders and rural assembling traders sell to wholesalers from elsewhere. Whether such a development actually occurs depends on a combination of factors which will be discussed in Sections 6.3 to 6.7.

While rural assembly markets have a collection function, urban wholesale markets have a distribution function. Retailers from urban retail markets in the same population centre as well as retailers from smaller population centres in the region come to buy produce from wholesalers based in the wholesale market. Some of these wholesalers buy their produce from farmers and traders in the production area, thus combining collection and distribution activities. Others focus either on the collection or distribution side. Distributing wholesalers remain in the market place and buy from collecting wholesalers who sell to them from the back of their truck in or in front of the market place.[2] The market place is operational six days a week.

Wholesale and retail trade

Although in theory a clear distinction exists between urban wholesale and retail markets, the situation is more complicated in reality, because wholesale activities in urban markets attract retailers who try to set up business in the same compound. Even in classified wholesale markets like the Nakuru wholesale market or the Kongowea wholesale market in Mombasa not all traders are pure wholesalers. Although these market places were primarily intended for wholesale trade when built, they were soon invaded by retailers who began trading on the ground, blocking the passageways with their small heaps of vegetables and fruits.

In Mombasa the authorities have tried to solve the problem by building a separate retail market adjacent to the wholesale market. The retailers were driven into this section and

---

[1] Sometimes these markets are also called roadside markets, but that is somewhat confusing. They are informal because they lack registration by the County Council, not because they are located on the side of a road. Both informal and registered rural markets may be located on the side of the road.

[2] In Kenya, traders who buy produce in the production area to sell in large towns are often called middlemen. This is confusing because these middlemen can be either collecting wholesalers (selling to distributing wholesalers), or wholesalers who combine collection and distribution activities (selling to retailers), or they can even be large retailers (selling to consumers). In the literature, the term *middlemen* usually refers to all traders operating in the marketing channel.

removed from the passageways by force. However, consumers keep on visiting the wholesale market and especially the smaller wholesale traders sell to them, although that is officially prohibited. It is very difficult for the market authorities to prevent this because of the lack of standardized wholesale units in horticultural trade.[3]

The authorities in Nakuru have not tried to get the retailers out of the wholesale market. Instead they have restricted the activities in the market place to the morning hours to deter competition with the retail market elsewhere in town. The retailers in the wholesale market are concentrated in the central open-air part, while the wholesalers have settled under the roofed part of the market place. Due to the presence of consumers, many of the wholesalers have also reverted to occasional retailing. Interestingly, some retailers in the central part of the market sell not only to consumers but also to traders. The traders they are dealing with come from poorer parts of town where they have small wooden kiosks alongside the road. The quantities they require per commodity are too small to buy from wholesalers.[4]

The thin dividing line between wholesale and retail trade exists not only in horticultural wholesale markets but also in the bigger market places without a defined wholesale character, such as the municipal markets in Kisii and Nyahururu. The traders in these market places are characterized not as wholesalers and retailers but as larger and smaller traders. The larger ones sell primarily in bulk to retailers from within the market and to retailers from other parts of town. After doing that in the morning, they may sell their remaining supplies in smaller units to consumers in the afternoon. The smaller traders sell primarily to consumers. They may sell to retailers from outside the market when commodities are scarce and the larger traders run out of supplies. The visiting retailers then revert to buying small quantities from various smaller traders instead of buying in bulk from one bigger trader.[5]

Allocation and sorting
The discussion on the dividing line between wholesalers and retailers stems from the definition of the two types of traders: wholesalers allocate commodities to businesses such

---

[3] A wholesaler may sell tomatoes either by the 50kg or 5kg box. Pineapples are usually sold by the dozen but no one can keep a wholesaler from selling them by the piece. A small retailer or a consumer may ask for the same quantities of one commodity. Most likely a retailer will come to buy every day and the consumer only once or twice a week, but traders are not registered and no one can tell whether a customer is a trader or a consumer.

[4] The kiosk retailers may buy only three heaps of tomatoes, five bundles of kale and two heaps of onions from one or more retailers to sell at a higher price in their kiosk. The traders they buy from are not pure retailers, because they also sell to traders, but neither are they true wholesalers, because they sell mainly to consumers.

[5] Combined wholesale and retail trade in food is not unique to Kenya. It was also found by Bryceson (1994), for instance, who studied grain traders in urban market places in Tanzania. To distinguish wholesale traders from retail traders, Kibera & Warungi (1988, 256) decided to define African food wholesalers as traders selling 'primarily' through retailers. This definition is difficult to use, even if we assume that 'primarily' refers to 50 per cent or more of the physical turnover. What do we call a trader, for instance, who sells most of her tomatoes to retailers and most of her onions to consumers? Comparing apples and oranges should be avoided. An alternative solution is to look at flows rather than actors. Each trader may participate in different flows, e.g. buying from farmers to sell to retailers (flow 1) or buying from farmers to sell to consumers (flow 2). In Chapters 7 and 8 below, flows instead of actors will be used to analyse vertical differentiation in horticultural marketing channels.

as retailers, and retailers allocate them to consumers. In Section 4.4, an additional criterion was mentioned to distinguish the two types of traders, namely their assortments. Wholesale assortments were defined in relation to physical handling characteristics during transport, and retail assortments in relation to consumer preferences. Thus, in theory a comparison of traders' assortments might define which traders are wholesaling and which are retailing. This approach does not work, however, for horticultural traders in Kenya. One reason for this is the differentiation into collecting and distributing wholesale trade that exists there. Distributing wholesalers do not transport commodities: both suppliers (collecting wholesalers) and buyers (retailers) come to them. A more important reason is the limited assortment of most collecting wholesalers, distributing wholesalers and retailers: the majority sell only one or a few commodities at a time (their allocation function is more important than their sorting function). As a consequence, the assortments of wholesalers and retailers who deal with each other are often quite similar, and a comparison of traders' assortments does not, in most cases, provide a clue to the type of trade (wholesale or retail) they are pursuing.

Characteristics of the market places in the present sample
Five types of Kenyan market places were introduced at the beginning of this section. Every market place can be characterized on the basis of its status (formal/informal), setting (rural/urban), frequency (periodic/daily) and main types of trade (wholesale/retail/ assembling).

The market places that were included in our trade survey can all be characterized in this way. To begin with, all of them are formal. Informal rural retail markets were not included in the sample because it was expected that traders in such markets would hesitate to cooperate due to the more or less illegal character of their activities.

Table 5.1 shows the further characteristics of the surveyed market places. Rural and urban, periodic and daily markets are included in the sample. The rural markets are all periodic ones, while the urban markets are either periodic or daily. The daily markets are found in the largest urban centres. The Kenyan CBS classifies population centres of 2,000 inhabitants and upwards as urban, but they are more rural then urban in appearance, and the trade activities that take place there are more similar to those in rural centres than in large cities. Both in the rural and small urban centres the markets are periodic. In markets in the small urban centres, some trade activities do usually take place outside official market days, while this is rare in the markets of rural centres.

Based on the CBS definition, two of the assembly markets in the sample are urban: Taveta and Kisii Daraja Mbili. This may seem strange because assembly markets have been characterized here as rural. Taveta is relatively large because it is a border town and it has a so-called second-level assembling function, as will be explained in Section 6.6. Daraja Mbili, the other urban assembly market, is officially part of Kisii town but it is located at the edge of town. It used to be located in the rural area but the expansion of Kisii town changed its setting. It retained its assembling function.

Table 5.1. Surveyed market places and their characteristics

District (Province)	market place	rural/ urban	periodic/ daily	main types of trade
Nyandarua (Central)	Nyahururu	urban	periodic*	retail/wholesale
	Engineer	rural	periodic	retail
	Magumu	rural	periodic	assembling/retail
Nakuru (Rift Valley)	Nakuru wholesale market	urban	daily	wholesale/retail
	Nakuru retail market	urban	daily	retail
	Njoro	urban	periodic*	retail
	Dundori	rural	periodic	retail
Taita Taveta (Coast)	Voi	urban	periodic*	retail
	Taveta	urban	periodic*	assembling/retail
	Wundanyi	urban	periodic*	retail
Kisii (Nyanza)	Kisii Municipal market	urban	daily	retail/wholesale
	Kisii Daraja Mbili	urban	periodic	assembling/retail
	Nyakoe	rural	periodic	assembling/retail
	Riochanda	rural	periodic	assembling/retail
	Kebirigo	rural	periodic	assembling/retail
	Keroka	urban	periodic*	retail
Mombasa (Coast)	Kongowea wholesale market	urban	daily	wholesale/retail
	Majengo retail market	urban	daily	retail

* Most market activities take place on periodic market days, but some retailing continues throughout the week.

Characteristics of the traders

The characteristics of horticultural traders who operate in the domestic market are analysed in some detail in Appendix 5.1. The findings show that over 95 per cent of the traders who sell horticultural commodities in rural market places and in market places in small urban centres have at least one thing in common: they are women. Only in daily markets in large urban centres do male traders become more numerous.

In terms of ethnic background, age and marital status, the composition of the horticultural trader population more or less coincides with that of the general population in the region where the traders operate. The majority of the traders are between 25 and 45 years of age. Many female traders are young women, single mothers, divorced women, widowed women, and women with absentee husbands.

The majority of the farmer-traders and professional traders derive low to moderate daily and monthly incomes from their trading activities. Two small groups of actors have high incomes, namely the collecting wholesalers, and those distributing wholesalers who operate in large wholesale markets (such as the Kongowea wholesale market in Mombasa).

Agents and facilitators

The most common horticultural agents in Kenya are **purchasing agents**. At the time of the trade survey, seven of them were interviewed in Kinangop Division, Nyandarua District.[6]

---

6   The total number of horticultural purchasing agents operating in Kinangop at the time of the trade survey was not known. It was estimated that there were 20 of them at most.

All but one of these dealt with potatoes, the most important horticultural crop in the area.[7] Four of the seven agents were also commercial horticultural farmers, and three were pure agents. All lived in the division where they carried out their agent activities. Their estimated buying radius was five to ten kilometres. They knew the farmers and the farmers knew them. This contrasted with the collecting wholesalers for whom they worked. These traders usually came from Nairobi or from other parts of the district. The agents' knowledge of the local situation gave them expert power.[8]

A collecting wholesaler informed his purchasing agent about the day he would come to collect produce and the price he was willing to pay farmers. The agent then started to look for produce. He bargained with farmers about quantities and prices on behalf of the wholesaler. Once the deal was settled, he instructed the farmer when to deliver the produce. The agent organized the packing of the produce in bags, the topping up and twining of bags,[9] if necessary the carrying of bags to a road that could be reached by truck, and finally the loading of the truck. In this way, he minimized the time the wholesalers needed to collect the produce. Without the agent the collecting process would have taken some two days, and with the help of the agent only half a day.

After loading the produce, the collecting wholesaler paid the agent, who in turn paid the farmers. Farmers always received cash. During periods of produce scarcity, all interviewed agents paid an advance to make sure that farmers did not sell their produce to another trader before the wholesaler arrived.[10] The agents, in turn, received the money in advance from the wholesaler. A farmer who received an advance could be dishonest to an agent, but this might backfire on him if he needed the agent in future. In general, a farmer was more prepared to cheat an unknown wholesaler than a well-known local person, which was an important reason, particularly for wholesalers from outside the district, to call in an agent. The agent might, of course, also cheat the collecting wholesaler, but word would then spread to other wholesalers and the agent would lose his job and his standing in the local community.

Five of the seven agents said they would deal with any reliable wholesaler that came along. The other two dealt with specific wholesalers only. The reason they gave was 'security': if they worked for these wholesalers during periods of high demand and low supply, the traders would also come to them during periods of low demand and high supply. The latter occurred, for instance, after a heavy shower during harvesting peaks, when the production area was difficult to access and the harvested crops began to perish.

---

7   Six of the interviewed agents dealt with potatoes. The seventh dealt with cabbages, the second most important crop in the area. Four of the six potato agents also handled cabbages. Agents handled one commodity at a time, because collecting wholesalers asked for either potatoes or cabbages.

8   See Section 4.6 on types of power.

9   Cabbages and potatoes were packed in the gunny bags also used for maize (containing 90 kgs of maize). After filling a bag with potatoes or cabbages a large heap of produce was put on top (the topping up). Then twine was used to make a kind of net that covered the heap and held it down to the bag. The extension of the bag could be one third to half the size of the bag itself.

10   The agent made an advance payment either before the crop was harvested or thereafter. The first possibility was adopted when crops was still immature and produce was not yet available in the area. The agent then tried to persuade farmers to harvest their crop prematurely in exchange for a good price, and, in the course of the negotiations, offered an ample prepayment to ease cooperation. The second kind of advance payment was made when only part of the crop in the area was mature, or when the harvest was poor.

All interviewed agents received a commission per collected bag which was agreed on in advance. The agents had to use part of the commission to cover their own costs, notably the hired casual labour needed for packing, topping up and twining.[11] The commission was not related to the negotiated buying price at the farm or the expected selling price in the Nairobi market.[12] Agents increased their profit by negotiating a lower buying price than the one agreed on with the wholesaler. Of course this practice was known to the wholesalers, and was used in the negotiation process to keep the commission rate low. The system remained advantageous to the agents because commission rates were known within the community, while people could only guess at the additional profits generated by the difference between agreed and actual buying prices.

Commission rates were negotiable, since wholesalers were not entirely dependent on their agent: agents were replaceable either by other agents or by direct buying from farmers. Engaging the services of agents was simply the result of weighing costs against benefits on the part of collecting wholesalers. The benefits included saved time, inside knowledge (expert power of the agent), and lower enforcement costs in cases of advance payments.

Whereas collecting wholesalers may use purchasing agents, distributing wholesalers may use **brokers**. Brokers are, however, less common in horticultural trade than purchasing agents. In Kenya they can be found, for instance, at the Wakulima wholesale market in Nairobi. The brokers are usually young men who do not have enough capital to go into trade themselves. They try to make some money by selling produce on behalf of collecting wholesalers who sell in the market place from the back of their truck, and distributing wholesalers who sell in the market from a stall. The brokers position themselves near the entrance of the market place and ask people who pass them what they want to buy. If a person wants to buy potatoes, a broker takes him to a potato trader he knows. He may either carry out the price negotiations on behalf of the trader, or assist the trader in the process. If the deal is on and the customer has paid, the broker gets a small commission from the trader.

In the Kongowea wholesale market in Mombasa an additional type of broker can be found, the auctioneer. They are the only horticultural brokers of their kind in Kenya.[13] They auction on behalf of collecting wholesalers, charging them a commission of 10 per cent of the selling price. Some fruits are auctioned throughout the year (e.g. bananas from Taveta), while others are only auctioned during peak periods of supply (e.g. a proportion of the oranges, mangoes and papayas from Kwale and Kilifi). The system guarantees quick selling at competitive prices. Buying, however, requires knowledge of the auction system and bidding skills.[14] This is beyond the scope of many retailers. Therefore, in addition to

---

[11] In two cases the agent also had to pay the hired labourers that loaded the bags into the trader's truck. Otherwise these costs, and any costs to carry the produce to an accessible road, were met by the wholesaler. In all cases the bags and string for twining were supplied by the wholesaler.

[12] The buying commission was either KSh 20 or Ksh 30 per bag, both for potatoes and cabbages. Since farm gate prices for potatoes were up to twice as high as those for cabbages, commissions were not in proportion to the value of the produce handled. Apparently agents were paid for their organizational efforts without regard to the value of the produce.

[13] In December 1991 nine auctioneers operated in the Kongowea wholesale market. Like wholesalers with stalls they paid a fixed monthly fee to the market authorities.

[14] Oranges and mangoes are sold in lots of one or more bags or baskets, and bananas in lots of some five to a dozen bunches (depending on supply and demand in the market). The auctioneer starts with a low price per bag, basket or bunch, and increases the price as long as more than one buyer shows interest.

retailers some distributing wholesalers have specialized in buying fruits at the auctions to sell to retailers.[15]

The most common facilitators in the marketing channel are **transporters** (in the broadest sense of the word). Porters are usually for hire for short distances. They carry bags, baskets, boxes and bunches on their head or back, from the farm to the road or from the bus stop to the market place. In addition to porters, transporters with donkeys and tractors may be available for short-distance transport in rural areas, and transporters with handcarts in urban areas.

For longer distances buses can be used. Minibuses (*matatus*) traverse production areas and urban centres, and run from one urban centre to another. They carry produce on their roofs. The driver is usually not the owner; one owner often having a whole fleet of *matatus*. Large coaches connect major cities. They carry produce in their cargo-hold and on their roofs. The bus companies to which they belong are owned by big businessmen. One parastatal used to run coaches (the so-called Nyayo buses), but halfway through the 1990s it was in the process of being sold off.

Instead of using a bus, which has to be shared with others, a trader may hire a truck. Transport companies that hire out trucks are usually located in cities. Most truck owners who live in rural areas are not primarily transporters but traders: they only rent out their trucks when they do not have business themselves. They own one or a few trucks, whereas urban truck companies may own a whole fleet of vehicles.

The most common trucks rented out to horticultural traders who want to collect produce in rural areas are 7- to 9-tonne trucks. Trucks of more than 10 tonnes are too heavy and too big. They easily get stuck on the narrow muddy roads in the rural areas. Pick-up trucks of 1 to 3 tonnes are economical only at short distances, that is, from farms to urban centres located in the production area.

Transporters finance the purchase of new trucks or buses through a loan from a commercial bank, on credit from a truck dealer, or, less often, by means of their own capital. They can get credit or a loan only if they are known, are able to provide collateral, and have proven themselves to be successful businessmen. Alternatively, they must have the right political connections.

Commercial **banks** are relatively unimportant as facilitators to horticultural traders. Lack of collateral and high trade risks make banks reluctant to issue loans to these traders. The limited working capital of the majority of the traders makes supplying credit unattractive.

If traders need a loan, other traders and informal savings and credit groups are their main sources. According to a small survey in Njoro market, nine of the 26 interviewed professional traders (35%) lent money to fellow traders. By contrast, only two (8%) admitted to borrowing money from colleagues, which could reflect people's reluctance to

---

The highest bidder does not have to take the entire lot but may also demand part of it. If this happens, the remaining bags, baskets or bunches are auctioned once more during the next round.

[15] A third, relatively small, category of buyers are agents who act on behalf of wholesalers from large urban centres up-country. They buy produce such as oranges, re-pack them, and put them on transport to Nairobi or Nakuru. The agents are relatively few in number, because most of the oranges and mangoes go directly from the coastal production areas to up-country markets without passing the Mombasa wholesale market.

talk about their debts. In addition to other traders, farmers were an important source of credit: seven of the professional traders (27%) received commodities on credit from farmers. In turn, seven professional traders said they provided credit to consumers.[16]

As many as 19 of the 26 professional traders (73%) participated in **savings and credit associations**. Nine of them belonged to two or more groups. The size of the association ranged from 6 to 33 traders, with 10 to 15 members being most common. The fixed weekly contribution could be as low as KSh 20 or as high as KSh 500 or more. Two systems existed, which were also found among traders in other parts of Kenya (e.g. Kisii District): members either borrowed money from an accumulating fund, or each member received the pool in turn.[17]

5.3. Horticultural marketing cooperatives

The Kenyan government has been promoting agricultural cooperatives since independence (Zeleza, 1990; GOK, 1997).[18] All over the arable parts of the country, agricultural cooperative unions and societies deal with input supply and the assembling stage of the marketing process. Both such activities are important for coffee, cotton, sugarcane and dairy products (the main areas of cooperative involvement) but also for horticultural commodities. Horticultural societies, however, have been rare in Kenya.[19] There are two reasons for this: a general reluctance of farmers to participate in any kind of group marketing due to negative experiences with cooperative structures (Appendix 5.3) and the availability of alternative marketing channels for horticultural commodities. Like it or not, until recently many non-horticultural farmers *had* to deal with cooperatives because these institutions were their only alternative. In the case of horticultural commodities alternative market outlets have been there all along. Moreover, they are reasonably reliable. Private traders usually come whenever they promise, and are ready to pay cash on delivery. Most farmers prefer these intermediaries to the theoretical alternative of cooperative marketing, even though traders may pay a lower price.

Most farmers do not believe that cooperative management is capable of successfully handling the marketing of horticultural commodities. By analysing the histories of the Horticultural Cooperative Union (HCU) and the Kinangop Agricultural Cooperative Society, one can show that this is not entirely unfounded. The HCU was at the centre of the cooperative approach of the Kenyan government towards the horticultural sector in the 1970s. The Kinangop Agricultural Cooperative Society is an example of a local initiative

---

16 As for the relatively small group of farmer-traders who operated in Njoro market: one of the five respondents lent money to another trader and none sold on credit to consumers.

17 In contrast with professional traders, none of the five interviewed farmer-traders participated in a savings and credit group.

18 According to Kohls & Uhl (1990) a cooperative is a business voluntarily owned and controlled by its member-patrons and operated for them on a non-profit or cost basis.

19 Until 1983, less than 12 societies focused on horticulture as their main activity, equalling less than five per cent of all registered societies in Kenya (Gyllström, 1991). Since then, the number of horticultural societies has most likely only decreased. They are not mentioned in recent statistics at all. So-called multi-produce societies may focus on horticulture in addition to, for instance, coffee, but such has been rare in the 1990s.

towards the cooperative marketing of horticultural commodities in the 1980s. Both failed, as explained in Appendix 5.4. In contrast to these two examples of failures, however, the Taita Horticultural Produce Cooperative Society is an example of an initiative that succeeded in the 1990s (Appendix 5.4).

A comparison of the three cooperative case studies can explain why the Taita initiative succeeded where the other two failed. This is of interest because the Kenyan government is still advocating agricultural marketing cooperatives, even though it recognizes that they must prove themselves in competition with private traders (GOK, 1997). One part of the explanation is immediately clear: the HCU and the Kinangop society had to cope with mismanagement, a fate which the Taita HPC has been spared. Obviously, it is more difficult to succeed while being mismanaged.

Another, less obvious, part of the explanation is found in marketing strategy. The HCU and the Kinangop society aspired to improve the equity in the marketing channel to the benefit of member-farmers. Their approach was to copy the buying activities of private traders. Both cooperatives failed because they proved to work less efficiently and to be more bureaucratic than the traders.

Like the HCU and the Kinangop society, the Taita HPC has also tried to get a better price for its members, but not by copying the activities of private traders. The Taita management has been aware that a cooperative can never be as flexible as an individual trader. It will lose the battle unless it delivers something new. And so it has done: a more effective marketing channel (a constant supply of superior-quality produce). Whether a similar strategy would have worked for the HCU and the Kinangop society cannot be said with certainty, but it is clear that a better strategy is needed than simply copying the activities of private traders.

5.4. Horticultural Export traders[20]

When produced for the world market, vegetables, fruits and cut flowers belong to the so-called non-traditional export crops (Appendix 5.5). Kenya is very successful in this field. In the late 1980s and early 1990s it developed into the largest African supplier of fresh vegetables and cut flowers to the European market, and the biggest African exporter of air-freighted fruits after South Africa (Appendix 5.6 shows Kenya's African competitors). In 1993 it exported 62,128 tons of fresh produce worth KSh. 4.8 billion, and 90,000 tons of processed produce worth KSh. 3.3 billion (Nyamiaka, 1995). Horticulture was the third foreign exchange earner in the Kenyan agricultural sector, after tea and coffee. Horticultural exports accounted for 11 per cent of Kenya's total foreign exchange earnings (CBS, 1995).

Kenya's chief export fruits are avocados, pineapples and mangoes, and the chief vegetables are French beans and the so-called Asian vegetables. The latter term refers to commodities such as chillies, okra, eggplants as well as more exotic species like karella, turia, tindori, dudhi, valore and guar. The most important types of cut flowers are roses,

---

20 An earlier version of this section has been published by the author in collaboration with T. D. Magori: 'Flowers and French Beans from Kenya. A Story of Export Success.' in S. Ellis & Y. A. Fauré (eds.) *Entreprises et entrepreneurs africains.* Karthala - Orstom, Paris, 1995, pp. 435-444.

spray and standard carnations, statice, alstroemeria, arabicum, solidaster, molucella, tuberose, ornithogalum, delphinium, ammi majus and orchids (see also Section 3.2).

All horticultural commodities are exported fresh, with the exception of some of the harvested French beans and pineapples, which are tinned. Whereas tinned produce is transported by sea, fresh commodities are usually air-freighted. The only major exception are irregular shipments of avocados to the Middle East in refrigerated containers.

The composition of fresh horticultural exports has changed over time: the relative importance of cut flowers increased at the expense of fruits and vegetables (Table 5.2). By 1993, over half the value of horticultural exports derived from cut flowers. Their export volume increased by about three-quarters in four years' time, while the export volume of fresh mangoes, pineapples, French beans and Asian vegetables either remained stable or declined (Table 5.3). Only avocados showed a major increase, due to rising sea transports.

The top seven countries that import fresh horticultural commodities from Kenya are all situated in Western Europe (Table 5.4). The most important export destination outside Europe is Saudi Arabia. Certain commodities have one main destination, such as Asian vegetables, of which over 90% are destined for the United Kingdom, where they wind up on the tables of British Asians in London and elsewhere. As for cut flowers, around 60% of the total exports are sent to the Netherlands to be auctioned near Schiphol Airport.[21]

The horticultural export sector in Kenya is the preserve of a limited number of traders and producers. In 1992, around 60 traders were exporting fruits and vegetables, of whom more than one-fifth were producers at the same time. The high degree of market concentration and vertical integration have been part of the success of horticultural exports, as we will see. In the case of cut flowers there is even greater concentration. Of the approximately 40 cut flower exporters who were in business in 1992, one-third owned a flower farm. Moreover, the four largest flower-producing exporters accounted for more than three-quarters of the total cut flower exports.

The involvement of foreign and multinational companies in the horticultural export sector is quite substantial indeed, especially in cut flowers. A quarter of the flower exporters are foreigners, while two of the four market leaders are multinationals, including Brooke Bond, a subsidiary of Unilever which is well-known throughout Africa. The other two leading flower exporting firms are Kenyan-owned.

In the case of vegetables and fruits, the importance of multinational and foreign companies is limited. The share of Kenyans of Asian origin, who have been in Kenya for more than one generation and have Kenyan nationality, is high. One-third of the fruit and vegetable exporters belong to this group, and this is partly related to the export of Asian vegetables. Kenyans of Asian origin are less prominent in flower exports, where they account for only one-sixth of all exporters and are not among the four leading exporters.

The secret of the Asian traders' success lies in their active promotion of small-scale production combined with detailed knowledge of the market. Market information is easier for Asians to acquire than other Kenyans because of their international family connections. Many Asian traders have family members in the United Kingdom who inform them about

---

21   A large portion of the Kenyan flowers do not stay in the Netherlands but are bought by Dutch exporters.

Table 5.2. Export value of fresh fruit, vegetable and cut flower exports, 1984-1993 (at current prices in KSh million)

Year	Fruits KSh mln	%	Vegetables KSh mln	%	Cut flowers KSh mln	%	Total KSh mln	%
1984	69.8	17	172.0	41	174.0	42	415.8	100
1985	54.2	12	200.8	43	209.2	45	464.2	100
1986	99.3	15	282.7	45	248.0	39	630.0	99
1987	104.3	12	293.4	33	502.4	56	900.1	101
1988	298.4	22	394.7	30	634.9	48	1328.0	100
1989	204.9	14	509.7	35	728.5	51	1443.1	100
1990	184.3	11	628.8	37	864.4	51	1678.5	99
1991	201.9	10	775.8	39	1033.5	51	2011.2	100
1992	359.0	14	909.7	36	1247.8	50	2516.5	100
1993	521.8	11	1771.7	37	2482.8	52	4776.3	100

Source: internal files HCDA

Table 5.3. Export volume of fresh horticultural exports, 1989-1993 (metric tonnes)

Commodity	1989	1990	1991	1992	1993
Mangoes	2,971	2,613	1,745	2,349	2,850
Avocados	3,438	3,311	4,193	6,310	6,676
Pineapples	3,255	767	580	568	757
French beans	15,227	16,330	14,855	15,196	14,468
Asian vegetables	8,614	9,276	9,244	9,445	9,095
Cut flowers	13,245	14,423	16,405	19,807	23,636
Other	2,753	2,427	2,826	3,688	4,646
Total	49,503	49,147	49,848	57,363	62,128

Source: internal files HCDA

Table 5.4. Destination of fresh Kenyan horticultural exports, 1989-1993 (%)*

Country	1989	1990	1991	1992	1993
United Kingdom	33.5	34.8	33.9	29.3	28.9
France	17.0	18.6	19.8	22.3	16.7
Netherlands	16.7	19.2	21.8	28.3	25.3
Germany	12.6	11.8	12.9	9.1	10.4
Belgium	3.6	6.8	3.6	3.8	2.7
Italy	6.3	0.4	0.6	0.4	0.1
Switzerland	2.1	1.9	1.9	2.1	4.0
Saudi Arabia	1.2	1.6	0.8	1.2	1.0
Other countries	7.0	4.9	4.7	3.5	10.9
	100.0	100.0	100.0	100.0	100.0

Source: internal files HCDA
* percentage of export volume

market developments or deal with the actual importation and distribution of the commodities concerned.[22] Other Kenyan traders normally lack contacts of this kind.

All Kenyan vegetable and fruit exporters rely at least in part on contract farmers. These are smallholders who buy seeds and various other inputs from certain traders or their agents, while committing themselves to sell the produce to them.[23] A smallholder will typically produce some 30 to 90 kilograms of French beans a week, receiving about KSh 1,000 to KSh 3,000 for this crop. These agreements, usually unwritten, are often the subject of disagreement. A farmer may decide to sell the commodities to another exporter who offers a slightly higher price. That is all the more tempting if the farmer has received inputs on credit. On the other hand, when the export market is depressed, a farmer may find that the trader fails to arrive to collect the crop. Export possibilities fluctuate weekly or even daily, notwithstanding the well-established contacts between most vegetable and fruit exporters and European importers. These fluctuations stem from the demand in Europe and competition from other countries.[24] As one export trader put it, 'If Morocco sends a boatload of French beans to France, I will not sell a single box of French beans the next day.' Exporters react to such market developments by staying at home, leaving their contract farmers with unsaleable produce that does not even have a local market.

In the case of cut flowers, small-scale production is less significant. A small-scale flower grower is one who harvests less than 10,000 stems a year, while large-scale farms produce anywhere between 5 and 250 million stems a year. Successful flower cultivation requires special skills, for which large-scale producers employ experts. Without such skills most smallholders cannot attain the standards of quality required in the European market and elsewhere, especially Japan, where quality regulations are even more stringent than in Europe. Consequently, smallholders normally sell to chance exporters who handle relatively small quantities.

The involvement of the government in horticultural exports is rather limited. The Horticultural Crops Development Authority (a parastatal) used to carry out exports, but stopped doing so in 1986. Now it has only a regulating, advisory and monitoring function on behalf of the Ministry of Agriculture (Appendix 5.7).

Conditions for success
In October and November 1992, four successful horticultural exporters were interviewed for a better understanding of the structure of the marketing channels in which this type of traders operate, and of the conditions for success in this part of the horticultural sector (Appendix 5.8).

---

22 Jaffee (1990; 1993; 1994) has shown that long-term and exclusive trading ties reduce the transaction costs faced by exporters. They do not have to identify the range of potential customers in different countries, negotiate individual sales terms with each, and enforce the ensuing agreements. Instead, they utilize a single contract and a single partner to make their sales, relying on this better informed and better positioned trader to coordinate sales and distribution operations.

23 An exporter normally deals with contract farmers though agents or employed truck drivers. The drivers are supposed to buy directly from the farmers, but some of them engage local agents to bring the produce from the farms to the collection points. The agent then pays the farmers 5 to 10 per cent less than the predetermined price, which sparks many complaints from the farmers (Njoro, 1993).

24 In 1992 the Kenyan export price for French beans, for instance, fluctuated between KSh 20 and KSh 60 per carton (Nyoro, 1993).

The case studies show that concentration and vertical integration are two factors that determine the success of horticultural exports. Only a strictly limited number of exporters are able to enter this multimillion dollar trade, which requires participants to have a minimum scale of operations. There are two reasons for this. First, exporters have to be able to deliver whatever quantities customers may require, at whatever moment. If an exporter proves unreliable in this respect, he will loose his customers rapidly, especially since competition by horticultural exporters from other African countries is rising. To make matters more difficult, exporters cannot stick to one customer, because importers switch from one source to another every week, putting exporters in trouble if they have no alternative market outlet.

The second reason why a minimum scale of operations is necessary derives from the need to have agents in the field, trucks on the road and cold stores in town or at the airport. These are essential to promote production, secure transportation to the airport, and maintain the quality of the commodities. Agents will only remain faithful if an exporter's turnover is large enough to guarantee them a reasonable commission. Heavy investments in transport and storage will only pay themselves back under the same conditions.

Besides money to invest, export traders require financial resources because of temporary losses they can incur during the initial stage of marketing or during periods of oversupply in the international market. The horticultural export assortment is to a large extent different from the assortment offered for sale in the domestic market. Therefore, rising exports of fruits, vegetables and cut flowers do not increase produce prices in the domestic market.[25] This in itself is positive, but it also has a negative side. The disparity between export assortments and domestic assortments makes the export trade even more risky than it already is. If traders fail to export their produce there is hardly any local market for it. In many cases it must be destroyed.[26] Solid financial backing is required to meet the losses involved. As a consequence, most successful exporters have been in business for a long time or have additional sources of income.

In addition to concentration, successful horticultural exports require vertical integration. The key to this is quality control (one aspect of a marketing channel's effectiveness, see Section 4.5). Unless exporters can guarantee delivery of highest-grade products, they will lose their customers. Quality can be regulated most easily when the exporters produce their commodities themselves. This requires major investments, however. The alternative is to rely on smallholders who are supplied with the right inputs and closely supervised by agents in the field. The chances of failure are greatest in the case of cut flowers, which explains why more exporters have reverted to their own production in this sector.

The phenomenon of diversification also exists in the Kenyan horticultural export trade. There are large exporters who act as transport operators, hiring out cargo space to smaller colleagues, and there are exporters who have diversified into the production of packing material. This is a sign of the flexibility of Kenyan export traders, who must be inventive in order to survive in an uncertain marketing environment. Their success is determined by commercial skill and their willingness to take risks, although the latter are

---

[25] In other words, the equity in serving market segments is not affected (see Section 4.6).

[26] Porter (1990) has pointed out that a home market is important to an industry with high levels of uncertainty. The interviews with traders have shown that high levels of uncertainty are characteristic for the export of fresh horticultural commodities from Kenya.

sometimes passed on to smallholders, labourers and the physical environment. The involvement of foreigners, multinationals and Kenyans of Asian origin is notably high, but the heavy investments that are required to become and remain successful suggest that most of the value added is ploughed back into the Kenyan economy. Exports of horticultural commodities have developed without any substantial support from the Kenyan government, thus reflecting the abilities of private entrepreneurs to generate employment and foreign exchange.

5.5. Horticultural processors

The present book focuses primarily on Kenyan marketing channels for fresh horticultural produce. That is because the largest proportion by far of the Kenyan horticultural commodities are marketed fresh, and only relatively small quantities are processed before reaching the consumer in Kenya or elsewhere. Nonetheless, we will now have a quick look at horticultural processors.

Kenya possesses canning, juice extraction and jam factories. Major products are tinned pineapples, tinned French beans, jams, ketchup, sauces, juices and juice concentrates (Table 5.5). The producers of jams and ketchup and the smaller producers of juices concentrate primarily on the domestic market. The producers of tinned beans and pineapples and the larger producers of fruit juices and fruit concentrates focus mainly on the export market. The profits of factories that trade in the domestic market depend to a large extent on economic developments in the country, which determine the purchasing power of potential consumers. The profits of export processors are closely related to their production costs relative to competitors in other countries, as well as to demand developments in the world market.

The domestic market is competitive, but competition does not reach the level experienced by producers for the world market. Many export processors have had problems surviving in recent decades. Two case studies show this: one concerns a vegetable dehydration factory in Naivasha, and the other a juice factory near Mombasa (Appendix 5.9). The examples illustrate how difficult it is to be a successful horticultural processor in Kenya. Quality standards in the international market are high, and competition can be lethal. Production costs are inflated by poor infrastructure in the production areas and by high costs of packing materials.[27] The raw materials offered for sale are often of poor quality, especially because farmers can sell their first-quality produce against higher prices in the local fresh market.

Sadly, the same problems that plague Kenya in the 1990s were already found in various developing countries three decades ago. Abbott (1988) cites a FAO study carried out in the second half of the 1960s which surveyed thirty-five vegetable and fruit processing enterprises that had not lived up to expectations. Two-thirds of them had problems with raw material supply, which were related to factors such as overestimation of potential supply and

---

[27] Porter (1990) cites infrastructure (including the transport and communication systems) as one of the factor conditions that determine an industry's competitiveness in the world market.

Table 5.5. Horticulture processing factories in Kenya

Industry	Location (District)	Manufactured products
Kabazi Canners Ltd.	Subukia (Nakuru)	canned vegetables, canned fruits, canned tomato juice, fruit salad
Del Monte Ltd.	Thika (Kiambu)	canned fruits, pineapple juice, pineapple slices and segments, frozen and canned vegetables, tomato sauce
Kenya Orchards Ltd.	Machakos	jams, marmalades, fruit juices, canned fruits and vegetables, tomato sauce, tomato ketchup
Kenya Fruit Processors Ltd.	Sotik (Kericho) Thika (Kiambu)	passion fruit juice
Trufoods Ltd.	Nairobi	jams, canned pineapple, tomato sauce, potato crisps, fruit squashes
Kenya Sunshine Products Ltd.	Ruaraka (Nairobi)	fruit squashes, passion fruit juice, black currant health drink, tomato sauce
Frozen Foods (K) Ltd.	Nairobi	canned fruit and vegetables
Feingold J. H.	Bahati (Nakuru)	strawberry jams, juices
Associated Packers Ltd.	Nairobi	fruit squashes, instant jellies
Pan African Vegetable Products Ltd.	Naivasha (Nakuru)	dehydrated vegetables
Limuru Canning Factory	Limuru (Kiambu)	canned & fresh peas
Cremex Ltd.	Nairobi	tomato sauce, spices, fruit squashes, tomato ketchup
Erskine & Price Manufacturing	Nairobi	passion fruit juice
Njoro Canning Factory (K) Ltd.	Njoro (Nakuru)	canned French beans
Agraphia Manufacturing Co. Ltd.	Nairobi	potato crisps, dried peas
Seven trees Farm Ltd.	Murang'a (Murang'a)	fruit juices, jams
Mt. Kenya Agro-Industries Ltd	Kiganjo (Nyeri)	canned fruits and vegetables
Mashambani Industries Ltd.	Kisii	processed juices and vegetables
Bawazir Food Processors Ltd.	Mtwapa (Mombasa)	fruit juice concentrates
Fri-O-Ken	Nairobi	canned beans
Highlands Canners Ltd.	Nairobi	canned beans

Sources: internal files HCDA, as consulted in 1990. The first five companies are also mentioned in Bhushan (1991, 1996).

lack of sufficient varieties for processing. Little less than one-third had problems with market demand, caused by factors such as overestimation of prospective demand, misjudgement of consumer tastes, and underestimation of competition from other sources. These are the same supply and demand problems found here for PanAVeg and Bawazir.

One final remark on horticultural processing in Kenya should be made. Processing is often mentioned by Kenyan policy makers as a means to get rid of seasonal oversupplies in the domestic market. It is important to stress that this is not by definition viable when the processed commodities are intended for export. Export processors require top-quality produce. Second-quality goods therefore remain unsold during periods of oversupply, either with or without the presence of export processors.[28]

5.6. Some comments on the channels from a SCP point of view

On the basis of the foregoing description of all the actors and institutions operating in the Kenyan horticultural marketing channels, a few observations can be made about the channels in terms of key words from structure-conduct-performance (SCP) analysis (Box 5.1).

Buyer and seller concentrations, entry barriers
In the domestic market, the structure of the horticultural marketing system is made up of large numbers of buyers and sellers operating at various marketing levels. Buyer and seller concentrations are generally low, especially in the rural and urban market places. Buyer concentrations are relatively high in less accessible production areas which have no assembly centres and where a limited number of collecting wholesalers deal with individual farmers at the farm gate.

The exact number of collecting wholesalers operating in a production area is difficult to estimate. However, according to Baumol et al. (1980), potential rather than actual competition counts, and imperfect competition is not a problem when entry and exit barriers are absent (see Section 4.4). Various entry barriers play a role in African horticultural trade, including economies of scale, capital requirements, cumulated experience, access to distribution channels and the expectations of potential entrants. These feature at the collecting wholesale level in particular.

In Kenya, one entry barrier seems to be most important: the lack of credit facilities which could provide potential collecting wholesalers with the working capital needed to get into business. Short-term credit is needed to pay a deposit to the truck owner for hiring a truck and to give farmers some down payment to ensure they do not sell their commodities

---

28 Processing is often seen as a medicine for all evils in Kenya. In Taveta, district officers advocated the building of a banana wine factory to solve the problem of banana surpluses and low farm-gate prices in the area. The reason for the surpluses and low prices was the poor condition of the road from Taveta to Mombasa. It caused high transport losses, and limited the number of transporters in the area. Bananas that did reach Mombasa without spoiling on the way did sell well. Whether banana wine would sell in the same market was never researched (nor whether the production of banana wine was technically feasible). Whether the transport of bottles of banana wine over the same road would be less of a problem than transport of fresh bananas was not looked into either. Banana wine had become a panacea that would bring prosperity to all.

Box 5.1. Structure-conduct-performance analysis

Structure-conduct-performance (SCP) analysis was developed by Bain (1959, 1968), Clodius & Mueller (1961) and Slater (1968). Market structure and trader conduct determine market performance. In turn, market performance will influence market structure and traders' conduct in the long run.

The key words used in relation to structure, conduct and performance differ greatly from one author to the other, depending on the sector and region being studied and the perceptions of the researcher. The key words used here are relevant to the agricultural sector in developing countries and are based on Clodius & Mueller (1961), Hill & Ingersent (1982), Van Tilburg (1981) and Van Tilburg et al. (1989).

Market structure refers to the organizational characteristics of the market, including seller and buyer concentration, conditions of entry, power distribution, and availability of market information. **Market conduct** refers to the set of competitive practices and tactics that traders deploy. It includes the methods employed by a trader or group of traders in determining prices and output; their attitudes towards grading, sorting, customer relations and adoption of innovations; the means by which price and product policies of competing traders are coordinated and adapted to each other; and the extent to which predatory and exclusionary tactics are directed against established rivals or potential entrants. **Market performance** refers to the economic result: product suitability in relation to product quality; rates of profit in relation to the margins at the different trading levels; level of output in relation to any deliberate restrictions to influence prices; and, finally, price integration between markets and the degree of unpredictable variation of prices in markets.

The SCP method has been subject to criticism, among other reasons because of its emphasis on narrowly defined economic goals such as efficient resource allocation and equitable income distribution (Bateman, 1976), its monodisciplinary approach (Harriss, 1982), and its inability to assess the contribution of agricultural markets to economic development. As for the last criticism, Janssen & Van Tilburg (1997) give three arguments for this inability: (1) SCP does not usually examine the costs and benefits of successful intervention, (2) SCP analysis normally does not include the process of change and instability through which most developing economies are passing, and (3) SCP criteria may be useful to review the existing agricultural marketing systems but are poor indicators of their potential for effecting change.

Some SCP studies on agricultural marketing in developing countries are Jones (1972), Van Tilburg (1981,1988), Van Tilburg et al. (1989), Dijkstra & Magori (1992b, 1994a, 1994b), Tollens (1992), Van Tilburg & Lutz (1992, 1995), Limbu (1993), Lutz (1994) and Goossens (1994).

---

to other traders. Long-term loans are needed for traders who decide to buy trucks for themselves.

Usually getting a loan from a commercial bank is impossible or very costly, because of the risky nature of the trade business and the requirement of collateral. The demand for collateral also affects transporters who want to buy a truck. In the past, title deeds for land were demanded, although they were not available. Nowadays title deeds are available in most areas, but many banks no longer accept them as collateral. Banks had meanwhile experienced problems in selling such title deeds because some local communities became very hostile to potential buyers. The lack of credit facilities to buy trucks results in a scarcity of transporters in the production areas. As a consequence, traders have to rely on urban transporters, but they do not like to send their trucks to horticultural production areas that are difficult to access. The vehicles get stuck easily and the wear and tear is high. Thus, financial and transport constraints impede the entry of new collecting wholesalers into the marketing channel, especially in less accessible production areas.[29]

Transport and finance are no real entry barriers to horticultural retailers. They use public transport (*matatus*), and their turnover is much smaller than that of wholesalers, meaning that they require less capital. Moreover, groups of traders may solve their credit problems by organizing informal savings and credit groups that provide financial aid to members whenever needed (see Section 5.2).

Finance is an important entry barrier when it comes to export trade. Capital requirements are high, because of the need for means of transport, cold storage facilities, and market information systems. Additional financial resources are required when traders focus on the export of processed horticultural commodities. Exporters of fresh and processed produce have better access to credit facilities from commercial banks than horticultural traders who concentrate on the domestic market. However, their capital requirements are also much higher (see Section 5.4). Often, potential exporters will only succeed in getting a substantial loan from a bank if they are part of one of the old-boys' networks in which bankers, captains of industry, bureaucrats and politicians participate. Lacking access to such a network, they will succeed only if they have substantial family resources.

Level of competition, power distribution, restrictions on output
The level of competition among traders in domestic market places is high, and prices are determined by supply and demand. A hierarchical power structure does not appear to exist. Horticultural traders are small-scale entrepreneurs who do not make themselves dependent on larger traders. Price cartels and deliberate restrictions on traded quantities were not found in our trade survey, even among collecting wholesalers who are relatively small in number and potentially more powerful.

Amongst horticultural retailers, price cartels would probably not limit competition even if they existed. Retail prices often refer to heaps and bundles which have no standard size. A heap of tomatoes can contain four to seven fruits, small or large, green or red, and any of five major varieties. All these distinguishable variables constitute means of competition among traders, without affecting the prices. A heap of tomatoes costs about the same from one retailer to the next, but the quantity and quality differ. Thus, any price agreements amongst traders do not hinder competition in the absence of standardized selling units. Moreover, even if such units existed, observance of the rules by all traders would be very difficult to control.

The threat of buying cartels, which would influence farm-gate prices and hence the incomes of the farmers, is most immediate at the collection stage because of recurrent accessibility problems in the production areas. Roads that change into mudpools after every shower discourage potential collecting wholesalers, and this decreases competition at the buying stage. Buying units also look more standardized at the wholesale level than at the retail level: potatoes are purchased by the gunny bag, tomatoes by the box, bananas by the

---

[29] Exit barriers are absent. Wholesalers, who want to quit can sell their truck second-hand at a fair price and use the money to repay loans; they have no other long-term financial obligations.

bunch and pineapples by the dozen. However, potato bags are extended, tomato boxes have different volumes, banana bunches vary in size and pineapples in weight. As a result there is no real standardization on the basis of which a price cartel could operate. Moreover, not all farmers have to rely on collecting wholesalers who come to their farms. Some may be able to sell their produce to local assembling traders (who in turn sell on to collecting wholesalers);[30] some farmers even sell to retailers who come to their farms. Others may be able to bring their produce to a rural assembly market where the number of potential buyers is larger, and price competition stronger. We will look in more detail at rural assembly markets in Sections 6.3 to 6.7, and at the rationale of collecting wholesalers in Sections 6.1 and 6.2.

Competition in the domestic market is not curtailed by law. The government tried to create a monopoly only once, in the second half of the 1960s when the Horticultural Cooperative Union was given a monopoly on onion marketing. The monopoly was never effective (Appendix 5.4).

The level of competition in the horticultural export branch is high, even though the number of exports is limited. Exporters try to secure their business through long-term vertical relationships with European importers, auctions, retail chains or overseas family branches, rather than developing horizontal ties with other exporters. Competition in the world market is rising, sometimes to the cut-throat level, and traders act each for themselves.

Customer relations, predatory and exclusionary trader tactics
Customer relations are not very important in domestic retail markets, although retail traders often try to befriend consumers by means of an extra dash after a deal is settled. Customer relations are more important at the collection stage. Farmers normally sell to whoever wants to buy instead of waiting for specific traders. When supply is scarce, however, collecting wholesalers try to hold onto producers by means of advance payments, while at the same time developing customer relations with local purchasing agents to secure supply and improve the efficiency of collection (see Section 5.2).

Customer relations are very important in the export trade. On the supply side, many exporters of fresh and processed produce use contract farmers who are supplied with inputs in return for their harvest (see Section 5.4). On the demand side, customer relations with importers, auctions and other institutions are nourished to secure markets.

Predatory and exclusionary tactics are uncommon in domestic horticultural trade. The only place where such things are known to take place is Nairobi wholesale market. The example of the Kinangop Horticultural Society, described in Appendix 5.4, shows that collecting wholesalers who supply this market may use all kinds of tactics to disrupt the activities of new competitors.

Exclusionary tactics probably play some role in the export trade. Export traders need a licence before they can start business and that can sometimes present problems. It is often said that ministers and former ministers who are in the horticultural export trade themselves are behind such problems, but this cannot be proven.

---

[30] When collecting wholesalers are not around and farmers are in need of money, assembling traders may be a solution. However, these traders are only able to store produce for a limited time. They will therefore not buy when they expect collecting wholesalers to stay away for too long, as when access roads to the production area are blocked.

Price information

Up-to-date information on prevailing prices in the domestic rural and urban markets is usually no problem for horticultural traders, because they go to these markets themselves or can ask other traders who have been there. The only constraint is that the prices apply to non-standardized selling units as explained above. Up-to-date price information is a bigger problem for horticultural farmers, especially those living in isolated production areas without assembly markets. They depend for their sales on collecting wholesalers who come to the farms, while they receive their price information from these same traders. This could in theory lead to price manipulation at the expense of the farmers.

A potential source of independent price information to the farmers is the radio. Several times a week the Kenyan Broadcasting Corporation, in collaboration with the Ministry of Agriculture, broadcasts commodity prices, data collected in major urban wholesale markets like Nairobi and Mombasa. Although these prices give only a rough idea what farm-gate prices to expect, they are supposed to improve farmers' bargaining position in dealing with traders. Unfortunately, fewer than 5 per cent of the horticultural farmers listened to the broadcasts at the time of our survey. Many lacked a radio or money to buy batteries, and if they had a working radio they usually listened only to their regional station that broadcasts in the local language. The price reviews were given on the national network in Kiswahili.[31]

An horticultural exporter can get up-to-date price information (e.g. auction prices for flowers) from various European institutes and companies — that is as long as he is prepared to pay for it. Such information is not available to contract farmers who sell their produce to exporters. They have no other choice than to accept what an exporter tells them, while trying to find out what other exporters are paying their outgrowers.[32]

Product suitability

Product suitability is related to the price-quality ratio of the traded horticultural commodities, and to attitudes of the traders towards grading, sorting and adoption of innovations. Although domestic prices are determined largely by market forces, the price-quality ratio is not optimal due to a generally low quality level in the surveyed markets. This is largely the result of factors outside the sphere of influence of individual traders. One of them is the physical conditions in the marketplaces. Lack of sheds, concrete floors and proper drainage adversely affect the quality of the fruits and vegetables sold in the market. The commodities, generally highly perishable, are displayed on the ground without protection against sun and rain. After a shower, the marketplace turns into a mudhole, and fruits and vegetables get as dirty as their surroundings.

The state of the roads also reduces the quality of the commodities. The rough roads in the production areas cause losses of fruits and vegetables destined for urban centres

---

31 This language barrier is not unique in Africa. A recent FAO study on market information services in developing countries came across the same problem in other countries, such as in Guinea Bissau, where prices are broadcast in Portuguese and the bulk of the farming community speaks Creole (Shepherd, 1997).

32 The exporter may pay the farmers a fixed price throughout the buying season or a price that fluctuates in relation to prices in the destination market. In both cases the farmers do not know whether the price they receive is fair in relation to the marketing costs and selling price of the exporter.

outside the district. Losses are aggravated by improper sorting and packing. For example, collecting traders and farmers in Taveta division carry tomatoes in large gunny bags all the way from the farms to Taveta market. By the time they get there the ripest tomatoes have turned to pulp. Collecting wholesalers usually repackage lots in boxes, but once again tomatoes of varying ripeness are often intermixed and most boxes are so big that tomatoes at the bottom get squashed. The use of gunny bags and large boxes does not arise from ignorance on the part of the farmers and traders. Wooden boxes are very expensive in Taveta as timber has to come from far away.

Tomato traders do try to innovate packing methods, especially when transport distances are large and potential losses are substantial. In the past few years, some tomato wholesalers have begun using plastic crates which were formerly used solely to transport bread. The crates have a longer lifespan than wooden boxes and tend to be less costly and easier to come by in some parts of the country.

An example of the rationale of poor packaging concerns cooking bananas. Collecting wholesalers in Kisii put bunches of cooking bananas on top of each other in the back of a truck without using boxes or cartons that would protect them against sun and rain. On arrival in Nairobi or Mombasa, the quality is often poor and consumers complain. Packing the cooking bananas would be expensive for two reasons. First, the trader needs to employ labourers to remove the hands from the stems and put them into cartons or boxes. Second, and more important, packing materials are scarce and costly. Packaging would therefore considerably increase the selling price of the fruits, raising the question of whether urban consumers would be able and willing to pay more in return for better quality. Of course, prices would not have to rise as much as the extra costs of packing, because of the anticipated lower losses during transport. Under the present circumstances, however, the smaller produce losses would probably not compensate the higher costs.

These examples deal with highly perishable commodities. In the case of less fragile commodities like potatoes and cabbages from Nyandarua, the quality of the vegetables remains reasonably good, even when they are packed in extended gunny bags of over 100 kilograms. However, the topping up of bags makes price formation in the production areas less transparent to farmers. Extensions differ from one bag to another, and farmers do not know the weight of their extended bags (especially because special labourers take care of the topping up). Farmers may get information on prices received by other farmers, but they do not know the sizes of the bags involved. Collecting wholesalers are not only their most important source of price information, but they also determine the size of the bag extensions.

The practice of extending bags is the result of the market fee system in the Wakulima wholesale market, Nairobi. Collecting wholesalers who enter this market are charged an amount per bag, regardless of size. They will not stop topping up bags until selling units in the Nairobi and other major wholesale markets have been forcefully standardized, or until market fees are based on the weight of each bag.

In contrast with domestic trade, sorting, grading and standard packing units are common in export trade. Without sorting and grading, exportation would not be possible, because of the high quality demanded by European importers, and the large quality fluctuations in harvested produce. Substandard produce is usually destroyed or dumped onto the local market. Packaging innovations that have been developed elsewhere in the world are introduced as quickly as possible to remain competitive. Importation of ready-made packing materials and inputs for the local manufacture of such packing materials used to be a bottleneck as a consequence of bureaucratic procedures and regulations with regard to foreign exchange. Nowadays the regime is not as strict. The high costs of good-quality packing materials still remain a problem, especially when the Kenyan Shilling is weak.

Profit rates
The profit rates of horticultural traders who operate in the domestic market are not excessive, as reflected in trader incomes. The majority of the traders in the local markets earn small to moderate incomes, and only a minority of the traders in the larger markets are fairly well-off (see Section 5.2). The group with the highest incomes is without a doubt the collecting wholesalers. Their substantial profits are at least partly related to the risks they have to endure.

As collecting wholesalers do not deliberately restrict output levels or operate buying cartels, the level of competition is determined by the number of traders who come to the production areas and the availability of transporters to carry the produce to the urban centres. Both factors depend on the accessibility of the areas. Improvement of the infrastructure will therefore not only permit smaller margins by reducing trade risks and transport costs, but it would also force wholesalers to decrease their margins because of rising competition.

Profit rates are potentially high in export trade, but they are commonly subject to large fluctuations. Trade risks are high due to local and intercontinental transport difficulties and recurring oversupplies in the world market. Most export traders are accustomed to temporary losses, and part of their normal profit must be reserved for such setbacks.

Price integration between markets and price fluctuations within markets
Analysis of price integration between domestic market places and price fluctuations in domestic markets requires longitudinal price data. Such data were not collected during the trade survey. Some general observations can nevertheless be made.

If commodities in a terminal market come from a rural assembly market, the degree of price integration between the terminal market and the rural assembly market is generally high because there are good infrastructural connections (see Sections 6.3 to 6.7) and no storage activities at any level of the marketing chain. If roads in the destination area are bad, the produce generally passes also through a market with a distribution function. The degree of price integration between the distribution market and the terminal market is high, because retailers have to collect fresh produce the day before each market day, and this keeps them informed about prevailing prices.

Horticultural commodities do not always pass through a rural assembly market on their way out of the production area. Under such circumstances prices at the farm gate and in the destination market have to be compared in order to analyse the level of integration. Interestingly, prices may fall at the farm level while remaining stable or rising at the destination market. This is the result of two factors, poor infrastructure and interregional substitution. Some collecting wholesalers divert their buying operations to other production areas during periods when roads are muddy or impassable. The consequent lower demand in the production area, in combination with higher transport costs, reduces farm-gate prices, while prices in the destination market remain stable when enough supplies from other parts of Kenya come in; otherwise they increase.

Seasonal price variations in the domestic markets are usually predictable, as they are related to the same rainfall fluctuations that determine harvesting periods. The direct relation between harvesting on the farm and supply in the markets derives from the general absence of storage facilities for horticultural commodities at all levels of the marketing chain, including the farm.

Price fluctuations in the international markets can be very volatile, especially when fresh produce is involved. Exporters can do little about that. They can try to get long-term contracts against a fixed price, but very few customers are willing to take such a risk. If the price is fixed, the contract will normally not stipulate the quantity, which means that importers will not buy from an exporter when they can get the goods cheaper elsewhere.

Price integration between local markets and international markets is normally not an issue. Most exported commodities do not pass a local market place, because production takes place at exporters' own farms or through contracted outgrowers. Only when commodities cannot be exported and are dumped on the local market does some price relationship exist.

Concluding remark
It can be concluded that horticultural farmers and traders succeed in operating within a marketing environment characterized by a poor physical infrastructure, poorly developed market places, scarcity of transport means, lack of credit facilities, lack of appropriate and affordable packing materials, and, in the case of farmers, lack of independent market information. Better market performance will require an improved marketing environment.

Horticultural Marketing Channels in Kenya: the Collection Stage

In the previous chapter various market intermediaries were reviewed. In this chapter we look in more detail at the collection stage of the horticultural trade, analysing two aspects: the rationale of collecting wholesalers (Sections 6.1 and 6.2), and the development of rural assembly markets (Sections 6.3 to 6.7).

6.1. The efficiency rationale of collecting wholesalers: the distributing wholesalers' perspective

Collecting wholesalers buy primarily from farmers in production areas to sell to distributing wholesalers in the wholesale markets of large towns. Their motive to go into business is clear: they want to make money and they have found a way to do so. Within a capitalistic system that is a legitimate reason. However, it raises the question of why distributing wholesalers and farmers do not go for the money themselves. Why do distributing wholesalers buy produce from collecting wholesalers instead of going to the production area, and why do farmers sell their produce to collecting wholesalers instead of taking it to the urban market? Both questions will be dealt with, starting with the first one.

Distributing wholesalers may have various reasons to leave the collection stage to collecting wholesalers. These reasons will be discussed in qualitative terms. The trade survey did not include enough wholesale markets and distributing wholesalers to come to a reliable quantitative analysis. The qualitative findings are based on observations in the Nairobi, Nakuru and Mombasa wholesale markets.

One important reason why wholesalers focus entirely on the distribution task — selling produce in the market place to retailers — is the daily character of market places in large urban centres. When the consumer population of an urban centre rises, periodic markets change into daily ones. Concentrating all trade on one or two market days is no longer necessary to attract enough customers per day. The change from a periodic into a daily market affects the mobility of the wholesalers in the market place. When the market was still periodic, wholesalers had sufficient time to collect produce in the production areas themselves. Not all of them did so, since some waited for suppliers to come to them, but they preferred to collect the produce because of the additional profits involved. Without collection, wholesalers would be idle on non-market days.[1]

Once a market has changed from a periodic into a daily one, the distributing wholesalers' time becomes scarcer. Various costs are involved if they continue buying produce from farmers in the production area rather than from collecting wholesalers in the market. One such cost involves lost sales on the days the wholesaler is on the road. A second cost derives from lower sales on the days the trader is in the market. Many urban horticultural retailers come to buy produce from wholesalers every day of the week, early in the morning before starting their own trading. For each commodity or group of related commodities they prefer to deal with one wholesaler whom they can trust in terms of prices and quality. They therefore prefer a distributing wholesaler who is available throughout the week to a part-time wholesaler, unless the latter offers substantially lower prices.

In some wholesale markets, being absent has an additional cost aspect. When a market changes from periodic to daily, the infrastructure of the market place tends to change as well. Permanent concrete stalls and halls replace temporary wooden stalls and selling on the ground.[2] Distributing wholesalers are charged by the market authorities for the use of these upgraded facilities. The details of the arrangements differ from one market to the other. In the new, spacious Mombasa wholesale market, distributing wholesalers sell either from an individual stall annex store or from a hall they share with other wholesalers. When they use a stall they pay a monthly rent, when they sell in a shared hall they do not pay anything.[3] In the Nakuru wholesale market, which is also relatively new but not as spacious as the Mombasa one, all distributing wholesalers sell from two halls and are charged on a daily basis. In the Nairobi wholesale market, which is old and small, all distributing wholesale traders have to rent a stall on a monthly basis.

As long as wholesalers are charged on a daily basis or not charged at all, being absent from the wholesale market does not affect their selling costs. If they have to pay a monthly rent, however, it becomes costly to leave the stall idle. Costs continue while revenues are absent. The costs of stall rent have to be added to the lost sales mentioned earlier. The total has to be compared with the profit made by going to the production area instead of staying in the market. Though figures are not available, the fact that collecting wholesalers are in business at all shows that buying from them can be more profitable for distributing wholesalers than going to the production area themselves.

---

[1]   If a wholesaler were to sell in different markets on successive days, time would be more scarce, but according to the trade survey horticultural traders in Kenya usually stick to one market place to sell their produce (unlike clothes traders, for example).

[2]   The market also gets properly fenced and guards look after stored produce at night.

[3]   At the time of the survey in 1991, wholesalers without stalls were only charged at the market gate when bringing produce into the market place. This meant that collecting wholesalers, who brought produce into the market to sell to distributing wholesalers, were charged while distributing wholesalers resident in the market were not. In 1993 the market authorities were in the process of changing the rules, which were considered unfair towards collecting wholesalers.

The further away the production area is from the urban centre, the longer it takes for a distributing wholesaler to collect horticultural commodities, and the more selling time that is lost. We might therefore expect collecting wholesalers to become more important as transport distances increase. This can indeed be observed. Collecting wholesalers are rare for commodities produced in divisions surrounding an urban centre, because wholesalers can easily combine collection and distribution activities in one day. Wholesale markets are operational in the morning, so traders can use the afternoon to collect produce.[4] When commodities are produced elsewhere in the region or outside it, collecting wholesalers are quite common. It would then take a distributing wholesaler at least one full day to collect produce and come back, raising opportunity costs in terms of lost sales, as explained earlier.

A wholesaler cannot buy commodities in the production area and sell them in the urban market at the same time. He could employ people to do the buying while himself focusing on the selling, or vice versa,[5] but that is rather uncommon due to the risks involved. Farmers usually have to be paid cash on delivery. Therefore, a substantial amount of money has to be taken to the production area to buy sufficient produce to fill a truck. Wholesalers find it risky to entrust such large sums of money to employees. They recall stories of an employee who absconded with all the money, and another who paid farmers half the price and promised to pay the rest within a few weeks. When farmers started to complain the latter employee also disappeared. Whether the stories are entirely true is not important. They show wholesalers' perceptions of the financial risks incurred by sending an employee to the production area with money. Even when an employee is given the benefit of the doubt, a wholesaler cannot verify everything the employee tells him. If the employee says he needs more money because farm-gate prices have suddenly gone up, the wholesaler either has to accept this or travel to the production area to check prices himself. To reduce all these financial risks wholesalers prefer to pay farmers personally.[6] An employee (or an agent) may do the negotiations, but the wholesaler finalizes the transactions.[7]

From the point of view of distributing wholesalers, then, the use of collecting wholesalers can be explained in efficiency terms: the benefits are thought to counterbalance the opportunity costs. Such costs would be lower if roads in the production areas were in better shape (less collection time), standardized selling grades existed (no visual inspection required), the banking system were better developed (no cash payment required), and farmers had telephones (smoother communication). In other words, the existence of collecting wholesalers is at least partly due to the poorly developed marketing environment.

---

4 Driving to the farms takes less than an hour, and buying produce and loading it into a truck can be finalized in half a day.

5 Someone has to go to the production area in person to do the buying. Ordering by phone is not possible, because farmers do not have phones and commodities do not have standardized grades.

6 The situation is different if, for instance, two brothers run a wholesale business. One of them can then focus on the collection stage and one on the distribution stage. According to the trade survey, however, shared family businesses are not very common in horticultural wholesale trade.

7 Similarly, wholesalers also prefer to finalize transactions personally with customers in the wholesale market. Employees (or brokers) may do the negotiations but the wholesaler will be around to supervise the transactions and collect the money. In retail trade the situation is different. It is not uncommon for retail traders to look after each other's businesses. The amount of money involved, however, is much smaller than in wholesale trade.

6.2. The efficiency rationale of collecting wholesalers: the farmers' perspective

Farmers could deliver their commodities to distributing wholesalers in the urban wholesale market, but they rarely do. According to the farm survey, very few horticultural farmers sell in large urban centres, even if such centres are within their district (as is the case for Kisii).[8] The reason is at least partly psychological. Farmers believe that urban wholesalers use unscrupulous bargaining methods and that urban markets are characterized by fierce competition. Such ideas are usually preconceived, which does not mean they are totally unfounded. To the extent that they are false, farmers are victims of a disturbed information flow and a psychological entry barrier based on mistaken expectations (see Section 4.4 on entry barriers). To the extent that the ideas are realistic, the trading practices in the urban market would increase farmers' marketing costs. The composition of these marketing costs is shown in the following example based on (1) information collected in Kinangop (Nyandarua District) in our farm survey, (2) observations in the Nairobi wholesale market, and (3) interviews with 24 potato-collecting wholesalers operating in the area.

Kinangop is situated some 100 kilometres from Nairobi, and is one of the main suppliers of potatoes to the Kenyan capital (see Section 3.3). Over 90 per cent of the farmers in the area were cultivating potatoes for sale at the time of the farm survey. As few as two percent of these farmers took their produce to Nairobi to sell to distributing wholesalers.[9] All others relied on collecting wholesalers who came to their farms. Calculations will show that the decision to sell to collecting wholesalers was a rational one: selling at the farm gate is more efficient than going to Nairobi.

Opportunity costs and marketing costs: the farmer's breakeven point
When a farmer sells his potatoes to collecting wholesalers at the farm gate he does not perform any marketing functions.[10] He receives a lower price, however, than if he sold the potatoes to distributing wholesalers in Nairobi. The difference between the farm-gate price and the price he would have received in the wholesale market can be regarded as an opportunity cost. In the analysis, this opportunity cost is compared with the marketing costs of selling potatoes in Nairobi. If the average marketing costs exceed the average opportunity costs, selling at the farm gate is more efficient.

During the main harvesting period of 1990, the farm-gate price in Kinangop was on average KSh 180 per bag, and the buying price of distributing wholesalers at the Nairobi

---

8 In Nyandarua, 5 of the 234 interviewed horticultural farmers (2%) went to such a centre, namely Nairobi (4x) and Machakos (1x). In Kisii, only 1 of the 1016 listed horticultural farmers went to Kisii town and three went to Kisumu (together less than 1%). In Taita, 5 of the 351 listed horticultural farmers (1%) went to Mombasa, and 7 (2%) to Voi. (Although Voi is the largest urban centre in the district, it is relatively small compared to Mombasa, Nairobi and Kisii.) In Taveta, none of the 182 listed horticultural farmers went to Mombasa or any other large urban centre.

9 None of these farmers sold their produce to retailers or to consumers. Selling to retailers requires a stall in the wholesale market and/or extensive knowledge of retail networks in the city. This is outside the scope of the farmers. Selling to consumers is not an option because harvests are too big to sell in retail quantities.

10 In Kinangop both men and women are involved in potato production and selling. References to male farmers in the present example also apply to female farmers.

wholesale market KSh 336. Both prices fluctuated, but the gross margin (KSh 156) appears to have stayed more or less constant during the observation period, because there was sufficient competition at the buying and selling stages and no speculative storage at any level of the marketing chain.[11] Hence, in the analysis the opportunity costs are set at KSh 156.

When a farmer takes his potatoes to Nairobi, instead of selling them at the farm gate, the marketing functions that have to be performed are as follows: physical possession (transport and storage), financing, risk taking, information, negotiation and payment (see Section 4.2). All functions are essential. To derive the farmer's total average marketing costs, the average costs of all functions are therefore added up.

The farmer has two alternative means of taking his potatoes to Nairobi: a hired truck and public transport.[12] The total marketing costs per bag of potatoes depend on the type of transport; transport costs differ, and so do the average costs in relation to other marketing functions (negotiation, payment, etc.). In Table 6.1 the average costs for each function are shown for a hired 7-tonne vehicle, and in Table 6.2 for public transport. The composition of each function-related cost is discussed in Appendix 6.1.

Figure 6.1 visualizes the total average cost curves in relation to the number of potato bags a farmer trades when hiring a 7-tonne truck and when using public transport. The figure also shows the farmer's average opportunity costs when he uses collecting wholesalers instead of going to Nairobi himself (KSh 156). Comparing the three alternatives, we see that selling to collecting wholesalers is more economical than going to Nairobi as long as the farmer has less than approximately 460 bags to sell (7.7 truckloads). In other words, his break-even point for hiring a truck is about 460 bags. We have to compare this with the actual sales per farmer. None of the interviewed farmers in Kinangop anticipated selling more than 300 bags of potatoes during the harvesting period under consideration. The average sales per potato farmer were expected to be 26 bags, and just seven per cent of all the potato farmers expected to sell over 60 bags. It can be concluded that collecting wholesalers were the best alternative for all potato farmers in Kinangop.

According to the farm survey, 98 per cent of the potato farmers in Kinangop indeed sold their potatoes to collecting wholesalers. Three of the 138 respondents took their potatoes by truck to Nairobi, and none did so by public transport. Two of the farmers that went to Nairobi carried not only their own potatoes but also potatoes they had bought from other farmers, thus acting primarily as collecting wholesalers. The third farmer reported sharing a hired truck with other potato farmers. It was the only case of group marketing found during the survey.

---

[11] Speculative storage at the farm level was uncommon for several reasons. First, farmers wanted to sell their harvest as soon as possible because they needed money. Second, harvests were big and farmers did not have enough storage space. Third, storage losses could be quite high due to humidity. Farmers preferred to postpone harvesting rather than store produce. However, the climate allowed two to three harvests a year, and postponing the harvest delayed field preparations for the next crop. Speculative storage at the wholesale level in Nairobi was absent because the city received supplies from all over Kenya, and harvesting periods differed from one part of the country to another. Therefore, fresh supplies were available most times of the year and seasonal storage was not cost-effective.

[12] A truck with a carrying capacity of 7 to 9 tonnes is best suited for the job. Buying such a truck is not an option to a farmer unless he wants to become a professional trader or transporter (none of the farmers in Nyandarua district grow enough produce to make buying a truck economically feasible).

Table 6.1. Function-related average marketing costs per bag of potatoes to a farmer hiring a 7-tonne truck, 1990 (KSh/bag)

no. of bags	transport	storage	finance	risk taking	informa- tion	negotia- tion	payment	total
20	283	0	64	4	67	17	9	444
40	166	0	38	4	67	8	5	284
60	127	0	29	4	67	0	3	230
80	164	0	22	4	59	4	5	258
100	141	0	17	4	54	3	4	223
120	125	0	14	4	51	0	3	200
140	147	0	12	4	48	2	4	217
160	134	0	11	4	46	2	3	200
180	125	0	10	4	45	0	3	187
200	140	0	9	4	44	2	4	203
220	131	0	8	4	43	1	3	190
240	125	0	7	4	42	0	3	181
260	135	0	7	4	39	1	3	189
280	128	0	6	4	36	1	3	178
300	123	0	6	4	34	0	3	170
320	131	0	5	4	32	1	3	176
340	126	0	5	4	30	1	3	169
360	122	0	5	4	28	0	3	162
380	129	0	5	4	27	1	3	169
400	125	0	4	4	25	1	3	162
420	122	0	4	4	24	0	3	157
440	128	0	4	4	23	1	3	163
460	124	0	4	4	22	1	3	158
480	121	0	4	4	21	0	3	153

Table 6.2. Function-related average marketing costs per bag of potatoes to a farmer using public transport, 1990 (KSh/bag)

no. of bags	transport	storage	finance	risk taking	informa- tion	negotia- tion	payment	total
3	81	0	23	2	67	34	78	285
9	81	1	8	2	45	34	78	249
18	81	4	4	2	28	34	78	231
30	81	8	3	2	17	34	78	223
42	81	12	2	2	12	34	78	221
54	81	13	2	2	9	34	78	219
66	81	15	2	2	7	34	78	219
78	81	17	2	2	7	34	78	221
90	81	20	2	2	6	34	78	223
102	81	23	2	2	5	34	78	225
114	81	27	2	2	4	34	78	228

Figure 6.1. Total average marketing costs to potato farmers in Kinangop, 1990 (KSh/bag)

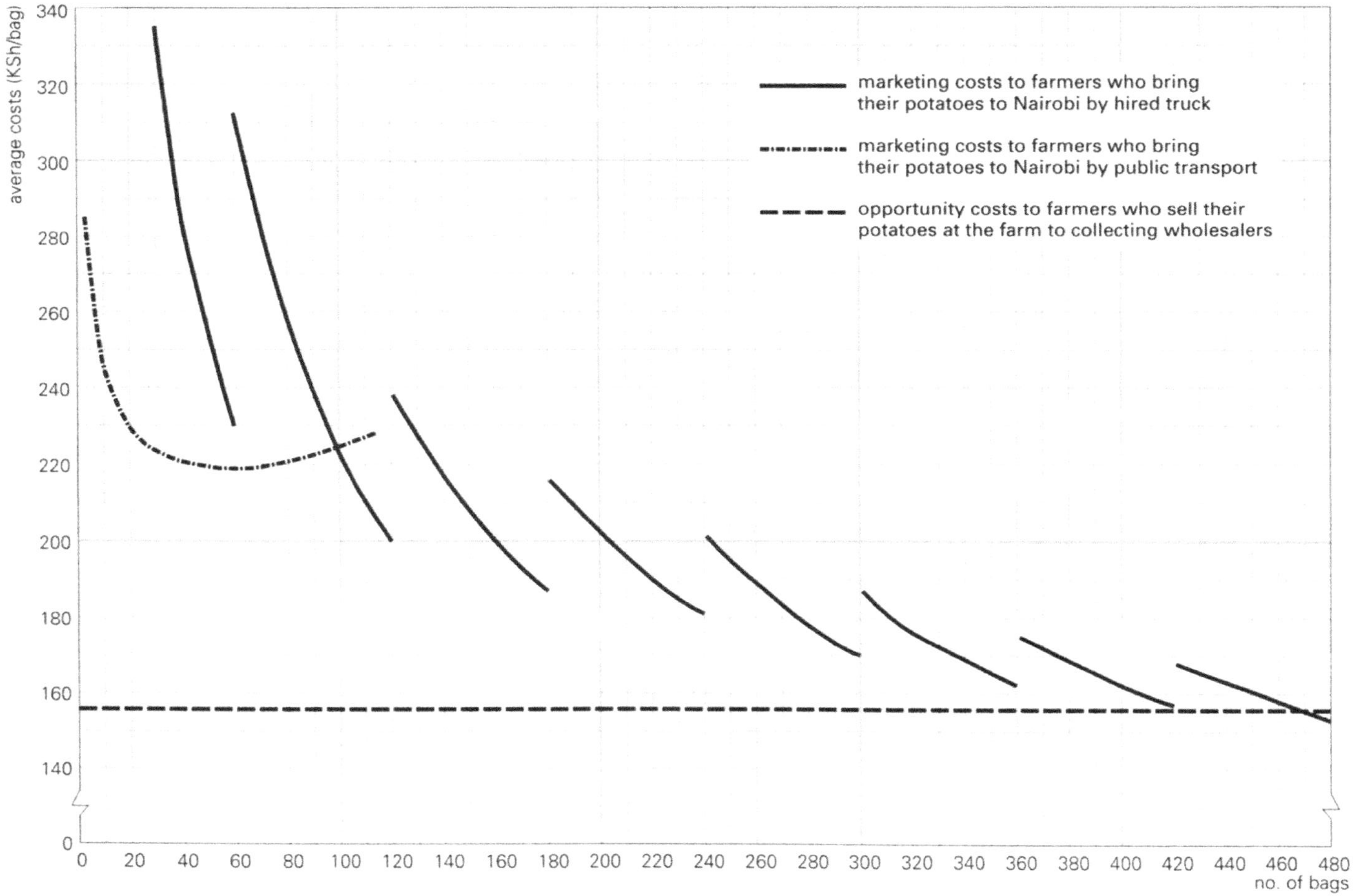

average costs (KSh/bag)
340
320
300
280
260
240
220
200
180
160
140
0
0
20
40
60
80
100
120
140
160
180
200
220
240
260
280
300
320
340
360
380
400
420
440
460
480
no. of bags
marketing costs to farmers who bring their potatoes to Nairobi by hired truck
marketing costs to farmers who bring their potatoes to Nairobi by public transport
opportunity costs to farmers who sell their potatoes at the farm to collecting wholesalers

Group marketing would be the obvious way to accumulate more than 460 bags of potatoes. Unfortunately, it has a negative reputation in Kinangop as a result of past experiences. Cooperative marketing of potatoes was tried there in the 1980s, but the initiative failed (see Section 5.3). Ever since, horticultural farmers in Kinangop have been reluctant to participate in any group marketing initiative.

The situation under an improved marketing environment

Apart from group marketing, it may be expected that selling in Nairobi would become economical to a larger number of Kinangop farmers if improvements were made to the marketing environment. For a farmer who hires a truck, the transport, information, and (initially) the finance function determine the bulk of the average costs (see Table 6.1 above). The high transport and information costs for the first few trips to Nairobi weigh heavily on the average transport and information costs for subsequent trips. If government policies were able to lower the costs in relation to these functions, the breakeven point would shift to the left.

Average transport and finance costs could be lowered through a credit scheme initiated by a parastatal or a private bank and backed up by the government. The credit scheme would issue loans to potential transporters. An increase in the number of trucks for hire would strengthen the bargaining position of farmers who require such a truck, thus lowering the hiring fees. The credit scheme would also have to issue loans to farmers who require working capital to take their commodities to Nairobi, and who otherwise rely on informal money lenders with high interest rates.

Average information costs could be lowered by developing a new kind of market information system. The radio has failed to be the appropriate medium for such a system in Kenya (see Section 5.6), and other methods should be tried, such as price information boards at strategic places in the production areas.[13]

Let us assume a significantly improved marketing environment for 1990 (the 'ideal' situation). Would selling in Nairobi have been economical to the majority of the Kinangop potato farmers under these circumstances (given that they acted as individuals and not as a group)? The answer is negative. Tables 6.3 and 6.4 show the revised average costs per bag of potatoes. It is assumed that hiring a truck would cost 10 per cent less because a larger number of trucks are available for hire, and that farmers pay the same fee from the start as collecting wholesalers (lower costs for the transport function).[14] In addition, farmers could get an official short-term loan to finance their business (lower costs for the finance function).[15]

---

[13] See also Shepherd (1997).

[14] The fee for collecting wholesalers was KSh 3850. Farmers paid this amount after the fourth trip when the transporter knew the farmer better (see Appendix 6.1, 'marketing costs in relation to the transport function').

[15] The nominal interest rate on short-term loans has been set at 16.5% per annum, and the real interest rate at 6.5% (see Appendix 6.1, 'marketing costs in relation to the finance function'). The farmer will need the loan for one week when selling up to 60 bags, for two weeks when selling up to 120 bags, etc. It is assumed that he can get a loan for such a short period, and that he pays no administration costs when applying for the loan. The real interest rate is then 0.125% per week. It can be calculated that the average interest costs per bag are negligible.

Table 6.3. Function-related average marketing costs per bag of potatoes to a farmer hiring a 7-tonne truck in an improved marketing environment, 1990 (KSh/bag)

no. of bags	transport	storage	finance	risk taking	informa- tion	negotia- tion	payment	total
20	244	0	0	4	0	17	9	274
40	147	0	0	4	0	8	5	164
46	133	0	0	4	0	8	4	149
60	114	0	0	4	0	0	3	121
80	144	0	0	4	0	4	5	157
100	125	0	0	4	0	3	4	136
120	113	0	0	4	0	0	3	120
140	130	0	0	4	0	2	4	140
160	120	0	0	4	0	2	3	129
180	112	0	0	4	0	0	3	119

Table 6.4. Function-related average marketing costs per bag of potatoes to a farmer using public transport in an improved marketing environment, 1990 (KSh/bag)

no. of bags	transport	storage	finance	risk taking	informa- tion	negotia- tion	payment	total
3	81	0	0	2	0	34	78	195
9	81	1	0	2	0	34	78	196
18	81	4	0	2	0	34	78	199
30	81	8	0	2	0	34	78	203
42	81	12	0	2	0	34	78	207
54	81	13	0	2	0	34	78	208
66	81	15	0	2	0	34	78	210
78	81	17	0	2	0	34	78	212
90	81	20	0	2	0	34	78	215
102	81	23	0	2	0	34	78	218
114	81	27	0	2	0	34	78	222

Finally, they could sell against current market prices in the Nairobi market from their first visit onwards due to an effective market information system (lower costs for the information function).[16]

The improved marketing environment would significantly reduce the farmers' total average costs. Collecting wholesalers would, however, also benefit from the improvements, especially the reduction in truck hire fees.[17] The lower costs would allow them to pay farmers more, thus reducing the gross margin. A 10 per cent reduction on truck hire allows a

[16] He receives the same price as collecting wholesalers. Therefore, his information costs are considered to be zero (see Appendix 6.1, 'marketing costs in relation to the information function').

[17] It is assumed that collecting wholesalers would not benefit form the credit scheme: it will only provide working capital to farmers who want to market their produce in Nairobi. The improved market information system would not be of much help to the collecting wholesalers either, since they are already well informed.

reduction of KSh 6 on the gross margin per bag.[18] The new gross margin would be KSh 150.

The assumed improvements in the marketing environment would lower the new break-even point substantially: from 460 to 46 bags. Even so, in 1990 this would still have made hiring a truck economical for only 12 per cent of the Kinangop potato farmers. Selling to collecting wholesalers thus remained the best alternative for 88 per cent of the farmers.

Conclusion

The Kinangop example shows that the rationale of collecting wholesalers can be explained from a farmers' perspective by analysing function-related marketing costs. Collecting wholesalers are able to perform transport, information and finance functions more efficiently than individual farmers. By being in business throughout the year or at least throughout the season, these traders are able to develop customer relations with transporters, accumulate knowledge about price developments, and level out high start-up costs.[19]

Mediation by collecting wholesalers is economical to all potato farmers in Kinangop because of the conditions in the marketing environment, especially with regard to transport, finance and information. However, even if these conditions should improve substantially, collecting wholesalers would remain the best alternative to the majority of the farmers. The supplies of most farmers are too small to make hiring a 7-tonne truck more attractive than selling to collecting wholesalers at the farm gate. Travelling to Nairobi by public transport is no alternative either, because of the distance involved and the limited number of bags that can be carried. Only if they operated as a group could farmers attain the same economies of scale as collecting wholesalers.

6.3. The development of rural assembly markets: introduction[20]

The second part of this chapter deals with rural assembly markets that often develop at the collection stage of horticultural marketing channels. The Kinangop example in the previous section has shown that farmers did not carry their potatoes to Nairobi but sold them to collecting wholesalers at the farm gate. The latter might also imply selling by a road near the farm, because many farms were inaccessible to vehicles. It did not imply selling to collecting wholesalers in a rural assembly market, because rural assembly markets are rare in Kinangop and elsewhere in Nyandarua District. This contrasts with districts like Kisii, where they are quite common. The question here, therefore, is under what circumstances rural assembly markets develop and how this relates to economic theory.

---

18   The price of the truck is reduced from KSh 3850 to KSh 3465, or KSh 6 per bag.

19   A collecting wholesaler can make three trips a week without problems, and four to five with some effort. In the case of four or five trips a week, however, he has to use purchasing agents who also have their price (in the case of three trips or fewer he may also use them; see Section 5.2). On the basis of three trips a week, a wholesaler can trade over 30 truckloads of potatoes per harvesting period. An individual farmer could never produce so many potatoes, and could only reach such an intensity of trading if he turned himself into a full-time collecting wholesaler.

20   An earlier version of sections 6.3 to 6.7 has been published by the author in the *British Food Journal*, Vol. 98, no. 9, 1996, pp. 26-34: 'Food Assembly Markets in Africa: lessons from the horticultural sector of Kenya.'

Rural assembly markets will develop under free market conditions when they increase the efficiency of a marketing system. A market place concentrates supply and demand, so that buyers need not travel all over the production area to meet suppliers. Nor do they have to travel around seeking potential sources of supply, because sellers come to the market place when their commodities are ready for exchange (Alderson, 1976). Thus, an assembly market potentially increases the efficiency of a marketing channel by decreasing transport costs to buyers. In addition, it increases channel efficiency by decreasing suppliers' and buyers' transaction costs. The concentration of supply and demand makes price developments more transparent. Such transparency may be expected to lower the costs of information (a transaction cost).[21] In sum, assembly markets should theoretically come into being when they reduce transport and/or information costs at the assembling stage. Whether this is indeed the case will be checked in the subsequent sections by comparing assembling trade in Nyandarua, Kisii, Taita and Taveta. The analysis looks at infrastructural conditions and supply factors, and links these to transport and information costs.

Market outlets in Nyandarua, Kisii, Taita and Taveta
In the research areas, households that sold horticultural commodities were asked where they sold them: at the farm gate, in a local market or in a large urban market (see Section 1.3). The latter alternative proved to be rare, as discussed in Section 6.2. The farmers involved in it are not included in the present analysis.[22] As for the other two alternatives, farm-gate sales were clearly more important among horticultural farmers in Nyandarua and Taita, and sales in a local rural market among those in Kisii and Taveta (Table 6.5). A combination of farm gate and market sales was also possible, but in all four research areas the majority of the farmers chose either the one or the other.[23]

The difference in market outlets between the four research areas will be explained after a look at the farmers' customers. Farmers who sold at the farm always dealt with traders. They sold primarily to collecting wholesalers but could also sell to retailers from a local rural market place, or to local assembling traders who then took the produce to the local market place to sell to collecting wholesalers. Farmers who went to the local market place themselves sold either to traders or directly to consumers. The traders were primarily collecting wholesalers but could also be retailers from the same or other local market places. The farmers carried the produce to the market on their head, by donkey or in one of the local minibuses that irregularly traverse the production areas. The traders who bought the produce used trucks and all kinds of public transport to take the commodities to other markets. Both farmers who sold at the farm and those who sold in the local market depended on the traders for information on current prices in other markets (see Section 5.6).

---

21   For a discussion of information problems as a source of transaction costs, see Nabli & Nugent (1989).
22   In Taita a fourth alternative existed, selling to the Taita Horticultural Produce Cooperative Society (see Section 5.3). During the survey, 35 of the 351 interviewed horticultural farmers said they did so. They are not included in the present analysis either.
23   In comparisons of 'selling at the farm' and 'selling in local market', differences between Nyandarua and Kisii, Nyandarua and Taveta, Taita and Kisii, and Taita and Taveta are statistically significant at the 0.01 level. When 'selling both at farm and local market' is included in the analysis, differences remain significant at the same level.

Table 6.5. Chief market outlets of horticultural farmers in the research areas*

	Nyandarua n	(%)	Kisii n	(%)	Taita n	(%)	Taveta n	(%)
1. selling at the farm	227	(99)	140	(14)	209	(69)	46	(25)
2. selling in local market	1	(0)	737	(73)	45	(15)	87	(48)
3. selling at farm and in local market	1	(0)	135	(13)	50	(16)	49	(27)
	229	(99)	1012	(100)	304	(100)	182	(100)

* Horticultural farmers who sold in large urban markets or who were members of the Taita HPCS are not included in the table.

In the farm survey, farmers who took their produce to the market were not asked whether they sold it to consumers or traders. However, during the trade survey, farmers who sold produce in the sampled market places were asked about their customers.

In Nyandarua, which has few rural markets of any significance in horticultural trading, two rural markets were surveyed: Engineer in the middle of the horticultural production area, and Magumu on the edge of the production area and district. Few farmers were encountered in Engineer market,[24] and the ones that were found sold small quantities to consumers (Table 6.6). This confirms the results of the farm survey, which identified the farm gate as the major market outlet in Nyandarua. Magumu market presented a different picture: almost half the suppliers in the market were farmers.[25] Most sold their commodities to traders, and any excess to consumers. Magumu market is somewhat atypical for Nyandarua because of its location near the Nairobi-Nakuru highway, which skirts the district in the extreme south. Local farmers come to the market because it is visited by collecting wholesalers who are looking for produce but do not want to enter the district.

In Kisii, where numerous rural horticultural markets can be found, four local market places were surveyed: Nyakoe, Daraja Mbili, Kebirigo and Riochanda. The farm survey findings for Kisii were confirmed: the majority of the suppliers in the markets were farmers.[26] These farmers sold primarily to traders. In Nyakoe and Daraja Mbili, the focus on traders was heavier than in Kebirigo and Riochanda (Table 6.6). Nyakoe and Daraja Mbili attracted more traders from other rural markets and from urban centres because of their location along the Kisumu-Kisii-Kericho highway.

---

24 Of the 25 horticultural traders in Engineer market, 21 were interviewed. Two were farmers, the others professional traders.

25 Of the 75 horticultural traders in Magumu market, 30 were interviewed. Thirteen were farmers, the others professional traders.

26 In Nyakoe market, 27 of the 225 horticultural traders were interviewed; 19 of them (70%) were farmers. In Daraja Mbili, 41 of the 286 horticultural traders were interviewed; 23 (56%) were farmers. In Kebirigo 38 of the 74 horticultural farmers were interviewed; 26 (68%) were farmers. In Riochanda 37 of the 307 horticultural traders were interviewed, 27 (73%) were farmers. Some of the interviewed farmers in the market places not only sold produce from their own farms but also commodities which they had purchased from neighbours.

Table 6.6. Farmers in the local market place, by customer

District	Market place	selling to consumers		selling to traders (and consumers)	
		n	(%)	n	(%)
Nyandarua	Engineer	2	(100)	0	(0)
	Magumu	1	(8)	12	(92)
Kisii	Nyakoe	2	(11)	17	(89)
	Daraja Mbili	2	(9)	21	(91)
	Kebirigo	8	(31)	18	(69)
	Riochanda	9	(33)	18	(67)
Taita	Wundanyi	15	(45)	18	(55)
Taveta	Taveta town	5	(28)	13	(72)

Both in Taita and Taveta only a few markets existed. Two of them were surveyed, Wundanyi in Taita and Taveta town in Taveta. In Wundanyi the proportion of farmers in the market place was higher (60%), and in Taveta lower (20%), than might be expected on the basis of the farm survey. Nearly half the farmers in Wundanyi market focused entirely on consumers, while almost three-quarters of the farmers in Taveta market sold to traders (Table 6.6). The situation in the Taita and Taveta research areas proved more complicated than in Nyandarua and Kisii. The analysis therefore focuses first of all on Nyandarua and Kisii (Section 6.4). Taita and Taveta are discussed separately (Sections 6.5 and 6.6).

6.4. Nyandarua and Kisii: accessibility and supply concentration

When looking for factors that explain the presence of rural assembly markets, Nyandarua and Kisii lend themselves well to comparison. In Nyandarua, farmers hardly go to local markets at all to sell horticultural commodities, except for the few that sell small quantities to local consumers. In Kisii, the majority do not wait for buyers at the farm but go to a local market place, and sell not primarily to consumers but to traders. In other words, the Kisii markets have an important assembling function which the Nyandarua ones do not have.

The relative absence of assembly markets in Nyandarua is attributable to two factors: accessibility and supply concentration. In Kisii, various tarmac roads cut across the production areas, and market places such as Daraja Mbili and Nyakoe have developed along these major roads. The minor roads to the farms are in poor shape and are virtually impassable after a heavy shower. In contrast with Kisii, the horticultural production areas in Nyandarua are not served by tarmac roads, and the nearest all-weather road is the highway from Nairobi to Nakuru skirting the production area in the south. A major road to a local market centre such as Engineer is often as difficult to negotiate as the minor roads to the farms. Once a trader has entered the production area, going to the farms is as risky as going to the market centre. Thus, a risk-wary trader going to Kisii will prefer to buy in a market place, while the same trader in Nyandarua might go to the farms as well. The only alternative in Nyandarua is Magumu market near the highway, but prices there are high because of its unique location, and traders not too averse to risks will try their luck in the interior.

Population density is very high in Kisii, both in absolute terms and in comparison to Nyandarua (see Section 4.3). As a consequence, holdings in Kisii are far smaller than in Nyandarua.[27] Besides horticultural commodities, Kisii farmers also grow maize, coffee and tea while Nyandarua farmers grow almost exclusively horticultural commodities. Both size of holding and cropping patterns affect the quantities of horticultural produce sold. The farm survey found that 83 per cent of the farmers in Nyandarua sold potatoes, and that the average number of bags sold per potato farmer per harvesting period was 36.[28] The potatoes were harvested in one or a few rounds. A collecting wholesaler normally had to visit fewer than 10 farmers to fill his 7-tonne truck. In Kisii, selling cooking bananas was almost as common as potato selling in Nyandarua: 69 per cent of all Kisii farmers sold cooking bananas. However, the average cooking banana farmer sold only 9 bunches a month,[29] and a collecting trader required 800 bunches to fill a 7-tonne truck. Even assuming that the banana farmers harvested just once a month (which is usually not the case), a collecting trader had to visit over 80 farmers. The comparison shows that supply concentration was much higher in Nyandarua than in Kisii, and that a cooking banana wholesaler would hence save much more time buying in a market place where farmers assembled than would a potato wholesaler. Theoretically, the banana wholesaler might also save time by buying other commodities from the banana farmers at the farms, thus filling his truck more quickly. However, collecting wholesalers who dealt in cooking bananas tended to specialize in that commodity alone, because other commodities such as sweet bananas, kale and tomatoes, also produced by the Kisii farmers, were intended for another market. They remained within the region (western Kenya), while cooking bananas were transported to large urban centres elsewhere in the country such as Nairobi, Nakuru and Eldoret.

The regional wholesalers who bought sweet bananas, kale and tomatoes in Kisii handled smaller quantities, and they had to rely on public transport or shared hired transport. Most of them did not go all the way to the farms because of transport constraints and because the supply concentration of these commodities was at least as low as that of cooking bananas.[30] As a consequence, most Kisii farmers who wanted to sell sweet bananas, kale or tomatoes had no alternative but to take them to the market. And as long as they were going, they might just as well take along their cooking bananas. The farm survey showed that

---

[27] The average holding of the horticultural farmers sampled was 3.4 acres in Kisii, compared to 11.0 acres in Nyandarua.

[28] Some differences existed between different parts of the district. In Kinangop, 92 per cent of the farmers sold potatoes and the average sales per harvesting period were 26 bags. In Ol Kalou, 73 per cent sold potatoes and the average sales per farmer was 79 bags. The potatoes from Ol Kalou were not only carried to Nairobi, but also to Nakuru in the adjacent district. In Geta, high up the slopes of the Aberdare range, spring onions were a more popular cash crop than potatoes. Nevertheless, 60 per cent of the farmers sold potatoes. The average sales per farmer per harvesting period was 9 bags.

[29] Bananas are harvested more or less throughout the year while potatoes are planted and harvested during specific periods.

[30] Twenty per cent of all Kisii farmers sold sweet bananas; the average number of bunches sold per month was 13. Thirty-two per cent of all farmers sold kale: the average number of bags sold per harvesting period was 5. The leaves were harvested almost continuously throughout the harvesting period. Nine per cent of the Kisii farmers sold tomatoes; they sold on average 406 kg per harvesting period (the equivalent of 9 crates). The tomatoes were harvested in two or more rounds.

almost all of them did so.[31] Thus, the importance of the market place as an assembly point for cooking bananas was determined not only by the supply concentration of cooking bananas but also by that of the other horticultural commodities grown for sale, and by the scale of operation of the wholesalers buying those commodities. This is confirmed by the findings for Nyandarua, where cabbages were grown as horticultural cash crop in addition to potatoes. Most cabbage wholesalers coming to the district used the same kind of 7-tonne truck as potato wholesalers did. Fewer horticultural farmers sold cabbages than sold potatoes, but the quantities offered for sale per farmer did not differ greatly.[32] As a result, neither potatoes nor cabbages required an assembly market in Nyandarua.

Concluding, in Kisii the relatively low accessibility of farms compared to market places, together with a low supply concentration, has caused assembly markets to develop. In Nyandarua equally poor accessibility of farms and local retail market places, combined with a high supply concentration, explains the general absence of such assembly markets.

6.5. Taita: a dual marketing system

As noted earlier, the situation in Taita and Taveta is more complicated than in Nyandarua and Kisii. An analysis of the collection system in the latter two regions makes it clear that, in addition to accessibility and supply concentration, other factors may play a role. In this section Taita will be discussed, and in the next section Taveta.

Similarly to Nyandarua and in contrast with Kisii, the majority of the horticultural farmers in Taita sold their produce at or near the farm (see Section 6.3). Nevertheless, Taita resembles Kisii more than it does Nyandarua: the population density is high, holdings are small, and supply concentration is relatively low.[33] Assembly markets are less important than farm-gate sales because of the location of the farms and the presence of specialized transporters. The Taita Hills are a relatively small but inaccessible area. Apart from a couple of main dirt roads, few tracks in the hills are accessible by truck due to their steep gradient and poor condition. Most horticultural farmers live within walking distance of one of the accessible roads. On specified days, collecting wholesalers wait at specified spots along these roads and horticultural farmers carry their commodities to them on their heads. The wholesalers do not concentrate on one kind of vegetable or fruit, but buy all sorts of commodities which are in high demand in Mombasa. After buying produce from the farmers, the wholesalers wait for transporters, who look for them up and down the roads. The transporters carry produce from different wholesalers directly from the hills to

---

[31] 98% of the farmers who sold other horticultural commodities than cooking bananas sold them in the market place. Over half of these farmers (53%) also cultivated cooking bananas for sale. 85% of the latter group sold these bananas in the market place.

[32] Thirty-five percent of all farmers sold cabbages. The average number of bags sold per cabbage farmer per harvesting period was 33. The crop was harvested in three rounds or less. A collecting cabbage wholesaler required 50 to 60 bags to fill a 7-tonne truck.

[33] The population density in the Taita Hills is 230 persons per square km (CBS, 1994b). According to the farm survey, the average holding size was 2.9 acres. Tomatoes, cabbages and kale, the most important horticultural commodities in Taita, were sold by 14%, 20% and 21% respectively of the farmers. The average selling quantities per harvesting period were 4 bags of kale, 215 kg of cabbage (approx. 2 bags) and 278 kg of tomatoes (or 6 crates).

Mombasa.[34] Thus, the few market places existing in the hills are not used to assemble produce destined for Mombasa, but to assemble produce for Mwatate and Voi town, located on the dusty plains at the foot of the hills. Traders from Mwatate and Voi buy their commodities in these market places from farmers who live within walking distance and come to the market to sell to both traders and consumers. The Mwatate and Voi traders do not buy their produce along the roads in the hills like the Mombasa wholesalers do, because there are no specialized transporters who operate to Mwatate and Voi. The Mwatate and Voi traders have to rely on public transport (*matatus*) that serves the market places.

In summary, a dual marketing system has developed in Taita, one focusing on the supraregional town Mombasa without using assembly markets, and one focusing on the regional towns Mwatate and Voi with the use of assembly markets. No system of this kind exists in Kisii, where both regional and interregional flows traverse assembly markets, nor in Nyandarua, where neither regional nor interregional flows do so. The reason for the development of the dual system is the location of the farms and the presence of specialized transporters.

6.6. Taveta: first- and second-level assembly markets

In Taveta the majority of the farmers in the farm survey reported selling their produce in a market place. The majority of sellers in Taveta market were professional traders (see Section 6.3). The reason for this situation is the presence of two additional, much smaller, market places in the production area, namely Chumvini and Mukuyuni. These serve as assembly markets for produce to be brought to Taveta market, which in turn serves as an assembly market for produce destined for Mombasa, Nairobi or elsewhere. Thus, a hierarchy of assembly markets can be distinguished, comprised of two first-level ones (Chumvini, Mukuyuni) and one second-level one (Taveta).

Taveta serves as a second-level assembly market because of its location at the head of the only interregional road to Mombasa. The production areas are located to the north and south of Taveta, and all traffic has to pass this centre on its way out. Transporters who hire out freight space like to assemble in Taveta because of its strategic location and because of the poor state of local roads. The majority of collecting wholesalers rely on these transporters because they do not own trucks themselves. Usually they share a truck and pay a fixed fee per box of tomatoes or bunch of bananas. They buy their commodities either from farmers in the first-level assembly markets or from assembling traders in Taveta. They do not go all the way to the farms, because these are located in swampy, inaccessible areas. When buying in the first-level market, they transport their commodities in small trucks and pick-ups hired from local transporters. On arrival in Taveta, the commodities are loaded onto one of the bigger trucks. When the collecting wholesalers buy from assembling traders in Taveta market, they do not have to bother about local transport. But they do buy at a higher price, because the assembling traders have bought the commodities at the first-level assembly market and transported them to Taveta, in either their own or hired vehicles. Like

---

34 The collecting wholesalers pay transport costs per kilogram of produce. They travel by public transport to Mombasa while the truck is carrying the commodities.

the collecting wholesalers, the assembling traders are not able to go all the way to the farms because of the inaccessibility of the area.[35]

Although the strategic role of Taveta as a second-level assembly market has to do primarily with its location at the beginning of the only interregional road to Mombasa, other factors are also at play. First, Taveta has a railway station, and every market day a few goods wagons of bananas leave for Nairobi. Second, Taveta is located on the border with Tanzania, and the market is therefore noted for its cheap imported goods such as radios, textiles, etc. Traders who come to buy these commodities may also carry some bananas or other horticultural commodities with them back home. This boosts demand, making the market more attractive to assembling traders. Third, in addition to means of transport, there are also sorting and packing facilities available to collecting wholesalers. Highly perishable commodities such as tomatoes are often delivered by the farmers in gunny bags. The fruits have to be sorted and repackaged in boxes before going on long-distance transport. Without the removal of overripe ones and proper repackaging, the whole lot would be rotten or mashed on arrival in Mombasa. In Taveta carpenters are available to supply new boxes and mend old ones, while experienced sorting boys can be hired to do the sorting. Of course, the sorting boys are not so much a cause as a consequence of Taveta's assembling function, but, now established, they further increase the attractiveness of the market to collecting wholesalers.

In Kisii, where assembly markets are also important outlets to farmers, no differentiation into first- and second-level assembly markets was found. None of the assembly markets had a more strategic location than the others, because all were located along routes to urban centres elsewhere in Kenya. In general, the phenomenon of second-level horticultural assembly markets is not very common in Kenya, because most horticultural production areas are less isolated than those in Taveta. However, at least two major second-level assembly markets do exist in addition to Taveta: the wholesale markets of Nairobi and Mombasa. The first serves as a second-level assembly market for commodities from the central highlands which are destined for the coast, and the second one for commodities from the coast destined for the central highlands. However, in both cases their assembling function is related not to accessibility but to a higher degree of vertical differentiation in the marketing channel, owing to the great transport distances of over 500 km. Rather than go all the way to Nyeri, Meru or Nyandarua, some coastal collecting wholesalers buy tomatoes, potatoes and cabbages from highland collecting wholesalers in Nairobi. By the same token, some highland collecting wholesalers buy mangoes and citrus fruits from coastal collecting wholesalers in Mombasa instead of searching for them in the coastal production areas. The further differentiation in the marketing channel is based not only on efficiency considerations but also on cultural and ethnic differences between the highland and the coastal people. Such differences make it harder for a collecting wholesaler from one region to deal directly with farmers and assembling traders from another.

---

[35] The only exception is Mboghoni sublocation, where small trucks can get reasonably near the farms. As a consequence, this sublocation does not have an assembly market and relatively many farmers sell their commodities at the farm. They constitute the major part of the 25% shown in Table 6.5, Section 6.3.

6.7. Explaining the development of rural assembly markets and assessing their future importance

In Section 6.3 it was observed that assembly markets develop when they reduce transport and information costs in the marketing channel. The research findings have shown that assembly markets for horticultural commodities tend to be found in surplus areas where farms are poorly accessible compared to market places, and where supply concentration is low. Clearly both factors are related to transport costs. When farms are relatively inaccessible and supply per farmer is small, traders who assemble produce at the farms face high transport costs. The creation of an assembly market will reduce these costs. Moreover, it will increase the efficiency of the marketing channel, because farmers who take their produce to the market use low-cost means of transport in comparison to traders who go to the farms (carrying their wares on their head, by donkey or local minibus as opposed to pick-up trucks or lorries).

To farmers who offer small quantities for sale, the assembly market ensures a price that more or less reflects current supply and demand conditions. The market thus reduces farmers' costs of imperfect information. When farmers sell their produce at the farm, such costs can run quite high. The trader who comes to buy the produce is usually the only one with up-to-date information on price developments in the urban markets. This gives him a decisive edge in price negotiations, especially because competing buyers are seldom around (in contrast with assembly markets, where all buyers are present simultaneously because of the periodic nature of the market).

For farmers who offer small quantities for sale in the more isolated parts of the production area, the assembly market may be the only selling outlet. Traders are not willing to travel all the way to their farms, and without a market place these farmers could not dispose of their produce. In this way, the assembly market not only increases the efficiency of the marketing channel, but it may also improve its effectiveness by stimulating a higher output.

When farms are just as accessible as the local market place and the supply per farmer is large, buying in the market will not reduce traders' transport costs. Most traders will then bypass the market. Farmers will wait for them at their farms, even though this may increase their costs of imperfect information. Taking the produce to the local market place would be costly to them in terms of transport. A farmer could not carry the entire load on their head or by donkey or *matatu*, and would thus require more expensive means (such as a pick-up truck hired from a local businessman). Failing to sell all the produce she took to the market, she would have to return home with it, again paying for transport. The extra trip would not do the produce any good either, especially in the case of highly perishable commodities.

It can be concluded that the development of rural assembly markets for horticultural commodities can be explained in terms of efficiency developments: they evolve in production areas with relatively poor farm accessibility and low supply concentration, because they reduce the transport and/or information costs of suppliers and buyers.[36]

---

[36] These findings will be useful to policymakers who are working to improve the efficiency (and effectiveness) of food marketing channels through the development of rural assembly markets. In deciding on regions where such markets should be established, they will no longer have to research

This finding can be used to assess the future importance of horticultural assembly markets in the research areas. If, in Nyandarua, roads to market centres such as Engineer are upgraded to all-weather roads, the relative accessibility of the farms will decrease. Under these circumstances, Engineer may be expected to develop into an assembly market similar to Magumu, all the more because population pressure in the district is on the rise, leading to a lower supply concentration.

In Kisii, minor market centres may develop into new assembly markets if roads to these centres are improved. As a consequence, existing assembly markets further up the road may lose importance. Only when the majority of the roads to the farms are improved will assembly markets be likely to lose ground. For the moment, however, this is rather hypothetical because of the high costs of such an operation.

In Taita, improvement of local roads may stimulate farmers who live in the more isolated parts of the hills to increase their horticultural production. The supply concentration will be relatively low, especially in the beginning, and that will call for new assembly markets. An increase in supply concentration may be hampered by rising population pressure.

In Taveta, some of the services now provided by Taveta town may be taken over by existing first-level assembly markets if roads to the latter are improved, and if production in the vicinity of these markets further increases through improved irrigation practices. Upgrading the tracks to the farms into all-weather roads seems out of the question in the swampy areas of Taveta, even more than elsewhere. The first-level assembly markets will therefore retain their significance.

It can be concluded that assembly markets will gain in importance, or at least maintain their current importance, in all four of our research areas. This applies to the coming decade. In the longer term, a new factor may come into play alongside accessibility and supply concentration. It will be related not to the efficiency of marketing channels but to their service output (effectiveness). It concerns a possible rise in the demand for high-quality produce. This will require quality control and may thus necessitate vertical coordination or integration in the marketing channel. Some vertical coordination and integration can already be observed in Kenya. A case of forward integration concerns a group of farmers in Taita have organized themselves into the Taita Horticultural Produce Cooperative Society (Taita HPC) (see Section 5.3). They sell their produce directly to retailers and institutions through a stall in the Mombasa wholesale market. At the time of the survey, they were achieving success because they endeavoured to supply superior-quality produce which was in high demand from tourist hotels. Their commodities fetched higher than average prices. The cooperative did not use local assembly markets, having instead its own collecting points where farmer-members brought their produce.

For the time being, the concept of the Taita HPC cannot easily be implemented in most other parts of Kenya because the demand for high-quality, higher-priced vegetables

---

transport and information costs, but can instead use farm accessibility and supply concentration as indicators. Developing rural assembly markets is predicted to have the desired impact in areas with three characteristics: (1) surplus production, (2) low supply concentration, and (3) poorly accessible farms. Dual systems or first- and second-level markets may need to be considered.

and fruits is still very limited among Kenyans. However, if Kenya develops further, and larger parts of the population get wealthier in the coming decade, things may change.

In addition to this forward integration, some backward coordination and integration can be observed in Kenya. It involves horticultural export traders who contract outgrowers or who go into production themselves. Their European customers, owners or suppliers of large retail chains, demand superior-quality French beans, avocados, mangoes, chillies, etc. Exporters will be sure of attaining the required standards only if they produce the commodities themselves or closely supervise selected outgrowers who are supplied with all the needed inputs (see Section 5.4). Harvested produce then goes directly from the farms to the airport, without passing assembly markets or other market places. Again, the prices of these commodities are still far beyond the purchasing power of most Kenyans, but this too may change.

In sum, forward and backward coordination and integration to attain higher quality standards are not yet widespread practices and are not expected to become so in the years to come. In the long run if quality gains importance in the domestic market, developments may turn in this direction, making assembly markets less important than at present and in the near future.

7

Vertical Differentiation of Horticultural Marketing Channels in Kenya: Model, Hypotheses and Data Set

This chapter and the following one deal with the vertical differentiation of horticultural marketing channels in Kenya. A model is built which is intended for African emerging economies. The first section explains why Kenya is an emerging economy where horticulture is concerned. The model and the hypotheses are then set out, and in the last two sections the data set is introduced and the independent variables are specified. The actual testing of the hypotheses will be reported on in the next chapter.

7.1. Horticulture in Kenya: an emerging economy

According to Janssen & Van Tilburg (1997) five stages of agricultural market development can be described, notably primitive, emerging, intermediate, industrialized and advanced. On the basis of the criteria laid down by these authors, the horticultural sector in Kenya can be characterized as an emerging economy. Horticultural farmers have shifted from a subsistence orientation to a mix of production for home consumption and production for the market. They have not yet reached the stage of pure commercial farming. The farmers have started to specialize (see Section 3.4), but the specialization is according to agro-ecological zone and not yet according to farm size or market contracts. Farm size is still unimportant, because all horticultural farms are small-scale family enterprises (see Sections 3.2 and 3.3). Large horticultural estates are found only when commodities for export are involved (see Section 5.4). Market coordination and integration is to a large extent restricted to this export market.

On the input side, many farmers are still replacing their seed stock only occasionally, although the demand for seed with specific commercial characteristics is rising. The application of fertilizers and pesticides is limited, and when used they are often applied incorrectly, as explained in Section 3.4. The only exception are again export farms, where expertise from outside is brought in whenever necessary, and capital is not a constraint.

Marketing channels serving the domestic market are still in a process of vertical differentiation. The market access of small farms is poor, and supply organizations such as marketing cooperatives are rare (see Section 5.3). Traders are able to enter the marketing chain because they accumulate produce from various producers. Due to economies of scale, this accumulation enables them to perform marketing functions such as transport, information and negotiation more efficiently than individual farmers (see Section 4.4). When traders aim for cost control, their activities minimize the number of transactions in the channel. Average transaction costs are reduced, though they may remain high. Contracts and futures markets are still distant prospects; credit may be used to secure verbal agreements (interlinked markets).

The channel differentiation process is not affected by factors such as government interventions, subsidies or laws, because horticultural commodities are regarded both as non-strategic and as too risky for intervention due to their perishability (see Section 4.1). Only horticultural exports are considered strategic and are hence subject to certain rules and regulations (see Section 5.4).

Backward integration in the marketing channel is practised for export crops, notably by exporters going into production. It is uncommon for commodities geared to the domestic market. Wholesalers do not go into large-scale production, but rely on field purchases from small-scale producers. Such purchases are hampered by the absence of grading at the production and assembling stages.

Supermarket chains are common only in the largest urban centres, where they sell limited quantities of horticultural produce.[1] Consumers prefer to buy their vegetables and fruits in the market place, where the high turnover assures them that the perishables will be fresh.

Product differentiation is still very low. The demand structure is defined by the urban or rural location of consumers rather than by income size. Kenya experienced rapid population growth and urbanization during previous decades (see Section 3.1), but its per capita income increased little. The per capita GNP was estimated at US $250 in the first half of the 1970s, and US $270 in the first half of the 1990s (current prices) (World Bank, 1995). The annual growth rate of the per capita GNP was a reasonable 3.1 per cent during the 1970s, but sank to a mere 0.3 percent in the 1980s (constant prices) (UNDP, 1994). The annual growth rate of per capita private consumption declined from 2.5 per cent in the 1970s to 0.8 per cent in the 1980s (constant prices) (UNDP, 1992). The income distribution did not change much. The top 20 per cent of the households earned 60 per cent of the national

---

[1]   In this respect the present situation in Kenya, and elsewhere in Africa, resembles the situation in Asia in the 1970s. Bucklin (1977) and Goldman (1974, 1981) studied supermarket chains in Asia at that time. The diffusion of modern supermarkets was low, because they served a much larger market than traditional shops, implying that customers had to travel a greater distance to get to them. This was only attractive if customers reduced their frequency of shopping, which they refused to do for various reasons. First, a large proportion of the foods sold was highly perishable and had to be purchased daily because of a lack of refrigerators. Second, the low-income consumers lacked storage space to keep foods for several days, and also could not afford to purchase more than one day's supply at a time. Both authors concluded that Western-style supermarkets were not widespread in Asia in the 1970s because they are were poorly suited to the needs of the low-income food buyer.

income in the first half of the 1970s, and 62 per cent in the early 1990s. The bottom 20 per cent earned 3 per cent of the income in both periods (World Bank, 1995). Under such conditions, the large majority of the consumers of horticultural commodities look for low prises rather than supreme quality. The market segment of the relatively wealthy consumers is still too small to trigger large-scale product differentiation. Some location-specific exceptions do exist. In Nairobi, the presence of many well-paid expatriates and reasonably paid government officials has led to a noticeable demand for first-class produce, especially in wealthier quarters, as well as to the introduction of new horticultural commodities such as strawberries and rhubarb into the domestic market. The same can be observed along the Kenya coast, where the international tourist industry is the source of innovation. Here we can also observe some fledgling attempts at seasonal control (see Section 5.3 on the Taita HPC). The value-added in processing and marketing remains limited, however.

The foregoing arguments demonstrate that in the emerging horticultural economy of Kenya the development of horticultural marketing channels is primarily an efficiency-based vertical differentiation process. Changes in the location and concentration of consumers are important determinants. Income is unimportant, because per capita incomes and income distributions have hardly changed over the past few decades. In some parts of the market, consumer incomes did rise: in the wealthier quarters of Nairobi, the tourist industry along the Kenya Coast and the export market. Here effectiveness (quality) featured alongside efficiency. The marketing channels that serve these newer market segments are not included in the following analysis.

7.2. Vertical differentiation of horticultural marketing channels in an African emerging economy: the model and the hypotheses

Our model of vertical differentiation includes one dependent variable, the degree of vertical differentiation of a channel, and five independent variables, notably the number of inhabitants of the market centre where the channel is directed, the population density of the rural hinterland of this market centre, the transport time of the commodity concerned, the keeping quality of this commodity, and the turnover of the trader concerned. Figure 7.1 summarizes the model. The dependent and independent variables will be introduced one by one, and the hypothesis relating to each independent variable will be presented.

Degree of vertical differentiation of a channel
Three steps are distinguished in the differentiation process. First, horticultural farmers sell directly to consumers (step 1). Then professional traders enter the marketing channel, mediating between farmers and consumers (step 2). Finally, these traders differentiate into wholesale traders and retail traders (step 3). In the latter situation, more than one wholesale level may evolve, e.g. collecting wholesalers and distributing wholesalers, but in our research model all channels with at least one wholesale level are defined as step-3 channels. Figure 7.2 shows the stepwise differentiation process.

Figure 7.1. Vertical differentiation of horticultural marketing channels in an emerging economy: a model

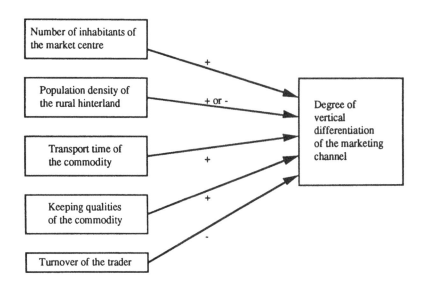

Figure 7.2. Steps of vertical differentiation in the model

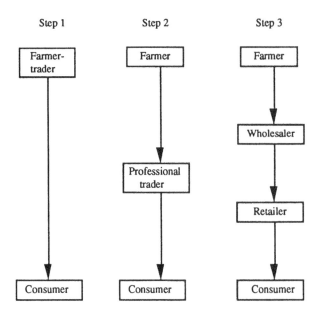

Number of inhabitants of the market centre

The history of food trade in Sub-Saharan Africa (Chapter 2) already showed a general relation between urbanization and urban growth on the one hand and the development of food marketing systems (including those for horticultural commodities) on the other. It did not, however, go into the exact relationship between urban demand and the structure of the channels.

According to Bucklin (1972) and Mallen (1977), marketing channels of food in emerging economies differentiate vertically when the size of the market increases. Market size is then defined in terms of market output. In Kenya, where incomes have not risen in the past few decades (see previous section), market output is directly related to the size of the consumer population. Consumers who buy horticultural commodities are found above all in urban centres. Most urban households lack food self-sufficiency, and earn their money through employment or self-employment in the formal and informal handicraft, industrial and service sectors. Their earnings usually allow purchases of horticultural commodities in addition to staple foods such as maize flour. When the number of inhabitants of a market centre increases the consumer population also grows. As a consequence, the output of the marketing channels supplying the centre increases, and the channels may be expected to differentiate vertically.[2]

The relationship between the population growth of a market centre and the vertical differentiation of horticultural marketing channels that supply the centre can be investigated by means of a longitudinal study, analysing marketing channels geared to one centre over a few decades' time. Within the time frame of the present study this was not possible. The second-best alternative is to carry out a cross-sectional survey comparing market centres of various population sizes, under the assumption that they develop along similar lines as to their population characteristics.

The hypothesis that will be tested is:

A horticultural marketing channel is more vertically differentiated when the centre served by the channel has more inhabitants.

Population density of the rural hinterland

As noted, the demand for horticultural commodities is primarily found in urban centres. Many rural households are either self-sufficient or they lack the purchasing power to buy the commodities. In rural areas with a high population growth, however, this situation is changing rapidly. Some rural households are losing their food self-sufficiency as a consequence of their shrinking holdings. Landless rural households are not yet a widespread problem in Kenya, but the cash revenues of rural households are derived to an increasing extent from off-farm employment (see Sections 3.3 and 3.4).

Rural households which are no longer self-sufficient in horticultural produce and which generate cash through other activities become potential buyers of vegetables and fruits. They go to the nearest market place to buy their commodities.[3] The total consumer population served by this market place includes both the inhabitants of the centre and part of

---

2   Should the growth of the centre be restricted to the slums, the demand for horticultural commodities might not increase because of the lack of purchasing power of the new citizens. In Kenya urban growth is not restricted to the slums.

3   They may also buy some from neighbours, but often these farmers are in the same position.

the rural population of 'the rural hinterland'. For the purpose of the present analysis, the rural hinterland is defined as the rural area that depends on this market place because there is no other market place (either rural or urban) nearer by.[4]

Which proportion of the population of the rural hinterland will actually go to the market place to buy horticultural commodities is difficult to say, but the population density gives an indication.[5] The higher the population density, the larger the potential number of rural consumers. A higher number of consumers increases the throughput of the marketing channels directed to the market centre, which in turn leads to more differentiated channels (as argued by Bucklin and Mallen; see the previous subsection).

So far we have been looking at the rural hinterland from the demand side. It also has a supply side. A higher population density in the rural hinterland implies the presence of more horticultural farmers, because horticulture has a higher value-added per unit of land than produce such as cereals or traditional cash crops such as coffee and tea.[6] Some horticultural farmers will take their produce to the market centre to which the rural hinterland belongs (by definition, no other markets are nearer).[7] Thus, a higher population density of the rural hinterland may increase the number of farmers selling produce to consumers in the market centre. In that case, some of the marketing channels directed to this centre are less differentiated than they would be if the rural hinterland were less densely populated.

In sum, the population density of the rural hinterland can have a two-way effect. On the demand side, it increases the consumer population served by the market centre, and thus the throughput of the marketing channels. As we saw before, a larger throughput leads to more differentiated marketing channels. On the supply side, however, greater rural population density increases the number of horticultural farmers in the vicinity of the market centre. Some of them then come to the centre to sell produce to consumers in the market place, thus forming less differentiated channels. Whether the demand or the supply effect will prevail cannot be determined in advance.

The hypothesis that will be tested is:

The vertical differentiation of a horticultural marketing channel that serves a population centre is influenced by the population density of that centre's rural hinterland.

Transport time

The description of the history of food trade in Sub-Saharan Africa (Chapter 2) has revealed the role of transport in the development of food marketing systems (including those for

---

[4] Any rural consumers that live closer to another rural or urban horticultural market place than the one in the surveyed market centre are assumed to go there to do their horticultural purchases. Consequently, they do not belong to the rural hinterland of the surveyed market centre. Thus, the radius of the rural hinterland depends here on the distribution of market places in the region, and not on the size of the market centre where the surveyed market place is located (as is often the case in geographical studies).

[5] An estimate of the total rural population that depends on the market place would require, to start with, a very detailed demarcation of the rural hinterland. This is not necessary when we use the population density of the rural hinterland.

[6] Only when agro-ecological circumstances do not allow horticulture do farmers have to look for other cash corps. However, under such circumstances most other kinds of commercial agriculture are not feasible either, and at least some of the farmers will migrate to other areas. As a consequence, the rural population density will be low.

[7] Other farmers will take their produce to other urban centres or sell it to traders at the farm gate.

horticultural commodities). It did, however, not show the precise effect that such transport has on the structure of the channels.

When an urban centre grows and demand rises, transport distances from the production areas to the centre may be expected to increase. First the production in the vicinity will grow, but when local producers are no longer able to satisfy demand, produce will be brought in from further away. Prices will rise due to an increase in demand, which in turn makes larger transport distances economically feasible, as was already shown by Von Thünen in the 19th century.[8]

Watts (1987) showed the relation between urban growth and increasing transport distances for Kano, Nigeria. He called it the regionalization of food trade. Braun et al. (1992) described the same development for another Nigerian town, Uyo (South East Nigeria). With the growth of the centre, supplies of basic foodstuffs like yams, cassava, gari and okra were brought in from further away.[9]

In emerging economies an increase in transport distances tends to increase the number of marketing intermediaries (Alderson, 1967; Bucklin, 1972). The new intermediaries will be able to work more efficiently with regard to transport and communication. A larger distance increases the relative importance of these factors in the total marketing costs and therefore the importance of economies of scale.

Alderson defines distance not in terms of miles but in terms of the time involved in communication and transportation.[10] This approach is appropriate in the case of developing countries, where one mile may take five minutes or one hour, depending on the state of the roads.

The hypothesis that will be tested is:
Horticultural marketing channels are more vertically differentiated when the transport from the production area to the market centre served by the channel takes more time.

Keeping qualities

It has been assumed thus far that horticultural commodities are a homogeneous group. Although all of them are perishables, they do, however, differ in their keeping qualities. Potatoes take considerably longer to go bad than bananas, and bananas can be kept longer than spinach. The keeping quality of a commodity could influence the structure of its marketing channels. After all, each transaction between channel members takes time, and that time will be more precious in the case of spinach than potatoes. Therefore, horticultural commodities with poorer keeping qualities may support less differentiated channels than horticultural commodities with better keeping qualities.

---

8   For the theory of Von Thünen see, for instance, Haggett (1983).
9   In the 1980s the principle supply areas of Uyo were located at a distance of 200 to 300 kilometres. This was also related to the increasing population density in the rural area surrounding the centre. In the course of time, the rural hinterland of Uyo had developed into a food deficit area, and part of the rural population had to rely on the same supplies brought in from elsewhere as did the inhabitants of Uyo. In this respect, the Nigerian case shows similar demand-side developments as outlined in the discussion of the rural population density factor in this chapter.
10   The use of travel time rather than travel distance can also be observed in certain gravity models used in regional marketing analysis (see Section 4.5).

Based on these considerations, the analysis should ideally be carried out for each individual commodity separately. This was not possible, however, given the presence of over 100 different horticultural commodities in the market places. The number of observations per commodity would be too small. Alternatively, commodities can be grouped according to their keeping qualities.

The hypothesis that will be tested is:

Horticultural marketing channels are more vertically differentiated when the commodities traded have better keeping qualities.

Turnover of the trader

Horticultural traders who sell produce in the market place of a consumer centre can be grouped on the basis of their respective turnovers.

Wholesalers are expected to have the largest turnover. If they sell produce from their own farm they are called farmer-wholesalers, otherwise they are professional wholesalers.

Next in hierarchy are mobile retailers, retailers who carry produce from the production area to the market place to sell to consumers. If they sell produce from their own farm they are called farmer-retailers, otherwise they are mobile professional retailers.

At the bottom of the hierarchy are immobile retailers, retailers who buy their produce from wholesalers in the same market where they sell their commodities. They are by definition professional retailers (farmer-retailers are always mobile).

The last two groups in the hierarchy (mobile retailers and immobile retailers) indicate that there is a relation between mobility and turnover. The explanation for this is economies of scale during transport. A retailer with a smaller turnover has higher average transport costs per selling unit in carrying produce from the production area to the consumer market. It is therefore more economical for him to stay in the market and buy from wholesalers than it is for a retailer with a larger turnover.[11]

Mobile and immobile retailers usually operate in channels of different lengths. Most of the immobile retailers operate in marketing channels with at least two intermediate levels (farmer -> *wholesaler* -> *retailer* -> consumer). Mobile retailers usually operate in channels with fewer levels: if they are farmer-retailers there is no intermediate level (farmer -> consumer), and if they are mobile professional retailers there is one intermediate level (farmer -> *retailer* -> consumer).[12] The following hypothesis can be formulated:

Horticultural marketing channels are more vertically differentiated when the retailers involved have a smaller turnover.[13]

---

[11] This argumentation is valid as long as the assorting function of the retailers is limited (e.g. they do not sell produce from different production areas). In Section 5.2 it was shown that this is indeed the case for most horticultural retailers in Kenya.

[12] Mobile professional retailers operate in channels with one intermediate level if they buy from farmers within the production area. The transaction may take place either at the farm gate or in a rural assembly market. Mobile professional retailers operate in channels with two intermediate levels if they buy in a rural assembly market from a rural assembling trader. That is less common, however (see Section 6.3).

[13] The hypothesis is only expected to be accepted when channels with two intermediate levels (step 3: farmer -> wholesaler -> retailer -> consumer) are compared to less differentiated channels. There is no reason to believe that it will be accepted when less differentiated channels are compared. Farmer-retailers (operating in a step-1 channel: farmer -> consumer) and mobile professional retailers (operating in a step-2 channel: farmer -> trader -> consumer) are not necessarily presumed to have different turnovers, since they are both mobile.

7.3. The data set

Horticultural traders in seventeen Kenyan market places are included in the analysis.[14] The randomly sampled traders in each market place were asked what kind of horticultural commodities they sold, both on the day of the interview and on other market days and during other parts of the year.

For each commodity traded, the traders were asked whether they or other family members had cultivated the commodity, or bought it. For each bought commodity, the traders were asked where and from whom they had bought it. If produce had been bought at farms, the place of purchase was to be specified up to the divisional level. If produce had been bought in a market place, the name of the market place was recorded. The people from whom the trader could buy the produce in such a market place were classified as either farmers or traders.[15]

A commodity could originate from more then one source of supply. A trader might, for instance, report having gone to farms to buy potatoes from farmers, and on to a local market place in the production area to buy additional potatoes from traders. A trader might also report buying potatoes from both farmers and traders who came to the sampled market. Or a trader might report selling potatoes from her own farm and potatoes she had bought from other farmers or traders. In all cases, all the sources of supply mentioned were recorded in the survey and included as separate transactions in the analysis.

In addition to sources of supply, respondents were also asked to whom they sold their commodities, either to consumers or other traders or both. They were asked about their customers only once, because horticultural traders in Kenyan market places do not have a commodity-specific selling strategy (selling one commodity exclusively to consumers and another exclusively to traders).

From sources of supply and customers to development steps
Five supply categories can be distinguished:
1. the supply comes from the respondent's own farm (he/she is a farmer-trader)
2. the supply is bought from farmers in the production area (either at the farm gate or in a rural market place)
3. the supply is bought from farmers in the sampled market place
4. the supply is bought from traders in the production area (selling in a market place)
5. the supply is bought from traders in the sampled market place
Two customer categories can be distinguished: traders and consumers. Ten different combinations can be made from the supply and customer categories. They are shown in Figure 7.3. Each combination represents one marketing channel. In most cases, only part of

---

14   The trade survey covered 18 market places (see Section 1.3), but the Kongowea wholesale market in Mombasa is not included in the analysis. In that market only traders that dealt with commodities from Taita Taveta were interviewed, so the sample was not random. In the other market places the traders were sampled randomly.

15   A trader distinguished a supplying farmer from a supplying trader on the basis of the language used during the bargaining. A trader would talk about the price paid in buying the commodity, while a farmer would talk about the money spent on inputs when cultivating it. Many farmers could also be recognized because they were less experienced negotiators and lacked up-to-date market information on supply and demand conditions, due to their irregular trading.

122

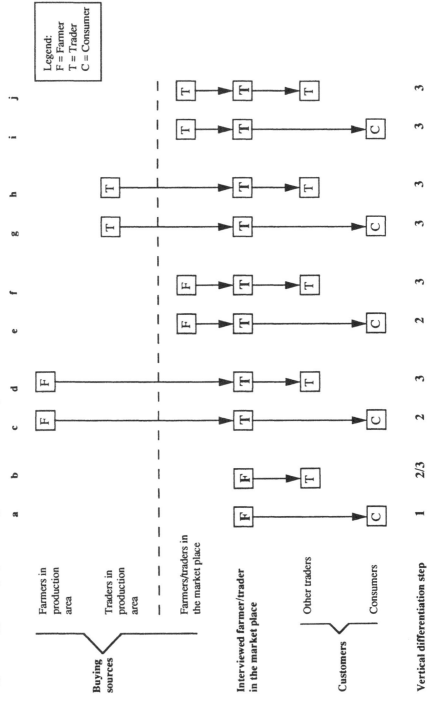

Figure 7.3. Types of buying-and-selling combinations according to the trade survey

the marketing channel from producer to consumer is shown. If produce is bought from farmers and sold to traders we are dealing with the upper part; if it is bought from traders and sold to consumers we are dealing with the lower part; and if it is bought from traders and sold to other traders, the middle part of the marketing channel is covered. Nevertheless, the rough structure of the entire marketing channel can be distilled from these channel segments.

Each combination in Figure 7.3 can be compared with the three differentiation steps outlined in Section 7.2 (Figure 7.2). All combinations but one are readily linkable to a specific development step. If the respondent is a farmer and her customers are consumers, we are dealing with a step-1 channel. If she is a trader, her source of supply are farmers and her customers are consumers, we are dealing with a step-2 channel. If she is a trader, and either her source of supply or her customers are traders, we are dealing with a step-3 channel.

If her source of supply is a trader, we do not know whether this is the only extra level between the farmer and the respondent. The trader from whom the respondent is buying could be buying her produce from another trader; for instance, she might be a distributing wholesaler buying from collecting wholesalers or a wholesaler buying from assembling traders. In the analysis, all these cases are defined as a step-3 marketing channel, that is, a channel in which vertical differentiation into wholesale and retail trade has occurred.

One particular combination of source of supply and customers can relate to more than one development step: a farmer selling to a trader. If that trader sells in turn to consumers, it will be a step-2 channel, but if she sells on to other traders it will be a step-3 channel. The customers of respondents' customers are, however, not known. Which alternative will prevail depends on the type of market place where the farmer is selling. The step-2 alternative is most likely to occur in market places without an assembling function. In those markets the buying trader is usually a retailer. The step-3 alternative is most probable in rural assembly markets. The buying trader there is usually a wholesaler who purchases produce from the farmers to sell on to distributing wholesalers and/or retailers in large population centres elsewhere in the region or the country.

Some assembling trade occurs in almost all rural markets in the sample. However, market places with a major assembling function are Magumu (Nyandarua District), Taveta (Taita Taveta District), Kisii Daraja Mbili, Nyakoe, Riochanda and Kebirigo (all Kisii District) (see Section 6.3). For the purpose of the analysis, they are labelled assembly markets.

Unit of analysis and sample size
The transaction is the unit of analysis. A transaction includes a trader, a commodity handled by this trader, a buying-and-selling combination in relation to this commodity, and a transport time in relation to this buying-and-selling combination. Thus, the number of transactions per trader depends on the number of commodities traded, the number of buying-and-selling combinations for each commodity, and the variation in transport time per buying-and-selling combination. An example: A respondent buys tomatoes from farmers at the farm gate in two different production areas and from traders in market places located in these two

areas. If she sells to consumers only, she represents four channels: two step-2 channels (combination 3 in Figure 7.3) and two step-3 channels (combination 7). If she sells to traders as well as consumers, she represents four more channels, all of them step-3 channels (combinations 4 and 8).

In total, 726 traders were interviewed in the 17 markets surveyed, representing 3776 transactions. Table 7.1 shows the number of traders interviewed per market, and the distribution of the transactions over the various buying-and-selling combinations as distinguished in Figure 7.3 (each buying-and-selling combination in Table 7.1 is represented by a letter that corresponds with a letter in Figure 7.3).

In Table 7.2, all buying-and-selling combinations have been translated into steps. Combination A in Table 7.1 represents a step-1 channel and combinations C and E represent step-2 channels. Combination B represents a step-3 channel in rural assembly markets and a step-2 channel otherwise. All other combinations are step-3 channels.

Not all 3776 observed transactions are included in the sample that will be used to test the vertical differentiation model. The reason is that some observations involve outgoing produce flows. Outgoing produce flows are ones that are directed not to the local consumer population living in the surveyed market centre and its hinterland, but to consumer populations elsewhere. The traders responsible for those flows buy commodities from the interviewed traders and farmers in the market place to take them to large urban centres such as Nairobi and Mombasa.

The outgoing produce flows cause a problem: we know how to characterize them according to the model (they are always step-3 channels), but we do not know the size of the consumer population they serve. In the trade survey respondents were not asked where traders who bought from them took their commodities. In many cases the respondents would not have known. As a consequence, we do not know to which consumer centres these flows are directed. This leaves two solutions: (1) to include only those flows which are definitely directed to local consumers (flows whose terminal market is known), or (2) to exclude market places where outgoing produce flows are known to be substantial.

For the first solution, five of the buying-and-selling combinations shown in Figure 7.3 are relevant, namely those ending at a consumer (combinations A, C, E, G and I). The consumer will be local, because consumers usually go to the nearest buying place to buy their horticultural commodities. Travelling to market places further away does not make sense, because the costs of transport are normally higher than possible benefits gained by lower prices in such markets. Thus, in the cases of these five combinations, the surveyed market place is without a doubt the terminal market and the consumer population is known. For the other combinations the surveyed market place may not be the terminal market and the consumer population is not known. Hence, these combinations are not included in the analysis.

The focus on combinations A, C, E, G and I in Figure 7.3 brings the sample size down to 2474 transactions (Table 7.3).[16] The number of step-1 channels remains the same, and the number of step-2 channels decreases by 11 per cent. The largest reduction is among

---

[16] Seventy-three traders from the original sample (10%) were omitted because they sold only to other traders and not to consumers.

Table 7.1. Number of buying-and-selling combinations by market place

market place	no. of traders interviewed	type of buying-and-selling combination*										total
		a	b	c	d	e	f	g	h	i	j	
Dundori	19	28	5	8	0	7	0	6	0	0	0	54
Magumu	30	29	49	30	32	4	0	7	4	2	0	157
Engineer	21	4	0	25	5	0	0	18	0	15	0	67
Riochanda	37	24	19	19	17	12	10	5	5	8	8	127
Kebirigo	38	28	20	9	8	12	9	5	5	7	4	107
Nyakoe	27	13	18	9	6	6	7	4	2	4	4	73
Keroka	35	9	10	15	12	16	5	9	5	20	6	107
Wundanyi	56	89	51	119	72	10	4	17	9	8	6	385
Njoro	31	13	13	17	17	45	28	5	5	62	53	258
Taveta	95	20	20	45	40	158	47	6	4	88	38	466
Voi	57	47	29	135	84	17	12	76	28	62	32	522
Nyahururu	21	13	5	29	12	3	0	3	3	16	12	96
Kisii Daraja Mbili	41	21	24	18	23	17	13	7	7	19	15	164
Kisii Municipal	39	11	8	37	34	14	8	11	10	16	9	158
Nakuru wholesale	96	2	3	66	85	30	34	17	17	106	100	460
Nakuru retail	24	7	2	3	0	127	3	2	0	217	5	366
Mombasa Majengo retail	59	0	0	0	0	3	0	0	0	203	3	209
Total all markets	726	358	276	584	447	481	180	198	104	853	295	3776

* For an explanation of the characters a, b, c, etc. see Figure 7.3.

Table 7.2. Number of recorded transactions by step and market place

market place	no. of traders in sample	recorded transactions Step 1	Step 2	Step 3	all
Dundori	19	28	20	6	54
Magumu	30	29	34	94	157
Engineer	21	4	25	38	67
Riochanda	37	24	31	72	127
Kebirigo	38	28	21	58	107
Nyakoe	27	13	15	45	73
Keroka	35	9	41	57	107
Wundanyi	56	89	180	116	385
Njoro	31	13	75	170	258
Taveta	95	20	203	243	466
Voi	57	47	181	294	522
Nyahururu	21	13	37	46	96
Kisii Daraja Mbili	41	21	35	108	164
Kisii Municipal	39	11	59	88	158
Nakuru wholesale	96	2	99	359	460
Nakuru retail	24	7	132	227	366
Mombasa Majengo	59	0	3	206	209
Total all markets	726	358	1191	2227	3776

step-3 channels (53 per cent). This is consistent with expectations, because, as argued, outgoing produce flows are always step-3 channels.[17]

Instead of removing some of the buying-and-selling combinations from the sample, we can alternatively remove market places where outgoing flows are prominent. This is the case in the market places with a major assembling function: Magumu, Taveta, Nyakoe, Kisii Daraja Mbili, Kebirigo and Riochanda. This reduces the sample size by about the same degree as the omission of some of the buying-and-selling combinations (Table 7.4). However, the number of traders in the sample is reduced more drastically, as is the number of step-1 and step-2 channels (in favour of step-3 channels). A further disadvantage is the loss of the bulk of the rural market places in the sample.[18]

The present analysis will apply both the focus on buying-and-selling combinations with known terminal markets and the removal of rural assembly markets.[19] The results of the two alternatives will be compared.

---

[17] It may be argued that removal of the combinations B, D, F, H and J is not only a solution to outgoing produce flows but is also necessary to avoid counting the same channel twice. In large subsamples within one market place, answers of traders may to some extent be interrelated. If a respondent reports selling tomatoes to traders in the market and another reports buying tomatoes from traders in the same market, the two may actually have been dealing with each other. They are thus part of the same channel, the first trader representing the upper part and the second trader the lower part of the channel.

[18] Of the six market centres with less than 2,000 inhabitants in the sample, four have a major assembling function (see Section 5.2).

[19] Appendix 7.1 shows the overlap and the differences between the samples used in the two analytical alternatives.

Table 7.3. Number of recorded transactions by step and market place, for trade flows
with known terminal markets*

market place	no. of traders in sample	recorded transactions Step 1	Step 2	Step 3	all
Dundori	19	28	15	6	49
Magumu	20	29	34	9	72
Engineer	21	4	25	33	62
Riochanda	33	24	31	13	68
Kebirigo	37	28	21	12	61
Nyakoe	17	13	15	8	36
Keroka	31	9	31	29	69
Wundanyi	56	89	129	25	243
Njoro	31	13	62	67	142
Taveta	80	20	203	94	317
Voi	57	47	152	138	337
Nyahururu	21	13	32	19	64
Kisii Daraja Mbili	30	21	35	26	82
Kisii Municipal	33	11	51	27	89
Nakuru wholesale	84	2	96	123	221
Nakuru retail	24	7	130	219	356
Mombasa Majengo	59	0	3	203	206
Total all markets	653	358	1065	1051	2474

* combinations A, C, E, G and I in Figure 7.3.

Table 7.4. Number of recorded transactions by step and market place, rural assembly
markets excluded

market place	no. of traders in sample	recorded transactions Step 1	Step 2	Step 3	all
Dundori	19	28	20	6	54
Engineer	21	4	25	38	67
Keroka	35	9	41	57	107
Wundanyi	56	89	180	116	385
Njoro	31	13	75	170	258
Voi	57	47	181	294	522
Nyahururu	21	13	37	46	96
Kisii Municipal	39	11	59	88	158
Nakuru wholesale	96	2	99	359	460
Nakuru retail	24	7	132	227	366
Mombasa Majengo	59	0	3	206	209
Total all markets	458	223	852	1607	2682

7.4. Specification of the independent variables

Number of inhabitants of the market centres and population density of their rural hinterlands
The latest Kenyan population census was used as the source of information to estimate the
populations of the centres where the surveyed market places were located and the population

density of their rural hinterlands (CBS, 1994b, 1994c). Although the census was carried out in 1989 and the trade survey was carried out between 1990 and 1992, the figures are thought to have sufficient accuracy for the analysis. Table 7.5 shows the populations of the surveyed centres.

The larger population centres have more than one market place. Nakuru has a wholesale market and a retail market which are both included in the analysis. Both the traders in the retail market and most of those in the wholesale market sell to consumers (see Section 5.2). Both types of traders serve the entire town. Therefore, for both markets the urban consumer population has been set at the total number of inhabitants of Nakuru.

Mombasa has a wholesale market and several retail markets. The wholesale market supplies primarily a number of retail markets on Mombasa Island and in Kisauni (Mombasa North Coast where the wholesale market is located). One of the retail markets on Mombasa Island, Majengo market, is included in the analysis. The consumer population for this market has been set not at the number of inhabitants of the quarter where the market is located, but at the total number of inhabitants of Mombasa Island and Kisauni. This is because all produce sold in the Majengo retail market passes through the wholesale market. The transport costs from the wholesale market to the retail market are small compared to those from the production areas to the wholesale market. Economies of scale during transport are one of the prime determinants of the vertical differentiation process (see Section

Table 7.5. Consumer population by market place

District (Province)	market centre	market place	inhabitants of market centre	population density of rural hinterland
Nyandarua (Central)	Nyahururu	Nyahururu	14,829	92
	Engineer	Engineer	446	111
	Magumu	Magumu	400*	147
Nakuru (Rift Valley)	Nakuru	wholesale market	163,928	124
		retail market	163,928	124
	Njoro	Njoro	9,026	148
	Dundori	Dundori	400*	182
Taita Taveta (Coast)	Voi	Voi	13,202	68
	Taveta	Taveta	10,378	66
	Wundanyi	Wundanyi	2,764	401
Kisii (Nyanza)	Kisii	Municipal market	44,149	572
		Daraja Mbili	22,075	572
	Nyakoe	Nyakoe	800*	589
	Riochanda	Riochanda	600*	526
	Kebirigo	Kebirigo	700*	546
	Keroka	Keroka	2,321	560
Mombasa (Coast)	Mombasa	Majengo	281,044	171

Based on CBS, 1994b, 1994c.
Note: Figures with an asterisk (*) represent our own estimates because specified information was lacking in the population census. The population for Majengo market equals the population of Mombasa Island and Kisauni. The population of Daraja Mbili has been set at half the population of Kisii town (see main text).

7.2). Therefore, the total number of consumers served by all retail markets that depend on the wholesale market is thought to determine the degree of vertical differentiation of the marketing channels directed to consumers in each of these retail markets.

Kisii town does not have a wholesale market, but it has two retail markets which are both included in the analysis. The Municipal market in the middle of town is a daily market and the Daraja Mbili market at the edge of town is a periodic one. The daily Municipal market serves all inhabitants of Kisii during the five days of the week that the periodic market is not operational. The survey in the Municipal market was carried out on one of these days. On days when the Daraja Mbili market is operational, some consumers go to there and some to the Municipal market. It is assumed that on such days each market serves half the population of Kisii. Therefore, the number of inhabitants served by Daraja Mbili market is set at half the number of inhabitants of Kisii town. The sensitivity of this assumption will be tested in the analysis.

In addition to the number of inhabitants of the sampled consumer centres, the population density of their rural hinterlands had to be ascertained. Rural hinterland has been defined above as the rural area that depends on a surveyed market place because there are no other market places (either rural or urban) nearer by. Defined in this way, the boundaries of a centre's hinterland often coincide with the boundaries of the administrative unit (division or subdivision) in which the centre is located. The exact shape of the hinterland is not so important, because population density is used rather than the absolute number of rural inhabitants, and population density changes only gradually. Table 7.5 shows the population densities used in the analysis.

Transport time
In the trade survey, farmer-traders (who sold produce from their own farm) were asked what their place of residence was. The transport time is estimated on the basis of this information and the location of the surveyed market. Professional traders were asked where they bought their commodities. If they bought commodities in production areas, the transport time was estimated on the basis of the place of purchase and the location of the surveyed market. If they bought commodities in the surveyed market, the transport time refers to traders who did go to the production area to buy these commodities in order to sell them to immobile traders in the surveyed market.

Keeping qualities
Three categories of horticultural produce are distinguished for the purpose of the analysis: commodities with poor, medium and good keeping qualities. The first and the last group have been entered as dummy variables. Both coincide largely with certain types of horticultural produce. All so-called leafy vegetables are categorized as poor, and all tubers, roots and bulbs as good. The leafy vegetables found in the surveyed market places were kale, spider flower, black nightshade, Amaranthus, cow pea leaves, bitter leaves, spinach, pumpkin leaves and lettuce. Once harvested, their keeping qualities outside the refrigerator are extremely poor. If they are not sold within one or two days after being harvested the trader has to decrease the price because the leaves start to flag and shrivel up.

In sharp contrast, tubers, roots and bulbs stay good for weeks, provided they are stored in a well-ventilated place. The most important tubers, roots and bulbs found in the market places surveyed were Irish potatoes, sweet potatoes, arrowroot, and red and white onions. Less known root crops such as beetroot and turnip are also part of the group. Pumpkins and the fresh herbs garlic and ginger were added because they have the same keeping characteristics. The entire category is named *tubers, roots and bulbs* for short.

All commodities that have keeping qualities better than leafy vegetables but poorer than tubers, roots and bulbs were grouped together into the third category. It includes commodities such as bananas, cabbages, mangoes, sweet peppers, passion fruit, tomatoes, carrots, eggplant, oranges and pineapples.

Turnover

The turnover of the traders in the sample is valued in Kenyan shillings and refers to the selling prices and selling quantities on the day the traders were interviewed. For each commodity the traders were asked how much they expected to sell on that day and what the average selling price would be. The average selling price was used in place of the going price at the moment of the interview because prices tend to change in the course of the day.[20]

All sampled traders in a particular market place were interviewed on the same market day. All market places in a region were surveyed when the bulk of the horticultural commodities were in harvest. During such periods the price fluctuations from one market day to another would be relatively small.[21]

---

[20] If current prices had been used, the calculated turnover would have been biased by the time of the day the interview was held. Usually prices are lower towards the end of the market day because traders do not like to take their perishable commodities home with them.

[21] At the beginning and towards the end of harvesting periods, price fluctuations become more volatile because supply is less steady.

Vertical Differentiation of Horticultural Marketing Channels in Kenya: Testing the Model

In the previous chapter a vertical differentiation model was put forward, and hypotheses were formulated to support it. The model and the hypotheses will now be tested by means of logistic regression (logit) analysis.

8.1. Logistic regression analysis

Two types of logit analysis can be distinguished: binomial (also called binary) and multinomial. Both work on the same principles, but binomial logit requires a dichotomous dependent variable, while multinomial logit allows dependent variables with more than two alternatives. The principles of logit analysis will be explained on the basis of the binomial variant.

Logit analysis is used to estimate the *probability* of some certain event. From the dichotomous value of the dependent variable the procedure predicts its estimate of the probability that the event will or will not occur. If the predicted probability is greater than 0.50 the prediction is 'yes', otherwise the prediction is 'no' (Hair et al., 1995).

The coefficients of the independent variables (B_0, B_1, B_2, etc) estimated by the procedure refer to a comparison of the probability of the event occurring with the probability of its not occurring. The mathematical expression is called 'the logit' because the coefficients are expressed in (natural) logarithms:

$$\text{logit} = \log (\text{Prob (event)} / \text{Prob (no event)}) = B_0 + B_1X_1 + B_2X_2 + \dots + B_pX_p$$

On the basis of the logit, the probability that the event will occur can be calculated:

$$\text{Prob(event)} = 1 / (1 + e^{-Z}) \quad \text{whereby} \quad Z = B_0 + B_1X_1 + B_2X_2 + \dots + B_pX_p$$

The signs of the coefficients B_0, B_1, etc are interpreted similarly to those in ordinary regression. A positive coefficient increases the probability that the event will occur, and a negative one decreases it.

The goodness-of-fit of the model can be assessed by means of the model chi-square. It tests the null hypothesis that the coefficients for all the terms in the model, except the constant, are zero (comparable to the overall F-test in ordinary regression analysis) (Norusis, 1990a). If the null hypothesis is rejected ($p<0.05$), the model is meaningful.

In addition to the model chi-square, the percentage of correctly classified observations gives an indication of the goodness-of-fit of the model. A t-test can be carried out on the classification table that compares observed and predicted values. The t-value is calculated as follows:

$t_{(n-1)} = (Q - P) / s_p$
$Q = (n_{11} + n_{22}) / n$
$P = (n_{1.}^2 + n_{2.}^2) / n^2$
$s_p = $ square root $((1 - P) * P / n)$

	Predicted		
	no event	event	
Observed			
no event	n_{11}	n_{12}	$n_{1.}$
event	n_{21}	n_{22}	$n_{2.}$
			n

The number of 'no-event' and 'event' observations entered in the analysis should not differ too much ($n_{1.} \approx n_{2.}$). When the number of 'no-event' and 'event' observations in the sample ($n_{1.}$ and $n_{2.}$) is approximately the same, and the model fits well, the number of correctly classified observations will be larger than the number of wrongly classified ones for both groups ($n_{11} > n_{12}$ and $n_{22} > n_{21}$). This will not be the case if group sizes considerably differ. In the case of, for instance, 20 'no event' observations ($n_{1.} = 20$) and 80 'event' observations ($n_{2.} = 80$) the model will focus primarily on the 'event' observations. As a consequence, both the 'event' and 'no-event' observations will be classified as 'event' occasions (n_{12} and n_{22}). When large differences exist in the sample, a random subsample must be taken from the biggest group (Maddala, 1992).

Once the model has been estimated, extreme cases have to be checked.[1] Conflicting or unrealistic answers by respondents may have led to the presence of these outliers. If this is the case they have to be removed from the sample. Correlations between the independent variables in the model have to be checked, too. When two independent variables show a strong correlation, the removal of one of them from the analysis must be considered.

The model has to be checked for heteroskedasticity. Logit analysis assumes homoskedasticity, meaning that the errors in the regression equation have a common variance. If error terms do not have a common variance they are heteroskedastic.

---

[1] A case is called extreme in the analysis when the studentized residual is greater than two (such in accordance with Norusis, 1990a).

Heteroskedasticity can be detected by separate regression analyses of the squared residuals of the model on each of the explanatory variables (X_1, ..., X_p), and by a regression analysis of the squared residuals on the predicted values of the dependent variable (Prob(event)) (Maddala, 1992). Absolute residuals may be used instead of squared residuals. The results are not necessarily the same, and therefore squared and absolute residuals are both used to detect heteroskedasticity in the present analysis. If heteroskedasticity is found for one or more explanatory variables, it can usually be resolved or diminished by substituting the logarithm or the reciprocal of these variables into the model (Norusis, 1990b; Maddala, 1992).

So far we have been talking about binomial logit analysis. Multinomial logit works according to the same principles. The biggest difference is that we no longer speak of 'no event' and 'event', but of 'event 1', 'event 2', 'event 3', etc. In binomial logit 'no event' was taken as a reference, and a positive sign of a coefficient increased the probability that the event would occur. In multinomial logit , 'no event' is not an option, and the model estimates the probability that one event occurs relative to another.

Whereas a binomial logit model consists of one logit function expressed as log (Prob (event) / Prob (no event)), a multinomial logit model consists of J-1 functions, whereby J stands for the number of possible events (Ben-Akiva & Lerman, 1985). One of the events is taken as the point of departure, and the model estimates the probability of the other events occurring relative to this one. If, for instance, we have three events and event 1 is taken as the point of departure, the model will be:

$$\log (\text{Prob (event 2) / Prob (event 1)}) = B_{10} + B_{11}X_{11} + B_{12}X_{12} + ... + B_{1p}X_{1p}$$
$$\log (\text{Prob (event 3) / Prob (event 1)}) = B_{21} + B_{21}X_{21} + B_{22}X_{22} + ... + B_{2p}X_{2p}$$

8.2. Analytic procedure

The analysis will be performed twice, with two different data sets. In Section 7.3 it was explained that these two sets originate from the need to solve the problem of outgoing flows. The first data set includes all surveyed markets, but in each market those flows are excluded whose terminal markets are unknown. The second data set excludes surveyed market places where outgoing flows are prominent (rural assembly markets), while including all recorded flows in the remaining markets.

The analysis seeks to estimate the probability of encountering step-1, step-2 and step-3 marketing channels. A step-1 channel stands for farmer -> consumer, a step-2 channel for farmer -> trader -> consumer, and a step-3 channel for farmer -> wholesaler -> retailer -> consumer (see Section 7.2). In logit terms, three events occur. In multinomial logit, all three events can be entered in one and the same analysis. For binomial logit, the analysis has to be split into three parts: step-1 channels are compared with step-2 channels, omitting step-3 channels; then step-2 channels with step-3 channels, omitting step-1 channels; and finally step-1 channels with step 3-channels, omitting step-2 channels.

Table 8.1 shows the distribution of the dependent variable for each data set. Not all the available observations will be used, however, because of the need for approximately equal group sizes (see Section 8.1). Random samples will be taken from the larger groups (step 2 and step 3) before carrying out the analyses.

Both binomial and multinomial logit will be used. The multinomial variant is the most straightforward alternative, but the binomial one has the advantage that a larger number of observations can be included in the analysis. In multinomial logit, where all three groups are entered into the same analysis, the numbers of step-2 and step-3 observations have to be brought back to 358 or 223, depending on the data set used (see Table 8.1). As a consequence, we lose the largest part of the step-2 and step-3 observations. In binomial logit, where steps are compared in pairs, the number of step-2 and step-3 observations has to be reduced in a similar fashion to compare each of them with step-1 observations, but that is not necessary for comparing step-2 with step-3 channels. From the first data set all step-2 and step-3 observations can be used, and from the second data set all step-2 observations and half of the step-3 observations. The larger the size of the sample, the greater the power of the statistical analysis (Hair et al., 1995).[2] Therefore, the power of a step-2 and step-3 analysis is expected to be greater in binomial logit than in multinomial logit. This makes it worthwhile to apply both approaches.

The binomial analysis will be performed first. After estimation of the model, the results will be checked for (1) extreme cases, (2) correlations between independent variables, (3) and heteroskedasticity (see Section 8.1). If heteroskedasticity is found, conversion of independent variables will be attempted. Once the right converted variables are found, they can be entered directly into the multinomial logit.[3]

The dependent and independent variables to be used in the analyses were already introduced in Section 7.2 and elaborated in Section 7.4. What remains is naming them. In the binomial analysis, where steps are compared one by one, the name of the dependent variable is equal to the highest step. For example, in the comparison of step-1 and step-2 channels, the dependent variable is called STEP2, which is equal to one in the case of a step-2 channel and zero in the case of a step-1 channel. In the multinomial logit, where all three steps are entered into the same analysis, the independent variable is called STEP, having a value of 1, 2 or 3.

Table 8.1. Sample population by vertical differentiation step and data set

	step 1 *	step 2 *	step 3 *	all
1. data set of trade flows with known terminal market **	358	1065	1051	2474
2. data set of all trade flows, rural assembly markets excluded	223	852	1607	2682

* step 1 = farmer -> consumer; step 2 = farmer -> trader -> consumer; step 3 = farmer -> wholesaler -> retailer -> consumer.
** buying-and-selling combinations A, C, E, G and I in Figure 7.3.
Note: the two data sets will both be analysed and the results compared.

---

2 The power of the statistical analysis is the probability that statistical significance will be indicated if it is present (Hair et al., 1995).
3 SPSS will be used for the binomial logit analyses, and LIMDEP for the multinomial logit analyses.

The names of the independent variables used in the analysis are:

POPSIZE   Number of inhabitants of the market centre where the surveyed market place is located [4]

POPDENSITY   Population density of the rural hinterland of the market centre where the surveyed market place is located [5]

TRANSTIME   Transportation time from the farm to the surveyed market place by vehicle

LEAVES   Dichotomous variable equalling one in the case of leafy vegetables

TUBERS   Dichotomous variable equalling one in the case of tubers, roots and bulbs

TURNOVER   Value of a trader's turnover on the day of the interview [6]

8.3. Testing the model using trade flows with known terminal markets

First, we focus on the marketing flows with known terminal markets (to avoid outgoing flows, see previous section). The analysis starts with binomial logit analyses of step-1 and step-2 channels, step-2 and step-3 channels, and step-1 and step-3 channels. Thereafter, the results are checked through multinomial logit analysis of step-1, -2 and -3 channels.

Binomial logit of step-1 and step-2 channels
Box 8.1 shows the binomial logit analysis for step-1 and step-2 channels. All independent variables are entered into the analysis at once. The variables POPSIZE and TRANSTIME are found to be significant at the 0.001 level. The other variables are not significant. The model chi-square is significant and high, and so is the t-value of the classification table. There is no reason to remove the extreme cases from the sample.[7] Correlations between independent variables are not disturbingly high. Heteroskedasticity is a problem, however, as shown when the squared and absolute residuals are regressed on each significant independent variable and on the predicted value of the dependent variable. The heteroskedasticity can to a large extent be resolved by taking the inversions of POPSIZE and TRANSTIME. The predicted residuals then no longer show heteroskedasticity. When the procedure is rerun with INVPOPSIZE (inversion of POPSIZE) and INVTRANSTIME (inversion of TRANSTIME), these variables become highly significant (0.001 level). In addition, the variables POPDENSITY and LEAVES become significant, though at lower levels (the first at the 0.05 level, and the second at the 0.10 level).

To check whether the results of the analysis are stable, the analysis is repeated with two different random samples from the step-2 cases. Each time the same variables are

---

[4]   The population figures are divided by one thousand before entering them into the analysis to avoid very small coefficients. Such coefficients are less exact in SPSS. The analysis will be repeated twice for different values of the population of Daraja Mbili because this figure is based on an assumption (see Section 7.4).

[5]   The population density figures are divided by one hundred before entering to avoid very small coefficients.

[6]   The turnover figures are divided by one thousand before entering to avoid very small coefficients.

[7]   The extreme cases involve commodities traded by three traders in Nakuru (one in the wholesale market and two in the retail market). They differed from the other sampled traders in the Nakuru markets because they not only bought the commodities they sold, but also grew them on their own farms. In the analysis, they are entered twice, once as professional traders and once as farmers. The extreme values occur for the farmer entries.

significant (Appendix 8.1). The analysis is also repeated for the two different assumptions about the size of the consumer population of Daraja Mbili. Again, the same variables remain significant (Appendix 8.1).

As explained in Section 8.1, the results of the analysis can be written as:

$$\log(\text{Prob(step 2)} / \text{Prob (step 1)}) = 1.4567 - 0.5205 \times \text{INVPOPSIZE} - 0.1115 \times \text{POPDENSITY} - 0.6178 \times \text{INVTRANSTIME} - 0.4365 \times \text{LEAVES}$$

The sign of INVPOPSIZE is negative, meaning that a larger value of this variable decreases

---

Box 8.1. Analysis of step-1 versus step-2 channels

A. Logistic regression analysis

Total number of cases	725
Number of selected cases	725
Dependent variable (0,1)	STEP2
Model Chi-Square	153.9 (df=6, p=0.0000)
Correctly classified observations	69.3% (t=10.3, p=0.000)
Number of extreme cases	8

Variables in the equation:	B	S.E.	Wald	Sig.
POPSIZE	0.0158	0.0025	39.93	0.0000
POPDENSITY	- 0.0627	0.0454	1.91	0.1668
TRANSTIME	0.9044	0.1526	35.11	0.0000
LEAVES	- 0.2686	0.2247	1.43	0.2320
TUBERS	- 0.0922	0.2262	0.17	0.6836
TURNOVER	- 0.0085	0.0081	1.09	0.2956
Constant	- 0.9501	0.2532	14.08	0.0002

Pearson correlation matrix

	STEP2	POPSIZE	POPDENS.	TRANST.	LEAVES	TUBERS
STEP2	1.00					
POPSIZE	0.33	1.00				
POPDENSITY	- 0.23	- 0.27	1.00			
TRANSTIME	0.31	0.29	- 0.37	1.00		
LEAVES	- 0.10	- 0.11	0.08	- 0.11	1.00	
TUBERS	0.03	0.02	- 0.02	0.04	- 0.20	1.00
TURNOVER	0.18	0.41	- 0.31	0.38	- 0.08	- 0.03

Separate bivariate regression analyses of the significant independent variables and predicted values with the squared residuals and the absolute residuals

	Squared residuals		Absolute residuals	
	t-value	p-value	t-value	p-value
POPSIZE	- 7.07	0.0000	- 13.68	0.0000
TRANSTIME	- 5.15	0.0000	- 8.96	0.0000
Predicted values	- 5.95	0.0000	- 11.27	0.0000

Continued on next page

Box 8.1 continued

B. Logistic regression analysis with inversions of POPSIZE and TRANSTIME

Total number of cases	725
Number of selected cases	725
Dependent variable (0,1)	STEP2
Model Chi-Square	113.9 (df=6, p=0.000)
Correctly classified observations	67.5% (t=9.4, p=0.000)
Number of extreme cases	0

Variables in the equation:	B	S.E.	Wald	Sig.
INVPOPSIZE	- 0.5205	0.1103	22.29	0.0000
POPDENSITY	- 0.1115	0.0457	5.96	0.0147
INVTRANSTIME	- 0.6178	0.1482	17.38	0.0000
LEAVES	- 0.4365	0.2238	3.80	0.0512
TUBERS	0.0388	0.2212	0.03	0.8609
TURNOVER	0.0060	0.0067	0.81	0.3695
Constant	1.4567	0.2371	37.73	0.0000

Separate bivariate regression analyses of the significant independent variables and predicted values with the squared residuals and the absolute residuals

	Squared residuals		Absolute residuals	
	t-value	p-value	t-value	p-value
INVPOPSIZE	- 2.59	0.0098	- 4.32	0.0000
POPDENSITY	0.59	0.5564	1.23	0.2206
INVTRANSTIME	- 0.82	0.4112	- 0.47	0.6399
LEAVES	2.18	0.0295	1.90	0.0581
Predicted values	1.07	0.2872	1.51	0.1315

the probability of encountering a step-2 channel. Since INVPOPSIZE is the inversion of POPSIZE, a larger value of INVPOPSIZE coincides with a smaller value for POPSIZE and vice versa. Thus, the negative sign in the equation means that a smaller value of POPSIZE decreases the probability of encountering a step-2 channel, and a larger value for POPSIZE increases this probability. In other words, the analysis shows that the probability of coming across step-2 channels relative to step-1 channels increases as the centre where the market is located has a larger population.

The same reasoning can be followed for INVTRANSTIME. It also has a negative sign, so that a smaller value of INVTRANSTIME (that is, a higher value of TRANSTIME) increases the probability of encountering a step-2 channel. In other words, the probability of encountering step-2 channels relative to step-1 channels increases as more time is required to transport the commodity from the production area to the consumer centre where the market is located.

The signs of POPDENSITY and LEAVES in the equation are also negative. The analysis thus shows that the probability of encountering step-2 channels relative to step-1 channels decreases as the population density in the rural hinterland of the market centre becomes higher, and when the traded commodities are (highly perishable) leafy vegetables. An explanation of these findings will follow.

On the basis of the logit, we can calculate the estimated probabilities of finding step-2 channels in market centres with different sizes, different population densities of the rural hinterland, different transport times of the commodity, and different perishability of the commodity (leafy vegetable or not). Before this, the equation has to be converted (see Section 8.1):

Prob (step 2) = $1 / (1 + e^{-Z})$
Z = 1.4567 - 0.5205 / POPSIZE - 0.1115 x POPDENSITY - 0.6178 / TRANSTIME - 0.4365 x LEAVES

Tables 8.2 and 8.3 show the results for different combinations of the independent variables. The probability of encountering step-2 channels increases in both tables as we move from top to bottom and from left to right. This again indicates that (1) an increase in the size of the consumer population, (2) an increase in transportation time, and (3) a less extreme perishability (non-leafy vegetables) all have a positive effect on the proportion of step-2 channels.

A comparison of the two tables shows that the direction of the changes is the same whether the hinterland is relatively scarcely or densely populated. However, the initial probability for step-2 channels is lower in the case of a densely populated hinterland. A high population density slows down the increase in step-2 channels (professional traders buying

Table 8.2. Estimated probability of encountering step-2 relative to step-1 channels in the case of a relatively sparsely populated hinterland (n=725)*

	POPSIZE = 0.6 LEAVES = 1	LEAVES = 0	POPSIZE = 100 LEAVES = 1	LEAVES = 0
TRANSTIME 0.5	0.22	0.31	0.40	0.51
2.0	0.42	0.53	0.63	0.73
5.0	0.47	0.57	0.69	0.77

* POPDENSITY = 1.5

Table 8.3. Estimated probability of encountering step-2 relative to step-1 channels in the case of a relatively densely populated hinterland (n=725)*

	POPSIZE = 0.6 LEAVES = 1	LEAVES = 0	POPSIZE = 100 LEAVES = 1	LEAVES = 0
TRANSTIME 0.5	0.15	0.22	0.30	0.40
2.0	0.31	0.42	0.52	0.63
5.0	0.36	0.46	0.57	0.67

* POPDENSITY = 5.5

from farmers and selling to consumers) in favour of step-1 channels (farmers selling to consumers).

Binomial logit of step-2 and step-3 channels

Box 8.2 shows the results when step-2 and step-3 channels are compared. All cases of both groups are included in the analysis. The variables POPSIZE, TRANSTIME and TURNOVER are significant at the 0.001 level, the variable POPDENSITY at the 0.05 level and the variable LEAVES at the 0.10 level. The model shows significant and high model chi-square and t-values. There is no case to remove the extreme values from the sample.[8] Correlations between independent variables do not disturb the analysis, but heteroskedasticity is again a problem. It is again resolved to a large extent by taking the inverse of POPSIZE and TRANSTIME.[9] The outcome of the logistic analysis is little affected by this change: the inverse of POPSIZE (INVPOPSIZE) and of TRANSTIME (INVTRANSTIME) become significant and the signs change as expected (see analysis of step-1 and step-2 channels). The variables TURNOVER, POPDENSITY and LEAVES remain significant (the latter two at higher levels).[10]

The results of the analysis can be written again as a logit:

log (Prob(step 3) / Prob (step 2)) = 1.5067 - 0.2267 / POPSIZE + 0.1239 x POPDENSITY -
1.9411 / TRANSTIME - 0.5822 x LEAVES - 0.0155 x TURNOVER

It can be interpreted as follows:
- The probability of coming across step-3 channels relative to step-2 channels increases as the centre where the market is located has a larger consumer population. This is the same as found in analysing step-1 and step-2 channels.
- The probability of encountering step-3 channels relative to step-2 channels *increases* as the population density of the rural hinterland of the market centre is higher. In the previous section the probability of finding step-2 relative to step-1 channels was found to *decrease* as the population density became higher. In Section 7.2 it was explained that a high rural population density may have both a negative effect (a higher density increases the number of horticultural farmers in the market place) and a positive effect on the differentiation process (a higher population density increases the consumer population dependent on the market place). It can be concluded that the positive effect (the 'consumer effect') is found in comparing step-2 and step-3 channels (removing the farmers from the sample), while the negative effect (the 'farmer effect') is found in comparing step-1 and step-2 channels. In other words, the analyses show that both effects exist.

---

[8] Some of the extreme cases are traders who bought directly from the farmers to sell to consumers (step 2), although the production area was 4 to 5 hours away. According to the model, they were expected to buy their produce from wholesalers in the selling market (step 3). The other extreme cases were traders who bought from wholesalers in the selling market (step 3), while the production area was only half an hour to one hour away. According to the model they were expected to go to the production area to buy directly from the farmers (step 2).

[9] When the squared residuals are regressed on the predicted values heteroskedasticity is no longer a problem, but for the absolute residuals it still is.

[10] The outcome does not change when other values are entered for the consumer population of Daraja Mbili market (Appendix 8.2).

- The probability of encountering step-3 channels relative to step-2 channels increases as transport from the production area to the consumer centre takes more time. This was also found in the analysis step-1 and step-2 channels.
- The probability of encountering step-3 channels relative to step-2 channels is lower when the commodities concerned are leafy vegetables (with relatively poor keeping qualities). This was also found for the step-1 and step-2 channels.

Box 8.2. Analysis of step-2 versus step-3 channels

A. Logistic regression analysis

Total number of cases	2116
Number of selected cases	2116
Dependent variable (0,1)	STEP3
Model Chi-Square	885.8 (df=6, p=0.0000)
Correctly classified observations	76.5 % (t=24.4, p=0.000)
Number of extreme cases	27

Variables in the equation:	B	S.E.	Wald	Sig.
POPSIZE	0.0051	0.0008	40.39	0.0000
POPDENSITY	0.0757	0.0312	5.88	0.0153
TRANSTIME	0.8757	0.0490	319.57	0.0000
LEAVES	- 0.3410	0.1888	3.26	0.0708
TUBERS	- 0.0424	0.1365	0.10	0.7562
TURNOVER	- 0.0354	0.0042	71.32	0.0000
Constant	- 2.0053	0.1431	196.34	0.0000

Pearson correlation matrix

	STEP3	POPSIZE	POPDENS.	TRANST.	LEAVES	TUBERS
STEP3	1.00					
POPSIZE	0.37	1.00				
POPDENSITY	- 0.12	- 0.21	1.00			
TRANSTIME	0.53	0.52	- 0.25	1.00		
LEAVES	- 0.15	- 0.12	0.14	- 0.20	1.00	
TUBERS	0.05	0.06	- 0.04	0.07	- 0.16	1.00
TURNOVER	0.00	0.21	- 0.21	0.21	- 0.12	- 0.07

Separate bivariate regression analyses of the significant independent variables and predicted values with the squared residuals and the absolute residuals

	Squared residuals		Absolute residuals	
	t-value	p-value	t-value	p-value
POPSIZE	- 10.69	0.0000	- 17.76	0.0000
POPDENSITY	3.21	0.0014	4.14	0.0000
TRANSTIME	- 11.52	0.0000	- 20.59	0.0000
LEAVES	0.64	0.5217	1.23	0.2189
TURNOVER	- 1.89	0.0591	- 2.89	0.0039
Predicted values	- 9.33	0.0000	- 16.19	0.0000

continued on next page

Box 8.2 continued

B. Logistic regression analysis with inversions of POPSIZE and TRANSTIME

Total number of cases	2116
Number of selected cases	2116
Dependent variable (0,1)	STEP3
Model Chi-Square	545.6 (df=6, p=0.000)
Correctly classified observations	73.4 % (t=21.6, p=0.000)
Number of extreme cases	69

Variables in the equation:	B	S.E.	Wald	Sig.
INVPOPSIZE	- 0.2267	0.0882	6.60	0.0102
POPDENSITY	0.1239	0.0332	13.97	0.0002
INVTRANSTIME	- 1.9411	0.1083	320.97	0.0000
LEAVES	- 0.5822	0.1951	8.90	0.0028
TUBERS	- 0.0598	0.1235	0.23	0.6285
TURNOVER	- 0.0155	0.0032	23.11	0.0000
Constant	1.5067	0.1133	176.71	0.0000

Separate bivariate regression analyses of the significant independent variables and predicted values with the squared residuals and the absolute residuals

	Squared residuals		Absolute residuals	
	t-value	p-value	t-value	p-value
INVPOPSIZE	- 0.39	0.6984	- 2.94	0.0033
POPDENSITY	3.81	0.0001	0.54	0.5863
INVTRANSTIME	-1.79	0.0733	- 7.25	0.0000
LEAVES	0.70	0.4836	- 1.92	0.0547
TURNOVER	- 1.28	0.2015	0.47	0.6373
Predicted values	- 1.88	0.0604	5.77	0.0000

- The probability of encountering step-3 channels relative to step-2 channels decreases as the trader (in the present analysis a retailer) has a larger turnover.[11] This was not found in the step-1 to step-2 analysis.

The model can be used to estimate the probability of encountering more step-3 channels relative to step-2 channels for differing values of the significant independent variables. To do this we have to rewrite the equation again:

Prob(step 3) = $1 / (1 + e^{-z})$
Z = 1.5067 - 0.2267 / POPSIZE + 0.1239 x POPDENSITY - 1.9411 / TRANSTIME - 0.5822 x LEAVES
  - 0.0155 x TURNOVER

On the basis of this equation we can analyse the impact of changes in the value of one significant independent variable while the value of all others remains constant (ceteris paribus conditions).[12] Tables 8.4 to 8.8 show the p-values for different values of the

---

[11] All traders are retailers since only the combinations A, C, E, G and I of Figure 7.3 are included.

[12] All continuous variables are set at their median, and the dummy variable LEAVES is set at zero. According to the equation, the estimated probability of coming across a step-3 channel is 0.64 under

Table 8.4. The probability of encountering step-3 channels relative to step-2 channels for different values of POPSIZE, under ceteris paribus conditions (n=2116)

	minimum value	lower quartile	median	upper quartile	maximum value
POPSIZE*	0.400	9.026	13.202	163.928	281.044
p-value	0.51	0.64	**0.64**	0.65	0.65

* POPSIZE = population of the market centre (1000s)

Table 8.5. The probability of encountering step-3 channels relative to step-2 channels for different values of POPDENSITY, under ceteris paribus conditions (n=2116)

	minimum value	lower quartile	median	upper quartile	maximum value
POPDENSITY*	0.660	0.680	1.240	1.710	5.890
p-value	0.63	0.63	**0.64**	0.66	0.76

* POPDENSITY = population density of the rural hinterland (100s)

Table 8.6. The probability of encountering step-3 channels relative to step-2 channels for different values of TRANSTIME, under ceteris paribus conditions (n=2116)

	minimum value	lower quartile	median	upper quartile	maximum value
TRANSTIME*	0.5	1.0	2.0	4.0	12.0
p-value	0.09	0.41	**0.64**	0.75	0.80

* TRANSTIME = transport time in hours

Table 8.7. The probability of encountering step-3 channels relative to step-2 channels for different values of LEAVES, under ceteris paribus conditions (n=2116)

	minimum value	maximum value
LEAVES*	0	1
p-value	**0.64**	0.50

* LEAVES = dummy variable: 1 in the case of leafy vegetables

these circumstances. While all other variables remain constant, the value of one of the variables is successively changed to its minimum, lower quartile, upper quartile and maximum. The corresponding probability of finding step-3 channels are shown in Tables 8.4 to 8.8.

Table 8.8. The probability of encountering step-3 channels relative to step-2 channels for different values of TURNOVER, under ceteris paribus conditions (n=2116)

	minimum value	lower quartile	median	upper quartile	maximum value
TURNOVER	0.100	2.783	5.400	13.50	100.0
p-value	0.66	0.65	**0.64**	0.61	0.29

* TURNOVER = turnover of a trader (x 1000 Kenyan Shillings)

independent variables. The leftmost column in each table represents the minimum value, and the rightmost column the maximum value found in the sample presently being analysed. In comparing the tables it becomes clear that changes in transportation time have the greatest impact: the difference in p-value between the minimum and maximum value of TRANSTIME is 0.71. Changes in turnover have the second strongest impact (0.37), while changes in all other variables have a relatively limited impact (POPSIZE: 0.14; POPDENSITY: 0.13; LEAVES: 0.14).

The values in Table 8.4 show that changes in the value of POPSIZE are of particular influence when a market centre is small. Once it is 'big' (over 10,000 inhabitants), any extra increase in size of the consumer population does not further increase the probability of our coming across step-3 channels. Similarly, the impact of changes in TRANSTIME is greater when the time required to transport the commodity from the production area to the consumer centre is short (Table 8.6). If it is 'long' (over 4 hours), any additional increase in time scarcely increases the probability of finding step-3 channels. This non-linear impact of the variables POPSIZE and TRANSTIME is the result of their inversion.

The continuous variables POPDENSITY and TURNOVER do show linear effects (a positive effect for POPDENSITY and negative one for TURNOVER). In both cases the effect is especially strong for high values of the independent variables. Such high values are, however, not very common in the sample. This is shown by the upper quartiles presented in the fourth column of the tables. Only beyond these upper quartiles do changes become consequential.

Binomial logit of step-1 and step-3 channels
Box 8.3 shows the results for step-1 versus step-3 channels. All step-1 cases are included and a random sample is taken from the step-3 cases. The variables POPSIZE, TRANSTIME and TURNOVER are significant at the 0.001 level, and the variable LEAVES at the 0.05 level. The model shows a significant and high model chi-square and t-value for correctly classified observations. There is no reason to remove the extreme cases.[13] The correlations between most of the independent variables are generally low. The correlation between POPSIZE and TRANSTIME is relatively high (0.66), but not high enough to remove one of

---

[13] All extreme cases involve step-3 channels found in relatively small market centres for commodities that had to be transported over relatively small distances. There is no need to remove such cases from the sample.

the two variables from analysis. Heteroskedasticity is again a problem, and can be tackled as before by taking the inversions of POPSIZE and TRANSTIME. When we enter the inverted variables into the analysis, they become significant, and the variables LEAVES and TURNOVER remain significant (the former becomes significant at a higher level).[14]

Box 8.3. Analysis of step-1 versus step-3 channels

A. Logistic regression analysis

Total number of cases	748
Number of selected cases	748
Dependent variable (0,1)	STEP3
Model Chi-Square	574.7 (df=6, p=0.0000)
Correctly classified observations	85.3 % (t=19.2, p=0.000)
Number of extreme cases	16

Variables in the equation:	B	S.E.	Wald	Sig.
POPSIZE	0.0195	0.0030	42.14	0.0000
POPDENSITY	0.0832	0.0621	1.80	0.1800
TRANSTIME	2.1851	0.2247	94.59	0.0000
LEAVES	- 0.7616	0.3598	4.48	0.0343
TUBERS	- 0.0712	0.3033	0.06	0.8144
TURNOVER	- 0.0782	0.0147	28.24	0.0000
Constant	- 3.1710	0.3681	74.23	0.0000

Pearson correlation matrix

	STEP3	POPSIZE	POPDENS.	TRANST.	LEAVES	TUBERS
STEP3	1.00					
POPSIZE	0.55	1.00				
POPDENSITY	- 0.34	- 0.33	1.00			
TRANSTIME	0.62	0.66	- 0.39	1.00		
LEAVES	- 0.24	- 0.16	0.13	- 0.22	1.00	
TUBERS	0.05	0.09	0.01	0.03	- 0.17	1.00
TURNOVER	0.16	0.21	- 0.31	0.28	- 0.06	- 0.06

Separate bivariate regression analyses of the significant independent variables and predicted values with the squared residuals and the absolute residuals

	Squared residuals		Absolute residuals	
	t-value	p-value	t-value	p-value
POPSIZE	- 6.05	0.0000	- 10.07	0.0000
TRANSTIME	- 8.23	0.0000	- 12.95	0.0000
LEAVES	0.45	0.6493	0.54	0.5919
TURNOVER	- 3.03	0.0025	- 4.13	0.0000
Predicted values	- 6.85	0.0000	- 10.65	0.0000

continued on next page

---

[14] Similar results are obtained for other random samples from the step-3 cases, and for the alternative figures for the consumer population of Daraja Mbili (Appendix 8.3). The results of the analysis are therefore stable.

Box 8.3 continued

B. Logistic regression analysis with inversions of POPSIZE and TRANSTIME

Total number of cases	748
Number of selected cases	748
Dependent variable (0,1)	STEP3
Model Chi-Square	415.6 (df=6, p=0.0000)
Correctly classified observations	81.8 % (t=17.3, p=0.000)
Number of extreme cases	35

Variables in the equation:	B	S.E.	Wald	Sig.
INVPOPSIZE	- 0.4833	0.1442	11.22	0.0008
POPDENSITY	0.0341	0.0614	0.31	0.5784
INVTRANSTIME	- 2.3960	0.1986	145.58	0.0000
LEAVES	- 1.0638	0.3371	9.96	0.0016
TUBERS	0.0069	0.2648	0.00	0.9791
TURNOVER	- 0.0237	0.0078	9.11	0.0025
Constant	2.9059	0.2525	132.46	0.0000

Separate bivariate regression analyses of the significant independent variables and predicted values with the squared residuals and the absolute residuals

	Squared residuals		Absolute residuals	
	t-value	p-value	t-value	p-value
INVPOPSIZE	- 3.47	0.0006	- 4.78	0.0000
INVTRANSTIME	2.74	0.0064	- 0.20	0.9841
LEAVES	0.61	0.5436	- 0.22	0.8257
TURNOVER	0.98	0.3279	2.69	0.0073
Predicted values	- 2.06	0.0400	0.38	0.7009

The results of the analysis can again be expressed in a logit:

$$\log (\text{Prob(step 3)} / \text{Prob (step 1)}) = 2.9059 - 0.4833 / \text{POPSIZE} - 2.3960 / \text{TRANSTIME} - 1.0638 \times \text{LEAVES} - 0.0237 \times \text{TURNOVER}$$

The interpretation is as follows:

- The probability of encountering step-3 channels relative to step-1 channels increases as the consumer population of the market centre where the market place is located becomes larger. The same was found in the comparison of step-1 and step-2 channels, and step-2 and step-3 channels.

- The probability of encountering step-3 channels relative to step-1 channels increases as the transport from the production area to the consumer centre requires more time. This was also found for the step-1 and step-2 channels and the step-2 and step-3 channels.

- The probability of encountering step-3 channels relative to step-1 channels is lower when the commodities concerned are leafy vegetables (with relatively poor keeping qualities). This was also found in the analysis of step-1 and step-2 channels, and step-2 and step-3 channels.

Table 8.9. Significance and direction of independent variables per binomial analysis, for trade flows with known terminal markets

	step 2 versus step 1 (n=725)	step 3 versus step 2 (n=2116)	step 3 versus step 1 (n=748)
POPSIZE	+	+	+
(INVPOPSIZE)	(-)	(-)	(-)
POPDENSITY	-	+	not sign.
TRANSTIME	+	+	+
(INVTRANSTIME)	(-)	(-)	(-)
LEAVES	–	–	–
TUBERS	not sign.	not sign.	not sign.
TURNOVER	not sign.	–	–

- The probability of encountering step-3 channels relative to step-1 channels decreases as a trader (in the present analysis a retailer) has a larger turnover. This was also found in the comparison of step-2 and step-3 channels, but not for the step-1 and step-2 channels.

The variable POPDENSITY is not significant, in contrast with the analyses of step-1 versus step-2 channels, and step-2 versus step-3 channels. The variable TUBERS is not significant either, similar to the findings in the other subanalyses. Table 8.9 above summarizes the results of all the binomial analyses thus far.

Multinomial logit of step-1, step-2 and step-3 channels
Multinomial logit of all three types of marketing channels will now be performed in an attempt to confirm the results of the binomial logit analyses. Three groups are distinguished (step = 1, 2 and 3), which means that the model consists of two logit functions (see Section 8.1). Box 8.4 shows the results of the analysis. In part A, step=1 is taken as the point of departure. It gives us the coefficients for the logit functions Prob (step=2) / Prob (step=1) and Prob (step=3) / Prob (step=1). In part B, step=2 is taken as the point of departure, showing the coefficients for the logit functions Prob (step=1) / Prob (step=2) and Prob (step=3) / Prob (step=2). The first function provides no additional information, as the coefficients are exactly the opposite of the coefficients for Prob (step=2) / Prob (step=1). The function Prob (step=3) / Prob (step=2) does provide information not found by taking step=1 as the point of departure, namely, on the relationship between step-3 and step-2 channels.

The results of the multinomial logit analysis largely confirm the results of the separate binomial analyses. Table 8.10 summarizes the significance and direction of the independent variables. The only difference vis-a-vis the binomial analyses (see Table 8.9) is that INVPOPSIZE loses its significance for step-2 versus step-3 channels. This is most probably due to the smaller sample sizes which had to be used in the multinomial analysis. In the binomial analysis, all step-2 and step-3 channels were included, whereas in the multinomial analysis subsamples were taken from the step-2 and step-3 channels (34 per

Box 8.4. Multinomial logit analysis of step-1, step-2 and step-3 channels

Total number of cases	1115
Number of selected cases	1115
Dependent variable	STEP
Model Chi-Square	519.6 (df=12, p=0.0000)
Correctly classified observations	62.2 % (X^2=448.3, p=0.000)

A. Step=1 as point of departure

Variables in the equation:	B	S.E.	t-ratio	Sig.
coefficients for step=2				
INVPOPSIZE	- 0.5336	0.1085	- 4.92	0.0000
POPDENSITY	- 0.1148	0.0467	- 2.46	0.0139
INVTRANSTIME	- 0.4940	0.1377	- 3.59	0.0003
LEAVES	- 0.3785	0.2217	- 1.71	0.0877
TUBERS	0.0237	0.2164	0.11	0.9129
TURNOVER	0.0056	0.0064	0.87	0.3851
Constant	1.3054	0.2259	5.78	0.0000
coefficients for step=3				
INVPOPSIZE	- 0.5574	0.1366	- 4.08	0.0001
POPDENSITY	0.0303	0.0541	0.56	0.5763
INVTRANSTIME	- 2.6710	0.1956	- 13.65	0.0000
LEAVES	- 1.0297	0.3195	- 3.22	0.0013
TUBERS	- 0.0934	0.2414	- 0.39	0.6989
TURNOVER	- 0.0160	0.0072	- 2.21	0.0271
Constant	3.1057	0.2399	12.95	0.0000

B. Step=2 as point of departure

Variables in the equation:	B	S.E.	t-ratio	Sig.
coefficients for step=1				
INVPOPSIZE	0.5336	0.1085	4.92	0.0000
POPDENSITY	0.1148	0.0467	2.46	0.0139
INVTRANSTIME	0.4940	0.1377	3.59	0.0003
LEAVES	0.3785	0.2217	1.71	0.0877
TUBERS	- 0.0237	0.2164	- 0.11	0.9129
TURNOVER	- 0.0056	0.0064	- 0.87	0.3851
Constant	- 1.3054	0.2259	- 5.78	0.0000
coefficients for step=3				
INVPOPSIZE	- 0.0238	0.1442	- 0. 17	0.8673
POPDENSITY	0.1450	0.0516	2.81	0.0049
INVTRANSTIME	- 2.1771	0.1840	- 11.83	0.0000
LEAVES	- 0.6511	0.3079	- 2.12	0.0344
TUBERS	- 0.1170	0.2104	- 0.56	0.5781
TURNOVER	- 0.0216	0.0055	- 3.89	0.0001
Constant	1.8003	0.1910	9.42	0.0000

Table 8.10. Significance and direction of independent variables according to multinomial logit analysis, for trade flows with known terminal markets (n=1115)

	step=2 versus step=1	step=3 versus step=2	step=3 versus step=1
POPSIZE (INVPOPSIZE)	+ (-)	not sign.	+ (-)
POPDENSITY	-	+	not sign.
TRANSTIME (INVTRANSTIME)	+ (-)	+ (-)	+ (-)
LEAVES	–	–	–
TUBERS	not sign.	not sign.	not sign.
TURNOVER	not sign.	–	–

cent of each). Sampling was necessary in the latter analysis because the number of step-1 observations was far smaller than the number of step-2 and step-3 observations, and all three groups had to be approximately the same size (see Section 8.2). (Sampling was not necessary in the case of binomial analysis of step-2 and step-3 channels because step-1 channels were not included.) The smaller number of observations decreased the power of the multinominal analysis, probably causing the lack of significance of POPSIZE for the step-2 versus step-3 channels.

The variables POPDENSITY, INVTRANSTIME, LEAVES and TURNOVER remain significant for step-2 versus step-3 channels, notwithstanding the smaller size of the sample. Although their level of significance is lower than those in the binary analyses, it remains sufficiently high (see Boxes 8.2 and 8.4).

Both the binomial and multinomial analyses reveal that INVTRANSTIME is by far the most significant variable in the comparison of both step-2 and step-3 channels and step-1 and step-3 channels (see Wald statistics in Boxes 8.2 and 8.3, and t-ratios in Box 8.4). The result is different in the case of step-1 versus step-2 channels. INVPOPSIZE is the most significant variable there, in both the binomial and the multinomial analysis, with INVTRANSTIME second best (see Wald statistics in Box 8.1 and t-ratios in Box 8.4).

8.4. Testing the model using all trade flows, rural assembly markets excluded

The analyses so far have focused on trade flows which were known to be directed to local consumers. While this solved the problem of outgoing flows headed for unknown terminal markets, it could have biased the results of the analyses by excluding a proportion of the observed transactions in each market. Therefore, a second approach will now be added: analysing all trade flows, but excluding those markets where outgoing flows are known to be especially important (the rural assembly markets). If the results of both approaches prove similar, we may conclude that no major biases are present.

The procedures are the same as those followed in the previous section. Therefore, the results of the binomial analyses are reported in the text in a summary table (Table 8.11), and the complete binomial analyses can be found in Appendix 8.4.[15] The results of the binomial analyses of all trade flows, rural assembly markets excluded, coincide largely with the results of the binomial analyses of trade flows with known terminal markets as presented in Table 8.9 above. Two differences appear, and they can both be explained. The first concerns the variable POPDENSITY, which is no longer significant for step-1 and step-2 channels nor for step-2 and step-3 channels (it was already nonsignificant for step-1 and step-3 channels). There is an explanation for this. When the rural assembly markets were omitted from the sample to solve the problem of outgoing flows, this cased the variable POPDENSITY to lose part of its variation. The four rural assembly markets in Kisii District have relatively densely populated hinterlands in comparison to other rural markets and most urban markets in the sample (see Section 7.4, Table 7.5). Removing those market places leaves only three markets with rural population densities over 400 (Wundanyi, Kisii Municipality and Keroka), while all others have densities below 200. Thus, the discriminating value of POPDENSITY declines and the variable loses its significance.

The second difference between Tables 8.9 and 8.11 is the lack of significance of the variable TURNOVER for step-1 versus step-3 channels in the latter table. There is an explanation for this, too. In the analyses of trade flows with known terminal markets, professional wholesalers who sold only to other traders and not to consumers (pure

Table 8.11. Significance and direction of independent variables per binomial analysis, for all trade flows with rural assembly markets excluded

	step 1 versus step 2 (n=465)	step 2 versus step 3 (n=1689)	step 1 versus step 3 (n=448)
POPSIZE (INVPOPSIZE)	+ (-)	+ (-)	+ (-)
POPDENSITY	not sign.	not sign.	not sign.
TRANSTIME (INVTRANSTIME)	+ (-)	+ (-)	+ (-)
LEAVES	-	-	-
TUBERS	not sign.	not sign.	not sign.
TURNOVER	not sign.	–	not sign.

---

[15] The results of the multinomial analysis do not differ much from the binomial analyses, and are therefore not reported. As far as differences exist, they are again thought to be the result of reduced power of the multinomial analysis due to a smaller sample size (see Sections 8.2 and 8.3). The results of the binary analyses are generally stable. The only exception is the significance of the variable LEAVES. Its significance is not confirmed in all cases when new samples of the largest group are taken (see Appendix 8.4, step-1 versus step-2 channels and step-1 versus step-3 channels).

wholesalers) were omitted. These traders operate in step-3 channels and have relatively large turnovers.[16] They are included in the analysis of all trade flows. As a consequence, the average turnover of step-1 channels is no longer significantly higher than the average turnover of step-3 channels.[17] It can be concluded that comparing the turnover of step-1 and step-3 traders only makes sense when the analysis focuses on the retail level.

The presence of pure wholesalers in the sample does not disturb the analysis of step-2 versus step-3 channels to any great extent. The turnovers of step-3 traders are still significantly smaller than those of step-2 traders, but the level of significance is lower. The variable TURNOVER is significant at the 0.05 level for all trade flows (Appendix 8.4) and at the 0.01 level for trade flows with a known terminal market (see Box 8.2).

8.5. Conclusions with respect to the model

Three levels of vertical differentiation have been compared in this chapter: farmer -> consumer (step 1), farmer -> retailer -> consumer (step 2) and farmer -> wholesaler -> retailer -> consumer (step 3). A model was tested which was based on five hypotheses (see Section 7.2). The first hypothesis was:

A horticultural marketing channel is more vertically differentiated when the centre served by the channel has more inhabitants.

It has been shown that the probabilities of encountering (1) a step-2 channel relative to a step-1 channel, (2) a step-3 channel relative to a step-2 channel, and (3) a step-3 channel relative to a step-1 channel are all higher when a centre has more inhabitants. It can therefore be concluded that this hypothesis is fully accepted. Two qualifications should be made, however. First, an increase in the number of inhabitants particularly is the most influential when centres are small. As they get bigger (over 10,000 inhabitants), further population increase has only a limited effect on the probability of finding more differentiated marketing channels there. Second, in the case of step-1 versus step-2 channels, population size is the most important variable of all endogenous variables in the model (it has the highest significance). Such is not the case otherwise: transport time is the most important endogenous variable when it comes to step-2 versus step-3 and step-1 versus step-3 channels.

The second hypothesis was:

The vertical differentiation of a horticultural marketing channel that serves a population centre is influenced by the population density of that centre's rural hinterland.

This hypothesis is also accepted. The findings show that a high population density of the rural hinterland has a negative effect on the probability of encountering a step-2 channel

---

[16] The average turnover of the pure wholesalers was KSh 918 (n=72), compared to KSh 175 for other traders who operated in step-3 channels (n=520). Analysis of variance shows that the averages differ significantly, at p<0.001 when turnover is used as a dependent variable, and at p<0.01 for log-transformed turnovers (without this transformation the distributions are positively skewed).

[17] Besides pure professional wholesalers, pure farmer-wholesalers were also left out of the analysis of trade flows with known terminal markets. The latter respondents, however, were also excluded from the analysis of all trade flows, since they were found only in rural assembly markets.

relative to a step-1 channel. This can be explained in terms of the supply-side effect described in Section 7.2. A higher population density leads to the presence of more horticultural farmers in the hinterland. Some of them come to the market place to sell to consumers, thus increasing the importance of step-1 channels.

A high population density of the rural hinterland has a positive effect on the probability of encountering a step-3 channel relative to a step-2 channel. This involves the demand-side effect: a high population density of the rural hinterland increases the consumer population served by the market centre because some of the rural households lack self-sufficiency (and a larger consumer population increases the probability of finding more differentiated marketing channels).

A high population density of the rural hinterland has no significant effect on the probability of finding a step-3 channel relative to a step-1 channel. This suggests that in this case opposing supply- and demand effects balance each other out.

The third hypothesis was:

Horticultural marketing channels are more vertically differentiated when the transport from the production area to the market centre served by the channel takes more time.
The analyses have shown that the probability of encountering a step-2 channel relative to a step-1 channel, a step-3 channel relative to a step-2 channel, and a step-3 channel relative to a step-1 channel is greater when transport takes more time. The hypothesis is therefore accepted. It should be noted that an increase in transport time has the strongest impact on the probability of coming across more differentiated marketing channels in cases where production and consumption centres are relatively near to each other. If they are far apart (over 4 hours' drive), any further increase in transport time has a weaker effect.

The fourth hypothesis was:

Horticultural marketing channels are more vertically differentiated when the commodities traded have better keeping qualities.
The results of the analyses show that this hypothesis can only partly be accepted. Three types of horticultural produce were distinguished: commodities with poor keeping qualities (leafy vegetables), medium keeping qualities and good keeping qualities (tubers, roots and bulbs). It has been shown that a significant difference exists between commodities with poor keeping qualities and other horticultural commodities: the probability of finding a more differentiated marketing channel is smaller when dealing with leafy vegetables.[18] Contrary to this, however, no significant difference was found between commodities with good keeping qualities (tubers, roots and bulbs) and other horticultural commodities. This is most likely due to the absence of storage at any level in the marketing chain, and transport distances that never go beyond a two-day journey. As a consequence, the time between harvesting and selling to consumers is almost always less than one week, even in the case of tubers, roots and bulbs.

The fifth and final hypothesis was:

Horticultural marketing channels are less vertically differentiated when the retailers involved have a larger turnover.
This hypothesis was formulated only for step-2 versus step-3 channels and step-1 versus step-3 channels. The analysis has shown that, for these two combinations, the hypothesis is

---

[18] It must be further noted that differences are only significant at the 0.10 level.

indeed accepted. The probability of encountering a *more* differentiated marketing channel becomes *smaller* (and the probability of finding a *less* differentiated marketing channel becomes *greater*) when the turnover of the retailer involved is larger.

All in all, it can be concluded that the hypotheses on (1) the number of inhabitants of the market centre, (2) the population density of the rural hinterland, (3) the transport time of the commodities, and (4) the turnover of the traders have been fully accepted, whereas the hypothesis on the keeping qualities of the commodities was partially accepted.

9

Summary and Conclusions

This book deals with horticultural marketing channels in Kenya. In particular, it studies the structure and development of such channels and the actors and institutions that operate within them. The rationale of collecting wholesalers and the development of rural assembly markets is analysed, and the vertical differentiation of the marketing channels is investigated in depth to identify factors that explain the process. The chapter to follow provides a summary of the research findings and general conclusions.

9.1. Summary of the research findings

Horticulture in Kenya
Kenya belongs to the middle-income countries of Sub-Saharan Africa.[1] It has a fast growing population, of which an increasing proportion lives in towns. The majority of the rural population lives in the fertile central and western highlands, and along the shores of Lake Victoria and the Indian Ocean. Pressure on land is mounting in these areas. Horticulture occupies over ten per cent of Kenya's total arable land.

Almost all horticultural producers in Kenya are smallholders who cultivate vegetables, fruits and tubers for family consumption and for the domestic market.[2] The limited number of large-scale farms in the country concentrate mainly on production for export. Most of them use irrigation. Smallholder production is generally rainfed.

The production of horticultural commodities for the domestic market was studied here in detail in three districts, namely Nyandarua in the central highlands, Kisii in the highlands of western Kenya, and Taita Taveta halfway between the central highlands and the coast.[3] Nyandarua is one of the chief suppliers of potatoes and cabbages to the Nairobi market, a 100 km to 140 km journey from the production area. Kisii is a key producer of bananas. The fruits find their way to urban centres in western Kenya, the Rift Valley and the

---

[1] Section 3.1.
[2] Section 3.2.
[3] Section 3.3.

central highlands 500 km further up the road. Taita Taveta has two centres of horticultural production, the wet Taita Hills and the farmland around the Taveta Springs in the otherwise dry lowlands. The Taita Hills are a major supplier of cabbages, tomatoes, capsicums and other vegetables to the Mombasa market, 170 km away. The Taveta area produces bananas, tomatoes, onions, mangoes and citrus fruits for the same market. That trip is some 80 km longer.

In all four research areas (Taita and Taveta taken separately) commercial horticulture has evolved gradually among smallholders over the past decades. Favourable agro-ecological circumstances and increasing land shortage in the production areas, in combination with growing urban demand and improvement of interregional road networks, have fostered the development process.

Our farm survey found high participation in commercial horticulture, not only near all-weather roads but also in more isolated parts of the research areas.[4] Among those involved, horticulture was on average the most important source of cash revenues on the farm. It was a core activity for low-, middle- and high-income households.

It has been argued that commercial horticulture offers a more sustainable source of income to smallholders than do export crops (coffee, tea, cotton) or off-farm employment.[5] The sustainability of the horticultural enterprise is, however, threatened by its present success. The rise of commercial horticulture initially led to diversification in the agricultural sector. When it proved profitable, farmers began to ignore other agricultural crops. This is not necessarily a problem, since horticultural crops are extremely varied in nature. However, the research shows that farmers tend to limit themselves to a few horticultural commodities (such as potatoes in Nyandarua and bananas in Kisii and Taveta), making their farming as poorly diversified and as vulnerable as before.[6] Specialization and lack of crop rotation lead to severe pest and disease problems. The problems are exacerbated by failing crop protection.

Horticultural marketing channels in Kenya

Once the commodities are produced they are brought into the marketing system. This system consists of marketing channels which are part of the marketing structures that operate within a marketing environment. The Kenyan environment is in many aspects quite similar to the marketing environment of horticultural marketing structures in other Sub-Saharan African countries.[7] The political and legal environment is weak. Government interventions, which until recently characterized the marketing of grains, are absent in the case of horticultural commodities. Vegetables, fruits and tubers are not regarded as strategic. Moreover, their perishability makes interventions risky, and requires cold storage facilities in the event of off-season storage. The demographic and economic environments have a greater impact on the horticultural marketing structures than the political and legal environment has. The size of the urban population, the degree of self-sufficiency of rural households, and the purchasing power of rural and urban households are all determinants of the size of the potential

---

4   Section 3.4.
5   Section 3.4.
6   Section 3.4.
7   Section 4.1.

consumer population. The physical environment (infrastructure) determines whether these consumers can actually be reached. The socio, cultural and ethnic environment influences the diet of consumers, as well as the characteristics of market intermediaries.

A wide variety of marketing intermediaries operate in the Kenyan horticultural marketing channels. Multiplicity of channels is quite common.[8] Marketing structures may encompass a wide range of channels.

Traders (merchants) are the most important marketing intermediaries because they take title to the produce. Different types of traders operate at different levels in the marketing channels and in different types of market places.[9] Farmer-traders and professional retailers serve local consumers in periodic retail markets in rural areas. Farmer-traders and assembling traders sell in rural assembly markets to wholesalers from elsewhere. Professional wholesalers in daily urban markets sell to professional retailers, who in turn sell in the same or in another daily urban market to consumers. The professional wholesalers may collect the produce themselves or act as distributing wholesalers, using collecting wholesalers as intermediaries.

The distinction between wholesale traders and retail traders, and between wholesale markets and retail markets, is rather artificial. One and the same trader or market may serve both traders and consumers. Traders' assortments give no clue to the type of trade (wholesale or retail). This is because the assortment of wholesalers and retailers is usually limited. The assorting function is relatively unimportant to both of them.

Our trade survey found that by far the majority of the horticultural traders are women.[10] Male traders appear only when remunerations are relatively high, as is the case in wholesale trade, or in retail trade carried out in daily retail markets of large urban centres. With regard to ethnic background, age and marital status, the composition of the trader population in a market place usually corresponds more or less to the composition of the general population in the region where the market is located.

The trade survey suggests that the majority of the horticultural traders derive low to moderate daily and monthly incomes from their trading activities. Three small groups have high incomes. Two of them concentrate on the domestic market, namely the collecting wholesalers, and those distributing wholesalers who operate in large wholesale markets (such as the Kongowea wholesale market in Mombasa). Horticultural export traders constitute a third group of relatively wealthy traders.

The horticultural export traders are a world apart.[11] They run multimillion companies which have various offices (e.g. in the production area, in the centre of Nairobi and at the airport), and which deal with transport, storage, sales, and promotion. They produce on large-scale farms, use smallholders as contract farmers, or combine both methods.

The Kenyan export assortment differs extensively from the assortment in the domestic market. This has the advantage that exports do not cause scarcity or inflate prices in the domestic market. The disadvantage is that exporters cannot sell unexportable produce in the local market either. The traders need a solid financial basis to cope with financial losses.

---

8   Section 4.2.
9   Section 5.2.
10   Section 5.2.
11   Section 5.4.

In addition they try to reduce risks through vertical integration and coordination (also beyond the export stage), diversification and flexibility.

In addition to traders, marketing intermediaries who do not take title to the produce operate in the horticultural marketing channels.[12] In the production areas, **purchasing agents** work on behalf of collecting wholesalers. They possess expert power because of their knowledge of the local situation. They reduce collection costs by identifying produce for sale, carrying out the negotiations and streamlining the process. In return they receive a commission. Brokers, who operate on the same basis, are less common. They are found, for instance, in the Nairobi wholesale market. A special kind of broker that operates in the Mombasa wholesale market is the auctioneer.

Porters and transporters are hired as **facilitating intermediaries** to get the produce from the farm to the destination market. The transporters use donkeys, tractors, handcarts, minibuses, coaches, and small and large trucks. In the export trade, cargo planes, airliners, and sometimes cargo vessels may be used (the latter only in combination with refrigerated containers).

Important financial facilitators in domestic horticultural trade are savings and credit associations. Commercial banks are relatively unimportant, because most payments are made in cash. The banks are reluctant to issue loans to horticultural traders because of their lack of collateral and their high trade risks. Other facilitating intermediaries such as warehouse firms, marketing research companies, insurance companies and advertising agencies are unimportant to horticultural traders (export traders being the exception to the rule for the first three).

Horticultural **marketing cooperatives**, marketing institutions which might best be classified as selling agents, are rare in Kenya.[13] Reasons for this are a general reluctance on the part of farmers to participate in any kind of group marketing as a result of negative experiences with cooperative structures, as well as availability of alternative marketing channels. Case studies of the Horticultural Cooperative Union and the horticultural marketing activities of the Kinangop Agricultural Cooperative society have shown that farmers' reluctance to participate in new initiatives is understandable. Both organizations failed due to mismanagement and the lack of successful marketing strategies. The Union thought it could improve the efficiency and equity in domestic and export marketing channels to the benefit of farmers. It lost the battle with private traders due to its bureaucratic payment procedures and inflexible commission rates. The Kinangop society, which was entirely equity-based, just copied the activities of collecting wholesalers, but without the required knowledge of the marketing system. However, one further case study of the Taita Horticultural Produce Cooperate Society has shown that cooperative marketing does not always fail. The Taita HPC has succeeded by bringing something new: improved service output (effectiveness) of the marketing channel through supplying superior quality produce. Other core elements of its strategy are the market-oriented planning of harvests, and direct access to retailers.

One more market intermediary needs be mentioned, **the processor**. Although by far the largest portion of the Kenyan horticultural commodities are marketed fresh, some are

---

12   Section 5.2.
13   Section 5.3.

processed before reaching consumers in Kenya or elsewhere. Kenya has canning, juice extraction and jam making factories.[14] Major products are tinned pineapples and tinned French beans for export, and jams, ketchup, sauces and tinned juices for the domestic market. In addition to large commercial firms, small cottage industries are involved, producing fresh fruit juices among other commodities. Many factories have experienced difficulties in surviving, especially when they produce for export. Case studies of Pan African Vegetable Products Ltd and of Bawazir Fruit Processors Ltd have shown that the quality of the Kenyan raw materials is poor, that farmers prefer to sell in the fresh market where they receive higher prices, that production costs are inflated by poor infrastructure and high costs of packing materials, and that competition in the world market is lethal.[15]

The collection stage of the marketing system deserves special attention because it is the most problematic and least understood part. African politicians like to question the rationale of **collecting wholesalers**. The mediation of these traders can, however, be efficient for distributing wholesalers and farmers. They allow distributing wholesalers to focus entirely on their urban clienteles. This is especially important in large urban centres where wholesale and retail markets operate six days a week. For such distributing wholesalers, being absent has its costs in terms of lost revenues and customer relations.[16]

Collecting wholesalers can also be efficient intermediaries for farmers, as shown by a case study of the collecting potato trade between Kinangop (Nyandarua) and Nairobi.[17] Farmers who carry the potatoes to the Nairobi wholesale market by themselves face costs with regard to transport, storage, finance, risk taking, information, negotiation and payment (the last three being transaction costs). Especially the high average costs in relation to transport, finance and information make reliance on collecting wholesalers more economical for farmers than going to Nairobi themselves.[18] The wholesale traders are able to perform these functions more efficiently because they have higher turnovers. They are in business throughout the season or year, which allows them to develop customer relations with transporters, accumulate knowledge about price developments, and level out high start-up costs.

Even if farmer's costs in relation to transport, finance and information are reduced through a credit scheme and an improved market information system, the majority are still better off selling their produce to collecting wholesalers, because their supply is simply too small. Only by operating as a group could they potentially achieve the same economies of scale as the traders.

Farmers and collecting wholesalers in Kinangop usually trade with each other at or near the farms, whereas in Kisii such transactions are concentrated in **rural assembly markets**. The difference can be explained in terms of transport and information costs. According to the findings of the farm and trade surveys, assembly markets tend to be found in surplus areas where farms are poorly accessible compared to market places, and where supply concentration is low.[19] Under these circumstances traders who assemble produce at

---

14 Section 5.5.
15 Section 5.5.
16 Section 6.1.
17 Section 6.2.
18 Section 6.2, Table 6.1 and Figure 6.1.
19 Section 6.4.

farms face high transport costs, and the development of an assembly market will reduce their costs.[20] It will also increase the efficiency of the marketing channel, because farmers who take their produce to the market use low-cost means of transport in comparison to traders who go to the farms. To the farmers, the assembly market ensures a price that more or less reflects current supply and demand conditions, thus reducing their costs of imperfect information.

Under certain circumstances, dual systems or first- and second-level assembly markets exist.[21] In Taita and Taveta these circumstances are specific infrastructural conditions and the presence of specialized transporters.

It is expected that assembly markets will gain in importance (Nyandarua, Taita), or at least maintain their current importance (Kisii, Taveta) for the coming decade.[22] Only in the long run, if a search for improved quality control leads to vertical coordination and integration in domestic marketing channels, may assembly markets become less important.

A few final comments on horticultural marketing channels in Kenya can be made, employing keywords from structure-conduct-performance analysis.[23] In the domestic market, buyer and seller concentrations are generally low, except in less accessible production areas without assembly markets where a limited number of collecting wholesalers deal with individual farmers at the farm gate. Financial constraints (lack of formal credit) and transport constraints (lack of trucks for hire in production areas) hamper the entry of new wholesalers, thus reducing competition at this stage.

The level of competition among traders in the domestic market is high. Price cartels and deliberate restrictions on traded quantities were not found during the trade survey. Any price agreements among traders would hardly hamper competition anyway because of the absence of standardized selling units.

In the export market, capital requirements are an important entry barrier, as is cumulated experience. The number of exporters is limited, but mutual competition is high. Competition in the world market is severe and still mounting. Customer relations are important both towards suppliers and buyers. Up-to-date price information is accessible to exporters, but not to contract farmers and independent smallholder producers.

Lack of up-to-date price information is also a problem to horticultural farmers in the domestic market, especially when they live in isolated production areas without assembly markets. They depend for their sales on collecting wholesalers who come to the farms, while receiving their price information from these same traders.

If farm-gate prices are low, this does not necessarily mean that profit margins of traders are high. Farm-gate prices are affected by high physical losses in the marketing process. The losses result from poorly developed rural market places and rural roads, and a lack of appropriate and affordable packing materials. Farm-gate prices are also affected by a strong seasonality of supply.

---

20 Section 6.7.
21 Sections 6.5 and 6.6.
22 Section 6.7.
23 Section 5.6.

Vertical differentiation of horticultural marketing channels

The horticultural sector in Kenya can be characterized as an emerging economy.[24] One of the characteristics of such an economy is that marketing channels directed to the domestic market are still in a process of vertical differentiation. A model has been developed here to find out which factors determine this process.[25] It distinguishes three steps of differentiation: (1) farmer -> consumer, (2) farmer -> retailer -> consumer, and (3) farmer -> wholesaler -> retailer -> consumer. The third step also includes channels with more than one wholesale level. The first two explanatory factors entered into the model are the number of inhabitants of the market centre where the surveyed market place is located and the population density of the rural hinterland. They are indicators of the consumer population served by the marketing channel. Other factors are transport time of the commodity from producer to consumer, keeping qualities of the commodity, and turnover of the trader concerned.

The unit of analysis is the transaction.[26] It refers to a trader, a commodity handled by this trader, a buying-and-selling combination in relation to this commodity, and the transport time in relation to this buying-and-selling combination. Each transaction is related to one of the three differentiation steps in the model.

The trade survey registered 3776 transactions. Not all of them are used in the present analysis. Some transactions represent channels that are not directed to the local consumer population but to unknown consumer populations elsewhere. These transactions have to be removed because the size of the consumer population is one of the explanatory variables in the model. Two approaches are applied. First, all surveyed market places are included in the analysis, but transactions with unknown terminal markets are removed from the sample, leaving 2474 transactions. Second, all transactions are included, but rural assembly markets, where outgoing flows are known to be important, are removed. This leaves 2682 transactions. The results of both approaches should ideally be similar. The analyses show that this is indeed the case.

Five hypotheses have been formulated here, which, on the basis of logit analyses, were all at least partly accepted. The first hypothesis proposes that a horticultural marketing channel is more differentiated when the centre served by the channel has more inhabitants. In general, the history of Sub-Saharan Africa shows a clear relation between urbanization and urban growth on the one hand and the development of food marketing channels on the other.[27] More specifically, the growth of the number of inhabitants of a centre increases the market output which in turn allows traders economies of scale when they differentiate.[28] According to the analysis, the relation between the number of inhabitants and the structure of the channels that serve them is non-linear: an increase in population has the strongest impact on the probability of encountering more differentiated channels when the centre is relatively small.[29]

---

[24] Section 7.1.
[25] Section 7.2.
[26] Section 7.3.
[27] Chapter 2.
[28] Section 7.2.
[29] Chapter 8.

The second hypothesis proposes that the differentiation of a horticultural marketing channel that serves a population centre is influenced by the population density of this centre's rural hinterland. The analysis shows that the effect is negative when step-2 and step-1 channels are compared. A higher rural population density implies more horticultural farmers, some of whom come to sell to consumers in the centre's market (a supply-side effect). The effect is positive when step-3 and step-2 channels are compared. A higher rural population density implies more rural consumers who depend on the centre's market (a demand-side effect).

The third hypothesis proposes that horticultural marketing channels are more differentiated when the transport from the production area to the market centre that is served by the channel requires more time. In general, the history of Sub-Saharan Africa shows a clear relation between transport conditions and food marketing structures.[30] More specifically, when commodities come from further away, and therefore require more transport time, this increases the opportunities of differentiating traders to gain from economies of scale in the process.[31] According to the analysis, the relation is again non-linear: the impact of an increase in transport time on the probability of encountering more differentiated channels decreases when transport time is already substantial.[32]

The fourth hypothesis proposes that horticultural marketing channels are more differentiated when the commodities traded have better keeping qualities. Every transaction takes time, but that time is less precious for commodities with good keeping qualities than for highly perishable ones. According to the analysis, the hypothesis is only accepted when leafy vegetables are compared with other horticultural commodities. The extremely poor keeping qualities of leafy vegetables imply less differentiated channels.

The fifth and final hypothesis proposes that horticultural marketing channels are less differentiated when the retailers involved have larger turnovers. Farmers who retail their produce (step-1) and professional retailers who buy from farmers (step-2) are expected to, and found to, have larger turnovers than retailers who buy from wholesalers (step-3). The latter have to rely on wholesalers because their selling quantities are too small to make their own transport from the production area to the market centre profitable.

Policy recommendations

On the basis of the problems of the horticultural sector,[33] the performance of the horticultural market[34] and the differentiation model presented above, policy recommendations have been formulated. These are presented in Appendix 9.1. They are intended for both private marketing intermediaries and the Kenyan government. At the production stage they relate to extension, credit and inputs. At the marketing stage they concern the exchange functions (recommendations on market infrastructure, group marketing), physical functions (road infrastructure, transport, cold storage) and facilitating functions (credit, packing, standardization, information systems).

---

[30] Chapter 2.
[31] Section 7.2.
[32] Chapter 8.
[33] Section 3.4.
[34] Section 5.6.

9.2. General conclusions

The marketing channel approach has been used here to study the trade of horticultural commodities in Kenya. This makes the study more holistic than a study of market places or traders as such. It is a kind of systems approach: all marketing steps from producer to consumer are taken as a system.

The marketing channel approach has allowed us to analyse efficiencies of the marketing process. We were able to calculate the costs of all marketing functions that have to be performed at different stages of the marketing channel. In this way, we could explain why collecting wholesalers are important, and indeed the best alternative, for potato farmers in Kinangop, Nyandarua District.

Through the channel approach we were also in a better position to understand the dynamics of the marketing process. It helped explain, for instance, the development of rural assembly markets for horticultural commodities. Consideration of the transport and information costs of farmers and wholesalers at the collection stage of the marketing channel showed when and where these markets are expected to emerge.

In particular, the channel approach made it possible to explain the number of trade levels observed in the marketing system (the degree of vertical differentiation of the channels). According to the findings, two of the principle explanatory factors are population size of the consumer centre, and transport time from producer to consumer. Interestingly, these two factors also feature in gravity models used in regional marketing analysis.[35] Such models were developed to explain not the structure of marketing channels, but the attractiveness of a city's shopping area. The present findings suggest that gravity models may also contribute to a better understanding of the structure of marketing channels in developing countries.

The vertical differentiation model proposed here helps to anticipate future developments in the marketing system in relation to expected trends in the demographic marketing environment (rural and urban population concentrations) and in the physical one (infrastructure). This is in contrast with approaches such as structure-conduct-performance analysis which usually do not go beyond the present state of affairs.[36]

The model used here will most likely have relevance not only for Kenya but also for other emerging economies in Sub-Saharan Africa. The horticultural marketing system in Kenya is further developed than those in many other African countries as a result of large urban demand, high pressure on arable land, and a relatively well developed road system. Many African countries are heading in the same direction, however. The model can be an aid to understanding how horticultural marketing channels in these countries are likely to develop.

The present analysis has shown that marketing channel theory, which has been applied extensively in developed countries, is of great relevance to the developing world as well. The analysis has focused on horticultural commodities, but studies on the marketing of other food crops such as grains can benefit from the same approach. These studies are

---

[35] Section 4.5.
[36] One of the criticisms of SCP analysis put forward by Janssen & Van Tilburg (1997) concerns its limited predictive power (see Section 5.6, Box 5.1).

needed now that state-controlled marketing is no longer the issue, and policymakers have put their faith in the free market.

Appendices

Appendix 2.1:
Causes of rural-urban migration in post-independence Africa

Becker et al. (1986) and UN (1989) identify a wide range of economic and non-economic causes of rural-urban migration in post-independence Africa. Among the economic factors are prices deliberately skewed against the agricultural sector (the urban bias), and a gap between urban and rural expected wages. A factor with both economic and environmental aspects is the rising population pressure on natural resources, as shown by indicators such as accelerating soil erosion, soil degradation and outright destruction, often associated with overstocking and overgrazing, and the breakdown of indigenous farming systems and smallholdings.

Geographical factors of rural-urban migration are the proximity of most urban centres to densely populated rural areas, and the short distances between villages and medium-size towns. The latter is said to stimulate stepwise migration (village - small town - big town), although there is no consensus on this.

Social factors are marital instability, short-term cash needs for dowries, and access to education and consumer goods and services in urban centres. In addition, the ease of adjusting to the urban milieu due to a support system provided by relatives is said to facilitate rural-urban migration.

Psychological factors are a desire for freedom from control of the older generation, the importance of prestige and the image of the city, and finally, distorted perceptions of the likelihood of success in the city. The ultimate goal of the rural youth, schooled in the formal education system, is the acquisition of a 'white collar' job in the city (Rempel & Todaro, 1973).

Political factors in some countries are rural insecurity and the expelling of nationals, mostly petty traders, of one country from another. Rural insecurity was experienced in countries such as Zimbabwe, Mozambique, Angola, Sudan, Liberia and Burundi. A mass exodus followed Ghana's Aliens Compliance Order in 1969 and Nigeria's Aliens Quit Order of 1983.

Additional factors in the rural-urban migration of women are the weak social position of childless women in traditional cultures, the desire to escape responsibilities for cultivation, the stifling social position imposed on women by men in villages, and better chances of finding a suitable partner in cities.

Appendix 3.1:
Commercial horticultural crops in Kenya[1]

Common Name	Botanical Name	Utilization
Apple	Pyrus malus (Rosaceae)	Fruit
Artichoke (Globe)	Cynara scolymus (Compositae)	Vegetable
Artichoke (Jerusalem)	Helianthus tuberosus (Compositae)	Vegetable
Asparagus	Asparagus officininalis (Liliaceae)	Vegetable
Aubergine	Solanum melongena (Solanaceae)	Vegetable
Avocado	Persea americana (Lauraceae)	Fruit
Banana (Sweet)	Musa sapientum (Musaceae)	Fruit
Banana (Cooking)	Musa paradisiaca (Musaceae)	Vegetable
Bean (Broad)	Vicia faba (Leguminosae)	Vegetable
Bean (Common or Kidney)	Phaseolus vulgaris (Leguminosae)	Vegetable
Beetroot	Beta vulgaris (Chenopodiaceae)	Vegetable
Breadfruit	Artocarpus altilis (Moraceae)	Fruit
Brinjal	Solanum melongena (Solanaceae)	Vegetable
Broccoli	Brassica oleracea var. botrytis (Cruciferae)	Vegetable
Brussels sprout	Brassica oleracea var. gemmifera (Cruciferae)	Vegetable
Cabbage	Brassica oleracea var. capitata (Cruciferae)	Vegetable
Carrot	Daucus carota (Umbelliferae)	Vegetable
Cape gooseberry	Physalis peruviana (Solanaceae)	Fruit
Cassava	Manihot esculenta (Euphorbiaceae)	Vegetable
Cauliflower	Brassica oleracea var. botrytis (Cruciferae)	Vegetable
Celery	Apium graveolens var. dulce (Umbelliferae)	Vegetable
Cherimoya	Annona cherimola (Annonaceae)	Fruit
Chora	Vigna unguiculata (Leguminosae)	Vegetable

---

[1]   Based on Kokwaro (1979). Cut flowers are not included in the list.

Common Name	Botanical Name	Utilization
Choyote	Sechium edule (Cucurbitaceae)	Vegetable
Cluster bean	Cyamopsis tetragonoloba (Leguminosae)	Vegetable
Coconut	Cocos nucifera (Palmae)	Edible nut
Coco yam (new)	Xanthosoma sagittifolium (Araceae)	Vegetable
Coco yam (old)	Colocasia esculenta (Araceae)	Vegetable
Cress (Water)	Nasturtium officinale (Cruciferae)	Vegetable
Cucumber	Cucumis sativus (Cucurbitaceae)	Vegetable
Dhania	Coriandrum sativum (Umbelliferae)	Pot herb
Dudi	Lagenaria siceraria (Cucurbitaceae)	Vegetable
Eggplant	Solanum melongena (Solanaceae)	Vegetable
Endive	Cichorium endivia (Compositae)	Vegetable
Fennel	Foeniculum vulgare (Umbelliferae)	Pot herb
Fig	Ficus carica (Moraceae)	Fruit
Galka	Luffa cylindrica (Cucurbitaceae)	Vegetable
Garlic	Allium sativum (Amaryllidaceae)	Pot herb
Gherkin	Cucumis sativus (Cucurbitaceae)	Vegetable
Golden grenadilla	Passiflora ligularis (Passifloraceae)	Fruit
Grape	Vitis vinifera (Vitaceae)	Fruit
Grapefruit	Citrus paradisi (Rutuceae)	Fruit
Guar	Cyamopsis tetragonoloba (Leguminosae)	Vegetable
Guava	Psidium guajava (Myrtaceae)	Fruit
Horseradish tree	Moringa oleifera (Moringaceae)	Vegetable
Jackfruit	Artocarpus heterophyllus (Moraceae)	Fruit
Jambolan	Eugenia cuminii (Myrtaceae)	Fruit
Kale	Brassica oleracea var. acephala (Cruciferae)	Vegetable
Karela	Momordica charantia (Cucurbitaceae)	Vegetable
Kohlrabi	Brassica oleracea var. (Cruciferae)	Vegetable
Leek	Allium ampeloprasum var. porrum (Amaryllidaceae)	Vegetable
Lemon	Citrus limon (Rutaceae)	Fruit
Lettuce	Lactuca sativa (Compositae)	Vegetable
Lime	Citrus aurantifolia (Rutaceae)	Fruit

Common Name	Botanical Name	Utilization
Loquat	Eriobotrya japonica (Rosaceae)	Fruit
Macadamia	Macadamia ternifolia (Proteaceae)	Edible Nut
Mandarin	Citrus reticulata (Rutaceae)	Fruit
Mango	Mangifera indica (Anacardiaceae)	Fruit
Marrow	Cucurbita pepo (Cucurbitaceae)	Vegetable
Methi	Trigonella foenum-graecum (Leguminosae)	Pot herb
Melon (Canteloupe)	Cucumis melo (Cucurbitaceae)	Fruit
Melon (Water)	Citrillus lanatus (Cucurbitaceae)	Fruit
Mint (Round-leaved)	Mentha rotundifolia (Labiatae)	Pot herb
Mulberry	Morus spp. (Moraceae)	Fruit
Mushroom	Psalliota campestris (Basidiomycetes)	Vegetable
Mzambarau	Eugenia cuminii (Myrtaceae)	Fruit
Okra	Hibiscus esculentus (Malvaceae)	Vegetable
Onion	Allium cepa var. cepa. (Amaryllidaceae)	Vegetable
Orange	Citrus sinensis (Rutaceae)	Fruit
Papaya or Pawpaw	Carica papaya (Caricaceae)	Fruit
Parsley	Petroselinum crispum (Umbelliferae)	Vegetable
Parsnip	Pastinaca sativa (Umbelliferae)	Vegetable
Passion fruit	Passiflora edulis (Passifloraceae)	Fruit
Pea	Pisum sativum (Leguminosae)	Vegetable
Pea (Pigeon)	Cajanus cajan (Leguminosae)	Vegetable
Peach	Prunus persica (Rosaceae)	Fruit
Pear	Pyrus communis (Rosaceae)	Fruit
Pepper (Red)	Capsicum frutescens (Solanaceae)	Spice
Pepper (Sweet)	Capsicum annum (Solanaceae)	Vegetable
Pineapple	Ananas comosus (Bromeliaceae)	Fruit
Plantain	Musa paradisiaca (Musaceae)	Vegetable
Plum	Prunus salicina (Rosacceae)	Fruit
Pomegranate	Punica granatum (Punicaceae)	Fruit
Pomelo	Citrus grandis (Rutaceae)	Fruit
Potato	Solanum tuberosum (Solanaceae)	Vegetable
Pumpkin	Cucurbita maxima (Cucurbitaceae)	Vegetable
Radish	Raphanus sativus (Cruciferae)	Vegetable
Radish (Moolee)	Raphanus sativus var. hortensis (Cruciferae)	Vegetable
Rape	Brassica napus (Cruciferae)	Vegetable

Common Name	Botanical Name	Utilization
Rhubarb	Rheum rhaponticum (Polygonaceae)	Dessert, Vegetable
Savoy	Brassica oleracea var. capitata (Cruciferae)	Vegetable
Shallot	Allium cepa var. aggregatum (Amaryllidaceae)	Pot herb
Snake Gourd	Trichosanthes cucumerina (Cucurbitaceae)	Vegetable
Spinach	Spinacia oleracea (Chenopodiaceae)	Vegetable
Spinach (Amaranthus)	Amaranthus spp. (Amaranthaceae)	Vegetable
Spinach (Beet)	Beta vulgaris (Chenopodiaceae)	Vegetable
Spring Onion	Allium cepa var. aggregatum (Amaryllidaceae)	Pot herb
Strawberry	Fragaria vesca (Rosaceae)	Fruit
Sweet corn	Zea mays var. saccharata (Gramineae)	Vegetable
Sweet potato	Ipomoea batatas (Convolvulaceae)	Vegetable
Saragwo	Moringa oleifera (Moringaceae)	Vegetable
Suran	Amorphophallus campanulatus (Araceae)	Vegetable
Tangerine	Citrus reticulata (Rutaceae)	Fruit
Tindora	Coccinia grandis (Cucurbitaceae)	Vegetable
Tomato	Lycopersicon esculentum (Solanaceae)	Fruit, Vegetable
Tomato (Cherry)	Lycopersicon esculentum var. cerasiformae	Fruit, Vegetable
Tomato Tree	Cyphomandra betacea (Solanaceae)	Fruit, Vegetable
Turia	Luffa acutangula (Cucurbitaceae)	Vegetable
Turnip	Brassica rapa (Crucifereae)	Vegetable
Val	Lablab purpureus (Leguminosae)	Vegetable
Valor	Lablab purpureus vat. benghalensis	Vegetable
Yam	Dioscorea spp. (Dioscoreaceae)	Vegetable
Youngberry	Rubus strigosus (Rosaceae)	Fruit

Appendix 3.2:
Production of cut flowers and cut foliage in Kenya, 1987-1992 (Hectares)

Type of flower	1987	1988	1989	1990	1991	1992
Spray Carnations	120.0	145.0	157.0	182.0	220.0	275.0
Standard Carnations	35.5	50.0	18.5	53.0	27.0	42.0
Roses	16.0	25.0	21.0	27.0	47.0	80.0
Statice (Limonium spp)	128.0	197.0	209.0	100.5	118.5	112.0
Alstroemeria	48.0	55.0	68.0	82.0	50.0	86.0
Tuberose	10.0	4.5	6.0	2.0	10.0	15.0
Arabicum (O. Saundersiae)	35.0	25.0	14.0	14.8	10.0	30.0
Molucella	12.0	7.0	5.3	1.5	7.5	15.0
Orchids (Cymbidium)	2.0	2.0	2.5	2.5	2.5	4.0
Ornithogalum (O. thysoides)	35.0	15.0	17.3	15.0	15.0	15.0
Gypsophila	5.5	2.0	1.0	1.1	5.0	6.0
Liatris	7.0	-	1.7	1.8	7.5	*
Lilies (Lilium spp)	3.0	-	3.5	3.6	2.5	7.0
Arum Lilies	5.5	5.0	1.3	2.5	2.5	4.0
Delphinium	86.0	38.0	55.0	12.0	*	20.0
Euphorbia Marginata	25.0	25.0	6.0	-	*	*
Dill	12.0	5.0	-	-	*	*
Ammi Majus	20.0	3.5	7.0	NR	35.0	33.0
Solidaster	-	15.0	19.0	12.0	2.8	26.0
Chrysanthemum	25.0	20.0	21.0	8.7	8.7	9.0
Cut foliage	-	15.0	5.0	5.8	16.0	30.0
Bulphleurum	-	10.0	-	-	-	40.0
Others	-	-	37.7	10.7	50.0	55.0
Total	630.5	664.0	676.8	538.5	638.3	860.0

Source: Nyamiaka, 1995.
*Included in Others
NR = Not Recorded

Appendix 3.3:
Some background information on Nyandarua, Kisii, Taita and Taveta

	Nyandarua	Kisii	Taita	Taveta
Area suitable for horticulture (sq km)	2,435	1,649	230	510
Altitude (m)	2400-3000	1500-2200	1400-1700	600-1000
Rainfall (mm)	850-1600	1400-2100	900-1200	480-700
Long rains	March - June	Feb. - June	March - May	March - May
Short rains	July - Dec.	July - Jan.	Oct. - Dec.	Nov. - Dec.
Soil type	deep, imperfectly to well-drained, clay loam / clay + humic topsoil	deep to very deep, well-drained clay + thick humic topsoil	moderately deep, well-drained clay loam + humic topsoil	very deep, well-drained clay loam / clay
Population density (persons/sq km)				
- Lowest density	51	330	83	29
- Average density	158	554	226	66
- Highest density	383	1068	705	393

Source: CBS, 1994b; Jaetzold and Schmidt, 1983.
Notes: All figures refer to the areas suitable for horticulture. The figures on population density refer to 1989, the year of the latest census.

Appendix 3.4:

Average annual net cash income of households selling horticultural commodities, by survey area, 1991

	Nyandarua (n=229) KSh	%	Kisii (n=144) KSh	%	Taita (n=87) KSh	%	Taveta (n=38) KSh	%
farm activities:								
- cereals, beans	0	0	600	7	0	0	100	1
- vegetables, fruits, tubers	10,200	42	3,000	35	3,600	34	5,300	54
- livestock, livestock products	7,900	32	1,100	13	2,100	20	200	2
- coffee, tea, pyrethrum, cotton	600	2	2,000	23	0	0	400	4
total net farm cash income	18,700	76	6,700	78	5,700	53	6,000	61
net off-farm cash income	5,800	24	1,900	22	5,000	47	3,800	39
net household cash income	24,500	100	8,600	100	10,700	100	9,800	100

Note: The net farm cash income consists of the value of cash received for the sale of agricultural commodities, animals and livestock products minus the costs of the goods and services purchased for farm use (FAO, 1980; MOA, 1989). The value of farm produce consumed within the household is not included. The off-farm cash income consists of the wages (when employed) and profits (when self-employed) of resident household members, plus the remittances and cash contributions of any part-time residents with jobs elsewhere. For more details see Appendix 3.5.

Appendix 3.5:
Calculation method for the household cash income

Net household cash income = net farm cash income + net off-farm cash income + net land cash income.
In the surveyed areas, the net land cash income (annual rent received for plots rented out) was on average negligible.
Remittances by household members with jobs away from home were included in the net off-farm cash income.

Gross farm cash incomes were calculated by multiplying selling quantities and average selling prices for the year under consideration.

Selling quantities of crops were recorded per plot:
- For annual crops (cereals, beans, vegetables, tubers, cotton) sales were recorded per season. Three seasons were distinguished: long-rains, short-rains and the intermediate period.
- For perennial crops with more or less continuous harvesting (tea, bananas) average sales were recorded per three months. The total annual sales were calculated by multiplying these figures by four.
- For perennial crops with harvesting periods in one part of the year (coffee, pyrethrum) average sales were recorded per three-month harvesting period. The total annual sales were calculated by multiplying these figures by 5/3 for coffee, and 7/3 for pyrethrum.

Fruit trees, other than bananas, were usually not grown on separate plots but scattered throughout the farm. Annual selling quantities were recorded per tree type.
Livestock sold was recorded per animal type. Livestock products sold were primarily milk. Average milk sales per day were recorded.

Average selling prices were estimated:
- For cereals and beans, estimated prices were based on average selling prices in local market places during harvesting periods. The (lower) official prices offered by the NCPB were not used, as small-scale farmers in the survey areas preferred to sell their limited surplus in the market place.

- For vegetables, fruits and tubers, average selling prices resulted from the weighted average of the recorded lowest and highest annual selling price and the price at the time of the interview.
- For livestock and livestock products, the selling prices were recorded.
- For coffee, tea, cotton and pyrethrum, local buying prices of the cooperatives and boards were used.

Net farm cash incomes were calculated by deducting the estimated costs of purchased inputs and services from the gross cash incomes.

For crops, the total costs per crop were estimated as a percentage of the gross income:
- for cereals, beans, coffee, tea, pyrethrum and cotton on the basis of interviews with extension officers;
- for vegetables, fruits and tubers on the basis of recorded costs.

The costs included:
- Purchased inputs: hybrid seeds, fertilizer, insecticides and fungicides.
- Purchased farm tools: e.g. spraying pump, hoe. Depreciation costs were calculated, based on a lifetime of five years. In most cases, the calculated depreciation costs were negligible.
- Services: hired casual labour for ploughing, planting, weeding and harvesting. Sometimes, hired tractor and ox services for ploughing and harrowing were used. In addition to casual labour, one or more permanent labourers might be in service.

For livestock and livestock products, costs of purchased services included veterinary services and hired permanent labour to look after the cattle. The total costs were estimated as a percentage of the gross income on the basis of interviews with extension officers.

The **net off-farm income** was estimated on the basis of the monthly income and number of months employed of each member of the household engaged in off-farm employment.

A distinction was made between full-time and part-time household members, and between local employment (in the compound or neighbourhood) and employment elsewhere:
- In the cases of full-time residents and local employment, the entire wage (when employed) or estimated income (when self-employed) was accounted to the household budget.
- In the cases of full-time residents and employment elsewhere, the wage or estimated income was accounted to the household budget, except for estimated travelling costs.
- In the case of part-time residents, the incomes were accounted to the household budget in relation to the frequency of visits to the household by the people concerned. It was assumed that less frequent visits resulted in lower cash contributions and remittances to the household (as a percentage of the income earned).

Appendix 3.6:
Net horticultural cash income by income category and survey area, 1991 (%)

| | Nyandarua (n=229) | | Kisii (n=144) | | Taita (n=87) | | Taveta (n=38) | |
	KSh	% of net hh. cash income	KSh	% of net hh. cash income	KSh	% of net hh. cash income	KSh	% of net hh. cash income
Low-income hh's	2,000	42	800	57	1,200	73	1,100	87
Middle-income hh's	8,100	40	2,000	34	2,400	34	4,600	65
High-income hh's	27,100	47	7,100	33	8,900	34	10,900	46

Abbreviations: hh = household
Note: The low-income households are the lowest 25% of the household cash income distribution (lower quartile), the middle-income households belong to the middle 50% (interquartile), and the high-income households are those in the highest 25% of the household cash income distribution (upper quartile).

Appendix 5.1:
Characteristics of horticultural traders in the domestic market

Our hypothesis is that horticultural traders in the domestic market are a cross-section of the local population. Trader characteristics such as gender, ethnic group, age, marital status and income will be analysed. Unless otherwise indicated, the information is based on the trade survey (see Section 1.3 in the main text).

Gender
As far as the gender of the traders is concerned, the hypothesis that horticultural traders are a cross-section of the local population has to be rejected. Over 95 per cent of the traders who sell horticultural commodities in rural market places and in market places in small urban centres have at least one thing in common: they are women. Only in daily markets in large urban centres do male traders become somewhat more numerous. In Kisii Municipal market, for instance, about 30 per cent of the traders were men at the time of the survey, and in the Majengo retail market in Mombasa about 40 per cent. The difference between markets in rural areas and small urban centres on the one hand and large urban centres on the other is most probably related to the incomes earned. In the former most female traders are so-called 'petty traders' who sell the surplus of a farm household or small quantities of bought produce, trying to earn a little money. For them trade is one of the rare opportunities to obtain cash. The remuneration per hour is low, but attractive when no other opportunities exist. Farm revenues from export crops such as coffee and tea are often controlled by the husbands, while trade revenues may provide a personal income to the women and give them some autonomy.

Husbands may be cultivating export crops, be absent because of jobs elsewhere, or have died or abandoned their wives. Those that are around and idle are often too proud (or, as some women say, too lazy) to work all day for such a small amount of money. According to men, cultural standards do not allow them to trade commodities while sitting on the ground (which is necessary due to absence of stalls). Selling clothing and cooking utensils in a similar way is, however, not a problem. Trading these commodities is usually more rewarding than retailing vegetables and fruits. The same is true for the wholesaling of horticultural commodities, and doing so without a stall is not a problem to men, either.[2]

---

2   It can be observed that men are more prominent in the distributing and collecting wholesale trade than in the retail trade of horticultural commodities. The gender ratio in neither of these types of wholesale trade is known.

In the Kisii Municipal market and in the Majengo retail market (Mombasa) a major part of the trade takes place in stalls. More important is that these are daily markets. Even if the income generated per market day is not higher than that in rural markets, the monthly income will be much higher because of the greater number of selling days. Apparently the monthly income is there high enough to attract both women and men (see also 'trader incomes').

Ethnic background

The hypothesis that horticultural traders are a cross-section of the local population is accepted in terms of the ethnic background of the traders. In most cases the ethnic composition of the trader population more or less conforms to that of the general population in the region where the traders operate. Almost all horticultural traders in the Nyandarua markets are Kikuyu, and in the Taita markets Taita. In all market places in Kisii District, except for Riochanda market, horticultural commodities are traded almost exclusively by Kisii. Riochanda market is located on the border of Kisii and Homa Bay Districts where Kisii and Luo territories meet. As a consequence, the market place is used as a trading ground by both ethnic groups.

In Nakuru District 60 per cent of the population belong to the Kikuyu, while about three-quarters of the horticultural traders in the Nakuru and Njoro markets belong to this ethnic group. In Taveta Division of Taita Taveta District, the Kamba outnumber the local Taveta, both among the general population and as horticultural traders in the market place. The only place where the ethnic composition of the traders in the market places differs from that of the general population is Mombasa. Over half the horticultural traders in the surveyed market places in Mombasa are Kamba or Kikuyu, while only one fifth of the general population belongs to those two groups. Mijikenda are hardly found selling horticultural commodities, although they are the biggest group, constituting one quarter of the general population. The Kamba are also major actors in the collecting wholesale trade between Taveta and Mombasa. This is to be expected, given the presence of supplying Kamba farmers and Kamba traders in Taveta and demanding Kamba traders in Mombasa.

Age

The hypothesis that horticultural traders are a cross-section of the local population is also accepted for age. In a small survey in three market places in Taita Taveta horticultural traders were asked their age. The markets were located in Voi, the largest urban centre in the district (13,000 inhabitants), Wundanyi, a smaller urban centre (3,000 inhabitants); and Mgambonyi, a rural centre (less than 500 inhabitants). In Voi and Wundanyi, traders were randomly sampled, and in Mgambonyi all traders were interviewed.

The age distribution of the traders did not differ significantly from one market place to another (Table A5.1). In all three markets none of the traders was younger than 18 or older than 55, while the majority were between 25 and 45 years of age. It can be concluded that the size of the market centres did not affect the age composition of the traders operating in the markets.

Table A5.1. Age distribution of horticultural traders by population size of the market centre in Taita Taveta*

age category	large urban centre		small urban centre		rural centre		all centres	
	n	(%)	n	(%)	n	(%)	n	(%)
18-24 years	5	(17)	7	(23)	5	(23)	17	(21)
25-34 years	12	(40)	12	(40)	5	(23)	29	(35)
35-44 years	7	(23)	6	(20)	7	(32)	20	(24)
45-55 years	6	(20)	5	(17)	5	(23)	16	(20)
all traders	30	(100)	30	(100)	22	(101)	82	(100)

*X^2 =2.73 (not significant).

Table A5.2. Age distribution of horticultural traders and the general population in Taita Taveta*

age category	traders		general population	
	n	(%)	n	(%)
18-24 years	17	(21)	25,013	(32)
25-34 years	29	(35)	25,005	(32)
35-44 years	20	(24)	16,632	(21)
45-55 years	16	(20)	12,230	(15)
all traders	82	(100)	78,880	(100)

Source for general population: CBS, 1994b.
*X^2 = 4.68 (not significant).

The age distribution of the trader population did not differ significantly from that of the entire district population between 18 and 55 years old (Table A5.2).[3] The absence of young and elderly people was to be expected, as this is common in most types of employment. It can therefore be concluded that the horticultural traders in the sampled markets show ordinary age characteristics.

Marital status
In the Taita Taveta study, the marital status of the traders was also investigated. The relatively small group of male traders in the market places (n=7) were all married except for one who was a widower. In contrast, about forty percent of the female traders were single

---

[3] The age distribution of the general population in Taita Taveta is based primarily on the rural situation because less than 15 per cent of the district population live in urban centres (CBS, 1994b, 1994c). The Voi and Wundanyi market places are situated in urban centres. None of the traders interviewed in the Wundanyi market lived in the centre itself, however. They lived in one of the surrounding locations and either possessed land themselves or lived on their parents' land. They were therefore part of the rural population. Twenty-three of the interviewed traders in the Voi market (77%) lived in Voi town; the others resided in rural areas. A comparison of the age distribution of the traders who lived in Voi with that of all inhabitants of Voi town reveals a similar picture to the one found in Table A5.2.

women. Approximately half of these were single mothers (Table A5.3).[4] All three market places showed the same picture.

Approximately half the female traders in all three markets were married. However, some had a husband who lived elsewhere due to employment. The percentage of absentee husbands was the lowest in the large urban centre (18%), followed by the small urban centre (25%) and the rural centre (37%). This hierarchy is probably related to the greater availability of local jobs in large centres.

The Kenya CBS regards women with husbands who reside elsewhere for work to be heads of their household, similarly to single mothers who live on their own.[5] A third group of female households consists of divorced women who have not gone back to their parents, and a fourth group is comprised of widowed women. A survey by the Kenyan CBS in the first half of the 1980s showed that 46 per cent of all rural households in Taita Taveta were female-headed (CBS, 1988). Our Taita Taveta survey shows that in Mgambonyi market 9 out of the 22 traders (41%) potentially represented female-headed households, and in Wundanyi 12 out of 30 traders (40%). A comparison of the two surveys therefore suggests that female-headed households were at least as common among the general rural population as amongst horticultural traders living in the rural areas.[6] In other words, going into horticultural trade was not specific to female heads of households. Our hypothesis that the trader population is a cross-section of the general population is therefore not rejected with respect to the gender of the head of household.

Table A5.3. Marital status of female horticultural traders by population size of the market centre in Taita Taveta

status	large urban centre		small urban centre		rural centre		all centres	
	n	(%)	n	(%)	n	(%)	n	(%)
single:								
- without children	5	(21)	6	(20)	4	(19)	15	(20)
- with children	5	(21)	7	(23)	4	(19)	16	(21)
married:								
- husband around	11	(46)	12	(40)	8	(38)	31	(41)
- husband elsewhere	2	(8)	3	(10)	3	(14)	8	(11)
divorced, widowed	1	(4)	2	(7)	2	(10)	5	(7)
all traders	24	(100)	30	(100)	21	(100)	75	(100)

4 Most single women without children are relatively young and still members of their parents' household. Single mothers have children from unknown fathers or fathers that do not recognize their children. In rural areas most such women live with their parents and a smaller number live on their own, while in urban areas the situation is the reverse. Those who live on their own are heads of their household. Female-headed households are believed to be poorer in most cases than male headed households.

5 In the scholarly literature, households with husbands who reside elsewhere for work are referred to as female-managed households rather than female-headed households, because the absentee men still feel responsible for their wife and children and support the household with regular or irregular remittances.

6 Wundanyi is a small urban centre, but all traders lived in the surrounding rural areas. Voi is not included in the analysis because most traders lived in town and the CBS did not cover urban areas in its survey.

Trader incomes

The hypothesis is also not rejected when it comes to the incomes earned, though we have to be a bit cautious here. According to our trade survey, only a small minority of the horticultural traders earn high incomes, as is similarly the case in other parts of the economy. In Wundanyi and Taveta, markets in relatively small population centres, one third to one half of the traders earned less than KSh 1,000 in November 1991 (Table A5.4).[7] By comparison, casual farm labour, which was regarded a poor man's job, yielded about KSh 900 per month at that time. In the same market places, slightly under half of the traders earned between KSh 1,000 and KSh 5,000, the incomes of drivers, office clerks and primary school teachers at the time. Only a small minority earned between KSh 5,000 and KSh 10,000, also earned by technicians, doctors and managers, while almost no one earned top incomes of over KSh 10,000.

We must be careful in drawing conclusions because most traders in Wundanyi and Taveta were part-time traders, selling produce two days a week (Table A5.5).[8] They were able to pursue other income-earning activities during the rest of the week. The most likely other activity would have been farming, because teaching, office work and the like are full-time jobs. Farming, however, only generates additional income when it concerns crops other than the ones brought to the market. We also have to use caution because incomes from horticultural trade may fluctuate from one month to another, in contrast with revenues from permanent jobs such as teaching.

In retail markets in larger urban centres, such as Voi and Majengo (Mombasa), almost all traders were involved full-time (Tables A5.5 and A5.6).[9] The majority earned again less than KSh 5,000 a month (Table A5.4). Monthly incomes of over KSh 5,000 were slightly more common than in Wundanyi and Taveta. This was, however, not the result of a

Table A5.4. Distribution of estimated monthly incomes of horticultural traders in selected market places, November 1991 (%)

monthly income (KSh)	Wundanyi (n=56)	Taveta (n=95)	Voi (n=57)	Mombasa		
				Majengo retail (n=59)	Kongowea wholesale (n=40)	collecting wholesalers (n=15)
<1,000	48	37	17	16	5	0
1,000-4,999	48	46	44	48	22	7
5,000-9,999	4	12	28	26	18	14
>=10,000	0	6	11	10	56	80
	100	101	100	100	101	101

---

7   Appendix 5.2 shows the method used to calculate daily and monthly incomes of the sampled traders.

8   These were the two official market days. Only a minority of traders were in business six or seven days a week. Most of them rented stalls (Table A5.5). They tried to be in business continuously because they paid rent on a monthly basis, in contrast with traders who displayed their commodities on the ground and paid on a daily basis.

9   In Voi market the majority of traders rent a stall and are in business throughout the week (Table A5.5). Only those without a stall stick to the official market days. In Majengo market in Mombasa every one rents a stall and in is business more or less the whole week (Table A5.6).

Table A5.5. Number of days per week traders are in business in Wundanyi, Taveta and Voi markets, by stall use (%)

| days per week | ---Wundanyi market---- | | | ---Taveta market------- | | | ---Voi market------------ | | |
	no stall (n=50)	stall (n=6)	all	no stall (n=67)	stall (n=28)	all	no stall (n=17)	stall (n=40)	all
1 or 2	84	17	77	70	11	52	94	5	31
3 to 5	0	0	0	9	4	7	0	3	2
6 or 7	16	83	24	20	86	40	6	93	67
	100	100	101	99	101	99	100	101	100

Table A5.6. Number of days per week traders are in business in the Mombasa markets (%)

days per week	Majengo retail (n=59)	Kongowea wholesale (n=39)	collecting wholesalers (n=15)
once every fortnight	0	0	7
1 or 2	0	0	93
3 to 5	2	13	73
6 or 7	98	88	0
	100	101	100

Table A5.7. Distribution of daily incomes of horticultural traders in selected market places, November 1991 (%)

| daily income (KSh) | Wundanyi (n=56) | Taveta (n=95) | Voi (n=57) | ------------Mombasa---------------------- | | |
				Majengo retail (n=59)	Kongowea wholesale (n=40)	collecting wholesalers (n=15)
<100	46	40	23	41	18	0
100-499	52	39	54	53	26	0
500-999	2	15	12	2	26	0
>=1,000	0	6	11	5	31	100
	100	100	100	101	101	100

higher income per selling day: the daily income distributions for Voi and Majengo retail markets were not very different from those for Wundanyi and Taveta (Table A5.7). The difference in monthly income was primarily the result of a larger number of selling days per week.

Two groups of horticultural traders in the sample had higher monthly incomes than the traders discussed so far, namely the distributing wholesalers based in the Mombasa wholesale market, and the collecting wholesalers who sold from the back of their truck to them and to visiting retailers (Tables A5.4, last two columns). Most collecting wholesalers came to the Mombasa wholesale market twice a week, and were busy collecting produce in the production areas during the rest of the week. Most distributing wholesalers sold produce throughout the week (Table A5.6). Not only the monthly incomes but also the daily incomes of both types of wholesalers were higher than those of the traders in the other markets (Table A5.7). The incomes of the wholesalers were in no way representative of all horticultural traders in the country, as the wholesalers were relatively few in number. Hence, our hypothesis is accepted, because only a small minority of the horticultural traders earn high incomes, as is the case in the Kenyan economy in general.

Appendix 5.2:
Calculation method for trader incomes

Daily income

In each surveyed market place, horticultural traders were interviewed on an official market day during the main harvesting period in the region (see also Section 1.3 in the main text). Through observation it was verified that the market day was not different from other market days in that period. The net daily income or daily profit of the interviewed traders was calculated by deducting the various costs from the gross daily income or gross daily margin. The gross daily margin equalled the selling price minus the buying price times the turnover on the day of the survey per traded commodity. Cost categories might include packing material, transport costs, produce losses during transport, market fees, costs of unsold produce and capital costs.

Traders used *packing material* such as boxes, bags, baskets, nets and crates during transport. Wholesaling traders also sold produce in such units. They either charged the buyer separately for the packing material, or included the costs of the packing material in the deal. Thus, their packing material costs were usually nil. Smaller traders usually sold their produce loose. They might wrap vegetables or fruits in a piece of old newspaper, which they had been able to get hold of at no cost. Some traders supplied plastic bags to their customers, but only if they paid for them. The packing material that was required during transport could be used until it had worn out. The depreciation costs were too small to be of significance.

Transport costs were the most important cost category to the traders (except for immobile traders, who bought produce in the same market place). Various types of *transport costs* were distinguished in the survey, including:
- hired labour for carrying to road
- hired transport to road
- hired labour for loading
- rent of hired vehicle
- running costs of own vehicle (including fuel and oil, salaries and allowances to driver and turnboys, repair and maintenance of truck, tyres, insurance, interest and depreciation, trade licence, administration)
- bus/*matatu* fees (one way, for the produce)
- bus/*matatu* ticket (to and fro, for the trader)
- hired labour for unloading/carrying

- hired handcart
- other transport costs (specified by the trader)

Produce losses during transport were generally low, except for collecting wholesalers who dealt with truckloads of highly perishable commodities such as bananas.

Besides transport costs, the main other marketing costs were *market fees*. Less frequent costs in relation to the market place were the rent of a store and the wages paid to a watchman. Watchmen were usually shared with other traders, thus reducing the costs involved.

Traders without stores usually sold (almost) all produce they brought to the market. Unsold produce was carried home, to be sold on the next market day or consumed in the household. The *costs of unsold produce* were usually negligible. Traders with stores also planned to sell all produce within one or two days, to avoid quality deterioration. Only tubers, onions, and bananas that required ripening might stay in the store a few days longer.

The traders' *costs of capital* were usually low due to absence of or limited storage, limited use of borrowed money, and low opportunity costs of their own capital. In comparison to other traders, collecting wholesalers might have relatively high costs of capital.

Monthly income

The monthly income was calculated by multiplying the net daily income by the number of days a week the trader was selling at the time of the survey, and multiplying that by 4.3, the number of weeks per month.

If traders in periodic markets sold commodities outside the official market days, it was presumed that the income during those days was one-third of the income on official market days.

Appendix 5.3:
Farmer Cooperatives in Kenya: a troubled history

The first farmer cooperatives in Kenya were established by white settlers in the 1920s. The formation of cooperatives by Africans was not permitted until 1945, when a new cooperative act was passed with the explicit aim of fostering marketing cooperatives among the African population. Initially African farmers focused on the cooperative marketing of cereals, eggs, poultry, vegetables and dairy produce. In the 1950s, when the administration started to promote smallholder production of export crops, coffee cooperatives, pyrethrum cooperatives and multipurpose cooperatives became more important. At independence, in 1963, approximately 460 societies were registered (Gyllström, 1991).

The newly independent Kenyan government continued the export-oriented agricultural policy. Coffee, pyrethrum and dairy societies east of the Rift Valley, and cotton and sugar societies west of the Rift valley, rated high in terms of registrations. The number of registered societies increased rapidly: in four years' time 645 societies were formed (Gyllström, 1991).

After 1966 the growth of the cooperative movement slowed down as the government imposed stringent regulatory controls on the movement 'partly in response to perceived problems of cooperative mismanagement and rampant corruption, and partly as a result of the state's own imperatives to regulate the economy in pursuit of "development" ' (Zeleza, 1990, 74). Through the Cooperative Societies Act (1966) and the Cooperative Societies Rules (1969), the Department of Cooperative Development was given exclusive rights of registration, dissolution and compulsory amalgamation of societies. It was also given the power to supervise budgets and accounts, and to dictate a society's mode of organization and activity orientation by prescribing the contents of the bylaws (Gyllström, 1991).

In the 1970s, the role of the cooperatives was redefined and widened in response to declining economic growth. The Department of Cooperative Development was upgraded into a Ministry in 1974, and increased since then both in size and complexity (Gyllström, 1988). Growing emphasis was placed on production credit and input supply with the intention of disseminating more productive, input-intensive technologies. This strategy was continued in the first half of the 1980s, although it had proved ineffective. According to Gyllström (1991) the policy may actually have slowed down the integration of smallholders into the market, for two reasons. First, loan defaulters tried to avoid dealing with their societies, which in practice meant that they ceased to produce the crops monopolized by the cooperatives. Second, as a consequence of the poor performance of societies, unions, and the Ministry of Cooperative Development in administering the loans — which resulted in widespread irregularities — farmers' confidence in the ability of cooperatives to serve their interests became seriously damaged, and their ideology questioned.

In the 1980s the number of agricultural societies increased from approximately 1,000 to over 2,000 (Zeleza, 1989; GOK, 1997). At the same time, the problems of the cooperative movement further escalated due to two factors. First, falling world market prices, of coffee in particular, exposed the inefficiencies in the cooperative marketing system. Second, corruption and clientalism became a threat to the very existence of the cooperative movement. As long as prices had been good, cooperatives had to some extent been able to deal with these conditions. When world market prices fell, the cooperatives continued as if nothing had happened, and the soft state, as Myrdall has called it, became rather destructive. Farmers might have been used to getting paid less than they were entitled to, but they never got used to not being paid at all or only after several years.

With the liberalization of agricultural trade in the 1990s, the societies faced a new challenge: competition with private collecting traders (e.g. for coffee and milk). Open competition did not do the cooperative movement any good. According to the Kenyan government, the proportion of agricultural produce marketed by the cooperatives declined from 59 per cent in 1991 to 21 per cent in 1995 (most probably in value terms, although this is not specified as such) (GOK, 1997).

Appendix 5.4:
Case studies of horticultural marketing cooperatives

Case 1. The Horticultural Cooperative Union

History, aims and activities

The Horticultural Cooperative Union (HCU) was established in 1951 by European settler-farmers, primarily to market members' produce.[10] In 1967 its mandate was enlarged. The HCU was given a monopoly over the marketing of onions in the country. The aim was to stabilize onion prices and ensure fair returns to small-scale growers. By selling the onions on behalf of the farmers, it claimed to get a better price for them, thus improving the equity in the channel.[11] In addition to onions, the HCU marketed other horticultural commodities of both members and non-members but without monopolizing the trade. Non-members paid a higher commission than members (15% versus 10% of the price realized by the HCU).

Table A5.8 shows the relative importance of the commodities handled by the HCU in 1975. As shown, onions were the core of the business. They were grown by both small-scale and large-scale farmers to be sold by the HCU in the domestic market. Of the other commodities, capsicums, French beans and asparagus were mainly grown by large scale farmers for export. The HCU also exported mangoes delivered by the Malindi Farmers Cooperative Society. Potatoes, strawberries, oranges, pineapples and eggs were meant for the domestic market. The potatoes and pineapples were grown by small-scale farmers, the strawberries and eggs by a small number of large growers, and the pineapples by the Delmonte plantation in Thika. Other fruits traded by the HCU included peaches, plums, apples and pears. Unlike the other commodities, these fruits were produced by the HCU itself on a 25.5 acre farm bought by the union in 1971.[12]

The HCU collected produce from suppliers by lorry at assembly points and sometimes at farms. All commodities were delivered to the HCU headquarters in the Nairobi industrial area, where the administration was located as well as the central depot with packing and cold storage facilities. Transport distances to the central depot could extend beyond 500 kms, for instance for onions from Bungoma and mangoes from Lamu and

---

[10] The story of the Horticultural Cooperative Union as presented here is based on Buaruhanga (1977).

[11] The Union would be able to offer larger volumes for sale than individual farmers, and have more market information, two aspects that determine the power of a marketing channel member (see Section 4.6 in the main text).

[12] The farm, which was called Pentlands Orchards, was located 18 miles northwest of Nairobi.

Table A5.8. Relative importance and main supply areas of commodities handled by the HCU in 1975

commodity	% of total volume	main supply areas
Vegetables		
Onions	60.1	Pekerra, Naivasha, Athi River, Bungoma
Capsicums	5.7	Naivasha, Athi River
Potatoes	3.0	Nakuru, Kinangop
French beans	6.5	Athi River, Limuru, Ngong
Asparagus	0.8	Naivasha, Athi River
Other vegetables	6.1	
Fruits		
Mangoes	4.0	Mombasa, Lamu, Malindi
Strawberries	0.7	Nakuru, Limuru
Oranges	2.1	Mombasa, Kitale, Machakos
Pineapples	5.5	Thika
Other fruits	4.4	
Eggs	1.1	Athi River, Muguga
	100.0	

Based on Buaruhanga, 1977, p. 10, Table 1.2.

Malindi. (Table A5.8 shows the main areas of supply per commodity.) Producers were supplied with crates, cartons, sacks, boxes or nets to minimize deterioration during transport. The costs of the packing materials were deducted from the payments, which took place after the consignment was sold. The grower received a return form that showed the quantity received and sold, the price obtained, the commission and costs deducted, and the net returns. Payments usually took four weeks from the moment the produce had left the farm.

As for its sales outlets, the HCU sold to Nairobi greengrocers from the Nairobi depot, and to consumers from a stall in the Nairobi City market and a supermarket it owned. The latter was opened in the Nairobi city centre in 1972. The HCU also had a branch office in Mombasa that was used mainly to sell onions and potatoes supplied by the Nairobi branch. The total domestic sales of the union were valued at approximately 5 million Kenyan Shillings in 1975.

The commodities that the HCU exported were sold mainly through wholesale markets in London, using two British agents.[13] Relatively small quantities were exported to Switzerland, Belgium, France, the Netherlands and Denmark. In 1975, the HCU handled approximately 3 per cent of Kenya's horticultural exports by volume.

Problems

By 1975 the HCU was in trouble. Suppliers and customers were deserting the union and financial losses were accumulating. Suppliers preferred private traders to the HCU for two

---

13 In 1974/75, 84 per cent of the HCU's exports by volume went to the UK. The British agents worked on a commission, charging 7.5 per cent and 10 per cent respectively.

reasons. The first was the long interval between delivery of the produce to the union and receiving the payment. Private traders usually paid cash on delivery. The second reason was the flat commission rate that was applied regardless of product quality, quantity, location, seasons and loyalty of the supplier. Private traders did take account of such characteristics when dealing with individual farmers. Even in the case of onions, for which the HCU was supposed to have a monopoly and for which unregistered production and selling was illegal, the union faced severe competition from private traders.[14]

As for exports, the HCU was unable to compete with private exporters and handled only a tiny part of the total horticultural export volume. Even in the case of mangoes, for which the HCU was the sole agent of the Malindi Farmers' Cooperative Society, exports were very limited because the society sold most of its mango supplies in the more remunerative domestic markets along the Kenya coast. The HCU only received the society's surpluses, that is, when such surpluses were present.

The HCU was rapidly losing customers to private traders. In the past it had had a large number of professional and institutional buyers, but all of them had deserted it by 1975 except for some thirty Nairobi greengrocers. The HCU supermarket, that was supposed to sell to high-income groups, hotels, restaurants and other institutions, had been incurring considerable losses from the moment it opened its doors, and eventually it folded in April 1975. Reasons for the débâcle were its unsuitable location and poor management.

The declining turnover of the HCU and the inability of the management to identify the bottlenecks led to rising financial losses. In 1976 the government decided to close down the business. The Horticultural Crops Development Authority (HCDA) took over some of its activities, including the sales of onions and the export of horticultural commodities (see Appendix 5.7). The other activities were left to the private sector.

Case 2. Horticultural marketing by the Kinangop Agricultural Cooperative Society

The Kinangop Agricultural Cooperative Society was a multipurpose society[15] that for a relatively short period in its history performed horticultural marketing activities. The initiative must have been taken sometime in the early 1980s. The society aimed to sell its members' horticultural commodities in the Nairobi market. Potatoes were the most important horticultural crop in the area, and the society focused to a large extent on this crop. Bags of potatoes were collected near the farms to be sold to wholesalers and retailers in the Wakulima wholesale market. In this it copied the activities of collecting wholesalers that were present in the area. The society probably started its new enterprise because farmers or local leaders felt exploited by these traders, who offered prices that were thought to be too

---

14 The problems the HCU had in maintaining its monopoly in the onion trade were not unique: the National Cereals Produce Marketing Board had similar problems in the maize trade (see Section 2.3 in the main text).

15 Core activities of the society were the collection of milk and pyrethrum from members. The milk was delivered to the Kenya Cooperative Creameries (KCC) (see also Section 2.3 in the main text) and the pyrethrum to the Pyrethrum Board of Kenya. Besides produce collection, the society irregularly dealt with input supply.

low as compared to prices in Nairobi. In other words, they wished to improve the equity in the marketing channel to the benefit of the farmers.

The society had purchased a truck to transport the produce to the market. The truck would collect members' produce near the farms and carry it to the Wakulima wholesale market in Nairobi. Whether all the money to buy the truck was brought together by members or an additional loan was received is not clear. What is clear, however, is that larger farmers donated more money, and therefore expected to have more rights. This was problem number one. During supply peaks, the larger farmers, who were also the leaders of the society, laid claim to the truck and smaller farmers had to await their turn. Local politicians and other leaders also thought they had privileges and demanded the truck for the transport of their crops and for other important activities such as moving furniture. In the end, many smaller members still had to sell their produce to collecting wholesalers.

A second problem concerned payment to members. In this the Kinangop society was no different from many other agricultural societies. Farmers were not paid immediately but only after weeks or even months, and the overhead charged by the society was high, at least according to the members. Quantitative information about the charges is not available, but in many Kenyan agricultural societies overhead costs have been inflated by the inefficient use of resources and by outright corruption on the part of staff members. In the case of Kinangop, part of the overhead on the horticultural marketing activities may have also been used to cover losses on other society activities such as input supply.

The horticultural marketing activities of the Kinangop society were further troubled by a lack of knowledge about the marketing system. The society just copied the activities of collecting wholesalers, following them to the Wakulima wholesale market in Nairobi. The collecting wholesalers, who did not appreciate this, began obstructing the society's activities in all kinds of ways. First, the Nairobi wholesale market is very small and trucks have to queue before entering the market place. Collecting wholesalers used their knowledge and connections to jump the queue. Second, the society representative who finally entered the actual market place might sell his load to a market intermediary whom he presumed to be a distributing wholesaler but who in reality worked for a collecting wholesaler — the same collecting wholesaler the society was trying to escape. Third, distributing wholesalers might refuse to buy the produce on the grounds of existing buying agreements with collecting wholesalers. The latter thus used their customer relations as part of their exclusionary tactics. Finally, distributing wholesalers might keep away customers by offering a lower price, temporarily accepting small margins. As a consequence, the society needed more than two days before they had sold out, and had to pay double or triple market fees for each bag as a result of the daily charges.[16]

The society had an especially hard time selling its produce during regional harvesting peaks. The number of collecting wholesalers supplying produce to the Wakulima market multiplied and competition reached a cut-throat level. The society had to realize peak sales because most of its members followed the traditional agronomic calendar, all planting and harvesting at the same time. The society did not monitor market prices, nor did it teach its

---

[16] Traders are charged at the market gate for each bag or other unit of produce they bring into the market place. The only traders who are allowed to leave their produce in the market overnight are resident wholesalers.

members to practise the production planning required to harvest when prices were high. After a few harvesting seasons most of the members had lost faith in the horticultural marketing activities of the society and turned back to the private traders.

Case 3. The Taita Horticultural Produce Cooperative Society

In contrast with the Horticultural Cooperative Union and the horticultural marketing activities by the Kinangop Agricultural Cooperative Society, the Taita Horticultural Produce Cooperative Society has been a success, that is at least until 1995.

History, aims and strategy
The Taita Horticultural Produce Cooperative Society, usually called Taita HPC for short, was established as part of a Kenyan Government programme to stimulate the productivity and efficiency of the horticultural sector.[17] It started operations in 1990 with the help of German technical assistance (GTZ) and a Nairobi-based consultancy firm called Technoserve.[18] Its head office was built near Wundanyi in the middle of the Taita Hills, an area with a long history of vegetable production for the Mombasa market (see Section 3.3 in the main text). Initially, it was part of the Taita Farmers Cooperative Society (TFCS), which concentrated primarily on coffee.[19] In 1992 the Taita HPC was registered as a separate cooperative society, the Taita Horticultural Produce Cooperative Society Ltd.[20]

The aims of the Taita HPC were twofold: to increase yields by providing technical know-how and inputs such as seed, fertilizers and pesticides through a seasonal credit scheme; and to streamline the marketing of farmers' produce by supplying transport to Mombasa, by producing at the right time for the market, by providing continuity in production, and by standardizing, grading and packing the produce before it went on transport.

The Taita HPC recruited 600 farmers, and instructed them when to sow. Various subgroups had differing sowing dates. Through this method, the cooperative applied a staggered production strategy. Farmers were allowed to select two types of vegetables per season from a limited crop package. From 1991 to 1993 the package was composed of

---

[17] The programme was already formulated in the 1970s (MOA, 1979), but was not launched until ten years later. HPCs were to be formed in various high potential horticultural production areas, and new wholesale markets established in Nairobi, Mombasa and Kisumu. Taita was the first to receive a HPC and Mombasa the first to open a new market (Kongowea wholesale market opened its gates in 1989). As of 1995 the other wholesale markets had not yet followed and no other HPCs had been established. The reasons were lack of donor funding and, in the case of the wholesale markets, ongoing discussions regarding the location of these markets.

[18] Unless otherwise indicated, the information on the Taita HPC presented here is based on Technoserve (1989, 1991, 1993).

[19] The newly established Taita HPC took over the limited horticultural marketing function of the TFCS (the TFCS had only about 20 regular horticultural suppliers who between them supplied 300 to 400 kilograms per delivery). The TFCS had taken over the horticultural marketing activities of the Ngangao Cooperative Society, liquidated in 1982. The Ngangao Cooperative Society had replaced the defunct Taita Vegetable Growers Cooperative Society in 1962. The later had been formed by colonial officers in 1941 (see Section 3.3 in the main text).

[20] When the Taita HPC had got off to a good start, it became clear to the management that it would have to become independent to avoid being used as a cash cow by the heavily indebted TFCS.

white cabbage, tomatoes, spinach, lettuce, capsicums, French beans, baby marrow, cucumber, cauliflower, leeks, garden peas, carrots, red cabbage, and Chinese cabbage. In the course of time tomatoes, cauliflower, capsicums, lettuce and spinach became more important, at the expense of carrots, baby marrow, French beans and garden peas. Tomatoes, white cabbage and spinach have remained the core of the business, not only because they are part of the traditional package of the member-farmers, but also because they are in high demand in the Mombasa market. In 1994, the Taita HPC began including maize and beans as rotational crops for three reasons: to battle seasonal shortages of food, to fix nitrogen in the soil, and to fight soil-borne diseases and pests like nematodes.

The Taita HPC set up collecting centres at Wundanyi, Mugange, and Werugha, and rented a wholesale stall at Kongowea wholesale market, Mombasa. The vegetables were collected from the farmers and transported by cooperative truck to Mombasa every day of the week except Friday.[21] This activity was continuous all the year round, with slack periods during the dry season and the early first rains, and a peak period towards the end of the first rains. A second peak occurred towards the end of the second rains but it was less extreme because the planting of maize has first priority for the farmers during this period.

Farmers were provided with farm inputs to make sure they used the correct ones. The aim was to sustain high yields and deliver good-quality produce. The emphasis on quality gave the cooperative a head start when competing in Mombasa with other suppliers from Taita and the central highlands of Kenya. A more or less continual supply of high-quality produce was something many customers favoured but few traders provided. The Taita HPC increased the effectiveness of the marketing channel.[22]

Produce of the cooperative sold well, and to wide cross-section of customers including retailers, institutional buyers (tourist hotels, ship chandlers) and consumers. In 1991 the cooperative handled 528 tonnes of produce worth KSh 3.1 million, and in 1992, 559 tonnes worth KSh 4.2 million. The commodities fetched higher than average prices in the Mombasa market because of their superior quality. The average payout ratio to the farmers was also high, namely 94 percent in 1991 and 86 per cent in 1992.

Characteristics of Taita HPC members
The concept of the Taita HPC allowed participation of relatively small as well as large horticultural farmers. Any farmer that had a quarter of an acre of land suitable for horticulture could join the cooperative. However, initially wealthier farmers with more land and higher incomes were in the majority. According to the HPC management this had two reasons. First, none of the farmers in the Taita Hills were very eager to join a new project under the umbrella of the Taita Farmers Cooperative Society because of their poor experiences with the latter institution. After some persuasion, farmers were found, but many of them were relatively wealthy. Apparently they were willing to take the risk because their resource base allowed them to do so.

A second reason for the prevalence of large farmers was the screening of the credit record of potential members. HPC members were supposed to receive inputs on credit. To

---

21 If the truck was not completely full, cargo space was offered to traders and farmers for rent. That provided an additional income flow to the cooperative.
22 See Section 4.5 in the main text on channel effectiveness.

minimize future problems of bad debts, only farmers with a good record of previous loan repayments were qualified for loans. Many small farmers were still indebted to the Taita Farmers Cooperative Society.[23]

Between 1991 and 1993 the membership of the society rose from six hundred in 1991 to slightly over a thousand. The influx of smaller horticultural farmers increased. There were two reasons for this. First, these farmers saw that the society was doing well, that members were receiving high prices and that the risks were limited. Second, the role of credit in the project diminished, and farmers with a poor loan record were also allowed to participate.

No success without problems
With its high payout ratios, increasing membership and rising turnover, the Taita HPC had developed into a prosperous horticultural marketing cooperative by 1993. At the same time, its progress had been slowed by various factors. The first factor was, according to Technoserve, a sociocultural one. In 1993, the Taita HPC was still producing only 25 per cent of its targeted annual output of 2,000 tonnes. Especially the older HPC members, who constituted the majority of the Taita HPC membership, were not fully utilizing their available land. According to Technoserve (1993, 30) 'some African traditions discourage industry and the older generation (over 40 years) is still bound by the tradition that instils fear and discourages financial success.' The report adds, however, that the older generation also has a lower demand for cash because it has no school bills to pay and does not have the same appetite for luxury items as the younger generation. The report also mentions the reason cited by the members themselves, which was labour shortage. Although Technoserve does not accept this, it could well be true since off-farm employment away from home is quite common in the Taita Hills (see Sections 3.3 and 3.4 in the main text).

A second factor that affected the performance the Taita HPC was weather conditions. Rainfall had become quite unreliable in the early 1990s, reducing yields. This in turn affected loan repayments by the farmers, a third factor of concern. As said, the role of credit in the project had diminished over time. The reason was a high default rate. Initially, participating farmers were supplied with inputs on credit. Loan repayments were poor for three reasons. The first was the erratic weather that affected farmers' yields and income. The second reason was the general misconception amongst farmers that the inputs on credit represented 'free money', which was based on their earlier experience with other credit schemes. Farmers did not feel obliged to deliver their produce to the Taita HPC in order to repay their loan. Some sold all or part of their produce to collecting wholesalers instead, and others did not use the inputs themselves, but sold them to other farmers. The project lacked tangible security that could be used to force the farmers to pay their debts. The third reason

---

23 Probably their loans had not been repaid after coffee prices had plunged and farmers had stopped harvesting the crop. Farmers neglected the coffee trees and interplanted them with bananas, maize and other crops. There is no reason to believe that large farmers did not have loans at the TFCS when coffee prices started to drop, but they probably continued to harvest the crop longer because of the money invested and because their larger holdings meant they had a less urgent need to use the land for other crops. They may also have been able to come to some agreement with the TFCS about the writing-off of their debts, whereas smaller farmers did not have the connections to do so.

for the high default rate was insufficient knowledge about proper use of the inputs among some farmers that were sincere in their efforts to produce and deliver to the cooperative.

To solve its loan default problems, the Taita HPC turned to commercial sales of inputs to its members (so-called self-sponsored supply) and to providing loans that were one hundred percent secured. The new policy did not affect the demand for inputs by established HPC members. It did, however, inhibit young, promising farmers from joining the project, because many of them had insufficient capital to finance their first crop produced for the cooperative.

In addition to sociocultural factors, the weather and loan defaulting, three further factors hampered the performance of the Taita HPC. The first was a lack of irrigated production. During the dry season, many vegetables fetch high prices in the Mombasa market. The Taita HPC therefore tried to maximize its turnover during these periods, but this required irrigated production by its farmers. Although parts of the Taita Hills have had experience with irrigated production for decades, it is still not a very common practice. As a consequence, the bulk of the vegetables were not supplied to the cooperative until towards the end of the rains when prices in the Mombasa market were low.

Another problem was the availability and rising costs of fertilizers. Fertilizer prices were liberalized as part of Structural Adjustment Policies in the early 1990s. The result was a sharp increase in wholesale and retail prices, that reduced HPC members' ability to buy them. To make matters worse, fertilizers were sometimes unavailable due to an unstable Kenyan Shilling which was hampering imports. All in all, fertilizer application by HPC members declined, which adversely affected the quality standards of the produce.

A last problem that impeded the performance of the Taita HPC was the fact that some HPC produce was sold by members to collecting wholesalers near the farms and to consumers and retailers in the local market. As noted above, some HPC members tended to sell their produce to traders to avoid repaying their loan. Others sold to traders because they required cash on a daily basis for current household needs. Most of the collecting wholesalers paid cash on delivery, while the cooperative paid at fixed intervals through bank accounts. Some collecting wholesalers were also said to advance substantial cash deposits for growing crops.

HPC produce was sold not only to collecting wholesalers but also to retailers and consumers in the Wundanyi market place. The reason for this was that prices in Wundanyi were sometimes higher than in Mombasa. Although Wundanyi market is located in the production area, prices of commodities such as tomatoes and cabbages can be higher than in Mombasa, because additional supplies from the central highlands of Kenya reach Mombasa and not Wundanyi. The Mombasa market is the main destination for all produce from up-country because of its large consumer population. The consumer population of Wundanyi is relatively small, and none of the collecting wholesalers from Nairobi dare to go to the Wundanyi market to sell an entire truckload of tomatoes or cabbages. Thus, prices in Wundanyi market can be high if supplies from the Taita Hills are limited. The Taita HPC did not benefit from high prices in the Wundanyi market, because it was focused entirely on the Mombasa market.

Explaining the Taita HPC's success

At first glance it seems likely that the success of the Taita HPC is related to the availability of Mombasa as a market outlet. The demand for high-value vegetables like cauliflower, lettuce, baby marrow and sweet pepper is greater in Mombasa than in other large cities because of the coastal tourist industry. The vegetables mentioned were indeed assigned a key place within the crop package when the Taita HPC started its activities in 1990. However, the HPC management soon found out that the demand for such high-value commodities was limited even in Mombasa, and that the market easily became flooded. Moreover, crops with a medium value like tomatoes, cabbage and spinach proved to sell very well in Mombasa as long as top quality was offered. With increasing transport costs due to rising fuel prices in subsequent years, the demand for tomatoes and cabbages from Taita Taveta further increased in Mombasa, because of the high prices asked for tomatoes and cabbages from Central Province. As a consequence, the Taita HPC began to concentrate even more on those medium value crops.

It can be concluded that the presence of the coastal tourist industry does not completely explain the success of the Taita HPC. At least as important are the superior-quality supply, a market-oriented planning of production, and access to retailers. This strategy can also be applied by groups of farmers in other parts of Kenya. Superior quality requires the use of proper inputs, improved grading and packing, and organization of transport. Market-oriented planning of production requires day-to-day scanning of the major urban markets, and the planning of planting and harvesting periods. Irrigation facilities may be needed for harvesting outside the main supply peaks. Finally, access to retailers must be gained by renting a stall in the wholesale market of the target city, thus bypassing distributing wholesalers who might otherwise boycott the farmers' initiative at the instigation of collecting wholesalers.

Appendix 5.5:
Some remarks on export diversification in Sub-Saharan Africa

Sustainable economic growth in Sub-Saharan Africa requires a steady increase of foreign exchange revenues, and for some time to come this will have to be derived from agriculture (Delgado, 1995). Unfortunately, world commodity prices for traditional export crops such as coffee and cocoa have been declining, and the prospects for price increases in real terms are poor (Duncan, 1993). Substantial agreement therefore exists that diversification of the agricultural export base should be central to long-term growth strategies in Africa (Boafo-Arthur, 1992; Delgado, 1995; Duncan, 1993). Diversification into non-traditional export crops is advocated, with fruits, vegetables and flowers being the prime candidates. The major macroeconomic and agricultural policy reforms realized in Africa during the last decade have created many of the right conditions. African exporters are now less subject to the heavy implicit taxation on non-traditional (and traditional) agricultural exports that comes with industrial protection and overvalued exchange rates (Delgado, 1995).

Having said that, we have to carefully weigh the idea of diversification into non-traditional exports and the role of this process in the development of Africa. Non-traditional exports may be helpful for income and may generate employment, but it will be some time before they can displace traditional agricultural exports as the chief providers of employment and growth in Sub-Saharan Africa (Delgado, 1995). Moreover, whilst export diversification has been an objective in a number of countries, it has proved a difficult and protracted process (UNCTAD, 1996). For one thing, success in promoting non-traditional exports may depend on specific policies to overcome obstacles at the early stages of breaking into new markets (so-called proactive policies) (Delgado, 1995). Researchers do not agree, however, on the extent to which governments should intervene in the production and marketing of non-traditional export crops. They are only agreed on the risks of any such intervention. There are many things governments can do to help develop new export activities, but there are also many things they are already doing with counterproductive results (Duncan, 1993).

In addition to the policy aspect, world market developments also have to be considered. Many scholars fear that Sub-Saharan Africa will be marginalized by the increasing economic and spatial integration of the European Union (Sommers & Mehretu, 1992). Some believe that diversification of exports can succeed only in combination with serious negotiations for realistic and binding trade and other concessions from the EU (Boafo-Arthur, 1992). Fact is that the EU is developing all sorts of rules that impede the import of vegetables, fruits and flowers from Africa. One such rule concerns the so-called maximum chemical residuals levels. Residues of pesticides in excess of set maximum residue limits (MRLs) or residues of banned pesticides, if detected, will result in the total rejection and return or destruction of a shipment at the expense of the exporter (Nyamiaka, 1995). The MRLs have a serious side-effect: they tend to reduce the involvement of small-scale producers. The rising minimum standards entail high production costs, resulting from the use of professional managers and costly inputs (Brown & Tiffen, 1992). In effect this means production on large-scale farms, and that implies the involvement of European and multinational companies.

Not only European integration, but also the globalization of trade systems forms a threat to Africa's non-traditional exports. According to the UNCTAD (1996), the yet unfinished Uruguay Round agenda on 'non-trade' issues, such as the relationship of trade to environmental and labour standards, could jeopardize the projected benefits of the Uruguay Round for Africa and other developing regions.

Appendix 5.6:
Horticultural exports from Africa

European consumers find all kinds of fruits in their baskets, vegetables on their plates and flowers in their vases which have been imported from Africa. French beans grown in Burkina Faso, pineapples from plantations in Ivory Coast, mangoes picked in Mali, avocados from orchards in Mozambique, grapefruits from Swaziland, bananas from Cameroon, strawberries packed in Kenya, grapes from South Africa, and roses cut in Zimbabwe are all exported from Africa to Europe. Per commodity, African countries can be listed in the order of importance based on the quantities exported fresh to Europe. In 1991, the situation was as follows:

A. Fruits

Pineapples	Ivory Coast, Ghana, South Africa
Avocados	South Africa, Kenya, Mozambique, Zambia
Bananas	Ivory Coast, Cameroon, Somalia
Mangoes, Guavas	South Africa, Mali, Ivory Coast, Kenya, Burkina Faso, Gambia, Mozambique, Guinee, Namibia
Grapefruits	South Africa, Swaziland, Mozambique
Oranges	Morocco, South Africa, Tunisia, Zimbabwe
Tangerines	Morocco, South Africa
Lemons	South Africa
Apples	South Africa
Strawberries	Morocco, Kenya
Grapes	South Africa, Namibia
Plums	South Africa, Namibia
Pears, Apricots	South Africa
Melons	South Africa, Morocco, Senegal
Watermelons	Somalia
Litchis	Madagascar, South Africa, Mauritius, Réunion, Namibia

B. Vegetables

French beans	Kenya, Burkina Faso, Morocco, Senegal, Ethiopia, Egypt
Aubergines	Kenya, Gambia
Peas	Morocco, Zimbabwe, Zambia, Nigeria, Morocco
Sweet corn	Zambia, Zimbabwe, Namibia
Onions	Egypt, South Africa
Artichokes, Garlic	Egypt
Courgettes, Leeks	Morocco
Asparagus, Tomatoes	Morocco

C. Cut flowers

Carnations	Kenya
Alstroemeria	Kenya, Zimbabwe
Asters	Kenya, Zimbabwe
Chrysanthemum	Zimbabwe, Nigeria
Roses	Zimbabwe, Kenya, Morocco, Zambia
Delphinium	Kenya, Zimbabwe
Gypsophila	Kenya
Gladioli	Zambia, Zimbabwe, Ivory Coast
Liatris	Kenya, Zimbabwe
Solidaster	Kenya, Zimbabwe
Orchids	South Africa, Kenya
Ammi majus	Kenya
Trachelium	Kenya, Zimbabwe
Statice	Kenya
Veronica	Zimbabwe
unspecified	Ethiopia, Tanzania, Namibia

(Sources: data from CBS, the Netherlands; DNSCE, France; HMSO, the United Kingdom; ISTAT, Italy; Ministerio de Economía y Hacienda, Spain; NIS, Belgium/Luxembourg; Stat. Bundesamt, Germany; and the association of Dutch flower auctions (VBN), the Netherlands)

Almost all fresh horticultural commodities exported from Africa to Europe are transported by air. Major exceptions are produce from northern Africa and bananas and pineapples from West Africa, which are transported in refrigerated ships (Van der Laan, 1997). For other horticultural produce, transport by sea was, at least until recently, non existent, either because it was not feasible due to the perishability of the commodities, or because it required sophisticated refrigeration techniques not yet available at African harbours. Hence, the growth of the horticultural export trade from Africa closely corresponds to the growth of air traffic over the past two decades. Cargo space has become more readily available at lower cost, due to the increasing number of diplomats, business people, development workers, tourists and others travelling to Africa.

Appendix 5.7:
The Horticultural Crops Development Authority

The Horticultural Crop Development Authority (HCDA) was established in 1967. Its initial objectives included fixing prices of horticultural commodities, marketing, and operating horticultural processing factories (Nyoro, 1993). As for the marketing and price fixing, the HCDA appointed the Horticultural Cooperative Union (HCU) as the monopolist buyer of onions and exporter of horticultural commodities (Appendix 5.4). The union failed and the HCDA reassumed the activities in 1976. The HCDA later lost its monopoly on onions, however, and became a buyer of last resort instead.

The HCDA remained actively involved in the export of commodities until 1986, when the government decided to leave all export trade to the private sector. The HCDA had become too much a competitor to private exporters rather than a provider. From then on, the HCDA was empowered to undertake the following key activities (HCDA, 1990):

1. the regulation of the horticultural industry through the licensing of exporters and application of rules as promulgated by the Ministry of Agriculture;
2. the provision of advisory services to the government and industry;
3. the provision of information about the market (market intelligence) to the industry;
4. the monitoring of prices and foreign exchange remittances to Kenya;
5. the supply of vital inputs to farmers, and assistance in grading, storage, collection, transportation and warehousing of produce (such only if approved and gazetted by the Minister of Agriculture).

The HCDA receives no subsidies from the Kenyan government, but finances its operating costs with export levies on fresh and processed produce and fees for export licensing. In 1993 the export levy was KSh 0.12 per kg for fresh produce, and was variable for processed produce. The HCDA also collects a levy on behalf of the Fresh Produce Exporters Association of Kenya (FPEAK), to which all exporters of fresh produce belong by virtue of paying the levy. In 1993, this levy was KSh 0.01 per kg of fresh produce. The FPEAK, whose purpose is to resolve problems affecting fresh produce exports by creating a unified voice, is a member of the HCDA board. The chairman of that board is appointed by the President of Kenya. Other members represent the Ministries of Agriculture, Finance, and Cooperative Development, as well as the industry (including growers, exporters and processors).

The HCDA is often criticized by producers and exporters for imposing export levies in return for too little action. According to Nyoro (1993), the HCDA has been unable to effectively disseminate market information to producers, although it receives information from the International Trade Centre (ITC) in Geneva. Producers and exporters have to rely on their own sources for the latest price developments in the various selling markets.

Nyoro characterizes the supply of inputs to farmers by the HCDA as erratic. He gives the example of a campaign in Coast Province against pests and diseases such as the mango weevil. The HCDA was to coordinate the spraying of nurseries and orchards. In 1990, however, it stopped supplying the inputs for the programme, and told farmers and export companies to look for the chemicals themselves. The campaign suffered badly from this change in policy.

Appendix 5.8:
Case studies of horticultural export traders

Case 1. An experienced flower producer-exporter

The first interviewed trader is a flower producer and exporter who emigrated from Germany around 1977. He worked for five years at Sulmac, Kenya's biggest flower exporter, and then started his own business. Today he has a 40-acre farm where he employs 210 people, producing about 20 million stems a year from irrigated land. The growing season lasts from October to March or April, which avoids the European summer during which European flower growers dominate the market.

The grower's main flowers are Alstroemeria and Solidaster, the latter of which is highly prized for use in bouquets because of its bright yellow colours. The future for Solidaster cultivation looks bright since bouquets are enjoying growing popularity in Europe. The only problem is that it needs about 16 hours of light a day, while the Kenyan day lasts no more than 12 hours. So extra illumination is required, and each plant has its own light bulb (and the farm a large generator). As well as flowers from his own farm, this trader exports other species which he buys from four other farms of 6 to 10 acres each, and from a farmers' cooperative of 300 small-scale producers, the only flower cooperative of its kind in Kenya.

The trader has a pre-cooling unit at his farm, in which cut flowers are chilled before being transported to the airport. Once they have arrived at the airport, they are stored in a cold store belonging to Oserean, another leading flower exporter, until being loaded into an aircraft chartered by Oserean. That firm charters more air cargo space than it needs and hires out part of it to smaller flower exporters.

Once exported, the flowers are sold either at an auction in Holland or on contract to importers in Switzerland and Germany. These two sales methods are complementary. Contracts specify price but not quantities, leaving the trader with unsold flowers in the event of low prices in the European market; the auction system allows the sale of variable quantities but at fluctuating prices.

When asked the main problem he was facing, this trader mentioned the high taxation on aeroplane fuel imposed by the Kenyan government. This inflates the Kenyan freight rates in comparison to other African countries competing in the international flower market, such as neighbouring Tanzania.

Case 2. An inexperienced flower producer-exporter with hired expertise

The second interviewed exporter is primarily an importer of agrochemicals, who went into rose farming and exporting some years ago. He has little expert knowledge of roses, but brings in a consultant from Israel twice a month. His rose farm consists of two hectares of greenhouses, producing five million stems per season. As roses are rather new in Kenya and established rose farmers were not willing to share their expertise, the selection of suitable varieties required a considerable investment of time and money. Post-harvest handling and transport also had to be developed by trial and error, as roses are delicate flowers that need to be kept at around three degrees centigrade during the entire length of transport.

The trader uses planes chartered by Oserean but, he says, there are problems in depending on others for cargo space, especially close to demand peaks in Europe (e.g. Christmas and Mother's Day). For those two high points in the market year, he has to be sure of getting his flowers to Europe in time, but he knows that Oserean will give priority to filling the aircraft with its own flowers. There is little point in approaching another large exporter to hire cargo space, since all are competing at such a prime market time. If he is unsuccessful in finding cargo space, the trader may have to send his flowers to auction two days after Christmas instead of two days before.

A future problem foreseen by the rose exporter involves complaints by European flower growers about increasing competition from countries like Kenya, Zimbabwe, Colombia and Israel. European growers are trying to stop the flower auction organizations, in which they are shareholders, from accepting flowers from those countries. At the same time they are urging the European Union (EU) to impose import restrictions. The EU has already developed rules requiring the destruction of imported flowers that originate from illegally multiplied planting material, the origin of which can be checked through the multiplication farms which sell such material.

The EU rule will affect the smallholders who work with illegally multiplied material because the royalties are too expensive for them. The multiplication farmers are also reluctant to deal with smallholders, because until 1995 Kenya had not signed the UPOV convention, an international treaty protecting their rights. Strict EU controls on planting material do not affect the large-scale producers, but they may be a sign of things to come (see also Appendix 5.5).

A factor that may contribute to further actions by the EU is the negative image of the Kenyan flower producers in certain European countries. One German organization, for example, has threatened to organize a boycott of Kenyan flowers because the labourers on Kenyan farms are thought to be not properly protected during the spraying of the flowers. Labour unions have raised questions about the wages paid to Kenyan labourers, and environmental organizations are criticizing the excessive use of agrochemicals, which pollute lakes near Kenyan flower farms. Such developments are of interest to European flower growers who want to keep African flowers outside the EU market.

Case 3. A producer-exporter of French beans

The third trader is a Kenyan exporter who has been in business for many years, chiefly exporting French beans. In addition, he exports some mangoes, avocados, passion fruit, and apple bananas (a small, sweet variety of banana), and he is trying his luck with snow peas. He has two irrigated farms of 100 and 50 acres respectively, on which he employs some 150 people all told. He buys French beans from about 100 smallholders and buys mangoes from agents in the coastal area of Kenya, but otherwise all his commodities originate from his own farms. During the off-season in the export market (June-September) he grows tomatoes on his farms, which he sells to a local supermarket chain (Uchumi).

The trader exports 3 to 10 tonnes of French beans per week, depending on demand. The commodities are flown to Europe the night after they are picked. Only if a flight is delayed are they stored in a cold store belonging to the airport. This is rather risky, because the cold store breaks down regularly. The trader uses an Air France cargo plane which flies to Nairobi twice a week, and he reserves space through a local cargo agent. His exports (between October and May) are destined for the United Kingdom, France, Belgium and Switzerland. Importers place their orders on a weekly basis, which makes long-term planning virtually impossible.

Lack of cargo space has been a problem in the past, but that is now no longer the case due to an overall business decline. The slump may be attributed, first, to the economic recession in Europe that has affected the demand for the commodities handled by the exporter, and second, to increasing competition from other African countries in the case of French beans, and Israel in the case of avocados. Since the trader is aware that cut flower exports are very profitable, he is thinking of converting his vegetable and fruit farms into flower estates.

Case 4. A vegetable and fruit exporter with no production of his own

The fourth interviewed trader has been in business for over 20 years, and deals with 15 different commodities, including French beans, courgettes, capsicums and all kinds of Asian vegetables. He relies on about a thousand contract farmers in various parts of Kenya, who supply him with about a hundred tonnes of produce a day. These smallholders receive seeds, fertilizers, pesticides and an advance payment in turn for selling the commodities to him.

The trader sells to importers, wholesalers and retailers whom he contacts at trade fairs in various European countries. He exports French beans seasonally and Asian vegetables throughout the year. For the latter he is given special treatment by airlines, which are willing to offer space in the high season in accordance with the trader's performance during the low season, when there is an over-supply of cargo space.

The exporter has a cooling device close to the airport which he uses only when flights are delayed, but he expects pre-cooling to become a standard procedure in the near future to enhance quality. Although this requires substantial investment, it is necessary to keep ahead of competitors from other African countries.

According to the trader, flexibility is a must at all stages of the export process. The destination of a commodity may change at any moment, even when it is already waiting at Nairobi airport. If a cargo of okra has to go to France instead of Britain, the vegetables have to be repacked on the spot, because French importers demand smaller boxes than British. French beans sold to large retailers such as supermarket chains are even packed in retail quantities (so-called pre-packing). The trader complains that the availability of cheap, good-quality packing material is a problem. To rectify this, several large exporters are planning to collaborate in building a packing material plant.

Appendix 5.9:
Case studies of horticultural export processors

Case 1. Pan African Vegetable Products Ltd.[24]

The history of Pan African Vegetable Products Ltd. in Naivasha goes back as far as 1964, when the Biddle and Sawer Company, a British firm that had been prominent in the marketing of Kenyan pyrethrum, started a vegetable dehydration factory on the edge of Naivasha town. The plant's aims were to earn Kenya foreign exchange by selling dehydrated vegetables overseas, to prolong shelf life of vegetable produce, to reduce its bulkiness in order to save cargo space and reduce transport costs, and last but not least to alleviate marketing problems of farmers in and around Naivasha. Those farmers resided predominantly in Kinangop Division, Nyandarua District.

From the moment the factory began operations, it showed erratic performance. Its capacity was small, but its turnover even smaller, its export markets were ad hoc, and it fetched low prices for its dehydrated vegetables and thus incurred financial losses. The company went into receivership for the first time in 1968. The Kenyan Government bought the factory and renamed it Pan African Foods.

The performance of the company improved somewhat over the following years, but the Kenyan produce was still sold at lower prices in the world market than that of other major suppliers, due to its poorer quality. In the early 1970s, the Bruckner Werke company, the largest producer of dehydrated vegetables in West Germany, was asked to come in, to provide finance, technical know-how and established distribution outlets. The new joint venture was called Pan African Vegetable Products Ltd., and it began operating in 1975.

The factory expanded and the government made land available to serve as nucleus estates for the company, where crops could be grown to supplement the produce supplied by farmers. Nevertheless, the performance of the company did not improve. The relations between 'PanAVeg' and Bruckner were troublesome from the start. The factory accused Bruckner of paying insufficient prices, providing insufficient market information, and curtailing the possibilities to develop promising distribution outlets. Bruckner in turn became annoyed by the factory's inability to maintain high quality standards and produce according to plan. Relations were further undermined by exogenous developments: oil prices increased dramatically, thus increasing production costs, and the demand for dehydrated vegetables in the world market stagnated due to an economic recession in Western Europe.

---

[24] The history of the vegetable dehydration plant until 1982 is based on Jaffee (1987), and the more recent history on interviews by the present author with the factory management in 1990.

In 1982 the company went into receivership for the second time, only to be revived in 1986 under the auspices of the Industrial and Commercial Development Corporation (ICDC), a government parastatal. In order to secure supplies, the management restarted a promotion campaign for carrot cultivation in Kinangop division. The company supplied carrot seed on credit to the farmers through their cooperative societies.[25] Moreover, the farmers were promised a guaranteed market outlet and the company was to take care of transport to the factory. So far so good, until the factory trucks did not turn up when the carrots had been harvested. Those farmers who organized transport to Naivasha themselves had to cope with further difficulties. The carrots had to meet all sorts of requirements. They were supposed to be of a certain size, colour, moisture content, variety, and to have been topped off in a particular way. Finally, the prices the farmers were offered were low compared to prices in the market for fresh carrots, and farmers did not receive cash on delivery as when they sold to collecting wholesalers. As a consequence, farmers ceased carrot cultivation or sold the crop in the fresh market.

After the outgrowers débâcle, the factory came to focus almost entirely on production on its own estates, which were too small to keep the factory running at anything near full capacity. Lack of buyers became a new bottleneck, however. There was no domestic market for dehydrated vegetables in Kenya, and the factory was unable to compete in the international market. The latter fact became especially clear when the German partner left the company in 1982, taking with it all its German contacts that had bought most of the produce up to then. The factory found no substantial long-term alternative market outlets due to severe competition in the international market and the higher quality standards of Asian competitors.

After half a decade of further financial losses and government subsidies to keep the factory running, the plant was put up for sale by the ICDC in 1991, as part of the national structural adjustment policy of the Government. It would take four years to find a buyer that would offer more than scrap value for the company's assets.

Case 2. Bawazir Fruits Processors Ltd.[26]

This factory was built in 1988 by an international company called Tropical Food Processors Ltd. In 1992 the company closed the factory due to increasing financial losses and sold it to a Kenyan business family in 1993. The factory restarted operations in April 1993 under the name Bawazir Fruits Processors Ltd.

The plant is able to produce mango, pineapple, grape, orange, passion fruit and tomato concentrates, as well as tinned juices, tomato paste, banana puree and various jams. The fruit concentrates and banana puree are intended for the export market, and the tinned juices, tomato paste and jams for the domestic market. The core of the business is production of the fruit concentrates.

---

25 Many people, including farmers and government officers, thought and still think that the seeds were supplied free of charge.

26 The story on Bawazir is based on interviews with the management in December 1993.

Less than a year after the restart of its engines, the factory was experiencing serious problems. They must have existed at least in part under the previous ownership. On the input side, Bawazir had problems acquiring sufficient fruit for its juice concentrates. The factory had an annual capacity of 30,000 tonnes of fresh fruit, but was running at one third of this. This was due to the low prices offered to farmers for their oranges, mangoes and pineapples. Farmers preferred to sell their fruit in the local markets to wholesalers and consumers. The factory was not able to pay as much as the local market because of the low prices for concentrates in the international market, the high transport costs to the factory, the high costs of the steel drums used for packaging, and the quality of the supplies offered. The high transport costs were due to the factory's location outside the main production areas of oranges, mangoes and pineapples, and the poor condition of many access roads to such areas.[27] The high costs of the drums were related to the depreciation of the Kenyan Shilling, which made the imported steel, used by a factory in Thika to make the drums, expensive. The quality of the produce was a problem in the case of mangoes and citrus. To get good-quality concentrate, the factory preferred large fruits produced by trees of a high-yielding variety. Most farmers, however, had indigenous trees that produced small fruits. The factory used the indigenous fruits for juice production, and to a limited extent for concentrate production.

In addition to its supply problems the factory had to deal with a lack of customers. Competition in the international market was strong, and when the factory closed in 1992, customers shifted to other suppliers. Almost a year after reopening, the management had not been able to get back any of them, nor had they been able to find new buyers.

The demand for juice concentrate in the domestic market was negligible. The demand for tinned fruit juices was much higher, but the factory was too big to produce only for the domestic market (it would only use a small part of its capacity, resulting in high fixed costs per selling unit). Moreover, competition was strong once again. The factory had to compete with a number of fruit juice tinning factories from up-country, and the demand for tinned juice from the tourist hotels at the coast had fallen during recent years because of competition by cottage industries.[28]

The juice of the cottage industries is cheaper, and it is fresh. The former owner of the present Bawazir factory had begun supplying fresh juices to tourist hotels in five-litre plastic containers, but after the cottage industries had taken over the idea, the factory was pushed out of the market. It was not able to compete with the small-scale entrepreneurs because of its capital-intensive method compared to the cheaper labour-intensive one used by the cottage industries. The latter use a squeezer and an electric blender of the kitchen type as their only mechanical tools. More advanced producers have a deep freeze in which they store the juice until it is ordered by their customers. Beginning producers only process the fruits after receiving an order. Both buy the fruit at the local market — the Kongowea wholesale market in the case of Mombasa and the Municipal market in the case of Malindi. The cottage businesses are located near those markets, so their transport costs are low.

---

27 The produce was usually bought from farmers near their farms. Some farmers organized transport to the factory themselves. Sometimes a farmers' cooperative society was also used as intermediary at the collection stage.

28 A cottage industry is a small-scale enterprise located in or around the house of the proprietor.

Appendix 6.1:
Specification of the marketing costs of a Kinangop farmer trading potatoes in the Nairobi wholesale market

Marketing costs in relation to the transport function

Seven-tonne trucks are for hire in Nairobi. To get hold of one of such a vehicle, the farmer has to take public transport to Nairobi to meet transporters. During his stay in Nairobi he has to pay for food and lodging. The first time he goes to Nairobi he needs at least two and a half days to travel to the city, find a willing transporter, and come back with the truck (and driver). Subsequent trips can be made in one and a half days because the farmer knows where to go.[29] During his absence his part of the work on the farm either has to be postponed or casual labour has to be hired. This has its (opportunity) costs.[30]

The transporter who agrees to hire out his truck for a trip to the production area and back charges the farmer a lump sum that includes petrol, a driver, and two turn boys. The first time the farmer deals with the transporter, he has to pay more than regular customers (such as professional collecting wholesalers). Only when the transporter gets to know the farmer better will he lower the price to the regular-customer level.[31]

The farmer has to bear other transport-related costs as well. He has to purchase gunny bags to pack the potatoes. He has to hire young men to extend (top up) filled bags with twined sisal.[32] The sisal has to be bought, too. The extended bags have to be loaded onto the truck by other hired young men. On arrival in Nairobi, market fees have to be paid

---

[29] The first trip will include half a day of travelling from the farm to Nairobi, one and a half days finding a truck for hire, and half a day returning to the farm with the truck. Subsequent trips will take the same travelling time, but only half a day to find a truck. Once the farmer knows the transporter well he might try to order a truck by phone, using a phone at the local post office. Transporters will be reluctant to honour such a request, however, because it means that they do not get an advance payment (see marketing costs in relation to the finance function).

[30] Labour has a price in Nyandarua because of the commercial cultivation of vegetables. The opportunity costs of the farmer's labour are set at the cost of hired casual farm labour in the area (thus assuming that a casual labourer will do the farm work as well as the farmer would do). Labour and travelling costs would not have to be included in the calculations if the farmer had to go to Nairobi anyway, for instance to visit a doctor or buy inputs. This will normally not be the case, however, because nearby Limuru and Naivasha offer the same services as Nairobi, and a farmer would prefer to stick to doctors and input suppliers he knows.

[31] After the farmer has hired a truck four times in subsequent weeks, the price will be lowered. The surcharge for the first four trips is estimated at 10 per cent.

[32] The topping-up of potato bags is standard procedure (see Section 5.6 in the main text, *product suitability*).

Box A6.1. Marketing costs in relation to the transport function, 1990

A. Hiring a 7-tonne truck
1. Costs of getting hold of the truck:
- one-way trip to Nairobi: KSh 15 for the local *matatu*, KSh 40 for the connecting *matatu* to Nairobi;
- food and lodging costs during stay in Nairobi: KSh 300 for first trip (2 nights out), KSh 150 for subsequent trips (1 night out);
- opportunity costs of farmer's own labour: KSh 83 (2.5 days) for first trip, KSh 50 (1.5 days) for subsequent trips.
2. Transport costs:
- Hiring fee for the truck: KSh 4235 per trip for first four trips, KSh 3850 for each additional trip.
3. Other transport-related costs:
- gunny bags: KSh 10 per bag;
- sisal for twining: KSh 10 per bag;
- hired labour for topping-up and twining bags: KSh 20 per bag;
- hired labour for loading truck: KSh 2 per bag;
- entry fee Nairobi market: KSh 6 per bag;
- hired labour for unloading truck: KSh 2 per bag.

B. Using public transport
1. Transport costs:
- transport fees: KSh 10 per bag for the local *matatu*, KSh 20 per bag for the connecting *matatu* to Nairobi.
2. Other transport-related costs:
- gunny bags: KSh 10 per bag;
- sisal for twining: KSh 10 per bag;
- hired labour for topping-up and twining bags: KSh 20 per bag;
- hired labour for carrying to the market: KSh 5 per bag;
- entry fee Nairobi market: KSh 6 per bag.

---

at the entrance to the Nairobi wholesale market. Once in the market men have to be hired once more to unload the truck. All these costs would have been met by the collecting wholesaler if the farmer had sold the potatoes at the farm-gate.

Section A of Box A6.1 above quantifies all transport-related costs to the farmer in hiring a 7-tonne truck. The second column of Table 6.1 in the main text shows the average transport costs in relation to the total number of potato bags the farmer wants to sell in Nairobi, based on a maximum of 60 bags per trip.[33]

Rather than hiring a truck, the farmer can use public transport (*matatu*). This has the advantage that the farmer does not have to make a separate trip to Nairobi to organize transport, and does not incur the costs involved. He has to bear the costs of empty gunny bags, sisal and twine, hired labour for topping-up and twining, transport fees for the local *matatu* and the connecting *matatu* to Nairobi,[34] hired labour for carrying the produce to the

---

[33] An extended potato bag weighs on average 125 kilograms. A 7-tonne truck should therefore officially carry no more than 56 bags per trip. Truck drivers do allow 60 bags without much fuss. Collecting wholesalers who own a 7-tonne truck load as many as 70 bags, which is technically possible but leads to higher costs from excessive wear and tear on the truck and the need to bribe policemen who check on overloading on the way to Nairobi.

[34] For each *matatu* the farmer pays a fixed transport fee per bag of potatoes. In addition he has to buy a ticket for himself. This tickets is, however, not included in the transport costs, because it is part of the payment function as will be explained later on.

wholesale market[35], and entry fees to the market (see Section B of Box A6.1). The total average marketing costs in relation to transport are constant, regardless the number of trips made (see second column of Table 6.2 in the main text).

Marketing costs in relation to the storage function
A farmer who travels to the market by *matatu* faces storage costs. The latter may consist of interest and depreciation on investments in a store, and costs arising from storage losses. To start with the first: most farmers in Nyandarua do not have a sophisticated vegetable store, and use their house or a low-budget general farm store instead. Therefore, their investments with regard to storage are nil, and so are their interest and depreciation.

This leaves costs in relation to storage losses. If a farmer hires a 7-tonne truck with a carrying capacity of 60 bags, all bags from one plot can easily fit into the truck and none of the potatoes have to be stored.[36] If a farmer travels to Nairobi by *matatu*, he can only carry 3 bags at a time (matatu drivers do not allow more bags to avoid excessive overloading). The other potatoes harvested from the same plot have to be stored, to be depleted gradually.[37] The storage period depends on the number of bags harvested and the number of trips the farmer is able to make per week. The farmer has to combine his travels with his farm work, and is therefore able to travel to Nairobi twice a week at the most (a trip requiring one and a half days).

The third column of Table 6.2 in the main text shows the average costs in relation to storage losses.[38] The table goes not further than 114 bags. To get 114 bags to Nairobi market would take 38 trips, or almost 5 months travelling twice every week. It is unlikely that any farmer could sustain such an effort. Moreover, the second potato crop of the year in Kinangop is usually harvested five to six months after the first one.

Marketing costs in relation to the finance function
A farmer who does not sell his potatoes at the farm gate to a collecting wholesaler will not get his money until he has reached the urban market and sold the produce to a distributing wholesaler. He has to finance the transport costs from his own resources or with a loan, which in both cases implies interest costs.[39] The money requirements are especially high for hiring a truck. He will need money to travel by *matatu* to Nairobi and for food and lodging

---

[35]   The *matatu* station is a few hundred metres away from the wholesale market, and casual labourers normally carry the bags to the wholesale market.

[36]   According to the farm survey a maximum of 42 bags were sold per plot in 1990. Farmers who sold more than 42 bags per harvesting period had planted more than one plot of potatoes (more than 42 bags per plot were sold in less than 4 per cent of all potato plots in the sample, N=299). If they sold less, they had planted all potatoes on one plot. Potatoes from one plot were all harvested at the same time, while potatoes from different plots could be harvested simultaneously or in phases. Phasewise harvesting required phasewise planting. The length of the rainy season allowed a maximum period of one month between the first and last planting.

[37]   According to field experiments by Durr & Lorenzl (1980) storage losses of potatoes in Kinangop average 2.3 per cent per week.

[38]   The value per bag has been set at KSh 180, the average farm-gate price in Nyandarua in 1990. This figure is taken instead of the cultivation cost, because the farmer has the alternative to sell the potatoes to a collecting wholesaler immediately after the harvest. Thus, the storage losses, when calculated on the basis of opportunity costs, have to be valued against the farm-gate price of the produce.

[39]   If he finances the trade from his own resources, the interest costs are opportunity costs.

while there. The transporter who hires out the truck will, in the beginning, ask for advance payment of the entire rent because he does not know the farmer and does not yet trust him. Finally, the farmer will need money to buy gunny bags and sisal twine and to pay casual labourers for the topping-up, loading and unloading.

The period the money is needed is rather short, since hiring a truck to sell one truckload of potatoes only takes a few days, and offloading the entire harvest will take two months at most. Nevertheless, getting a loan may be costly. It has already been noted in Section 5.2 that commercial banks do not like to deal with horticultural farmers who want to go into trade. Such farmers therefore have to rely on informal money lenders, who charge higher interest rates, but do not require collaterals.[40] The fourth column of Table 6.1 in the main text shows the average interest costs per bag in truck transport.

If the farmer takes public transport instead of hiring a truck, the capital requirements are much lower, including only the transport-related costs (see Section B of Box A6.1) and the costs of a ticket to Nairobi.[41] In addition to this, the farmer faces a minor financial cost because he has to store the potatoes. If he sells the potatoes to a collecting wholesaler he can earn interest on the money received. If he bypasses the collecting wholesaler and uses a *matatu*, the potatoes have to be stored, and the lost interest must be treated as an opportunity cost. The average interest per bag is quite low, however.[42] The fourth column of Table 6.2 in the main text shows the total average costs in relation to the finance function (including interest on the loan and opportunity costs of stored produce) to a farmer using public transport.

Marketing costs in relation to the risk-taking function
Two types of risks are normally mentioned in textbooks on marketing, namely physical and market risks. The first concern the destruction or deterioration of the product itself, while the second relate to changes in the value of a product as it is marketed. The latter changes can be caused by unfavourable price movements, as when changes in consumer taste make the product less desirable (Kohls & Uhl, 1990).

In the case of the potato trade in Kenya, the market risks are small compared to the physical risks. Although potato prices in Nairobi fluctuate considerably, that is due mainly to seasonal cycles (Durr & Lorenzl, 1980). Such cycles do not cause large market risks

---

[40] In 1990, the interest rate at commercial banks on so-called short-term loans was 16.5 per cent per annum. Informal money lenders charged approximately 25 per cent interest on all seasonal loans, regardless of the precise term. To get the real interest rate, the nominal rate has to be corrected for inflation, which was approximately 1 per cent per month in 1990. Thus, the real interest rate on an informal loan for two months was 23 per cent.

[41] The farmer needs to buy a one-way *matatu* ticket to accompany the produce (KSh 55). He can pay his return ticket from the money earned from the sales. A farmer who hires a truck incurs no extra costs in this respect because he accompanies his produce in the truck. The costs of accompanying produce will be explained further under the payment function.

[42] The farmer can bring his money to the local branch of a commercial bank to be put in a savings account. He receives 14 per cent interest on an annual basis, of which 4 per cent is left after correction for inflation. It can be calculated that the average interest per bag is nil up to 54 bags, and KSh 1 between 54 bags and 114 bags. The interest would be much higher according to the short-term real interest rate in the informal market (23 per cent). However, it is unlikely that an ordinary farmer could turn into a successful money lender from one day to the next.

Box A6.2. Marketing costs in relation to physical risks, 1990

To calculate the average costs per bag in relation to physical risks, one must know the frequency that vehicles get into trouble. It is difficult to generalize these chances because they not only depend on the weather but they also differ from one vehicle to the other, depending on the age of the vehicle and the experience of the driver. Our general impression in the 1990 harvesting season in Kinangop was that one out of every 9 journeys (11%), both by truck and by *matatu*, was delayed because a vehicle broke down or got stuck in the mud.

In order to quantify the value losses involved, a few assumptions must be made. First, 5 per cent of the trips are delayed because of a breakdown and 6 per cent because the vehicle gets stuck. Second, quality deterioration of potatoes is highest in the event of a broken-down truck (30% loss in value), followed by a stuck truck (20%), a broken-down *matatu* (15%), and a stuck *matatu* (10%). Pulling a vehicle out of the mud takes less time than repairing a vehicle, and both take less time for a *matatu* than a truck. Moreover, changing to another passing *matatu* is easier than organizing another hired truck.

Before calculating the average loss per bag of potatoes in relation to type of transport, we have to define what value we mean. For the storage losses discussed above, the average farm-gate price of KSh 180 was used for the alternative of selling to collecting wholesalers. The same average applies to losses in relation to vehicle breakdown, because this is assumed to occur throughout the year independent of the weather conditions. Getting stuck in the mud, however, is clearly related to the weather, and so are the farm-gate prices that collecting wholesalers are willing to offer. During heavy rains with their high risks of getting stuck, traders offer lower prices. These prices must also be applied to farmers who would organize transport at that time. Consequently, possible losses due to a stuck vehicle are valued here at KSh 80, the farm-gate price in 1990 during periods of low accessibility.

Based on the above assumptions, it can be calculated that the total average loss per bag of potatoes is:

(5% x 30% x KSh 180) + (6% x 20% x KSh 80) = KSh 3.7 in transport by hired truck, and (5% x 15% x KSh 180) + (6% x 10% x KSh 80) = KSh 1.9 by *matatu*.

---

because there is no seasonal potato storage between harvesting and selling in the urban market.[43]

That physical risks are much larger than the market risks is mainly due to weather and road conditions. Tarmac roads are nonexistent in the production areas of Kinangop, and vehicles break down regularly due to the rough roads. Moreover, the high precipitation of over 800 mm per annum causes regular floods that block roads and leave vehicles stuck in the mud for days. Whenever such things happen, the quality of a perishable good like potatoes deteriorates rather quickly, especially because the load is unprotected against sunshine and rain. If a farmer sells his produce at the farm-gate to a collecting wholesaler, the latter has to bear the costs of such quality losses. The farmer who transports his own potatoes to Nairobi bears the risk himself. Box A6.2 above explains the calculations of the average loss per bag in transporting the potatoes by hired truck and by *matatu*.

Marketing costs in relation to the information function (a transaction cost)
A farmer who bypasses collecting wholesalers to sell his potatoes to distributing wholesalers in Nairobi has to develop a knowledge of the Nairobi market. He has to know who the

---

43 The short-term risks are slightly greater in transport by *matatu* than by truck because depletion of a farmer's stock may then take several months. However, it is difficult to make accurate estimates of price fluctuations during such a period, because short-term price movements depend on unpredictable factors such as the weather.

distributing wholesalers are in the market, and who their brokers are, and how such traders should be approached. In addition he needs to know what price he can expect on the day he brings his potatoes to the market. The problem is that such knowledge can only be gained through experience. Traders in the market do not have a signboard, and prices are neither fixed nor announced in the market.[44] Only when the farmer brings potatoes to the market regularly will he gain a sense of the trading practices, trader strategies and price developments.

Due to his lack of information on his first trips to Nairobi, the farmer receives a lower price than collecting wholesalers. These lost revenues can be defined as the farmer's information costs.[45] On subsequent trips the farmer's knowledge increases and he will make a better price.[46] The sixth column of Table 6.1 in the main text shows the average information costs (revenue losses) per bag of potatoes when he hires a truck. The costs are constant up to 60 bags, the maximum number carried in one trip.[47] Thereafter the average costs decrease as a result of the lower information costs on subsequent trips and the levelling out of the high information costs of the first trip. The sixth column of Table 6.2 in the main text shows the average information costs when he uses public transport.

Marketing costs in relation to the negotiation function (a transaction cost)
Prices in the Nairobi wholesale market are determined through negotiation. The results of the negotiations depend on two factors. The first is knowledge of the market system and price developments. The costs of the negotiation function coincide here with those of the information function. The second factor is the number of bags of potatoes offered for sale. Collecting wholesalers always arrive in Nairobi with a fully loaded truck, both to reduce their average transport costs and to have a strong bargaining position vis-à-vis distributing wholesalers. The more bags the latter traders can buy at one go, the shorter their average negotiating time per bag, and hence the greater their willingness to offer a higher price per bag.[48] This is a matter of concern to a farmer who hires a truck but is not able to fill it completely, and even more so for one that brings three bags of potatoes by *matatu* to the market. The latter will never be able to get the same price as a collecting wholesaler, even if

---

[44] Prices in the Nairobi wholesale market are announced on the radio, but these are selling prices, not buying prices. Moreover, many people have their doubts about the accuracy of the broadcasted prices (see Section 5.6 in the main text, *price information*).

[45] It is estimated that, during his first trip, the farmer receives some 20 per cent less than the average price made by collecting wholesalers. The latter traders report that a farmer may even end up selling his produce to one of these collecting wholesalers while assuming he is dealing with a distributing wholesaler. That is because the market place is too small to bring all produce in, and part of the produce changes hands without entering the market.

[46] It is estimated that he receives 10 per cent less during his second, third and fourth trip. On subsequent trips he receives the same price as collecting wholesalers. For the purpose of our calculations, his information costs for such subsequent trips are considered to be zero, because by then he is familiar with trading practices and strategies in the wholesale market, and he acquires the latest information on price developments by accompanying his produce there. The costs of accompanying produce will be dealt with under the payment function (see 'marketing costs in relation to the payment function' below).

[47] It may be expected that in quantities up to 60 bags the farmer will carry all produce by hired truck to Nairobi in one go. Hiring a truck three times to carry 20 bags a trip would be very costly indeed.

[48] The negotiating time per bag is lower when more bags are bought at once because a trader will negotiate approximately as long about the price for 60 bags of potatoes as about the price of 40 bags. Negotiations for 30 bags will probably take longer than for 3 bags, but not ten times as long.

he frequents the market as much as the wholesaler.[49] The average negotiation costs per bag of potatoes are shown for a hired truck in the seventh column of Table 6.1 in the main text and for a *matatu* in the seventh column of Table 6.2.[50]

Marketing costs in relation to the payment function (a transaction cost)
To bypass the collecting wholesalers, the farmer carries the potatoes to Nairobi himself. In theory the farmer might also ask somebody he knows who is going to Nairobi anyway to accompany the produce and do the selling. However, he will prefer to travel to Nairobi himself, for two reasons. First, knowledge about the market system and price developments will only accumulate when the same person does the selling all the time. Second, the distributing wholesalers pay cash on delivery and the farmer will only trust himself (or his close relatives) when it comes to bringing the money back home. He will therefore accompany the produce as part of the payment function.[51]

The costs of accompanying the produce are related to the type of transport used. When using a hired truck, the farmer can sit in the truck on the journey out. He has to travel back home by *matatu*.[52] The entire trip takes one and a half days, including half a day to load the truck and travel to Nairobi, and one day to sell the produce and return home. The farmer does not spend the night in a hotel but in the truck to make sure the potatoes are not stolen. The truck is parked in the queue with other produce trucks in front of the wholesale market. Since he has no lodging costs, only food costs remain.[53] On top of the travel and food costs, the opportunity costs of the farmer's labour have to be counted.[54] The eighth column of Table 6.1 in the main text shows the average payment costs (costs of accompanying the produce) per bag when using a hired truck.

When using public transport instead of a hired truck, the farmer must buy tickets to and from Nairobi. The entire trip will again take one and a half days. The farmer will travel during the afternoon and night, and return the next day after selling the potatoes. Based on three bags per trip, the average payment costs when the farmer uses public transport are shown in the eighth column of Table 6.2 in the main text.

---

[49] The difference in price in relation to lot size is estimated to be 10 per cent for those offering fewer than 10 bags for sale, 5 per cent for less than 30 bags (half a truckload), and 2.5 per cent for less than 60 bags (1 truckload). For the purpose of our calculations, the negotiation costs are considered to be zero for a full truck (60 bags). In reality the negotiation costs are then equal to the costs of the time spent by the farmer in the negotiation process. However, that is part of the total time required to accompany the produce to the wholesale market. The latter costs are dealt with under the payment function (see 'marketing costs in relation to the payment function' below).

[50] A farmer who takes a *matatu* will always get 10 per cent less (KSh 34) because he offers 3 bags for sale at a time (it is assumed he will try to minimize transport costs by carrying the maximum number of bags allowed by the *matatu* driver).

[51] If he does not collect the money himself but entrusts it to someone else, he could face high enforcement costs to get the money later. Accompanying the produce and collecting the money saves the farmer these enforcement costs (see also Section 6.1 in the main text on perceptions of distributing wholesalers with regard to the risks involved).

[52] A one-way trip by *matatu* costs KSh 55 (see costs in relation to the transport function).

[53] The food costs are KSh 50 per day out. Strictly speaking, the food costs until the bags are sold (half a day: KSh 25) should also to be included in the loan mentioned under the finance function. The related interest costs per bag of potatoes are, however, very small or negligible and therefore ignored.

[54] The opportunity costs of the farmers own labour are KSh 33 per day (see 'marketing costs in relation to the transport function' above).

Appendix 7.1:
Sample overlap and difference between the two analytic alternatives

		analysis of all trade flows, rural assembly markets excluded		
		no. of cases included in sample	no. of cases excluded from sample	all cases
analysis of trade flows with known terminal markets	no. of cases included in sample	1838	636	2474
	no. of cases excluded from sample	844	458	1302
	all cases	2682	1094	3776

Appendix 8.1:
Additional analyses of step-1 versus step-2 channels for trade flows with known terminal markets

A. Alternative values of the variable POPSIZE for Daraja Mbili market

A1. Results for first alternative (POPSIZE = 11.037)

Total number of cases	725			
Number of selected cases	725			
Dependent variable (0,1)	STEP2			
Model Chi-Square	114.1 (df=6, p=0.000)			
Correctly classified observations	67.5% (t=9.4, p=0.000)			
Number of extreme cases	0			

Variables in the equation:	B	S.E.	Wald	Sig.
INVPOPSIZE	- 0.5237	0.1106	22.43	0.0000
POPDENSITY	- 0.1104	0.0457	5.85	0.0156
INVTRANSTIME	- 0.6182	0.1482	17.41	0.0000
LEAVES	- 0.4361	0.2238	3.80	0.0513
TUBERS	0.0413	0.2213	0.03	0.8518
TURNOVER	0.0059	0.0067	0.79	0.3728
Constant	1.4571	0.2372	37.74	0.0000

A2. Results for second alternative (POPSIZE = 33.112)

Total number of cases	725			
Number of selected cases	725			
Dependent variable (0,1)	STEP2			
Model Chi-Square	113.9 (df=6, p=0.000)			
Correctly classified observations	67.5% (t=9.4, p=0.000)			
Number of extreme cases	0			

Variables in the equation:	B	S.E.	Wald	Sig.
INVPOPSIZE	- 0.5194	0.1102	22.24	0.0000
POPDENSITY	- 0.1118	0.0457	5.99	0.0144
INVTRANSTIME	- 0.6177	0.1482	17.37	0.0000
LEAVES	- 0.4366	0.2238	3.80	0.0511
TUBERS	0.0379	0.2212	0.03	0.8640
TURNOVER	0.0060	0.0067	0.81	0.3684
Constant	1.4565	0.2371	37.72	0.0000

B. Other random samples of step-2 channels

B1. Results for first alternative

Total number of cases	754	
Number of selected cases	754	
Dependent variable (0,1)	STEP2	
Model Chi-Square	131.3 (df=6, p=0.0000)	
Correctly classified observations	69.0% (t=10.4, p=0.000)	
Number of extreme cases	0	

Variables in the equation:	B	S.E.	Wald	Sig.
INVPOPSIZE	- 0.5886	0.1120	27.64	0.0000
POPDENSITY	- 0.0976	0.0461	4.49	0.0342
INVTRANSTIME	- 0.5781	0.1471	15.45	0.0001
LEAVES	- 0.6094	0.2270	7.21	0.0073
TUBERS	0.1652	0.2144	0.59	0.4411
TURNOVER	0.0080	0.0067	1.43	0.2322
Constant	1.4404	0.2371	36.92	0.0000

B2. Results for second alternative

Total number of cases	698	
Number of selected cases	698	
Dependent variable (0,1)	STEP2	
Model Chi-Square	117.8 (df=6, p=0.000)	
Correctly classified observations	66.8% (t=8.9, p=0.000)	
Number of extreme cases	0	

Variables in the equation:	B	S.E.	Wald	Sig.
INVPOPSIZE	- 0.4514	0.1073	17.69	0.0000
POPDENSITY	- 0.1452	0.0477	9.26	0.0023
INVTRANSTIME	- 0.7323	0.1536	22.73	0.0000
LEAVES	- 0.4489	0.2305	3.79	0.0519
TUBERS	0.0540	0.2217	0.06	0.8075
TURNOVER	- 0.0002	0.0071	0.00	0.9749
Constant	1.6272	0.2465	43.58	0.0000

Appendix 8.2:
Additional analyses of step-2 versus step-3 channels for trade flows with known terminal markets

A. Alternative values of the variable POPSIZE for Daraja Mbili market

A1. Results for first alternative (POPSIZE = 11.037)

Total number of cases	2116
Number of selected cases	2116
Dependent variable (0,1)	STEP3
Model Chi-Square	545.5 (df=6, p=0.000)
Correctly classified observations	73.4 % (t=21.6, p=0.000)
Number of extreme cases	69

Variables in the equation:	B	S.E.	Wald	Sig.
INVPOPSIZE	- 0.2258	0.0884	6.53	0.0106
POPDENSITY	0.1243	0.0332	14.03	0.0002
INVTRANSTIME	- 1.9411	0.1083	321.00	0.0000
LEAVES	- 0.5815	0.1951	8.88	0.0029
TUBERS	0.0593	0.1235	0.23	0.6315
TURNOVER	- 0.0155	0.0032	23.09	0.0000
Constant	1.5059	0.1133	176.65	0.0000

A2. Results for second alternative (POPSIZE = 33.112)

Total number of cases	2116
Number of selected cases	2116
Dependent variable (0,1)	STEP3
Model Chi-Square	545.6 (df=6, p=0.000)
Correctly classified observations	73.4 % (t=21.6, p=0.000)
Number of extreme cases	69

Variables in the equation:	B	S.E.	Wald	Sig.
INVPOPSIZE	- 0.2270	0.0882	6.63	0.0100
POPDENSITY	0.1238	0.0331	13.94	0.0002
INVTRANSTIME	- 1.9411	0.1084	320.96	0.0000
LEAVES	- 0.5824	0.1951	8.91	0.0028
TUBERS	- 0.0599	0.1235	0.24	0.6275
TURNOVER	- 0.0155	0.0032	23.11	0.0000
Constant	1.5070	0.1134	176.73	0.0000

Appendix 8.3:
Additional analyses for step-1 versus step-3 channels for trade flows with known terminal markets

A. Alternative values of the variable POPSIZE for Daraja Mbili market

A1. Results for first alternative (POPSIZE = 11.037)

Total number of cases	748
Number of selected cases	748
Dependent variable (0,1)	STEP3
Model Chi-Square	415.8 (df=6, p=0.0000)
Correctly classified observations	81.8 % (t=17.3, p=0.000)
Number of extreme cases	35

Variables in the equation:	B	S.E.	Wald	Sig.
INVPOPSIZE	- 0.4888	0.1446	11.42	0.0007
POPDENSITY	0.0353	0.0614	0.33	0.5645
INVTRANSTIME	- 2.3959	0.1985	145.68	0.0000
LEAVES	- 1.0635	0.3371	9.95	0.0016
TUBERS	0.0092	0.2648	0.00	0.9722
TURNOVER	- 0.0237	0.0078	9.16	0.0025
Constant	2.9066	0.2525	132.49	0.0000

A2. Results for second alternative (POPSIZE = 33.112)

Total number of cases	748
Number of selected cases	748
Dependent variable (0,1)	STEP3
Model Chi-Square	415.5 (df=6, p=0.0000)
Correctly classified observations	81.8 % (t=17.3, p=0.000)
Number of extreme cases	35

Variables in the equation:	B	S.E.	Wald	Sig.
INVPOPSIZE	- 0.4814	0.1441	11.16	0.0008
POPDENSITY	0.0337	0.0614	0.30	0.5830
INVTRANSTIME	- 2.3960	0.1986	145.55	0.0000
LEAVES	- 1.0638	0.3371	9.96	0.0016
TUBERS	0.0062	0.2648	0.00	0.9813
TURNOVER	- 0.0237	0.0078	9.10	0.0026
Constant	2.9056	0.2525	132.45	0.0000

B. Other random samples of step-3 channels

B1. Results for first alternative

Total number of cases	720
Number of selected cases	720
Dependent variable (0,1)	STEP3
Model Chi-Square	413.4 (df=6, p=0.0000)
Correctly classified observations	82.1 % (t=17.2, p=0.000)
Number of extreme cases	30

Variables in the equation:	B	S.E.	Wald	Sig.
INVPOPSIZE	- 0.4498	0.1509	8.88	0.0029
POPDENSITY	0.0245	0.0628	0.15	0.6970
INVTRANSTIME	- 2.4968	0.2114	139.44	0.0000
LEAVES	- 1.1157	0.3476	10.30	0.0013
TUBERS	0.0042	0.2684	0.00	0.9875
TURNOVER	- 0.0225	0.0079	8.11	0.0044
Constant	2.9068	0.2624	122.69	0.0000

B2. Results for second alternative

Total number of cases	719
Number of selected cases	719
Dependent variable (0,1)	STEP3
Model Chi-Square	416.5 (df=6, p=0.000)
Correctly classified observations	81.5 % (t=16.9, p=0.000)
Number of extreme cases	35

Variables in the equation:	B	S.E.	Wald	Sig.
INVPOPSIZE	- 0.5192	0.1501	11.97	0.0005
POPDENSITY	0.0250	0.0640	0.15	0.6958
INVTRANSTIME	- 2.4648	0.2101	137.68	0.0000
LEAVES	- 0.9772	0.3515	7.73	0.0054
TUBERS	0.0436	0.2705	0.03	0.8718
TURNOVER	- 0.0200	0.0082	5.91	0.0151
Constant	2.8283	0.2613	117.19	0.0000

Appendix 8.4:
Binary analyses using all trade flows, rural assembly markets excluded[55]

A. ANALYSIS STEP-1 VERSUS STEP-2 CHANNELS

A1. Results of analysis

Total number of cases	465
Number of selected cases	465
Dependent variable (0,1)	STEP2
Model Chi-Square	66.7 (df=6, p=0.0000)
Correctly classified observations	63.9% (t=5.9, p=0.000)
Number of extreme cases	1

Variables in the equation:	B	S.E.	Wald	Sig.
INVPOPSIZE	- 0.6265	0.1958	10.24	0.0014
POPDENSITY	- 0.0122	0.0682	0.03	0.8585
INVTRANSTIME	- 0.6703	0.1812	13.69	0.0002
LEAVES	- 0.4658	0.2763	2.84	0.0918
TUBERS	0.4321	0.2863	2.28	0.1312
TURNOVER	0.0046	0.0083	0.31	0.5749
Constant	1.1263	0.3025	13.86	0.0002

A2. Results of analysis with other random samples of step-2 channels

A21. Results for first alternative

Total number of cases	442
Number of selected cases	442
Dependent variable (0,1)	STEP2
Model Chi-Square	43.0 (df=6, p=0.0000)
Correctly classified observations	62.0% (t=5.0, p=0.000)
Number of extreme cases	0

---

[55] Heteroskedasticity occurred in all the analyses, similar to that found in the analysis of trade flows with known terminal markets. It could be solved as before by taking the inversions of POPSIZE and TRANSTIME. Daraja Mbili market is not included in the present analyses because it is a rural assembly market (in the analysis of trade flows with known terminal markets, the analysis had to be repeated for different POPSIZE values of this market).

Variables in the equation:	B	S.E.	Wald	Sig.
INVPOPSIZE	- 0.6467	0.2047	9.98	0.0016
POPDENSITY	- 0.0165	0.0671	0.06	0.8085
INVTRANSTIME	- 0.4651	0.1756	7.01	0.0081
LEAVES	- 0.4152	0.2623	2.51	0.1135
TUBERS	0.0124	0.3013	0.00	0.9671
TURNOVER	0.0087	0.0094	0.85	0.3575
Constant	0.7577	0.3240	5.47	0.0194

A22. Results for second alternative

Total number of cases	446
Number of selected cases	446
Dependent variable (0,1)	STEP2
Model Chi-Square	47.5 (df=6, p=0.0000)
Correctly classified observations	62.1% (t=5.1, p=0.000)
Number of extreme cases	2

Variables in the equation:	B	S.E.	Wald	Sig.
INVPOPSIZE	- 0.6750	0.2070	10.63	0.0011
POPDENSITY	0.0204	0.0677	0.09	0.7630
INVTRANSTIME	- 0.4674	0.1830	6.53	0.0106
LEAVES	- 0.2205	0.2583	0.73	0.3932
TUBERS	0.3641	0.2950	1.52	0.2172
TURNOVER	0.0108	0.0089	1.48	0.2234
Constant	0.6575	0.3193	4.24	0.0395

B. ANALYSIS STEP-2 VERSUS STEP-3 CHANNELS

B1. Results of analysis

Total number of cases	1689
Number of selected cases	1689
Dependent variable (0,1)	STEP3
Model Chi-Square	332.5 (df=6, p=0.0000)
Correctly classified observations	68.9% (t=15.5, p=0.000)
Number of extreme cases	24

Variables in the equation:	B	S.E.	Wald	Sig.
INVPOPSIZE	- 0.3704	0.1288	8.27	0.0040
POPDENSITY	0.0574	0.0370	2.41	0.1205
INVTRANSTIME	- 1.4451	0.1027	197.96	0.0000
LEAVES	- 0.4060	0.1829	4.93	0.0265
TUBERS	- 0.0937	0.1419	0.44	0.5088
TURNOVER	- 0.0075	0.0030	6.38	0.0116
Constant	1.2482	0.1245	100.46	0.0000

B2. Results of analysis with other random samples of step-3 channels

B21. Results for first alternative

Total number of cases	1727
Number of selected cases	1727
Dependent variable (0,1)	STEP3
Model Chi-Square	335.2 (df=6, p=0.0000)
Correctly classified observations	70.0% (t=16.6, p=0.000)
Number of extreme cases	22

Variables in the equation:	B	S.E.	Wald	Sig.
INVPOPSIZE	- 0.3240	0.1228	6.96	0.0083
POPDENSITY	0.0501	0.0373	1.81	0.1789
INVTRANSTIME	- 1.4139	0.1003	198.60	0.0000
LEAVES	- 0.4390	0.1829	5.76	0.0164
TUBERS	- 0.0454	0.1393	0.11	0.7446
TURNOVER	- 0.0072	0.0029	6.07	0.0137
Constant	1.2669	0.1239	104.51	0.0000

B22. Results for second alternative

Total number of cases	1705
Number of selected cases	1705
Dependent variable (0,1)	STEP3
Model Chi-Square	307.8 (df=6, p=0.0000)
Correctly classified observations	68.6% (t=15.4, p=0.000)
Number of extreme cases	24

Variables in the equation:	B	S.E.	Wald	Sig.
INVPOPSIZE	- 0.3295	0.1235	7.12	0.0076
POPDENSITY	0.0575	0.0367	2.46	0.1167
INVTRANSTIME	- 1.3629	0.0988	190.31	0.0000
LEAVES	- 0.3832	0.1779	4.64	0.0312
TUBERS	- 0.1907	0.1430	1.78	0.1824
TURNOVER	- 0.0071	0.0030	5.54	0.0186
Constant	1.2230	0.1239	97.37	0.0000

C. ANALYSIS STEP-1 VERSUS STEP-3 CHANNELS

C1. Results of analysis

Total number of cases	448
Number of selected cases	448
Dependent variable (0,1)	STEP3
Model Chi-Square	194.9 (df=6, p=0.0000)
Correctly classified observations	76.3% (t=11.2, p=0.000)
Number of extreme cases	18

Variables in the equation:	B	S.E.	Wald	Sig.
INVPOPSIZE	- 0.7375	0.3160	5.45	0.0196
POPDENSITY	0.1350	0.0824	2.69	0.1013
INVTRANSTIME	- 2.0379	0.2313	77.60	0.0000
LEAVES	- 0.6092	0.3602	2.86	0.0908
TUBERS	0.3123	0.3440	0.82	0.3640
TURNOVER	- 0.0097	0.0089	1.19	0.2745
Constant	2.0352	0.3028	45.17	0.0000

C2. Results of analysis with other random samples of step-3 channels

C21. Results for first alternative

Total number of cases	443
Number of selected cases	443
Dependent variable (0,1)	STEP3
Model Chi-Square	190.0 (df=6, p=0.0000)
Correctly classified observations	74.3% (t=10.2, p=0.000)
Number of extreme cases	5

Variables in the equation:	B	S.E.	Wald	Sig.
INVPOPSIZE	- 0.5989	0.2766	4.69	0.0304
POPDENSITY	0.0234	0.0864	0.07	0.7867
INVTRANSTIME	- 1.8576	0.2239	68.82	0.0000
LEAVES	- 0.8049	0.3685	4.77	0.0289
TUBERS	0.0673	0.3301	0.04	0.8384
TURNOVER	- 0.0031	0.0085	0.13	0.7209
Constant	2.0461	0.3084	44.00	0.0000

C22. Results for second alternative

Total number of cases	464
Number of selected cases	464
Dependent variable (0,1)	STEP3
Model Chi-Square	192.5 (df=6, p=0.0000)
Correctly classified observations	75.4% (t=10.9, p=0.000)
Number of extreme cases	12

Variables in the equation:	B	S.E.	Wald	Sig.
INVPOPSIZE	- 0.4634	0.2327	3.97	0.0464
POPDENSITY	0.0175	0.0822	0.05	0.8312
INVTRANSTIME	- 1.9076	0.2185	76.21	0.0000
LEAVES	- 0.4104	0.3456	1.41	0.2350
TUBERS	0.1901	0.3333	0.33	0.5683
TURNOVER	- 0.0107	0.0082	1.70	0.1919
Constant	2.2018	0.2935	56.27	0.0000

Appendix 9.1:
Policy recommendations

In this appendix some ideas are developed for short-term improvements in the horticultural sector (first part) and for long-term policies (second part). Recommendations are made which may be of use to actors and institutions operating in the sector as well as to the Kenyan government. Private market intermediaries must carry out the job, but some state regulation is advocated, for instance when it comes to the standardization of wholesale units. In addition, state investments in facilities such as roads, market places and improved information systems are seen as important. Finally, it is argued that extension services and training are needed to improve the sector's capacity to solve its own problems.

Short-term improvements in market performance

Various problems and constraints hamper the present performance of the sector. Some recommendations will be made that may apply not only to Kenya but also to other African countries with similar horticultural production and marketing systems.

The domestic market and the export market are dealt with separately. Their producers and market intermediaries differ, and their marketing problems and constraints are not necessarily the same.

The domestic market
The first constraint that demands attention in the domestic market is the quality of produce entering the market. Marketing channels may be very efficient and effective but that is to no avail if the quality of the produce is poor to start with. The quality is poor for various reasons.[56] Farmers use uncertified seeds and planting material, because certified ones are either not available or too expensive. The crop is attacked by pests and diseases, which prosper due to a lack of crop rotation, scarcity of affordable agro-chemicals, and untimely and indiscriminate use of them. Fertilizer applications are low because farmers lack knowledge about the use of fertilizers or do not have the money to buy them. Agro-chemicals are sprayed right until the last moment, and sometimes even after harvesting, leaving high chemical residues in the food of consumers. In sum, poor quality is the result of lack of financial means, failing supply and inadequate knowledge. It is recommended that

---

[56] Section 3.4 (in the main text).

the lack of financial means be tackled through some kind of credit system, as will be discussed more in general later on. In addition, farmers need to be educated by extension officers about proper input use. Finally, local seed companies, and government and private nurseries require support in their efforts to supply farmers with certified and affordable seeds and planting material.

Once the produce is harvested, marketing problems arise. Poor infrastructure in the production areas causes accessibility problems.[57] The obvious solution is to improve the physical infrastructure. Roads, however, are expensive, especially in horticultural production areas located in hilly or mountainous areas with a high precipitation. In some parts of Kenya a system has been introduced whereby groups of people are responsible for the maintenance of certain stretches of rural roads. They receive a small reward in return. The same is being done in other parts of Africa as part of food-for-work programmes. The system is recommendable for horticultural production areas.

As well as by poor roads, the collecting stage of the marketing process is affected by the state of rural market places.[58] Most of them lack essential facilities such as stalls, toilets, fences, and proper drainage systems. They are usually too small, so that many traders sell their produce outside the official trading area. The areas themselves change into mudpools after every shower. The poor conditions affect the quality of the commodities traded. One does not expect every rural market place to have concrete stalls, but it is recommended that they at least have a concrete floor, toilets, and a proper drainage system. If the fenced area were big enough to harbour all traders, the latter could be required to trade only in the official market place. This will make collection of market fees easier. Such fees are only fair, however, if the local authorities use at least part of the revenues to improve and maintain the marketplace.

Transport is also a major constraint. Trucks for hire are scarce in the production areas, and this restricts the possibilities for farmers and collecting wholesalers to get the commodities from production areas to large urban centres.[59] Improved availability of trucks would increase competition among collecting wholesalers, which may lead to better prices to farmers. It would also give groups of farmers the opportunity to go into trade. Again, some kind of credit system is needed that enables issuing loans to farmer groups and traders to purchase trucks, even if they lack collateral.

Produce losses during transport are usually high due to perishability of the horticultural commodities and lack of adequate sorting, grading and packing. The Taita HPC has shown that such activities repay their costs.[60] Improper packing usually does not arise from ignorance of farmers and traders, but from a scarcity of timber and the high costs of ready-made crates and boxes. The practice of packing vegetables and fruits in very large units like extended bags of over 120 kgs and wooden boxes of 80 kgs also stems from the present market fee system in the urban wholesale markets, which is based on transport units regardless of their size. It is recommended that extension services sensitize farmers and traders to the advantages of proper sorting, grading and packing. In advice on appropriate

---

[57] Section 5.6 (in the main text).
[58] Section 5.2.
[59] Sections 5.6 and 6.2.
[60] Section 5.3.

packaging means, both technical and financial aspects have to be taken into account. Standardization of selling units in the urban wholesale markets has to be realized, for example by allowing only non-extended bags and wooden boxes of less than 40 kg to enter the market place.[61]

Capital is a constraint both in horticultural production and in marketing. Financial institutions are reluctant to supply credit for smallholder horticulture.[62] Collateral is often a problem. In some parts of Kenya (e.g. Taita Taveta), farmers have not yet received their title deeds. In other parts, financial institutions have experienced problems in selling land mortgaged as collateral because local communities became very hostile to potential buyers (e.g. in Kisii). Financial institutions ought to develop a positive attitude towards horticultural smallholders. Loans need to be made available both for buying inputs and financing trade. Group lending may be recommendable when title deeds are absent or cannot be used as collateral.[63]

Collecting wholesalers play a crucial role when it comes to marketing horticultural commodities, and most farmers cannot do without them.[64] However, if farmers organized themselves into farmer groups and went into trade themselves, they would receive the trade profits that are now being made by the traders. Group marketing by farmers is feasible, as is shown by the example of the Taita HPC.[65] It requires an elaborate concept that may need to include not only organized transport, but also production planning based on the monitoring of market prices; input supply; improved sorting, grading and packing; direct selling to retailers; and last but not least, independent business-oriented management. Whether all aspects of the concept are required depends on the type of horticultural commodities handled and the market targeted. It is recommended that group marketing only be supported when it is based on a well thought-out marketing strategy.

The bargaining power of horticultural farmers towards traders depends not only on supply and demand conditions, as reflected in average farm-gate and market prices, but also on knowledge among the farmers about these conditions. The Kenyan government has tried to improve the farmers' knowledge by regularly broadcasting the prices prevailing in selected urban markets.[66] The effect has been minimal, since very few horticultural farmers listen to the broadcasts. Most of them either do not have a wireless set or batteries, or they do not know about the broadcasts, or they listen only to programmes in their tribal language which do not include this kind of information. It is therefore recommended that price information be broadcasted on regional stations that use local languages. Extension workers should sensitize the farmers to the price broadcasts on the radio. They can also listen to the

---

[61] The alternative to standardization is to weigh all produce when it enters, but this does not seem a practical option. Standardization must be introduced simultaneously in the largest wholesale markets (Nairobi, Mombasa, Kisumu). The other markets will then follow suit without problems.

[62] Section 5.2.

[63] Farmers or traders could organize themselves into associations to open savings accounts. Fixed weekly or monthly contributions could be used to generate enough capital for them to eventually apply for loans, for instance to develop irrigation channels or buy a truck. Meanwhile, the money could be used to issue short-term credit to members who want to start or expand their horticultural farm or trade business.

[64] Section 6.2.

[65] Section 5.3.

[66] Section 5.6.

broadcasts themselves and pass on the information to farmers who have no radios or batteries. They could, for instance, write the prices on blackboards in local marketplaces and at the Chief's office.[67]

Similarities exist between the constraints in horticultural marketing and those in the marketing of grains. To improve the performance of liberalized grain marketing in Africa, projects and programmes focus on the development of marketplaces, storage structures and rural financial markets; on long-term infrastructural policies to reduce transport costs; and on investment in market-support systems, marketing research, and quality grades and standards.[68] It is recommended that such initiatives not confine themselves to grains, but be expanded to horticultural commodities. As has been shown, they require the same measures. Horticulture deserves not to be forgotten.

The export market

Although producers and market intermediaries that deal with export commodities are generally performing well, they also have problems to cope with. In the production sphere, the problems of small-scale producers especially need attention. A major part of the production is concentrated on large farms run by export traders. However, small-scale farmers are also involved, either as contract farmers or as independent producers who sell to export traders.[69] The latter group is small but important from a development point of view. They act as forerunners of a much larger groups of smallholder producers who are considering switching to horticultural export crops. A major problem for them is scarcity of appropriate planting material. Local nurseries do not produce the right materials, and international breeders are reluctant to deal with small-scale farmers because of risks of illegal multiplication. Moreover, certified material that has to be imported is expensive, and small-scale farmers cannot afford to buy it without receiving some kind of credit. Additional credit is required to buy agro-chemicals. Therefore, the recommendations formulated above with regard to planting material and credit also apply for smallholders focusing on the export market.

The farmers also need to be advised, above all on chemical residues. The European Union is implementing very stringent rules on maximum residue levels, and smallholders stand an increasing chance that their crop will be rejected by exporters, or destroyed on arrival in Europe.[70] Information is also required on post-harvest handling: proper treatment and packing are essential to guard quality. Scarcity of affordable packing materials is a problem which is not easy to solve because local low-cost alternatives do not meet the required international standards.

To produce the right varieties, smallholders need to have access to market information about demand developments in the international market. At present they are not

---

[67] At present, the prices are broadcasted only a few times a week. A daily routine would be better, as prices of vegetables and fruits fluctuate substantially from one day to another. The most appropriate time would be immediately after the news because farmers who want to save batteries switch off the radio after the news. At present broadcasted prices apply only to urban markets. It would be better if prices at the major rural assembly markets were included in the broadcasts, as they are nearer to the farm-gate price that most farmers have to negotiate for. See also Shepherd (1997).

[68] Section 2.3.

[69] Section 5.4.

[70] Appendices 5.5 and 5.8.

abreast of things. Local extension officers cannot help them because they know as little as the farmers. It is recommended that a group of extension workers be trained to deal specifically with horticultural export crops.

Large-scale producer-exporters are well capable of solving their own production problems. Like exporters who have not gone into production, they do face persistent international transport constraints due to scarcity of cargo space.[71] The availability of cargo space is partly related the number of the number of scheduled passenger flights to Kenya, partly to the stopover of cargo planes on their way North, and partly to the willingness of charter companies to bring in their planes. One of the decisive factors with regard to the latter two categories is the local taxation of jet fuel. The tax used to be much higher in Kenya than in neighbouring counties. Although it has been reduced now, a further reduction may have to be considered.

A second problem the exporters face is the negative image of Kenyan horticultural produce in Europe.[72] Efforts have been put into reducing the use of agro-chemicals and improving labour conditions on large-scale farms, but the results have not yet been communicated to European consumers. It is recommended that this issue be taken up, for instance by the Horticultural Crops Development Authority.

Long-term horticultural policies

The domestic market

On the basis of our vertical differentiation model, some recommendations can be made for the longer term. Two premises underlie them. First, horticultural production for the domestic market is expected to remain a smallholder business. Second, the commodities are to be traded in a free-market system. Given these conditions, the model that has been proposed in this book predicts that changes in urban population, transport time, and rural population density have the strongest impact on the marketing system.[73]

Based on present trends, further urban growth may be expected in Kenya.[74] According to the model, it will increase the importance of more differentiated marketing channels, especially if smaller towns are the centres of urban growth. Farmer-traders will become scarcer and wholesale traders will arise, partly because some of the produce will be brought in from further away (increasing transport time). The growth in wholesale trade demands improved market places. The Kenyan government has focused so far on building separate wholesale markets, but once established these markets have been found to also develop as centres of retail trade.[75] The distinction between wholesale and retail horticultural trade is rather artificial, and it is therefore recommended that markets be built where both types of trade have a place. To ensure that farmers retain direct access to consumers, the new

---

[71] Section 5.4.
[72] Section 5.4.
[73] Section 8.5.
[74] Section 3.1.
[75] Section 5.2.

market places should have both stalls that are rented out on a monthly basis and a section where part-time (farmer-)traders can sell commodities by paying a daily fee.

At some moment in time, large urban market places will require cold storage facilities. Local market authorities may take the initiative to build and manage the facilities. It is recommended that they do so only after a thorough feasibility study. Once they are built, accountable management and transparent procedures are a prerequisite for running the cold stores to the benefit of all market participants. The initiative could also be left to large traders. They would probably run the facilities more efficiently and effectively, but at the expense of accessibility to smaller traders. Whether private traders or the local market authorities take the lead is partly a political choice.

The presence of cold stores will increase the shelf life of highly perishable commodities such as leafy vegetables. According to the model, this will lead to more differentiated marketing channels. Farmer-traders will become less important and wholesalers more important in the trade of these commodities. This has its bearing on the desired infrastructure of the market places where such cold stores would be located.

In addition to urban growth, rising pressure on rural land may be foreseen. More rural households will embark on the horticultural enterprise, which requires relatively little land, but the output per farmer will decline.[76] According to the research findings, the consequent lower supply concentration will increase the need for rural assembly markets.[77] The location of such a market within a region has to be based on its relative accessibility: it should be better accessible by road or rail than its hinterland. Most assembly markets that already exist in Kenya had been small local markets before they evolved their assembling function. This suggests that it is better to upgrade a well-situated local market place than to establish a new one. Upgrading means improving its accessibility, preferably by means of all-weather roads. Investments will pay themselves back, as rural assembly markets are expected to maintain their importance at least for the coming decade.

Beyond the coming decade it is difficult to predict what will happen. For one thing, it is hoped that per capita incomes will have increased in the intervening period. This would probably lead to a more substantial demand for high-quality produce. As a consequence, vertical coordination and integration may become more common in the domestic market. Farmer groups could take the lead, using a similar strategy to that presently applied by the Taita HPC. To become successful, the groups will require technical and managerial support. For the rest, they should be able to develop without being shackled by political forces.

Export market

Long-term developments in the horticultural export market depend on the future structures of world supply and demand, and on Kenya's competitiveness. In addition, the production of export crops will depend on local developments such as an increasing demand for food, accumulating pressure on land, and the rise of a rural proletariat that needs jobs.

It is difficult to say what the role of Kenyan policymakers could be. One thing may be important. At present the horticultural export assortment is largely different from the assortment offered for sale in the domestic market. To remain a successful exporter in the

---

[76] Section 3.4.
[77] Section 6.7.

long term, it may be important to have a solid home market.[78] The Kenyan government could play a role in promoting the local consumption of commodities that have hitherto only been exported.

---

[78] Section 5.4.

References

ABBOTT, J. C. (1987) *Agricultural Marketing Enterprises for the Developing World*. Cambridge: Cambridge University Press.

ABBOTT, J. C. (1988) *Agricultural Processing for Development*. Aldershot: Avebury.

ABBOTT, J. C. & H. C. CREUPELANDT (1966) *Agricultural Marketing Boards: Their Establishment and Operation*. Rome: Food and Agricultural Organization of the United Nations.

ABIR, M. (1970) 'Southern Ethiopia.' In R. Gray & D. Birmingham (eds.) *Pre-Colonial African Trade; Essays on Trade in Central and Eastern Africa before 1900*. London: Oxford University Press, pp. 119-138.

ACHROL, R. S., T. REVE & L. W. STERN (1983) 'The Environment of Marketing Channel Dyads: a Framework for Comparative Analysis.' In *Journal of Marketing*, vol. 47, Fall, pp. 55-67.

ADEBAYO, A. G. (1991) 'The Kola Nut Trade in West Africa: A Note on the Nigerian End of the Trade under British Rule, 1900-45.' In *Frankfurter Afrikanistische Blätter*, no. 3, pp. 94-109.

ADEDEJI, A. (1984) 'The Economic Evolution of Developing Africa.' In *The Cambridge History of Africa, Volume 8, from c. 1940 to c. 1975*, Cambridge: Cambridge University Press.

AFRICAN WORLD (1954) 'Kenya Tribe's Co-operative Effort, Vegetable Growing in the Teita Hills.' In *African World*, February, p. 15.

AHMED, R. (1988) 'Pricing Principles and Public Intervention in Domestic Markets.' In J. W. Mellor & R. Ahmed (eds.) *Agricultural Price Policy for Developing Countries*, Baltimore: Johns Hopkins, pp. 55-80.

AKASAKA, M. (1992) 'Small Urban Centers and the Development of Periodic Markets in Rural Mali.' In *African Urban Studies II*, Tokyo: Institute of the Study of Languages and Cultures of Asia and Africa, vol. 2, pp. 1-42.

ALDERSON, W. (1967) 'Factors Governing the Development of Marketing Channels.' In B. Mallen (ed.) *The Marketing Channel, A Conceptual View Point*. New York: Wiley, pp. 35-40.

ALPERS, E. A. (1968) 'The Nineteenth Century: Prelude to Colonialism.' In B. A. Ogot & J. A. Kieran (eds.) *Zamani, A Survey of East African History*, Nairobi: East African Publishing House, Longmans of Kenya, pp. 238-254.

ANDERSON, E., L. M. LODISH & B. A. WEITZ (1987) 'Resource Allocation Behavior in Conventional Channels.' In *Journal of Marketing Research*, vol. XXIV, February, pp. 85-97.

ANDRAE, G. (1992) 'Urban Workers as Farmers: Agro-links of Nigerian Textile Workers in the Crisis of the 1980s.' In J. Baker & P. O. Pedersen (eds.) *The Rural-Urban Interface in Africa; Expansion and Adaptation*, Uppsala: Scandinavian Institute of African Studies.

ANTONY, G. & E. FLEMING (1991) 'Statutory Marketing Authorities in the Third World: Recent Changes and Conclusions.' In *Journal of International Food & Agribusiness Marketing*, vol. 3, no. 3, pp. 43-54.

AREDO, D. (1994) 'Income Diversification Behaviour of Farm Households in an Ethiopian Village.' Paper given at a workshop on De-agrarianization and Rural Employment, African Studies Centre, Leiden, 10-12 May.

ARHIN, K. (1990) 'Trade, Accumulation and the State in Asante in the Nineteenth Century.' In *Africa*, vol. 60, no. 4, pp. 525-537.

ARNDT, J. (1983) 'The Political Economy Paradigm: Foundation for Theory Building in Marketing.' In *Journal of Marketing*, vol. 47, Fall, pp. 44-54.

AZAM, J., P. COLLIER & A. CRAVINHO (1994) 'Crop Sales, Shortages and Peasant Portfolio Behaviour: An Analysis of Angola.' In *The Journal of Development Studies*, vol. 30, no. 2, pp. 361-379.

BAIN, J. S. (1959) *Industrial Organization*. New York: Chapman and Hall.

BARRETT, H. R. (1988) *The Marketing of Food Stuffs in The Gambia, 1400-1980*. Aldershot: Avebury, Gower.

BATEMAN, D. I. (1976) 'Agricultural Marketing: A Review of the Literature of Marketing Theory and the Selected Applications.' In *Journal of Agricultural Economics*, vol. 27, pp. 171-224.

BATES, R. H. (1989) *Beyond the Miracle of the Market; The Political Economy of Agrarian Development in Kenya*. Cambridge: Cambridge University Press.

BAUMOL, W. J., J. C. PANZAR & R. D. WILLIG (1988) *Contestable Markets and the Theory of Industrial Structure*. Revised edition. San Diego: HBJ Publishers.

BECKER, C. M., C. N. DE BODISCO & A. R. MORRISON (1986) *Urban Africa in Macro-Economic and Micro-Economic Perspective: Issues and Options*. Washington: The World Bank, Discussion Paper.

BEN-AKIVA, M & S. R. LERMAN (1985) *Discrete Choice Analysis; Theory and Application to Travel Demand*. Fourth edition. Cambridge, MA: MIT Press.

BENNETT, G. (1965) 'Settlers and Politics in Kenya, up to 1945.' In V. Harlow, E. M. Chilver & A. Smith (eds.) *History of East Africa, Volume II*. London: Oxford University Press, pp. 265-332.

BERG, E. (1985) 'Why Don't LDC Governments Liberalize Agricultural Markets?' Alexandria, VA: Elliot Berg Associates, Paper prepared for the Economic Institute of the World Bank.

BERG, E. (1989) 'The Liberalization of Rice Marketing in Madagascar.' In *World Development*, vol. 17, no. 5, pp. 719-728.

BERG, F. J. (1968) 'The Coast from the Portuguese Invasion.' In B. A. Ogot & J. A. Kieran (eds.) *Zamani, A Survey of East African History*. Nairobi: East African Publishing House, Longmans of Kenya, pp. 100-118.

BERRY, B. J. L. & W. L. GARRISON (1958) 'Recent Developments of Central Place Theory.' In *Papers and Proceedings of the Regional Science Association*, vol. 4, pp. 107-120.

BEYNON, J., S. JONES & S. YAO (1992) 'Market Reform and Private Trade in Eastern and Southern Africa.' In *Food Policy*, vol. 17, no. 6, pp. 399-408.

BHUSHAN, K.(1991) *Kenya 1991 Factbook, Uhuru 28, 12th Edition*. Nairobi: Newspread International.

BHUSHAN, K. (1996) *Kenya 1995/1996 Factbook, Uhuru 32, 14th Edition*. Nairobi: Newspread International.

BIRMINGHAM, D. (1970) 'Early African Trade in Angola and Its Hinterland.' In R. Gray & D. Birmingham (eds.) *Pre-Colonial African Trade; Essays on Trade in Central and Eastern Africa before 1900*. London: Oxford University Press, pp. 163-174.

BIRMINGHAM, D. (1981) *Central Africa to 1870; Zambezia, Zaire and the South Atlantic*. Cambridge: Cambridge University Press.

BOAFO-ARTHUR, K. (1992) 'Europe 1992: A Challenge to Sub-Saharan Africa Development.' In *Africa Development*, vol. XVII, no. 2, pp. 27-43.

BOEKHOLT, J. M. C., R. H. F. JANSEN & P. VAN DER VEEN (1983) *Vegetable and Milk Marketing in Developing Countries. A Case Study of its Spatial Organizational Aspects in Mysore City, India*. Groningen: University of Groningen, Geographic Institute.

BRAUN, M. , W. FRICKE & G. MALCHAU (1992) 'The Double Function of Periodic Markets in Densely Populated Areas of Uyo/SE-Nigeria.' In L. Cammam (ed.) *Traditional Marketing Systems: Proceedings of an International Workshop, Feldafing July 6-8, 1992*. Bonn: German Foundation for International Development, pp. 62-69.

BRETT, E. A. (1973) *Colonialism and Underdevelopment in East Africa; The Politics of Economic Change 1919-39*. London: Heinemann.

BROWN M. B. & P. TIFFEN (1992) *Short Changed. Africa and World Trade*. London: Pluto Press, with the Transnational Institute.

BRYCESON, D. F. (1993) *Liberalizing Tanzania's Food Trade; Public & Private Faces of Urban Marketing Policy, 1939-1988*. Geneva & London: UNRI & James Currey.

BRYCESON, D. F. (1994) 'Too Many Assumptions: Researching Grain Markets in Tanzania.' In *Nordic Journal of African Studies*, vol. 3, no. 1, pp. 29-45.

BRYCESON, D. F. (1996) 'Deagrarianization and Rural Employment in Sub-Saharan Africa: A Sectoral Perspective.' In *World Development*, vol. 24, no. 1, pp. 97-111.

BRYCESON, D. F. & C. VAN DER LAAN (1994) *De-Agrarianization in Africa: Proceedings of the 'De-Agrarianization and Rural Employment' Workshop held at the Afrika-Studiecentrum, Leiden, May 1994*, Leiden: African Studies Centre, Working Paper no. 20.

BUARUHANGA, J. (1977) *The Performance of the Horticultural Cooperative Union of Kenya*. Nairobi: University of Nairobi.

BUCKLIN, L. P. (1970) 'The Classification of Channel Structures.' In L. B. Bucklin (ed.) *Vertical Marketing Systems*. Glenview, IL: Scott, Foresman, pp. 16-31.

BUCKLIN, L. P. (1972) *Competition and Evolution in the Distributive Trades*. London: Prentice Hall International.

BUCKLIN, L. B. (1977) 'Improving Food Retailing in Developing Asian Countries.' In *Food Policy*, May, pp. 114-122.

CAMPBELL, G. (1993) 'The Structure of Trade in Madagascar, 1750-1810.' In *The International Journal of African Historical Studies*, vol. 26, no. 1, pp. 111-148.

CARLSEN, J. (1980) *Economic and Social Transformation in Rural Kenya*. Uppsala: Scandinavian Institute of African Studies.

CARR-HILL, R. A. (1990) *Social Conditions in Sub-Sahara Africa*. Basingstoke: Macmillan Academic and Professional Ltd.

CBS (1981) *Kenya Population Census 1979, Volume I*. Nairobi: Central Bureau of Statistics.

CBS (1984) *Statistical Abstracts 1983*. Nairobi: Central Bureau of Statistics.

CBS (1988) *Economic Survey 1988*. Nairobi: Central Bureau of Statistics.

CBS (1990) *Statistical Abstracts 1990*. Nairobi: Central Bureau of Statistics.

CBS (1994a) *Economic Survey 1994*. Nairobi: Central Bureau of Statistics.

CBS (1994b) *Kenya Population Census 1989, Volume I*. Nairobi: Central Bureau of Statistics.

CBS (1994c) *Kenya Population Census 1989, Volume II*. Nairobi: Central Bureau of Statistics.

CBS (1995) *Statistical Abstracts 1995*. Nairobi: Central Bureau of Statistics.

CHALON, T. W. (1994) 'Kenya Sugar Industry: the Effects of Liberalization.' In *Proceedings of the Conference on Market Reforms, Agricultural Production and Food Security, held at the Kenya Commercial Bank, Institute of Banking and Finance, Nairobi, June 22-23, 1994.*, Nairobi: Egerton University, Policy Analysis Matrix, pp. 44-80.

CHAMBERS, R. (1969) *Settlement Schemes in Tropical Africa.* London: Routledge & Kegan Paul.

CHANDLER, T. & J. D. TARVER (1993) 'Urbanization in Colonial Africa.' In *Africa Insight*, vol. 23, no. 4, pp. 250-254.

CHOLE, E. (1991) 'Introduction: What is Social Development?' In D. Mohammed (ed.) *Social Development in Africa: Strategies, Policies and Programmes after the Lagos Plan.* Tripoli & London: African Centre for Applied Research and Training in Social Development & Hans Zell Publishers, pp. 4-21.

CLODIUS, R. L. & W.F. MUELLER (1961) 'Market Structure Analysis as an Orientation of Research in Agricultural Economics.' In *Journal of Farm Economics*, vol. 43, no. 3, pp. 515-553.

COHEN, D. W. (1983) 'Food Production and Food Exchange in the Precolonial Lakes Plateau Region.' In R. I. Rotberg (ed.) *Imperialism, Colonialism, and Hunger: East and Central Africa.* Lexington, MA: Lexington Books, D. C. Heath, pp. 1-18.

COQUERY-VIDROVITCH, C. (1991) 'The Process of Urbanization in Africa; From the Origins to the Beginning of Independence.' In *African Studies Review*, vol. 34, no. 1, pp. 1-98.

COULTER, J. & P. GOLOB (1992) 'Cereal Marketing Liberalization in Tanzania.' In *Food Policy*, vol. 17, no. 6, pp. 420-430.

DAAKU, K. Y. (1971) 'Trade and Trading Patterns of the Akan in the Seventeenth and Eighteenth Centuries.' In C. Meillassoux (ed.) *The Development of Indigenous Trade and Markets in West Africa.* London: Oxford University Press, International African Institute, pp. 168-181.

DAVISON, J. (1986) 'Gender Relations of Production in Collective Farming in Mozambique.' Paper given at the 29th Annual Meeting of the African Studies Association, Los Angeles, Oct. 30 - Nov. 2.

DE JANVRY, A. & E. SADOULET (1994) 'Structural Adjustment under Transaction Costs.' In F. Heidhues & B. Knerr (eds.) *Food and Agricultural Policies under Structural Adjustment.* Frankfurt: Peter Lang Verlag.

DE MORÉE, D. (1985) *A Comparative Analysis of Marketing and Consumption of Cassava and Potatoes in Bucaramanga; the Possibilities of the Introduction of a Storage Technology for Cassava.* Cali, Colombia: CIAT.

DELGADO, C. L. (1995) 'Agricultural Diversification and Export Promotion in Sub-Saharan Africa.' In *Food Policy*, vol. 20, no. 3, pp. 225-243.

DELISLE, H. (1991) 'Urban Food Patterns.' In *Food, Nutrition and Agriculture*, vol. 1, pp. 7-10.

DIAS, L., M. I. MUGABE, R. VARELA, T. FINAN, D. TSCHIRLEY & M. WEBER (1991) 'Informing the Process of Agricultural Market Reform in Mozambique: A Progress Report.' In M. Rukuni & J. B. Wyckoff (eds.) *Market Reforms, Research Policies and SADCC Food Security.* Harare: University of Zimbabwe, UZ/MSU Food Security Research in Southern Africa Project, pp. 183-197.

DIJKSTRA, T. (1990) *Marketing Policies and Economic Interests in the Cotton Sector of Kenya.* Leiden: African Studies Centre, Research Report no. 40.

DIJKSTRA, T. (1995) *Food Trade and Urbanization in Sub-Saharan Africa: From the Early Stone Age to the Structural Adjustment Era.* Leiden: African Studies Centre, Working Paper no. 22.

DIJKSTRA, T. (1996) 'Food Assembly Markets in Africa: Lessons from the Horticultural Sector of Kenya.' In *British Food Journal*, vol. 98, no. 9, pp. 26-34.

DIJKSTRA, T. (1997) 'Commercial Horticulture by African Smallholders: A Success Story from the Highlands of Kenya.' In *Scandinavian Journal of Development Alternatives and Area Studies*, vol. 16. no. 1, pp. 49-74.

DIJKSTRA, T. & H. L. VAN DER LAAN (1990) 'The Future of Africa's Raw Material Marketing Boards: Will Local Factories Make Some of Them Redundant?' In *Journal of International Food & Agribusiness Marketing*, vol. 2, no. 2, pp. 47-76.

DIJKSTRA, T. & T.D. MAGORI (1991) *Horticultural Production and Marketing in Kenya; Part 1: Introduction, Research Objectives and Methodology.* Nairobi & Leiden: Ministry of Planning and National Development & African Studies Centre, Food and Nutrition Studies Programme, Report no. 41.

DIJKSTRA, T. & T.D. MAGORI (1992a) *Horticultural Production and Marketing in Kenya; Part 2A: Horticultural Production in Nyandarua District.* Nairobi & Leiden: Ministry of Planning and National Development & African Studies Centre, Food and Nutrition Studies Programme, Report no. 47.

DIJKSTRA, T. & T.D. MAGORI (1992b) *Horticultural Production and Marketing in Kenya; Part 2B: Horticultural Marketing in Nyandarua District.* Nairobi & Leiden: Ministry of Planning and National Development & African Studies Centre, Food and Nutrition Studies Programme, Report no. 48.

DIJKSTRA, T. & T.D. MAGORI (1994a) *Horticultural Production and Marketing in Kenya; Part 3: Taita Taveta District.* Nairobi & Leiden: Ministry of Planning and National Development & African Studies Centre, Food and Nutrition Studies Programme, Report no. 51.

DIJKSTRA, T. & T.D. MAGORI (1994b) *Horticultural Production and Marketing in Kenya; Part 4: Kisii & Nyamira Districts.* Nairobi & Leiden: Ministry of Planning and National Development & African Studies Centre, Food and Nutrition Studies Programme, Report no. 52.

DIJKSTRA, T. & T.D. MAGORI (1995a) 'Flowers and French Beans from Kenya; A Story of Export Success.' In S. Ellis & Y. A. Fauré (eds.) *Entreprises et entrepreneurs africains.* Paris: Karthala, pp. 435-444.

DIJKSTRA, T. & T.D. MAGORI (eds.) (1995b) *Horticultural Production and Marketing in Kenya; Part 5: Proceedings of a Dissemination Seminar at Nairobi, 16-17th November 1994.* Nairobi & Leiden: Ministry of Planning and National Development & African Studies Centre, Food and Nutrition Studies Programme, Report no. 53.

DIKE, A. A. (1979) 'Misconceptions of African Urbanism: Some Euro-American Notions.' In R. A. Obudho & S. El-Shakhs (eds.) *Development of Urban Systems in Africa.* New York: Praeger.

DINHAM, B. & C. HINES (1983) *Agribusiness in Africa; A Study of the Impact of Big Business on Africa's Food and Agricultural Production.* London: Earth Resources Research Ltd.

DUDLEY, B. J. (1984) 'Decolonisation and the Problems of Independence.' In M. Crower (ed.) *The Cambridge History of Africa, Vol. 8: from c. 1940 to c. 1965.* Cambridge: Cambridge University Press, pp. 52-94.

DUE, J. M. (1971) 'Efficiency of Resource Use - the Case of the Ghanaian Rice Farms.' In *East African Journal of Rural Development,* vol. 4, no. 2, pp. 77-93.

DUNCAN R. C. (1993) 'Agricultural Export Prospects for Sub-Saharan Africa.' In *Development Policy Review,* vol. 11, pp. 31-45.

DURR, G. & G. LORENZL (1980) *Potato Production and Utilization in Kenya.* Nairobi, Berlin & Colombia: University of Nairobi, Technical University Berlin & Centro Internacional de la Papa.

DURRANT, A. E. , C. P. LEWIS & A. A. JORGENSEN (1981) *Steam in Africa.* London: Hamlyn.

ECA (1989) *African Alternative Framework to Structural Adjustment Programmes for Socio-Economic Recovery and Transformation.* Addis Ababa: United Nations, Economic Commission for Africa.

EGGERTSSON, T. (1990) *Economic Behavior and Institutions.* Cambridge: Cambridge University Press.

EHRLICH, C. (1965) 'The Uganda Economy, 1903-1945.' In V. Harlow & E. M. Chilver (eds.) *History of East Africa, Volume II.* London: Oxford University Press, pp. 395-475.

ELKAN, W. & R. VAN ZWANENBERG (1975) 'How People Came to Live in Towns.' In P. Duignan & L. H. Gann (eds.) *Colonialism in Africa, 1870-1960. Volume 4: The Economics of Colonialism.* Cambridge: Cambridge University Press, pp. 655-672.

ELLIS, F. (1983) *Agricultural Marketing and Peasant-State Transfers in Tanzania.* Norwich: University of East Anglia, School of Development Studies, Discussion Paper no. 16.

ELLIS, F. (1993) *Peasant Economics. Farm Households and Agrarian Development.* Second edition. Cambridge: Cambridge University Press.

ENSMINGER, J. (1992) *Making a Market; The Institutional Transformation of an African Society.* Cambridge: Cambridge University Press.

ETGAR, M. (1976) 'Channel Domination and Countervailing Power in Distributive Channels.' In *Journal of Marketing Research,* vol. 13, August, pp. 254-262.

EVANGELOU, P. (1984) *Livestock Development in Kenya's Maasailand: Pastoralists' Transition to a Market Economy.* Boulder: Westview.

FAGAN, B. M. (1970) 'Early Trade and Raw Materials in South Central Africa.' In R. Gray & D. Birmingham (eds.) *Pre-Colonial African Trade; Essays on Trade in Central and Eastern Africa before 1900.* London: Oxford University Press, pp. 24-38.

FALOLA, T. (1991) 'The Yoruba Caravan System of the Nineteenth Century.' In *The International Journal of African Historical Studies,* vol. 24, no. 1, pp. 111-132.

FAO (1980) *Farm Management Research for Small Farmer Development.* Rome: Food and Agriculture Organization, Agricultural Services Bulletin no. 41.

FAO (1985) 'List of Government and Cooperative Marketing Organizations for Agricultural Produce and Production Inputs in Developing Countries.' Rome: Food and Agriculture Organization, Agricultural Services Division.

FAO (1995) *Food for Consumers: Marketing, Processing and Distribution.* Rome: Food and Agriculture Organization, Report WFS 96/TECH/4.

FEARN, H. (1955) 'The Problems of the African Trader.' East Africa: Institute of Social Research Conference Papers, unpublished report.

FLEMING, E. & G. ANTONY (1991) 'Statutory Marketing Authorities in the Third World: Background and Assessment.' In *Journal of International Food & Agribusiness Marketing,* vol. 3, no. 1, pp. 65-91.

FODOUOP, K. (1988) 'La Contrabande entre le Cameroun et le Nigeria.' In *Les Cahiers d'Outre-Mer*, no. 161, pp. 5-26.

FOEKEN, D., P. LEEGWATER, R. NIEMEIJER, W. VEERMAN & J. HOORWEG (1989) *Seasonality in the Coastal Lowlands of Kenya Part 3: Socio-Economic Profile*. Nairobi & Leiden: Ministry of Planning and National Development & African Studies Centre, Food and Nutrition Studies Programme, Report no. 32.

FOEKEN, D. & N. TELLEGEN (1994) *Tied to the Land; Living Conditions of Labourers on Large Farms in Trans Nzoia District, Kenya*. Aldershot: Avebury, African Studies Centre Research Series no. 1/1994.

FOEKEN, D. & L. VERSTRATE (1992) *Labour Conditions on Large Scale Farms in Trans Nzoia District, Kenya*. Nairobi & Leiden: Ministry of Planning and National Development & African Studies Centre, Food and Nutrition Studies Programme, Report no. 43.

FREEMAN, D. (1988) *Informal Urban Agriculture in the Open Spaces of Nairobi, Kenya*. York, Ontario: York University, Department of Geography.

FRENCH, J. R. P. JR. & B. RAVEN (1959) 'The Bases of Social Power.' In D. Cartwright (ed.) *Studies in Social Power*. Ann Arbor: University of Michigan, pp. 150-167.

FRONTERA, A. E. (1978) *Persistence and Change: A History of Taveta*. Waltham, MA: Brandeis University, African Studies Association.

GANN, L. H. (1975) 'Economic Development in Germany's African Empire, 1884-1914.' In P. Duignan & L. H. Gann (eds.) *Colonialism in Africa, 1870-1960. Volume 4: The Economics of Colonialism*. Cambridge: Cambridge University Press, pp. 213-255.

GIBSON, G. D. (1962) 'Bride Wealth and Other Forms of Exchange among the Herero.' In P. Bohannan & G. Dalton (eds.) *Markets in Africa*. Evanston: Northwestern University Press, pp. 617-639.

GODIN, F. (1986) *Bénin 1972-1982, La Logique de l'Etat Africain*. Paris: L'Harmattan.

GOK (1964) *Development Plan 1964-1970*. Nairobi: Government of Kenya, Government Printer.

GOK (1966) *Development Plan 1966-1970*. Nairobi: Government of Kenya, Government Printer.

GOK (1987) *Directory of Industries*. Nairobi: Government of Kenya, Government Printer.

GOK (1997) *National Development Plan, 1997-2001*. Nairobi: Government of Kenya, Government Printer.

GOLDMAN, A. (1974) 'Outreach of Consumers and the Modernization of Urban Food Retailing in Developing Countries.' In *Journal of Marketing*, October, pp. 8-16.

GOLDMAN, A. (1981) 'Transfer of a Retail Technology into the Less Developed Countries: The Supermarket Case.' In *Journal of Retailing*, vol. 57, no. 2, pp. 5-27.

GOOSSENS, F. (1994) *Performance of Cassava Marketing in Zaire*. Leuven: Catholic University of Leuven, PhD thesis.

GRAY, R. & D. BIRMINGHAM (1970) 'Some Economic and Political Consequences of Trade in Central and Eastern Africa in the Pre-Colonial Period.' In R. Gray & D. Birmingham (eds.) *Pre-Colonial African Trade; Essays on Trade in Central and Eastern Africa before 1900*. London: Oxford University Press, pp. 1-23.

GRETHER, E. T. (1983) 'Regional-Spatial Analysis in Marketing.' In *Journal of Marketing*, Fall, pp. 36-43.

GSAENGER, H. G. & G. SCHMIDT (1977) 'Decontrolling the Maize Marketing System in Kenya?' In *Zeitschrift für auslandische Landwirtschaft*, vol. 16, no. 3, pp. 268-284.

GUGLER, J. & W. G. FLANAGAN (1978) *Urbanization and Social Change in West Africa*. Cambridge: Cambridge University Press.

GUYER, J. I. (1987) 'Introduction.' In J. I. Guyer (ed.) *Feeding African Cities; Studies in Regional Social History*. Manchester: Manchester University Press, International African Institute, pp. 1-54.

GYLLSTRÖM, B. (1988) 'Government Versus Agricultural Marketing Cooperatives in Kenya.' In H. Hedlund (ed.) (1988) *Cooperatives Revisited*. Uppsala: Scandinavian Institute of African Studies.

GYLLSTRÖM, B. (1991) *State-administered Rural Change: Agricultural Cooperatives in Kenya*. London: Routledge.

HABTU, Y. (1994) 'Landlessness and Rural Labor Markets: A Study of Households in Northern Shewa Region of Ethiopia.' Paper given at a workshop on De-agrarianization and Rural Employment, African Studies Centre, Leiden, 10-12 May.

HAGGETT, P. (1983) *Geography; A Modern Synthesis*. Revised Third edition. New York: Harper and Row.

HAIR, J. F., R. E. ANDERSON, R. L. TATHAM & W. C. BLACK (1995) *Multivariate Data Analysis*. Fourth edition. Englewood Cliffs: Prentice Hall.

HANCE, W. A. (1970) *Population, Migration and Urbanization in Africa*. New York: Columbia University Press.

HANSEN, K. T. (1989) 'The Black Market and Women Traders in Lusaka, Zambia.' In J. L. Parpart & K. A. Staudt (eds.) *Women and the State in Africa*. Boulder: Rienner Publishers, pp. 143-160.

HARMS, R. W. (1981) *River of Wealth, River of Sorrow; The Central Zaire Basin in the Era of the Slave and Ivory Trade, 1500-1891*. New Haven: Yale University Press.

HARRISS, B. (1982) *Agricultural Marketing in the Semi-arid Tropics of West Africa*. Norwich: University of East Anglia, Development Studies Paper.

HCDA (1990) *Horticultural Development and Marketing Policy Guidelines*. Nairobi: Horticultural Crops Development Authority.

HEIDE, J. B. & G. JOHN (1988) 'The Role of Dependence Balancing in Safeguarding Transaction-Specific Assets in Conventional Channels.' In *Journal of Marketing*, January, pp. 20-35.

HESP, P. & L. VAN DER LAAN (1985) 'Marketing Boards in Tropical Africa: A Survey.' In K. Arhin, P. Hesp & L. van der Laan (eds.) *Marketing Boards in Tropical Africa*. London: KPI Ltd, Monograph of the African Studies Centre, pp. 1-36.

HESSELMARK, O. & G. LORENZL (1976) 'Structure and Problems of the Maize Marketing System in Kenya.' In *Zeitschrift für ausländische Landwirtschaft*, vol. 15, no. 2, pp. 161-179.

HILL, B. E. & K. A. Ingersent (1982) *An Economic Analysis of Agriculture*. Second edition. London: Heinemann.

HILL, F. (1977) 'Experiments with a Public Sector Peasantry: Agricultural Schemes and Class Formation in Africa.' In *African Studies Review*, vol. 20, no. 3, pp. 25-41.

HILL, P. (1971) 'Two Types of West African House Trade.' In C. Meillassoux (ed.) *The Development of Indigenous Trade and Markets in West Africa*. London: Oxford University Press, International African Institute, pp. 303-318.

HODDER, B. W. (1969) 'Markets in Yorubaland.' In B. W. Hodder & U. I. Ukwu (eds.) *Markets in West Africa*. Ibadan: Ibadan University Press.

HODDER, B. W. (1971) 'Periodic and Daily Markets in West Africa.' In C. Meillassoux (ed.) *The Development of Indigenous Trade and Markets in West Africa*. London: Oxford University Press, International African Institute, pp. 347-358.

HOGENDORN, J. S. (1975) 'Economic Initiative and African Cash Farming: Pre-Colonial Origins and Early Colonial Development.' In P. Duignan & L. H. Gann (eds.) *Colonialism in Africa, 1870-1960. Volume 4: The Economics of Colonialism*. Cambridge: Cambridge University Press, pp. 283-328.

HOLLIER, G. P. (1980) *Rural Markets and Central Place Theory in West Cameroon*. Glasgow: University of Strathclyde, Department of Geography, Research Seminar Series no. 4.

HOLLIS, H. E. (1975) *A History of the Taita of Kenya to 1900*. Indianapolis: Indiana University, PhD thesis.

HOOGERVORST, J., C. ROELANDS & A. VAN TILBURG (1988) *Senegal; Verslag van een literatuurstudie naar het Senegalese beleid inzake voedselvoorziening*. Wageningen: Landbouwuniversiteit Wageningen, Vakgroep Marktkunde en Marktonderzoek.

HOORWEG, J. (ed.) (1993) *FNSP Studies 1985-1992: Results and Recommendations*. Nairobi & Leiden: Ministry of Planning and National Development & African Studies Centre, Food and Nutrition Studies Programme, Report no. 50.

HOORWEG, J., D. FOEKEN & W. KLAVER (1995) *Seasons and Nutrition at the Kenya Coast*. Aldershot: Avebury, African Studies Centre Research Series no. 7/1995.

HOORWEG, J., R. NIEMEIJER, D. FOEKEN, W. OKELLO & W. VEERMAN (1991) *Economic and Nutritional Conditions at Settlement Schemes in Coast Province*. Nairobi & Leiden: Ministry of Planning and National Development & African Studies Centre, Food and Nutrition Studies Programme, Report no. 36.

HOPKINS A. G. (1973) *An Economic History of West Africa*. London: Longman.

HRBEK, I. (ed.) (1992) *General History of Africa III; Africa from the Seventh to the Eleventh Century*. Abridged edition. London & Paris: James Currey & UNESCO.

HUFF, D. L. (1964) 'Defining and Estimating a Trading Area.' In *Journal of Marketing*, vol. 28, July, pp. 34-38.

HUTT, M. D., M. P. MOKWA & S. J. SHAPIRO (1986) 'The Politics of Marketing: Analyzing the Parallel Political Marketplace.' In *Journal of Marketing*, vol. 50, January, pp. 40-51.

ILIFFE, J. (1979) *A Modern History of Tanganyika*. Cambridge: Cambridge University Press.

JAETZOLD, R. & H. SCHMIDT (1983) *Farm Management Handbook of Kenya Vol. II: Natural Conditions and Farm Management Information (Part A: West Kenya, Part B: Central Kenya, Part C: East Kenya)*. Nairobi: Ministry of Agriculture.

JAFFEE, S. (1987) *Case Studies of Contract Farming in the Horticultural Sector of Kenya*. Binghampton, NY: Institute of Development Anthropology, IDA paper no. 83.

JAFFEE, S. (1990) *Alternative Marketing Institutions for Agricultural Exports in Sub-Saharan Africa with Special Reference to Kenyan Horticulture*. Oxford: University of Oxford, PhD thesis.

JAFFEE, S. (1993) 'Kenya's Horticultural Export Marketing: A Transaction Cost Perspective.' In J. Abbott (ed.) *Agricultural and Food Marketing in Developing Countries: Selected Readings*. Wallingford, UK & Wageningen: CAB International & Technical Centre for Agricultural and Rural Cooperation, pp. 388-403.

JAFFEE, S. (1994) 'Contract Farming in the Shadow of Competitive Markets: The Experience of Kenyan Horticulture' In P. D. Little and M. J. Watts (eds.) *Living under Contract; Contract Farming and Agrarian Transformation in Sub-Saharan Africa*. Madison: The University of Wisconsin Press, pp. 97-139.

JAFFEE, S. (1995) 'Perishable Profits: Private Sector Dairy Processing and Marketing in Kenya' In S. JAFFEE & J. MORTON (eds.) *Marketing Africa's High-Value Foods; Comparative Experiences of an Emergent Private Sector*, Dubuque, IA: Kendall/Hunt Publishing Company, pp. 199-254.

JANSSEN, W. & A. VAN TILBURG (1997) 'Marketing Analysis for Agricultural Development: Suggestions for a New Research Agenda.' In B. Wierenga, A. van Tilburg, K. Grunert, J-B. E. M. Steenkamp & M. Wedel (eds.) *Agricultural Marketing and Consumer Behavior in a Changing World.*, Dordrecht: Kluwer Academic Publishers, pp. 75-91.

JAYNE, T. S. & M. CHISVO (1991) 'Unravelling Zimbabwe's Food Insecurity Paradox; Implications for Grain Reform in Southern Africa.' In *Food Policy*, vol. 16, no. 4, pp. 319-329.

JIRIYENGWA, S. J. (1993) 'Grain Market Liberalization and Social Goals; The Grain Marketing Board of Zimbabwe.' In *Food Policy*, vol. 18, no. 4, pp. 316-324.

JOHN, C. (1970) 'Kazembe and the Tanganyika-Nyasa Corridor, 1800-1890.' In R. Gray & D. Birmingham (eds.) *Pre-Colonial African Trade; Essays on Trade in Central and Eastern Africa before 1900*. London: Oxford University Press, pp. 202-227.

JONES, S. & J. BEYNON (1992) 'Review Paper - Market Reform and Private Trade in Eastern and Southern Africa.' In J. Beynon (ed.) *Market Liberalization and Private Sector Response in Eastern and Southern Africa*. Oxford: University of Oxford, Food Studies Group, International Development Centre, Working Paper no. 6, pp. 1-15.

JONES, W. O. (1972) *Marketing of Staple Food Crops in Tropical Africa*. London: Cornell University Press.

JONES-DUBE, E. D. (1991) 'The Influence of Entrepreneurs on Rural Town Development in Botswana.' In *Botswana Notes & Records*, vol. 23, pp. 11-32.

KALINGA, O. J. M. (1990) 'Rice Production and Marketing in Colonial Malawi in the Inter-War Period.' In *Transafrican Journal of History*, vol. 19, pp. 61-72.

KALUWA, B. & W. CHILOWA (1991) 'Malawi: Food Marketing Liberalisation and Household Food Security - Preliminary Results from Baseline Surveys.' In M. Rukuni & J. B. Wyckoff (eds.) *Market Reforms, Research Policies and SADCC Food Security*. Harare: University of Zimbabwe, UZ/MSU Food Security Research in Southern Africa Project, pp. 104-119.

KANDOOLE, B. (1991) 'Household Food Security and Market Liberalization in Blantyre Agricultural Development Districts.' In M. Rukuni & J. B. Wyckoff (eds.) *Market Reforms, Research Policies and SADCC Food Security*. Harare: University of Zimbabwe, UZ/MSU Food Security Research in Southern Africa Project, pp. 90-103.

KANOGO, T. (1989) 'Kenya and the Depression, 1929-1939.' In W. Ochieng' (ed.) *A Modern History of Kenya, 1895-1980*. Nairobi: Evens Brothers (Kenya) Ltd., 112-143.

KATZENELLENBOGEN, S. E. (1975) 'Miner's Frontiers, Transport and Economic Development.' In P. Duignan & L. H. Gann (eds.) *Colonialism in Africa, 1870-1960. Volume 4: The Economics of Colonialism*. Cambridge: Cambridge University Press, pp. 360-426.

KIBERA, F. N. & B. C. WARUINGI (1988) *Fundamentals of Marketing; An African Perspective*. Nairobi: Kenya Literature Bureau.

KOHLS, R. L. & J. N. UHL (1990) *Marketing of Agricultural Products*. Seventh edition. New York: Macmillan.

KOKWARO, J. O. (1979) *Classification of East African Crops*. Nairobi: Kenya Literature Bureau.

KONGSTAD, P. & B. MIKKELSEN (1983) 'Fagbevaegelse og samfundsudvikling i Kenya.' In *Den Ny Verden*, no. 17.

KONINGS, P. (1986) *The State and Rural Class Formation in Ghana: A Comparative Analysis*. London: Routledge and Kegan Paul, Monograph of the African Studies Centre.

KOSINSKI, L. A. & J. I. CLARKE (1982) 'African Population Redistribution - Trends, Patterns and Policies.' In J. I. Clarke & L. A. Kosinski (eds.) *Redistribution of Population in Africa*. London: Heinemann Educational Books, pp. 1-14.

KOTLER, P. (1988) *Marketing Management: Analysis, Planning, Implementation, and Control*. Sixth edition. Upper Saddle River, NJ: Prentice Hall International.

KOTLER, P. (1997) *Marketing Management: Analysis, Planning, Implementation, and Control*. Ninth edition. Upper Saddle River, NJ: Prentice Hall International.

KRISHNAN, P. (1994) 'Getting By and Getting On: Income Diversification in Rural Ethiopia.' Paper given at a workshop on De-agrarianization and Rural Employment, African Studies Centre, Leiden, 10-12 May.

LADO, C. (1991) 'Rural Periodic Markets: A Case Study from North Malakisi Location, Bungoma District, Kenya.' In *Eastern & Southern Africa Geographical Journal*, vol. 2, no. 1, pp. 37-55.

LAMPHEAR, J. (1970) 'The Kamba and the Northern Mrima Coast.' In R. Gray & D. Birmingham (eds.) *Pre-Colonial African Trade; Essays on Trade in Central and Eastern Africa before 1900*. London: Oxford University Press, pp. 75-102.

LARSON, T. J. (1991) 'Six-day Markets of the Kabiye of North Togo.' In *South African Journal of Ethnology*, vol. 14, no. 4, pp. 115-121.

LAW, R. (1991) *The Slave Coast of West Africa 1550-1750. The Impact of the Atlantic Slave Trade on an African Society*. Oxford: Clarendon Press.

LAW, R. (1992) 'Posthumous Questions for Karl Polanyi: Price Inflation in Pre-Colonial Dahomey.' In *Journal of African History*, vol. 33, pp. 387-420.

LAW, R. (1995) 'Introduction.' In R. Law (ed.) *From Slave Trade to ' Legitimate' Commerce; The Commercial Transition in Nineteenth-Century West Africa*. Cambridge: Cambridge University Press, pp. 1-31.

LAWSON, R. M. (1971) 'The Supply Response of Retail Trading Services to Urban Population Growth in Ghana.' In C. Meillassoux (ed.) *The Development of Indigenous Trade and Markets in West Africa*. London: Oxford University Press, International African Institute, pp. 377-398.

LEWIS, I. M. (1962) 'Trade and Markets in Northern Somaliland.' In P. Bohannan & G. Dalton (eds.) *Markets in Africa*. Evanston: Northwestern University Press, pp. 365-385.

LIMBU, F. (1993) *Efficiency of the Rice Marketing System in Tanzania*. Berlin: Verlag Köster, Schriften zur internationalen Agrarentwicklung, vol. 5.

LITTLE, P. D. (1992) 'Seasonality and Rural-Urban Linkages in Southern Somalia.' In J. Baker & P. O. Pedersen (eds.) *The Rural-Urban Interface in Africa; Expansion and Adaptation*. Uppsala: The Scandinavian Institute of African Studies.

LITTLE, P. D. & I. B. L. DE COLOANE (1992) *Petty Trade and Household Survival Strategies: a Case Study of Fruit and Vegetable Traders in the Peri-Urban Area of Maputo, Mozambique*. Binghamton, NY: Institute of Development Anthropology, Working paper no. 90.

LIVINGSTONE, I. (1991) 'A Reassessment of Kenya's Rural and Urban Informal Sector.' In *World Development*, vol. 19, no. 6, pp. 651-690.

LONSDALE, J. (1985) 'The European Scramble and Conquest in African History.' In R. Oliver & G. N. Sanderson (eds.) *The Cambridge History of Africa; Volume 6: from 1870 to 1905*. Cambridge: Cambridge University Press, pp. 680-766.

LOVEJOY, P. E. (1980) 'Kola in the History of West Africa.' *Cahiers d'Etudes africaines*, vol. 20, no. 77-78, pp. 97-134.

LOW, D. A. (1965) 'British East Africa: The Establishment of British Rule, 1895-1912.' In V. Harlow & E, M. Chilver (eds.) *History of East Africa, Volume II*. London: Oxford University Press, pp. 1-56.

LUTZ, C. H. M. (1989) 'l'Analyse du functionnement des marchés: comment estimer leur efficacité? Etude des cas du marché de maïs au Benin en 1988.' Paper for 21st European Seminar of Agricultural Economists, Montpellier, 29 May-2 June.

LUTZ, C. H. M. (1994) *The Functioning of the Maize Market in Benin: Spatial and Temporal Arbitrage on the Market of a Staple Food Crop*. Amsterdam: University of Amsterdam, Department of Regional Economics, PhD thesis.

MADDALA, G. S. (1992) *Introduction to Econometrics*. Second edition. Englewood Cliffs: Prentice Hall.

MALLEN, B. (1973) 'Functional Spin-Off: A Key to Anticipating Change in Distribution Structure.' In *Journal of Marketing*, vol. 37, July, pp. 18-25.

MALLEN, B. (1977) *Principles of Marketing Channel Management*. Lexington, MA: Lexington Books.

MANDALA, E. C. (1990) *Work and Control in a Peasant Economy; A History of the Lower Tchiri Valley in Malawi, 1859-1960*. Madison: The University of Wisconsin Press.

MANGAT, J. S. (1969) *A History of the Asians in East Africa, c. 1886 to 1945*. Oxford: Carendon Press, Oxford Studies in African Affairs.

MANU, F. A. (1992) 'The State and Marketing in African Countries: A Case Study of Ghana.' In *Journal of International Food & Agribusiness Marketing*, vol. 4, no. 2, pp. 67-82.

MARITIM, K. A. (1976) *Analysis of Produce Flows to Wakulima Wholesale Market Nairobi*. Nairobi: University of Nairobi, MA thesis.

MARK, P. (1986) 'Quantification of Rubber and Palm Kernel Exports from the Casamance and the Gambia, 1884-1914.' In G. Liesegang, H. Pasch & A. Jones (eds.) *Figuring African Trade; Proceedings of the Symposium on the Quantification and Structure of the Import and Export and Long Distance Trade in Africa 1800-1913*. Berlin: Dietrich Reimer Verlag, pp. 321-342.

MAXWELL, D. & S. ZZIWA (1992) *Urban Farming in Africa; The Case of Kampala, Uganda*. Nairobi: Acts Press, African Centre of Technology Studies.

MBOGHO, S. G. (1977) *The Potato Industry in Kenya*. Nairobi: University of Nairobi, Agr. Ec. Studies no. 1.

McCARTHY, E. J. (1964) 'Effective Marketing Institutions for Economic Development.' In S. A. Greyser (ed.) *Towards Scientific Marketing*. Chicago: American Marketing Association 1963 proceedings.

McGOWAN, W. (1990) 'The Establishment of Long-Distance Trade between Sierra Leone and its Hinterland, 1787-1821.' In *Journal of African History*, vol. 31, pp. 25-41.

MEAGHER, K. (1990) 'The Hidden Economy: Informal and Parallel Trade in North Western Uganda.' In *Review of African Political Economy*, vol. 47, pp. 64-83.

MEILINK, H. (1985) *Agricultural Pricing Policy in Kenya: Scope and Impact*. Nairobi & Leiden: Ministry of Planning and National Development & African Studies Centre, Food and Nutrition Studies Programme, Report no. 11.

MEILINK, H. (1987) *Food Consumption and Food Prices in Kenya: a Review*. Nairobi & Leiden: Ministry of Planning and National Development & African Studies Centre, Food and Nutrition Studies Programme, Report no. 21.

MEILLASSOUX, C. (1971) 'Introduction.' In C. Meillassoux (ed.) *The Development of Indigenous Trade and Markets in West Africa*. London: Oxford University Press, International African Institute, pp. 9-86.

MEULENBERG, M. T. G. (1989) 'Structuur en Ontwikkeling van Afzetkanalen: een Literatuuroverzicht.' In *Recente Ontwikkelingen in het Marktonderzoek, Jaarboek '89-90 van de Nederlandse Vereniging van Marktonderzoekers*, Haarlem: De Vrieseborch, pp. 247-263.

MEULENBERG, M. T. G. (1997) 'Evolution of Agricultural Marketing Institutions, a Channel Approach.' In B. Wierenga, A. van Tilburg, K. Grunert, J-B. E. M. Steenkamp & M. Wedel (eds.) *Agricultural Marketing and Consumer Behavior in a Changing World.*, Dordrecht: Kluwer Academic Publishers, pp. 95-108.

MFP (1971) *Statistical Abstracts 1971*. Nairobi: Ministry of Finance and Planning, Statistical Division.

MIDDLETON, J. (1962) 'Trade and Markets among the Lugbara of Uganda.' In P. Bohannan & G. Dalton (eds.) *Markets in Africa*. Evanston: Northwestern University Press, pp. 561-578.

MITTENDORF, H. J. (1982) 'Topics for Studies on Agricultural and Food Marketing in Developing Countries.' In *Quarterly Journal of International Agriculture*, vol. 21, no. 2, pp. 139-154.

MOA (1979) *Horticultural Development Studies: Wholesale Market Feasibility Studies*. Nairobi: Ministry of Agriculture.

MOA (1989) *Farm Management Handbook of Kenya, Vol. V: Horticultural Production Guidelines*. Nairobi: Ministry of Agriculture.

MOKHTAR, G. (ed.) (1990) *General History of Africa II; Ancient Civilizations of Africa*. Abridged edition. London & Paris: James Currey & UNESCO.

MOUSTIER, P. (1992) 'Is the Urban Vegetable Supply Performant in Africa? Some Evidence from Congo, Central African Republic and Madagascar.' Paper presented at the XIIth International Symposium on Horticultural Economics, Montpellier (France), 7-11 September.

MPND (1989) *Kisii District Development Plan 1989-1993*. Nairobi: Ministry of Planning and National Development.

MTAWALI, K. M. (1993) 'Trade, Price and Market Reform in Malawi; Current Status, Proposals and Constraints.' In *Food Policy*, vol. 18, no. 4, pp. 300-307.

NAJIB, A. & B. NINDI (1988) *The Problem of Efficiency and Pursuance of Public Food Marketing Systems in the Sub-Saharan African Countries*. Uppsala: Swedish University of Agricultural Sciences, International Rural Development Centre, Issue paper no. 6.

NABLI, M. K. & J. B. NUGENT (1989) 'The New Institutional Economics and Its Applicability to Development.' In *World Development*, vol. 17, no. 9. pp. 1333-1347.

NAZZARO, A. A. (1974) *Changing Use of the Resource Base among the Taita of Kenya*. East Lansing: Michigan State University, PhD thesis.

NDC (1992) *Sector Aid and Structural Adjustment: the Case of Sugar in Tanzania*. The Hague: Netherlands Development Cooperation, Operations Review Unit.

NGENO, S. Z. T. K. (1978) *Structure, Conduct and Performance of Transport of Fruit and Vegetables in Kenya*. Nairobi: University of Nairobi, MA thesis.

NKERA, R. W. A. & B. G. SCHOEPF (1991) 'Unrecorded Trade in Southeast Shaba and Across Zaire's Southern Borders.' In J. MacGaffey (ed.) *The Real Economy of Zaire; The Contribution of Smuggling & Other Unofficial Activities to National Wealth*. London & Philadelphia: James Currey & University of Pennsylvania Press, pp. 72-96.

NOAH, M. E. (1989) 'Inland Ports and European Trading Firms in Southeastern Nigeria.' In *African Affairs*, vol. 88, no. 350, pp. 25-40.

NORTH-COOMBES, A. (1993) *A History of Sugar Production in Mauritius*. Mauritius: Mauritius Printing Specialists (Pte) Ltd.

NORTHRUP, D. (1978) *Trade without Rulers; Pre-Colonial Economic Development in South-Eastern Nigeria*. Oxford: Clarendon press.

NORUSIS, M. J. (1990a) *SPSS Advanced Statistics User's Guide*. Chicago: SPSS Inc.

NORUSIS, M. J. (1990b) *SPSS Introductory Statistics Student Guide*. Chicago: SPSS Inc.

NYAKAANA, J. B. (1993) 'Organisation and Regulation in the Urban "Informal Sector": the Street Traders of Kampala City, Uganda.' In *Eastern and Southern Geographical Journal*, vol. 4, no. 1, pp. 17-22.

NYAMIAKA, P. M. (1995) 'Horticultural Production for Export.' In Dijkstra, T. and T. D. Magori (eds.) *Horticultural Production and Marketing in Kenya Part 5: Proceedings of a Dissemination Seminar at Nairobi, 16-17th November 1994*, Nairobi & Leiden: Ministry of Planning and National Development & African Studies Centre, Food and Nutrition Studies Programme, Report no. 53, pp. 32-37.

NYORO, J. (1993) 'Production of Horticultural Export Crops in Kenya.' In *Proceedings of the Conference on Agricultural Exports and Market Development, Nairobi, June 23-24, 1993*. Nairobi: Egerton University-PAM, pp. 11-83.

OAU (1980) *Lagos Plan of Action for the Economic Development of Africa 1980-2000*. Addis Ababa: Organization for African Unity.

OBUDHO, R. A. (1983) *Urbanization in Kenya; A Bottom-Up Approach to Development Planning*. Lanham, MD: University Press of America.

OBUDHO, R. A. & P. P. WALLER (1976) *Periodic Markets, Urbanization, and Regional Planning*. Westport, CT: Greenwood Press, Contributions in Afro-American and African Studies, no. 22.

ODINGO, R. S. (1971) *The Kenya Highlands, Land Use and Agricultural Development*. Nairobi: East African Publishing House, African Geographical Studies no. 1.

OLIVER, R. & A. ATMORE (1967) *Africa since 1800*. Cambridge: Cambridge University Press.

OMER-COOPER, J. D. (1978) *History of Southern Africa*. London & Portsmouth, NH: James Currey & Heinemann

OVPMPND (1994a) *Kisii District Development Plan 1994-1996*. Nairobi: Office of the Vice-President and Ministry of Planning and National Development.

OVPMPND (1994b) *Nyamira District Development Plan 1994-1996*. Nairobi: Office of the Vice-President and Ministry of Planning and National Development.

OVPMPND (1994c) *Nyandarua District Development Plan 1994-1996*. Nairobi: Office of the Vice-President and Ministry of Planning and National Development.

PAM (1995) 'Liberalization of Processing and Marketing of Industrial Crops and Export Diversification.' In *Proceedings of the Conference on 'Towards 2000: Improving Agricultural Performance', held at the Kenya Commercial Bank, Institute of Banking and Finance, Nairobi, September 21, 1995*, Nairobi: Egerton University, Policy Analysis Matrix, pp. 35-67.

PEDLER, SIR F. (1975) 'British Planning and Private Enterprise in Colonial Africa.' In P. Duignan & L. H. Gann (eds.) *Colonialism in Africa, 1870-1960. Volume 4: The Economics of Colonialism*. Cambridge: Cambridge University Press, pp. 95-126.

PORTER, G. (1984) 'Traders' Travel Patterns: The Case of Part-Time Trade Among the Kanuri of Bornu.' In *The Nigerian Geographical Journal*, vol. 27, no. 1/2, pp. 98-111.

PORTER, G. (1986) 'Periodic Rural Markets in Borno, North-East Nigeria.' In *Annals of Borno*, vol. 3, pp. 107-125.

PORTER, M. E. (1980) *Competitive Strategy: Techniques for Analyzing Industries and Competitors*. New York & London: The Free Press, Macmillan.

PORTER, M. E. (1990) *The Competitive Advantage of Nations*. London: MacMillan.

POWER, J. (1993) 'Race, Class, Ethnicity, and Anglo-Indian Trade Rivalry in Colonial Malawi, 1910-1945.' In *The International Journal of African Historical Studies*, vol. 26, no. 3, pp. 575-607.

PRESTON, L. E. (1970) 'Marketing Organization and Economic Development: Structure, Products and Management.' In L. P. Bucklin (ed.) *Vertical Marketing Systems*. Glenview, IL: Scott, Foresman and Co.

REILLY, W. J. (1931) *The Law of Retail Gravitation*. Austin: The University of Texas.

REMPEL, H. & M. P. TODARO (1973) 'Rural-to-urban Labour Migration in Kenya.' In S. H. Ominde & C. N. Ejiogu (eds.) *Population Growth and Economic Development in Africa*. London: Heinemann, pp. 214-231.

REUSSE, E. (1987) 'Liberalization and Agricultural Marketing: Recent Causes and Effects in Third World Economies.' In *Food Policy*, vol. 12, pp. 299-317.

REVZAN, D. A. (1967) 'Marketing Organization through the Channel.' In B. Mallen (ed.) *The Marketing Channel, A Conceptual View Point*. New York: Wiley, pp. 3-19.

REVZAN, D. A. (1971) *A Marketing View of Spatial Competition*. Berkeley: University of California, School of Business Administration.

RIMMER, D. (1983) 'The Economic Imprint of Colonialism and Domestic Food Supplies in British Tropical Africa.' In R. I. Rotberg (ed.) *Imperialism, Colonialism, and Hunger: East and Central Africa.* Lexington, MA: Lexington Books, D. C. Heath, pp. 141-166.

ROBBINS, S. R. (1984) *Pyrethrum: a Review of Market Trends and Prospects in Selected Countries.* London: Tropical Development and Research Institute.

ROBERTS, A. (1970) 'Nyamwezi Trade.' In R. Gray & D. Birmingham (eds.) *Pre-Colonial African Trade; Essays on Trade in Central and Eastern Africa before 1900.* London: Oxford University Press, pp. 39-74.

ROBERTS, R. (1980) 'The Emergence of a Grain Market in Bamako, 1883-1908.' In *Canadian Journal of African Studies,* vol. 14, no. 1, pp. 37-54.

ROSS, R. (1986) 'The Relative Importance of Exports and the International Market for the Agriculture of the Cape Colony.' In G. Liesegang, H. Pasch & A. Jones (eds.) *Figuring African Trade; Proceedings of the Symposium on the Quantification and Structure of the Import and Export and Long Distance Trade in Africa 1800-1913.* Berlin: Dietrich Reimer Verlag, pp. 247-261.

ROTWEG, R. I. (1962) 'Rural Rhodesian Markets.' In P. Bohannan & G. Dalton (eds.) *Markets in Africa.* Evanston: Northwestern University Press, pp. 581-600.

RUIGU, G. M. (1988) *Large-Scale Irrigation Development in Kenya: Past Performance and Future Prospects.* Nairobi & Leiden: Ministry of Planning and National Development & African Studies Centre, Food and Nutrition Studies Programme, Report no. 23.

RUTTEN, M. M. E. M. (1992) *Selling Wealth to Buy Poverty; The Process of Individualization of Landownership among the Maasai Pastoralists of Kajiado District, Kenya, 1890-1990.* Saarbrücken: Verlag Breitenbach.

SALAU, A. T. (1979) 'Urbanization, Planning, and Public Policies in Nigeria.' In R. A. Obudho & S. El-Shakhs *Development of Urban Systems in Africa.* New York: Praeger, pp. 196-214.

SANDEE, H. & H. WEIJLAND (1986) 'Dual Production and Marketing of Vegetables in Swaziland: A Case of Marginalization of Female Traders.' In *Scenes of Change: Visions on Developments in Swaziland.* Amsterdam: Free University, Papers presented at the seminar Social Sciences in Swaziland, Free University, Amsterdam, February 1986, pp. 150-162.

SANTORUM, A. & A. TIBAIJUKA (1992) 'Trading Responses to Food Market Liberalization in Tanzania.' In *Food Policy,* vol. 17, no. 6, pp. 431-442.

SCHERER, F. M. & D. ROSS (1990) *Industrial Market Structure and Economic Performance.* Third edition. Boston: Houghton Mifflin.

SCHIFF, M. & A. VALDÉS (1992) *A Synthesis of the Economics in Developing Countries, Vol. 4: The Political Economy of Agricultural Pricing Policy.* Baltimore: Johns Hopkins University Press.

SCHILTER, C. (1991) *L'agriculture urbaine à Lomé.* Paris & Geneva: Karthala & l'Institute Universitaire d'Etudes du Developpement (IUED).

SEARING, J. F. (1993) *West African Slavery and Atlantic Commerce. The Senegal River Valley, 1700-1860.* Cambridge: Cambridge University Press.

SEIERUP, S. (1994) *Small Town Entrepreneurs and their Networks in Kenya.* Copenhagen: Centre for Development Research, CDR Working Paper no. 94.1.

SHAWA, J. J. (1993) 'Trade, Price and Market Reform in Zambia; Current Status and Constraints.' In *Food Policy,* vol. 18, no. 4, pp. 294-299.

SHECHAMBO, F. (1993) *The Search for Transaction Mechanisms for Agricultural Products in Tanzania. The Case of Lushoto District.* Berlin: Verlag Köster.

SHEPHERD, A. W. (1989) 'Grain Marketing in Africa Under Conditions of Structural Adjustment.' In *Journal of International Food & Agribusiness Marketing,* vol. 1, no. 2, pp. 25-34.

SHEPHERD, A. W. (1997) *Market Information Services: Theory and Practice.* Rome: Food and Agriculture Organization, Agricultural Services Bulletin no. 125.

SHETH, J. N., D. M. GARDNER & D. E. GARRETT (1988) *Marketing Theory: Evolution and Evaluation.* New York: Wiley.

SKINNER, E. P. (1986) 'Urbanization in Francophone Africa.' In *African Urban Quarterly,* vol. 1, no. 3/4, pp. 191-195.

SKINNER, G. W. (1964) 'Marketing and Social Structure in Rural China.' In *International Journal of Asian Studies,* vol. 24, no. 1, pp. 5-31.

SLATER, C. C. (1968) 'Marketing Processes in Developing Latin American Societies.' In *Journal of Marketing,* July, pp. 50-55.

SLATER, C. C. (1970) 'Market Channel Coordination and Economic Development.' In L. B. Bucklin (ed.) *Vertical Marketing Systems.* Glenview, IL: Scott, Foresman and Co., pp. 135-157.

SMITH, C. A. (1985) 'How to Count Onions: Methods for Regional Analysis of Marketing.' In S. Plattner (ed.) *Markets and Marketing.* Lanham, MD: University Press of America, Monographs in Economic Anthropology no. 4.

SMITH, L. D. (1992) 'Problems of Liberalizing Cereals Markets: the Kenya Case.' Paper presented at a Rural Development Studies seminar on 22nd Jan 1992, Institute of Social Studies, The Hague.

SOMMERS L. M. & A. MEHRETU (1992) 'Trade Patterns and Trends in the African European Trading Area: Lessons for Sub-Saharan Africa from the Era of the Lomé Accords.' In *Africa Development*, vol. XVII, no. 2, pp. 5-26.

SOSNICK, H. (1958) 'A Critique of Concepts of Workable Competition.' In *The Quarterly Journal of Economics*, 72, 380-423.

SPAULDING, J. & L. KAPTEIJNS (1987) *The Periodization of Precolonial African History*. Boston: Boston University, African Studies Centre Working Papers no. 125.

STAATZ, J. M., J. DIONÉ & N. NANGO DEMBÉLÉ (1989) 'Cereal Market Liberalization in Mali.' In *World Development*, vol. 17, no. 5, pp. 703-718.

STATISTISCHES BUNDESAMT (1990) *Länderbericht Äthiopien 1990*. Wiesbaden & Stuttgart: Statistisches Bundesamt (Federal Statistical Office) & Metzler-Poeschel.

STERKENBURG, J. J. (1987) *Rural Development and Rural Developing Policies: Cases from Africa and Asia*. Utrecht: University of Utrecht, PhD thesis.

STERN, L.W., A.I. EL-ANSARY & A. T. COUGHLAN (1996) *Marketing Channels*. Fifth edition, Upper Saddle River, NJ: Prentice Hall International.

STERN, L.W. & T. REVE (1980) 'Distribution Channels as Political Economies: A Framework for Comparative Analysis.' In *Journal of Marketing*, vol. 44, Summer, pp. 52-64.

STIGLER, G. J. (1951) 'The Division of Labor is Limited by the Extent of the Market.' In *Journal of Political Economy*, vol. 54, pp. 185-193.

SUTHERLAND-HARRIS, N. (1970) 'Zambian Trade with Zumbo in the Eighteenth Century.' In R. Gray & D. Birmingham (eds.) *Pre-Colonial African Trade; Essays on Trade in Central and Eastern Africa before 1900*. London: Oxford University Press, pp. 231-242.

TAKAVARASHA, T. (1993) 'Trade, Price and Market Reform in Zimbabwe; Current Status, Proposals and Constraints.' In *Food Policy*, vol. 18, no. 4, pp. 286-293.

TALBOTT, I. D. (1990) *Agricultural Innovation in Colonial Africa: Kenya and the Great Depression*. Lewiston, NY.: Edwin Mellen Press.

TARVER, J. D. & H. M. MILLER (1993) 'Urbanization in Pre-Colonial Africa'. In *Africa Insight*, vol. 23, no. 3, pp. 176-178.

TECHNOSERVE (1989) *Taita Horticultural Produce Centre, Taita Farmers Cooperative Society; Marketing Improvement Strategies*. Nairobi: Technoserve Inc., Consultancy report no. 2.

TECHNOSERVE (1991) *Taita Horticultural Produce Centre, Taita Farmers Cooperative Society; Performance and Progress Report; January to June 1991*. Nairobi: Technoserve Inc., Consultancy report no. 7.

TECHNOSERVE (1993) *Taita Horticultural Produce Centre (THPC); Progress Report; Production, Marketing and Financial Performance for Period 1990 to May 1993*. Nairobi: Technoserve Inc.

TELLEGEN, N. (1993) *Rural Employment in Sub-Sahara Africa, a Bibliography*. Leiden: African Studies Centre, ASC Working Paper no. 18.

TIMMERMANS, H. (1993) 'Retail Environments and Spatial Shopping Behavior.' In T. Gärling & R. G. Golledge (eds.) *Behavior and Environment; Psychological and Geographical Approaches*, Amsterdam: North-Holland, pp. 342-377.

TOLLENS, E (1992) 'Cassava Marketing in Zaire: An Analysis of its Structure, Conduct and Performance.' In L. Cammann (ed.) *Traditional Marketing Systems*. Feldafing: German Foundation for International Development (DSE), p. 113-127.

TORRES, E. B. & F. A. LANTICAN (1977) 'Middlemen and Their Operation in Fruit and Vegetable Marketing.' In *Journal of Agricultural Economics and Development*, vol. 7, no. 1, pp. 79-95.

TOSH, J. (1970) 'The Northern Interlacustrine Region' In R. Gray & D. Birmingham (eds.) *Pre-Colonial African Trade; Essays on Trade in Central and Eastern Africa before 1900*. London: Oxford University Press, pp. 103-118.

TURRITIN, J. (1988) 'Men, Women and Market Trade in Rural Mali, West Africa.' In *Canadian Journal of African Studies*, vol. 22, no. 3, pp. 583-604.

UKWU, U. I. (1969) 'Markets in Yorubaland.' In B. W. Hodder & U. I. Ukwu (eds.) *Markets in West Africa*. Ibadan: Ibadan University Press.

UN (1989) *Patterns, Causes and Consequences of Urbanization in Africa*. Addis Ababa: United Nations Economic Commission for Africa.

UN (1993) *Statistical Yearbook Thirty-Eighth Issue*. New York: United Nations.

UNCTAD (1996) *The Least Developed Countries 1996 Report*. Geneva: United Nations Conference on Trade and Development.

UNDP (1992) *African Development Indicators*. New York: United Nations Development Programme.

UNDP (1994) *Human Development Report 1994*. New York & Washington: United Nations Development Programme & The World Bank.

VAN DEN BERG, P. (1994) *The Marketing of Horticultural Commodities to Urban Areas in Kenya; The Case of Nakuru Town.* Wageningen: Wageningen Agricultural University, Department of Marketing and Marketing Research, Unpublished MA thesis.

VAN DER LAAN, H. L., & W. T. M. VAN HAAREN (1990) *African Marketing Boards under Structural Adjustment.* Leiden: African Studies Centre, Working papers no. 13.

VAN DER LAAN, H. L. (1997) *The Trans-Oceanic Marketing Channel: A New Tool for Understanding Tropical Africa's Export Agriculture.* Binghampton, NY: International Business Press (Haworth Press).

VAN DIJK, R. A. (1992) *Young Malawian Puritans; Young Puritan Preachers in a Present-day African Urban Environment.* Utrecht: University of Utrecht, PhD thesis.

VAN DONGE, J. K. (1992) 'Waluguru Traders in Dar es Salaam: An Analysis of the Social Construction of Economic Life.' In *African Affairs*, vol. 91, no. 363, pp. 181-205.

VAN TILBURG, A. (1981) 'Evaluation of the Performance of the Existing Marketing System for Highland Vegetables in West Java, Indonesia.' Paper for 1981 annual meeting of the European Academy for Advanced Research and Marketing, Copenhagen, 25-27 March.

VAN TILBURG, A. (1988) 'Performance Measurement in Respect of Periodic Markets and Marketing Agents Operating at these Markets in South-west Benin, West-Africa.' In *Proceedings of the European Marketing Academy Conference*, Bradford (UK), pp. 625-646.

VAN TILBURG, A. & C. LUTZ (1992) 'Competition at Rural and Urban Markets in South Benin.' In L. Cammann (ed.) *Traditional Marketing Systems.* Feldafing: German Foundation for International Development (DSE), pp. 101-112.

VAN TILBURG, A. & C. LUTZ (1995) 'Framework to Assess the Performance of Food Commodity Marketing Systems in Developing Counties.' Paper for the conference of the Réseau SADAOC on Sustainable Food Security in West Africa, Accra, 13-15 March 1995.

VAN TILBURG, A., M. MULDER & G. VAN DIJKEN (1989) 'Performance of LDC's Domestic Vegetable Marketing Systems: Effectiveness and Efficiency.' Paper given at a seminar at the Centro Internacional de Agricultura Tropical (CIAT), Cali, Colombia, 16-20 October.

VENNETIER, P. (1972) 'La Poussée Urbaine en Afrique Noire et à Madagascar.' In *La Croissance Urbaine en Afrique Noire et à Madagascar.* Paris: Centre National de la Recherche Scientifique, pp. 45-64.

VON BRAUN, J., J. MCCOMB, B. K. FRED-MENSAH & R. PANDYA-LORCH (1993) *Urban Food Insecurity and Malnutrition in Developing Countries: Trends, Policies, and Research Implications.* Washington, D.C.: International Food Policy Research Institute.

VON BRAUN, J. & L. PAULINO (1990) 'Food in Sub-Saharan Africa; Trends and Policy Challenges for the 1990s.' In *Food Policy*, vol. 15, no. 6, pp. 505-517

WADINAMBIARATCHI, G. (1967) 'Channels of Distribution in Developing Economies.' In B. E. Mallen (Ed), *The Marketing Channel; A Conceptual Viewpoint.* New York: Wiley.

WAGNER, M. D. (1993) 'Trade and Commercial Attitudes in Burundi before the Nineteenth Century.' In *The International Journal of African Historical Studies*, vol. 26, no. 1, pp. 149-166.

WAMBUGU, S. K. (1994) 'Spatial Distribution Patterns of Market Places and Market Provision in Nyeri District, Kenya.' In *Journal of Eastern African Research & Development*, vol. 24, pp. 1-14.

WAMBUGU, S. K. (1995) 'A Spatio-temporal Analysis of Periodic Markets in Nyeri District, Kenya.' In *Eastern and Southern Africa Geographical Journal*, vol. 6, no. 1, pp. 60-73.

WATTS, M. (1987) 'Brittle Trade: a Political Economy of Food Supply in Kano.' In J. I. Guyer (ed.) *Feeding African Cities; Studies in Regional Social History.* Manchester: Manchester University Press, International African Institute, pp. 55-111.

WEEKLY REVIEW (1993) 'Coffee: A Troubled Industry.' In *The Weekly Review*, June 1 (1990), pp. 46-54.

WHITE, R. R. (1989) 'The Influence of Environmental and Economic Factors on the Urban Crisis.' In R. E. Stern & R. R. White (eds.) *African Cities in Crisis; Managing Rapid Urban Growth*, Boulder: Westview Press, African Modernization and Development Series, pp. 1-36.

WIENER, L. (1931) *Les chemins de fer coloniaux de l'Afrique.* Brussels & Paris: Goemaere & Dunod.

WILD, V. (1992) 'An Outline of African Business History in Colonial Zimbabwe.' In *Zambezia, the Journal of the University of Zimbabwe*, vol. 19, no. 1, pp. 19-46.

WILKS, I. (1975) *Asante in the Nineteenth Century; the Structure and Evolution of a Political Order.* Cambridge: Cambridge University Press.

WILSON, F. A. (1969) *The Marketing of Fruits and Vegetables in Kenya.* Nairobi: University of Nairobi, Institute of Development Studies.

WILSON, F. A. (1973) *Some Economic Aspects of the Structure and Organization of Small Scale Marketing Systems - Marketing of Fruit and Vegetables in Kenya.* Nairobi: University of Nairobi, Institute of Development Studies, Discussion Paper no. 176.

WOLF, T. P. (1985) 'State Intervention at the Cabbage-Roots; A Case Study from Kenya'. Paper presented at the seminar on Sate Economic Intervention in Third World Polities, Institute of Development Studies, University of Sussex, UK, July 1985.

WORLD BANK (1991) *World Bank Development Report 1991, The Challenge of Development*. Washington DC: The World Bank.

WORLD BANK (1994) *World Development Report 1994*. Washington, DC: The World Bank.

WORLD BANK (1995) *Social Indicators of Development 1995*. Baltimore: Johns Hopkins University Press.

WRIGLEY, C. C. (1965) 'Kenya: The Patterns of Economic Life, 1902-1945.' In V. Harlow & E, M. Chilver (eds.) *History of East Africa, Volume II*. London: Oxford University Press, pp. 209-264.

YIMAM, A. (1990) *Social Development in Africa 1950-1985: Methodological Perspectives and Future Prospects*. Aldershot: Avebury.

ZELEZA, T. (1989) 'Kenya and the Second World War, 1939-1950.' In W. Ochieng' (ed.) *A Modern History of Kenya, 1895-1980*. Nairobi: Evens Brothers (Kenya) Ltd., pp. 144-172.

ZELEZA, T. (1990) 'The Development of the Cooperative Movement in Kenya since Independence.' In *Journal of Eastern African Research & Development*, vol. 20, pp. 68-94.

Research Series of the African Studies Centre, Leiden, The Netherlands

1. Dick Foeken & Nina Tellegen   Tied to the land. Living conditions of labourers on large
    1994   farms in Trans Nzoia District, Kenya

2. Tom Kuhlman   Asylum or Aid? The economic integration of Ethiopian
    1994   and Eritrean refugees in the Sudan

3. Kees Schilder   Quest for self-esteem. State, Islam and Mundang
    1994   ethnicity in Northern Cameroon

4. Johan A. van Dijk   Taking the waters. Soil and water conservation among
    1995   settling Beja nomads in Eastern Sudan

5. Piet Konings   Gender and class in the tea estates of Cameroon
    1995

6. Thera Rasing   Passing on the rites of passage. Girls' initiation rites in the
    1995   context of an urban Roman Catholic community on the
                                      Zambian Copperbelt

7. Jan Hoorweg, Dick Foeken   Seasons and nutrition at the Kenya coast
    & Wijnand Klaver
    1995

8. John A. Houtkamp   Tropical Africa's emergence as a banana supplier in the
    1996   inter-war period

9. Victor Azarya   Nomads and the state in Africa: the political roots of
    1996   marginality

10. Deborah Bryceson &   Farewell to farms. De-agrarianization and employment
    Vali Jamal, eds.   in Africa.
    1997

11. Tjalling Dijkstra   Trading the fruits of the land: horticultural marketing
    1997   channels in Kenya.

12. Nina Tellegen   Rural enterprises in Malawi: necessity or opportunity?
    1997

Copies can be ordered at: Ashgate Publishing Ltd.
                            Gower House
                            Croft Road
                            Aldershot
                            Hampshire GU11 3HR
                            England

For Product Safety Concerns and Information please contact our EU
representative GPSR@taylorandfrancis.com Taylor & Francis Verlag GmbH,
Kaufingerstraße 24, 80331 München, Germany

Printed and bound by CPI Group (UK) Ltd, Croydon, CR0 4YY
08/05/2025
01864370-0019